Penal Exceptionalism?

In the growing field of comparative criminal justice, the Nordic countries are regularly used as exceptions to the global move towards growing rates of imprisonment and tougher, less welfare-oriented crime-control policies.

Why are the Nordic penal institutions viewed as so 'different' from a non-Nordic vantage point? Are Nordic prisons and penal policies in fact positive exceptions to the general rule? If they are, what exactly are the exceptional qualities, and why are the Nordic societies lucky enough to have them? Are there important overlooked examples of Nordic 'bad practice' in the penal area? Could there be a specifically Nordic way of doing prison research, contributing to the gap between internal and external perspectives?

In considering – among others – the above questions, this book explores and discusses the Nordic jurisdictions as contexts for the specific penal policies and practices that may or may not be described as exceptional.

Written by leading prison scholars from the Nordic countries as well as selected researchers from the English-speaking world 'looking in', this book will be particularly useful for students of criminology and practitioners across the Nordic countries, but also of relevance in a wider geographical context.

Thomas Ugelvik is a post-doctoral research fellow at the Department of Criminology and Sociology of Law at the University of Oslo, Norway. His Ph.D. is an ethnography of prisoner-subjectivation processes in and through the everyday life and power struggles of the institution. His research interests also include crime and the media, gender issues, and cultural criminology. He has published on violence against prison officers, power–resistance relationships in prison, and masculinity theory.

Jane Dullum is a post-doctoral research fellow at the Department of Criminology and Sociology of Law at the University of Oslo, Norway. In her Ph.D. she analysed the development of the psychiatric institutions in Norway, with a special focus on the decarceration of the mentally ill. She has done research on economic crime, restorative justice, topics regarding the rule of law, prisons and prison education, and miscarriages of justice.

Penal Exceptionalism?
Nordic prison policy and practice

**Edited by Thomas Ugelvik
and Jane Dullum**

LONDON AND NEW YORK

First published 2012
by Routledge
2 Park Square, Milton Park, Abingdon, Oxon, OX14 4RN

Simultaneously published in the USA and Canada
by Routledge
711 Third Avenue, New York, NY 10017

Routledge is an imprint of the Taylor & Francis Group, an informa business

© 2012 Thomas Ugelvik and Jane Dullum; individual chapters, the contributors

All rights reserved. No part of this book may be reprinted or reproduced
or utilized in any form or by any electronic, mechanical, or other means,
now known or hereafter invented, including photocopying and recording,
or in any information storage or retrieval system, without permission in
writing from the publishers.

Trademark notice: Product or corporate names may be trademarks or
registered trademarks, and are used only for identification and explanation
without intent to infringe.

British Library Cataloguing in Publication Data
A catalogue record for this book is available from the British Library

Library of Congress Cataloging in Publication Data
Nordic prison practice and policy, exceptional or not? : exploring penal
exceptionalism in the Nordic context / edited by Thomas Ugelvik and
Jane Dullum.
    p. cm.
1. Corrections—Scandinavia. 2. Prisons—Scandinavia. I. Ugelvik, Thomas.
II. Dullum, Jane, 1960–
HV9718.N67 2011
365′.948—dc22   2011000228

ISBN: 978-0-415-66869-9 hbk
ISBN: 978-0-415-67295-5 pbk
ISBN: 978-0-203-81327-0 ebk

Typeset in Times New Roman
by Keystroke, Station Road, Codsall, Wolverhampton

Printed and bound in Great Britain by the MPG Books Group

Contents

Notes on the contributors vii
Preface xi

1 Introduction: exceptional prisons, exceptional societies? 1
JANE DULLUM AND THOMAS UGELVIK

PART I
Exceptions or not? 11

2 Scandinavian exceptionalism in penal matters: reality or wishful thinking? 13
THOMAS MATHIESEN

3 A critical look at Scandinavian exceptionalism: welfare state theories, penal populism and prison conditions in Denmark and Scandinavia 38
PETER SCHARFF SMITH

4 Media, crime and Nordic exceptionalism: the limits of convergence 58
DAVID A. GREEN

PART II
Commodification of exceptional penal systems 77

5 'The most progressive, effective correctional system in the world': the Swedish prison system in the 1960s and 1970s 79
RODDY NILSSON

6 Comparisons at work – exporting 'exceptional' norms   100
   ANDREW M. JEFFERSON

PART III
Closing in on the Nordic I: cultures of equality?   119

7 The dark side of a culture of equality: reimagining communities in a Norwegian remand prison   121
   THOMAS UGELVIK

8 Imprisoning the soul   139
   CECILIE BASBERG NEUMANN

9 A blessing in disguise: attention deficit hyperactivity disorder diagnosis and Swedish correctional treatment policy in the twenty-first century   156
   ROBERT ANDERSSON

PART IV
Closing in on the Nordic II: prison management and prison cultures   173

10 Are liberal-humanitarian penal values and practices exceptional? 175
    BEN CREWE AND ALISON LIEBLING

11 Prison size and quality of life in Norwegian closed prisons in late modernity   199
    BERIT JOHNSEN AND PER KRISTIAN GRANHEIM

12 A harsher prison climate and a cultural heritage working against it: subcultural divisions among Swedish prison officers   215
    ANDERS BRUHN, ODD LINDBERG AND PER-ÅKE NYLANDER

PART V
Scandinavian exceptionalism revisited   233

13 In defence of Scandinavian exceptionalism   235
    JOHN PRATT AND ANNA ERIKSSON

Index   261

Contributors

Robert Andersson has a Ph.D. in criminology and works as a senior lecturer in criminology at the Institute of Police Education, Linnæus University, Växjö, Sweden. His publications mostly concern crime policy and his latest publication, co-written with Roddy Nilsson, *Svensk Kriminalpolitk* [Swedish crime policy] is a study of Swedish crime policy during the twentieth century.

Anders Bruhn is an associate professor in sociology at Örebro University, Sweden. His main field of research is work and organization. He has published on individualization and collective action in working life, work environment, work environment regulation and inspection, organizational and occupational change, and prison work.

Ben Crewe is a senior research associate at the Institute of Criminology, University of Cambridge. He has published on various aspects of prison life, including staff–prisoner relationships, the drugs economy within prison, and the 'inmate code'. His most recent book, *The Prisoner Society: Power, Adaptation and Social Life*, was published in 2009.

Anna Eriksson is a lecturer in criminology at Monash University, Melbourne, Australia. Originally from Sweden, she has conducted research in Northern Ireland, England, and Australia on restorative justice and alternative approaches to punishment. She is the co-investigator with Professor John Pratt on the 'Scandinavian Exceptionalism' project.

Per Kristian Granheim is an adviser and teacher at the Correctional Service of Norway Staff Academy. Since 2007 he has been working on the study 'The quality of life in Norwegian closed prisons'. He has an MD in social psychology from the Norwegian University of Science and Technology.

David A. Green is an assistant professor of sociology at John Jay College of Criminal Justice, City University of New York, and a 2010–11 Fellow at the Straus Institute for the Advanced Study of Law and Justice, New York University. He won the European Society of Criminology's Young Criminologist Award in 2007 and the 2009 British Society of Criminology Book Prize for his first book, *When Children Kill Children: Penal Populism and Political Culture* (2008).

Andrew M. Jefferson is a senior researcher at the Rehabilitation and Research Centre for Torture Victims in Copenhagen, Denmark, specializing in prison practices and justice sector reform beyond the West. He is a co-editor of *State Violence and Human Rights: State Officials in the South* and a co-founder of the Global Prisons Research Network.

Berit Johnsen is a researcher at the Correctional Service of Norway Staff Academy. Since 2007 she has been working on the study 'The quality of life in Norwegian closed prisons'. Besides prison sociology, her research interests include new criminal sanctions in the Norwegian Criminal Code, such as preventive detention and the drug court programme.

Alison Liebling is a professor of criminology and criminal justice at the University of Cambridge and Director of the Institute of Criminology's Prisons Research Centre. She has published several books, including: *Suicides in Prison* (1992); *Prisons and their Moral Performance: A Study of Values, Quality and Prison Life* (2004); and (with Shadd Maruna) *The Effects of Imprisonment* (2005). She has recently published the second edition of *The Prison Officer* and is presently completing a study of public and private sector prisons, with Ben Crewe, and a repeat of a study of staff–prisoner relationships at Whitemoor high-security prison.

Odd Lindberg is a professor of social work and Director of the Centre for Criminological Research at Örebro University, Sweden. He has published several articles and book chapters concerning women in prison, careers in drug misuse, and bullying in schools. Lindberg is also a member of the Swedish Prison and Probations Service's Scientific Board.

Thomas Mathiesen became a professor of sociology of law at the University of Oslo in 1971, and has been a professor emeritus since 2003. He is the author of a number books on sociology of law, criminology, media, prisons, power and counter-power, six of them in English (including *Prison on Trial*, 3rd edn, 2006). He is the founder of KROM – the Norwegian prisoners' association, in which he is still active.

Roddy Nilsson, Ph.D., is a senior lecturer in criminology and an associate professor in history at Linneæus University, Växjö, Sweden. He has published books and articles on prison history, criminal politics, and historical criminology. He has also written articles on historiography and historical theory and an introduction to the works of Michel Foucault.

Cecilie Basberg Neumann, Ph.D., is a senior researcher at the Work Research Institute, Oslo, Norway. She has published a book on prison officers, and a book and articles on the Norwegian health-visiting service, the Norwegian child-care services, and equality and discrimination issues. She has a particular interest in class, gender, care, and power, and in methodological questions and challenges.

Per-Åke Nylander, MA in social work, is a lecturer and Ph.D. candidate in social work at Örebro University, Sweden. He has published in the fields of prison work and drug abuse treatment. Nylander has also held the position of Coordinator for the educational programme for prison officers at Örebro University.

John Pratt is a professor of criminology and James Cook Research Fellow in Social Science at the Institute of Criminology, Victoria University of Wellington, New Zealand. He is also a Fellow at the Straus Institute for Advanced Legal Studies and Justice, Faculty of Law, New York University 2010–11. He has published extensively on the history and sociology of punishment. His 2008 two-part *British Journal of Criminology* article – 'Scandinavian Exceptionalism in an Era of Penal Excess' – received the Sir Leon Radzinowicz Memorial Award in 2009.

Peter Scharff Smith, Ph.D., is a senior research fellow at the Danish Institute for Human Rights. He has published books and articles on prisons, punishment, and human rights, including works on prison history, children of imprisoned parents, and the use of solitary confinement in prisons. He has also written books and articles on the Second World War and the Nazi war of extermination on the Eastern front.

Preface

The Scandinavian Studies of Confinement (SSC) research network was established by Peter Scharff Smith and Andrew M. Jefferson as a joint initiative of the Danish Institute for Human Rights and the Rehabilitation and Research Centre for Torture Victims in Copenhagen in 2005. The network grew steadily in numbers over the first few years. When the third meeting was held, also in Copenhagen, in May 2007, it was not only a Scandinavian, but a truly Nordic forum, with participants from all Nordic countries, as well as a few specially invited 'honorary Scandinavians' from the UK. Originally, the network was designed to particularly encourage younger scholars doing prison studies. The 2007 meeting represented an expansion of the network, both to include senior scholars, and in the terms of expanding beyond imprisonment in the narrow sense, to include studies of confinement broadly speaking. The network had also become truly multidisciplinary, bringing together perspectives from the fields of sociology, criminology, social work, law, anthropology, psychology, and history. This book is the first joint publication by this still-growing group of scholars joined together by their common interest in penal policy, practice, and politics in the Nordic countries.

As editors, we wish to express our gratitude to some of the institutions and people who have made the project possible. We have received generous grants from the Scandinavian Research Council for Criminology and from the Faculty of Law at the University of Oslo (Lovsamlingsfondet and UiOs stimuleringsmidler). Thanks are due also to the administrative staff at our department, the Department of Criminology and Sociology of Law in Oslo, especially Turid Eikvam and Per Jørgen Ystehede. Kristin Hobson has also done an invaluable job towards the end.

We also wish to thank the entire SSC network, not only those who ended up writing chapters. The productive juxtaposition of different perspectives on different practices has made us all reflect in new ways, something which will continue for years to come.

Lastly, we would like to thank John Pratt. Your two-part article on Scandinavian exceptionalism in the *British Journal of Criminology* set this whole thing in motion. The discussions inspired by your work have been, and will continue to be, interesting and rewarding.

Oslo, March 2011
Thomas Ugelvik and Jane Dullum

1 Introduction
Exceptional prisons, exceptional societies?

Jane Dullum and Thomas Ugelvik

In the growing field of comparative criminal justice, the Nordic countries are regularly used as exceptions. As the story goes, Nordic societies somehow seem to resist the global move towards growing rates of imprisonment and tougher, less welfare-oriented crime-control policies (e.g. Cavadino and Dignan 2006; Lacey 2008; cf. Garland 2001). In an award-winning two-part article in the *British Journal of Criminology*, New Zealand-based criminologist John Pratt (2008a, b) describes the Nordic countries as exhibiting a specifically Nordic 'culture of control', resulting in what he calls 'Scandinavian exceptionalism' in the penal area; consistently low rates of imprisonment and comparatively humane prison conditions. The Scandinavian or Nordic[1] countries have taken over as the preferred 'beacon of tolerance' in a world moving steadfastly towards the dusk of ever-increasing levels of punitiveness (Nelken 2009).

Compared to such outsider accounts, Nordic prison researchers have traditionally been far less positive in their descriptions of prison conditions and penal policies, focusing more on the pains of imprisonment and the complex processes of social marginalization the penal system is part of. From within the Nordic societies, Nordic prisons are often seen as part of a governmental system of legitimized pain delivery, as described by Nils Christie (2007), or, as Thomas Mathiesen (2006) would have it, a control effort with very serious (technical, theoretical, moral) shortcomings.

The high material standard of Nordic prison facilities is certainly controversial even in Nordic societies themselves. A complaint commonly voiced in Nordic public debates is that (at least the newer) prisons are far too good for the prisoners. Echoing the traditional call for 'less eligibility' as a prison design principle, such critical voices claim that Nordic prisons look more like spa hotels or cruise ships, making the punishment element of the prison experience almost non-existent. In contrast, Nordic prison researchers have consistently produced critical accounts of the pains of imprisonment, often focusing on issues such as isolation, violence or suicide. Compared to prisons in other parts of the world, Nordic prisons, especially the new ones, may seem luxurious. Then again, in other jurisdictions, even indoor plumbing in a prison is an unthinkable luxury. So what do we do when we compare prisons? What is the point of comparisons, and what are the results?

What are researchers in the Nordic countries to make of the considerable gap between the Nordic prison research, and the story told in Pratt's articles? This book is the result of the problem of what to do with this tension. It obviously has something to do with the nature of comparisons in general; what the world looks like is at least partly dependent on where you stand. But is Pratt's exceptionalism based on something more substantial than this truism? Why are the Nordic penal institutions viewed as so 'different' from a non-Nordic vantage point? And why have several Nordic researchers reacted quite badly to his use of Nordic prisons as positive examples? Are Nordic prisons and penal policies in fact positive exceptions to the general rule, and if they are, what exactly are the exceptional qualities, and why are Nordic societies lucky enough to have them? Or should the external perspectives be nuanced? Are there important examples of Nordic 'bad practice' in the penal area that are overlooked? Are the Nordic countries even similar enough to warrant such comparisons? Or, on yet another level, is it even possible to still talk of a specifically Nordic penal model, bearing in mind the way prison service bureaucrats have eagerly imported policies, practices and programmes from the various Anglo-American jurisdictions over the last decades? And, finally, could it be that a specifically Nordic way of doing prison research makes the gap between internal and external perspectives widen?

These were the questions raised in the invitation to the third biannual conference of the Scandinavian Studies of Confinement (SSC) research network. Using Pratt's award-winning articles as a starting block, we explored and discussed the tension between insider and outsider perspectives on our Nordic societies and their prisons. Prison scholars from the Nordic countries, as well as selected researchers from the English-speaking world 'looking in' (John was himself one of them), came together for two days to discuss what a specifically Nordic culture of control might look like, if it is best described as exceptional, and if it is indeed a reality at all. Are the exceptional qualities observed about empirical differences, different analytical views, different theoretical perspective or different political objectives? All of the above? None? This book is the result of the dialogue that followed.

Comparative criminology

One way of understanding different incarceration rates and penal forms has been to see them as a reflection of different crime levels in different societies. However, the sociology of punishment has challenged this view. Inspired by canonical texts such as those of Marx, Durkheim and Weber, the social sciences have shown how punishment is a complex social institution, deeply embedded in a society's cultural and historical forms and no simple expression of the crime rate.

In recent years, we have seen a renewed interest in the question of the disparate incarceration rates worldwide. Influential contributions to the tradition of comparative criminology are well known; influential titles are Nils Christie's *Crime Control as Industry* (2000), Michael Cavadino and James Dignan's *Penal Systems: A Comparative Approach* (2006) and Nicola Lacey's *The Prisoners' Dilemma* (2008). It is important, however, to remember that comparative criminology has deep roots in the social science tradition. Cavadino and Dignan's book is a case in point; they seek to synthesize aspects of the Marxist, Durkhemian and Weberian traditions. In their outline, there is a significant difference between different types of state, and different levels of incarceration. They go on to give an overview of some of the major differences in 'punitiveness' between four different types of state formation: neoliberal states, conservative corporatist welfare states, social democratic corporatist welfare states and oriental corporatist states.

When it comes to incarceration rates, Nordic social democratic welfare states certainly stand out as exceptional when compared to Anglo-American countries. Sweden is leading the Nordic pack with a prison rate of 78 per 100,000 of the total population, with Denmark and Norway following at 71. Measured this way, Finland and Iceland are among the least punitive societies in Europe, at 60 and 55 respectively. In comparison, England and Wales combined are at a rate of 154, almost double that of Sweden. We are all dwarfed by the world leaders, however: Russia takes the European prize at 588, while the US is the imprisonment world leader at 748 prisoners per 100,000 inhabitants.[2]

However influential, the growing comparative penology often confine its analyses to the macro level of prison rates and political and economic systems. Enter John Pratt: one of the great strengths of Pratt's project is that he wants to connect the macro levels of prison rates with the experiential level of humane prison conditions. As a project, we acknowledge that this is both ambitious and bold, and very, very difficult.

What is so exceptional? By the term 'exceptionalism' Pratt both refers to the low prison rates in the Nordic countries and their relatively humane prison conditions, compared to the poor and degrading living conditions often characteristic of prisons in the Anglo world. The roots of both the exceptionally low prison rates and the exceptionally humane prison conditions are, according to Pratt, to be found in the '*highly* egalitarian cultural values and social structures in these countries' (2008a: 120). The still quite well-functioning welfare state safety net provided in these countries are also seen as an important part of the foundation for exceptionalism.

In the second article, Pratt's focus is on recent trends. He acknowledges the fact that levels of imprisonment are increasing even in Nordic countries, and he maintains that what lies behind this increase is a development towards new values attached to crime, crime control, and penality. The Nordic societies may be at a crossroads. The same forces that have contributed to penal excess elsewhere can also be seen in here: a reduced belief in experts, decline in trust in government, tabloidization of the media, and sensational media reporting. These forces 'produce new forms of knowledge and understandings about crime and punishment, new power relations that determine policy' (2008b: 277). The Scandinavian welfare model is also restructured, resulting in reduced levels of security and increased differences along class and ethnic lines. Furthermore, this development may be seen as connected to a growth in intolerance and more pronounced feelings of punitiveness directed towards outsider groups.

Pratt's article gives important contributions to comparative criminology. It also reminds us that the penal excesses we see in other parts of the world are not a universal phenomenon. However, the articles have evoked reactions among Scandinavian scholars. Several of the authors in this book question whether Nordic prisons and penal policies are indeed positive exceptions to the general rule, or if Pratt has in fact painted too rosy a picture of Scandinavian penal practices. Regardless of the answer, it begs the question: how has this picture been produced?

Making sense of the difference

The question of the production of a certain picture of Nordic societies and penal systems as exceptional relates to issues of how to analyse and compare different cultures and societies. There are several methodological and theoretical challenges involved in comparative research.

Most basically: what is a comparison? In a certain perspective, comparisons are what the production of meaning is all about; to turn it on its head, meaning has, at least since Ferdinand de Saussure (1983 [1906–11]), been seen as itself fundamentally a product of difference. Introducing new differences will inevitably produce new meanings. Better meanings, perhaps, but any comparison must be understood as part of the context in which it is made. We can, like David Nelken, argue that 'there is no "view from nowhere", and no "global" or "world view", even if there can be less, or more, parochial perspectives' (2010: 10).

Studies of the rising punitiveness and 'culture of control' have been criticized for being ethnocentric, for making sweeping generalizations based on a narrow and specific material. Often the focus is on Anglo-American practices. But, as questioned by Lucia Zedner: is the Anglo-American response to the problem of crime 'the only or indeed the dominant response of late modernity' (2002: 353)? Well, it is obviously not the only response, although its dominance may be up for discussion. In his oft-cited paper on the eclipse of prison ethnography, Loïc Wacquant (2002) charges the prison research community with being far too Anglo-centric. This seems strange, writes Wacquant, given the fact that the US in particular should best be described as an extreme or exceptional case when it comes to penal policies and practices. Relatively too much effort has been spent on describing what he calls 'the glaring *carceral exceptionalism* of the United States', leaving almost nothing for research on the far more typical cases of almost everywhere else. Many have made this point, that prison research has been a field where everything not American or British tends to fall under the radar (Sparks *et al.* 1996; Nelken 2009).

If we instead of looking for convergence towards a more or less uniform worldwide punitive culture of control argue a view with multiple cultures, what would the Nordic one look like? And what would be, if anything, specifically 'Nordic' about it? Or is 'the Nordic' too wide a category – are the differences (cultural and other) between the Nordic countries so great as to make 'the Nordic' an untenable generalization? Comparisons between phenomena on a higher level will often contribute to erasing differences on lower ones. 'Scandinavian prisons' are obviously not all the same. Talking about differences between two distinct models, a Scandinavian model and an Anglo-American one, will for instance play down the differences between the Scandinavian countries, as well as differences

Exceptional prisons, exceptional societies? 5

between, let's say, Cardiff and Los Angeles. Lindberg, Bruhn and Nylander's chapter (Chapter 12) shows some of the diversity between regimes and practices within just one of the Nordic countries – in this case, Sweden.

Another question deals with the assumed comparability of prison rates, and the way prison rates are used to say something about the level of punitiveness in general. For instance, will comparably low prison rates necessarily be connected to humane prison conditions? The Democratic Republic of Congo (or Congo-Kinshasa) has prison conditions well known to Norwegian media consumers, at least through an ongoing case in which two Norwegian nationals were tried and convicted of murdering their local driver, which seems to illustrate the point: bad conditions, at least materially speaking, *and* lower prison rate than most Nordic countries at 57 per 100,000 of the total population.[3] Only Iceland has a slightly lower rate. What this says about similarities between DRC and Iceland is, however, unclear. But what can be stated is that low imprisonment rates do not equal humane conditions.

Yet another point: what about other forms of social control, sometimes working together with the formal system of punishment? Should we include these other forms of social control in an overall account of a society's punitiveness? We think it may be fruitful to try. Low levels of official, public, state control do not necessarily equal low levels of control. More individualist and more collective societies can each have their own sort of pathologies, for example dealing with the difference by excluding it or by enforced assimilation (Young 1999). Different societies may be excluding different populations in different ways, and it may be that the Nordic societies just specialize in different forms of control – Ugelvik's and Andersson's chapters in this book (Chapters 7 and 9, as well as Dullum 2009) both point in this direction. As does Nelken:

> By contrast, some other countries, such as the allegedly more 'inclusive' and tolerant Scandinavian countries, are currently idealised because of their relatively low incarceration rates. But such places are much more complicated when taken in their own terms and not only treated as exemplars of leniency.
> (2010: 29)

Nordic societies may be more inclusive on the level of official policy, but what about practice? One researcher can at the programmatic level get one picture, another looking into prison practices, a totally different one.

Comparisons across cultures and societies are inevitably reductions. This does not mean that they may not be incredibly useful for different purposes. One of the risks is that of ethnocentrism – that people may automatically assume that their own local arrangements, the system they are in a sense part of, is the 'natural' or best way to do things, superior to foreign alternatives. An opposite danger is, however, xenocentrism, where a foreign way of reasoning or doing is taken a priori to be superior to one's own. Are Pratt's articles xenocentric, assuming that everything Nordic is superior? Is the Scandinavian exceptionalism thesis based on the same sort of rose-tinted stereotype that Nilsson describes in his chapter, or does the fault lie elsewhere; are domestic scholars too caught up with domestic politics to recognize a good thing when they see it?

Or may it be that Pratt and the Nordic researchers are equally xenocentric in their denouncement of their 'own' prison systems, both reacting to similar ethnocentrism internal to their respective home societies and criminal justice systems? Jefferson's and Nilsson's chapters (Chapters 6 and 5) both show how Nordic societies may exhibit a kind of 'welfare nationalism'; many feel that our modern and humane systems should be exported, for instance, for the good of the world. Nordic researchers have based entire careers on criticizing such an ethnocentric view, so no wonder Pratt's articles have been much discussed.

This also relates to the more fundamental question of how one conducts comparative research, and the methodological question Pakes (2010: 23) describes as the problem of how to 'touch base': 'It relates to questions such as: who do you talk to? What do you read? What do you observe?' A researcher will gain different insights depending on who she talks to. Usually prisoners and prison officers will have opposing views. Zedner (1995) cautions against what she calls 'criminological tourism', which is that comparative researchers may misread or oversimplify local customs based on rather thin and random material.

And what about the researcher's own position? What does the researcher see as humane conditions? According to Christie (2007), one should be very cautious about the grading of different kinds of pain. Prison conditions and the resulting pains may not be experienced in and of themselves, but relative to the wider historical, cultural and social context, as Neumann argues (Chapter 8). Prison conditions will of course affect prisoner's experience of the conditions. But other things will factor in as well. Could prison suicides be a good indication of perceived pains of imprisonment? If so, the humane conditions in Nordic prisons may be nuanced. A benevolent-looking system on the policy level might perfectly well be compatible with a relatively large number of prison suicides. The road to a certain hot place is, as should be well known, paved with the best intentions.

Comparisons between systems might also be part of an (implicit or explicit) normative or political argument. As Nelken puts it: 'For reform purposes, comparative researchers deliberately use accounts of practices elsewhere as a foil. Lacey's (2008), for example, deploys evidence of differences in prison rates in Europe so as to prove that growing punitiveness is not the only game in town' (2010: 12). Are the differences between insider and outsider accounts of Nordic prisons the results of different political goals, or maybe 'the same' goal, but on different levels? Depending on who we as prison researchers want to influence (and taking as given the problematic assumption that prison researchers necessarily want to influence someone), 'the same' practices and policies may be seen and portrayed in very different ways. Pratt's comparisons may not even be first and foremost intended for a Nordic readership. 'Like culture itself, legal culture is about who we are, not just what we do' (Nelken 2004: 1). And, at least as important, who we *are not*, we might add. Comparisons might help make us into something else – the transformative political power of the Nordic countries as contrast may be what Pratt ultimately is seeking?

Introducing the chapters

Reflecting the variety of backgrounds and disciplines represented in the network, the book is multidisciplinary, exploring the exceptionalism thesis from different angles. The book is divided into five parts.

In Part I, the very idea that Scandinavian prisons and penal policies are exceptionally humane is challenged. Thomas Mathiesen – focusing in some detail on penal practices in Norway – points at features which partly contradict the exceptionalism thesis (Chapter 2). As for Denmark, Peter Scharff Smith also points to prison practices which could be described as inhumane rather than humane (Chapter 3). The Danish (and Scandinavian) tradition of using pre-trial solitary confinement is an example that seems to contradict the traditional view of a humane Scandinavian prison policy. David Green expands the scope of discussion about exceptionalism by drawing in comparative scholarship about media convergence (Chapter 4). He offers examples of how Nordic media practice and coverage of crime have come to reflect Anglo-American trends; however, he argues that the homogenization of media content and practice has been significantly tempered in Nordic countries.

In Part II, the focus is not on whether a Scandinavian exceptionalism exists or not, but rather on how such an image has been produced. Roddy Nilsson's thesis (Chapter 5) is that the image of Swedish prisons and penal policies as humane and 'modern' historically to a large extent has been the result of a successful marketing campaign. A tradition of discourse travelling back and forth over the Atlantic worked to present an image of Sweden as a progressive country when it comes to penal matters. Andrew Jefferson (Chapter 6) considers the way ideas and discourses travel even as they are implicitly located within practices, and embodied in particular professionals, institutions, and policies. He also discusses the nature of comparisons, and the politics of comparisons. He makes an important point: comparisons *perform*, they are productive.

Are Nordic countries cultures of equality, or do they have mechanisms for excluding different populations in different ways than the English-speaking world? If this is so, does this imply that the exceptionalism thesis has to be nuanced? In Part III, Thomas Ugelvik, Cecilie Basberg Neumann and Robert Andersson (Chapters 7–9) explore forms of social control in Norway and Sweden other than that exerted by the penal system. Andersson argues, using the example of the ADHD diagnoses in Sweden, that Scandinavian exceptionalism is not a culture of equality, but rather a 'culture of intervention'.

In Part IV, the question of whether prison conditions can be more or less humane, and under what circumstances this can be the case, is raised. Pratt's original article may be criticized for leaving the basis for comparison mostly implicit – the contrast is, at least in that text, left as a ghostly referent behind his descriptions of Nordic reality. Ben Crewe and Alison Liebling's chapter (Chapter 10) is partly an attempt to remedy this: they discuss the exceptionalism thesis from the point of view of Pratt's implicit Anglo prison reference. Their argument is that prison conditions in the UK under what is conventionally seen as the period of penal welfarism, was far from liberal and humane in practice. Today, however, the relationship between official rhetoric and practice is much closer than it was. Managerial reforms have narrowed the range of professional orientations. Berit Johnsen and Per Kristian Granheim (Chapter 11) explore the quality of life in Norwegian prisons seen through the eyes of the prisoners. The study shows that there are differences; small prisons have more positive scores on several dimensions. This goes against the trend in Norwegian penal policy today, where the 'new penology' is influencing the leading discourses regulating penal policy. This entails the closing down of older and smaller prisons. Managerial considerations seem to lie behind this development. There are also differences between Swedish prisons, and between different prison wings and units. This is outlined in Bruhn, Lindberg and Nylander's chapter on subcultural divisions among Swedish prison officers (Chapter 12). In closed prisons, the wings have been more specialized, resulting in a division of labour into treatment, regular and specialized security wings. Their chapter illustrates the aforementioned: 'Scandinavian prisons' are not all the same. The chapter also discusses how a development of more specialized wings and treatment prisons may threaten a culture of equal treatment of prisoners.

Finally, in Part V, John Pratt and Anna Ericsson (Chapter 13), based on the discussions that the original articles in the *British Journal of Criminology* generated, expand on the exceptionalism thesis. They acknowledge the need for some adjustment and refinements, but they also conclude by validating the overall thesis: the Scandinavian countries are exceptional.

In conclusion

We prefer to see this book as a contribution to the growing literature on comparative criminology, understood more widely than comparisons of prison rates. One goal of the anthology is to widen Pratt's perspective, to 'thicken' (cf. Geertz 1973) his description and analyses. Another is to contribute to the opening up of the international research field to include new geographic areas of interest.

So are Nordic prison practices and policies exceptional or not? Yes and no. We couldn't really decide on one answer. One of the strengths of this book, we feel, is that it really is a discussion, that the question in the title really is an open one. The one thing uniting us all is that we see Pratt's two-part article as interesting and important enough to respond to in some way. Our chapters sometimes strengthen his argument, at other times challenge it. Exceptional or not? If yes, how? Readers must make up their own mind. We hope that our book can make that process at once more fruitful and more complicated.

Notes

1 Scandinavia as a geographical area consists of Denmark, Norway and Sweden. These countries also have a common cultural heritage and can understand one another's languages reasonably well. The Nordic countries on the other hand also include Iceland

and Finland. Although part of the same linguistic family, most Scandinavians cannot understand Icelandic. And Finnish is another story entirely – being part of a totally separate family of languages it is, as the proverb goes, Greek to Scandinavians, although Greek is actually a closer relative. In common English usage, however, the difference between Scandinavia and the Nordic countries is often blurred. Pratt's article is mostly based on data from Norway, Sweden and Finland.
2 All this according to the excellent World Prison Brief of the International Centre for Prison Studies at King's College, London.
3 The total prison population is of course also something to consider: DRC has 30,000 prisoners, Iceland 175.

References

Cavadino, Michael and James Dignan (2006) *Penal Systems: A Comparative Approach*. London: Sage.
Christie, Nils (2000) *Crime Control as Industry: Towards Gulags, Western Style*. London: Routledge.
—— (2007) *Limits to Pain*. Eugene: Wipf & Stock.
Dullum, Jane (2009) 'Fengslene og de psykiatriske institusjonene: like eller forskjellige?' ['Prisons and psychiatric institutions: how different? how similar?'], *Nordisk Tidsskrift for Kriminalvidenskab*, 96(1): 35–53.
Garland, David (2001) *The Culture of Control: Crime and Social Order in Contemporary Society*. Chicago: University of Chicago Press.
Geertz, Clifford (1973) 'Thick description: toward an interpretive theory of culture', in Clifford Geertz: *The Interpretation of Cultures: Selected Essays of Clifford Geertz*. New York: Basic Books.
Lacey, Nicola (2008) *The Prisoners' Dilemma: Political Economy and Punishment in Contemporary Democracies*. Cambridge: Cambridge University Press.
Mathiesen, Thomas (2006) *Prison on Trial*. Winchester: Waterside.
Nelken, David (2004) 'Using the concept of legal culture', *Australian Journal of Legal Philosophy*, 29(1): 1–28.
—— (2009) 'Comparative criminal justice', *European Journal of Criminology*, 6(4): 291–311.
—— (2010) *Comparative Criminal Justice: Making Sense of Difference*. Los Angeles, London, New Delhi, Singapore, Washington, DC: Sage.
Pakes, Francis (2010) *Comparative Criminal Justice*. Collumpton: Willan.
Pratt, John (2008a) 'Scandinavian exceptionalism in an era of penal excess: Part I: The nature and roots of Scandinavian exceptionalism', *British Journal of Criminology*, 48(2): 119–37.
—— (2008b) 'Scandinavian exceptionalism in an era of penal excess: Part II: Does Scandinavian exceptionalism have a future?', *British Journal of Criminology*, 48(3): 275–92.
Saussure, Ferdinand de (1983) *Course in General Linguistics*. London: Duckworth.
Sparks, Richard F., Will Hay and A. E. Bottoms (1996) *Prisons and the Problem of Order*. Oxford: Clarendon Press.
Wacquant, Loïc J. D. (2002) 'The curious eclipse of prison ethnography in the age of mass incarceration', *Ethnography*, 3(4): 371–97.
Young, Jock (1999) *The Exclusive Society: Social Exclusion, Crime and Difference in Late Modernity*. London, Thousand Oaks, New Delhi: Sage.

Zedner, Lucia (1995) 'Comparative research in criminal justice', in Lesley Noaks, Michael Levi and Mike Maguire (eds): *Contemporary Issues in Criminology*. Cardiff: University of Wales Press.
—— (2002) 'Danger of dystopias in penal theory', *Oxford Journal of Legal Studies*, 22(2): 341–66.

Part I

Exceptions or not?

2 Scandinavian exceptionalism in penal matters
Reality or wishful thinking?

Thomas Mathiesen

In the footsteps of Margaret Mead

When I began reading John Pratt's two articles on Scandinavian exceptionalism, an old part of one of my first courses in sociology and social anthropology came to mind. The year was way back, 1953, and the site was the University of Wisconsin, where I plunged into my first courses in social science as an undergraduate student. A book came out which soon became very famous. It was one of the major works of the late grand lady of social anthropology, Margaret Mead.

The title of Margaret Mead's volume was *The Study of Culture at a Distance* (Mead and Métraux 1953). It was in her late period, when she turned away from Samoa and similar places, and over to contemporary European and American societies during the 1940s and 1950s. Margaret Mead's concern was the many ways in which social scientists were barred from access to other societies by wars and other calamities during the Second World War, and certainly by the Cold War after the Second World War. The book was widely read and praised. But it was also criticized by many. How could society be studied without close observation and other techniques fostered by social scientists? Margaret Mead responded by moulding a string of methods by which it could be done, precisely without direct access, 'at a distance'.

John Pratt's account of Scandinavian exceptionalism is not exactly a study of culture at a distance as Margaret Mead conceptualized it, because he has to some extent been able to study Norway, Sweden and Finland at close hand. He has been there, talked with many people, observed what is going on. But it reminds one a little of Margaret Mead's approach, because he has had to read a lot about the Nordic countries and their politics. I take it he has had to read historical and contemporary works as they have appeared in English, and he has had conversations in English. Our English is pretty good, so this has been fairly easy, but, nevertheless, it must have created some distance.

Above all, he has for the most part – I am sure there are exceptions – been barred from communication with people who do not speak English. I will come back to this, but first I wish to congratulate John Pratt with a courageous attempt, along lines – if not identical with Margaret Mead – to study culture, shall we say, at some distance. It takes courage to undertake such a research project.

Macro-sociology

There is a second point that I think is important, and which should be put to the forefront. This is one of the few attempts I have seen at studying criminal policy in macro-sociological terms. Whether we are natives or foreigners – I leave that distinction behind now – we so easily become immersed in the details of criminal policy and criminology, even in sociology of law, which is my own approach. And it is important to dig deeply into the details. But it has the disadvantage of blurring the distinction between figure and ground, to use a parallel from Gestalt theory. Essentially, John Pratt has studied the ground – criminal policy interpreted boldly in terms of whole societies – whereas we often end up concentrating so much on the details of criminal policy that we forget the larger issues of societal underpinnings. He has studied these societal underpinnings in a grand way and seen the criminal policy of three societies relative to (as I understand it) the Anglo world (Britain, North America and other parts of the world which are predominantly English speaking). Thus he also has been able to see some important general trends emerge in contrast to the Anglo world, which could not have been seen had he – or we – gone about it in the usual figure-oriented detail. The macro-sociological slant Pratt has chosen brings a new dimension to criminology, and probably also to sociology of law.

While true, such a macro-sociological approach in the context of a study of culture at a distance (or some distance) is open to problems. *The core problem lies in the very coupling of macro-sociology with distance.* A macro-sociological approach invites a strong emphasis on general social trends. It is an important but difficult art to engage in. The researcher is at risk to be caught up in sweeping generalizations. He is able to manage if he or she is intimately familiar with the case. John Pratt is not intimately familiar with his case. He has become familiar with it at a distance. In a sense, then, he has been doubly distanced, which makes him vulnerable. While I have praised him for a courageous attempt, I am now obliged to turn to important features which partly contradict his main thesis, as far as Norway goes. His main thesis is that Scandinavian penal policy is exceptionally mild, and that the mildness is caused by a few general social underpinnings. I question the mildness – the 'dependent variable' if you like. Norwegian penal policy is hardly as mild as John Pratt has imagined.

Before I begin the essential criticism, let me note the following: John Pratt talks of 'Scandinavia' as including Finland, Norway and Sweden. 'Scandinavia', however, includes Norway, Sweden and Denmark, whereas 'the Nordic countries' include in addition Finland, Iceland and the Faeroe Islands. This is not just a trifle. There are some important historical, cultural and political differences between Finland on the one hand and the Scandinavian countries on the other. International influences and national history are different, Finland being inter alia much more tied to and influenced by Russia (though also at war with Russia right before the Second World War). Languages are also widely different, Finnish (the majority language in Finland) being Finno-Ugric, which is very different from the so-called north Germanic languages including Danish, Swedish and Norwegian in addition to Icelandic and Faroese. Scandinavians (Danes, Swedes and Norwegians) cannot at all understand Finnish, but Scandinavians can more or less understand and certainly read one another. I do not go further into this, though it may be of some importance to Pratt's comparisons and research design.

In this chapter, I concentrate on developments in my own country, Norway, which I know best. My discussion is specifically related to the two articles on 'Scandinavian exceptionalism' which Pratt produced in the *British Journal of Criminology* in 2008, and which the editors of this book have already brought to the forefront of the debate. I generally refer to the two articles as 'Part I' and Part II', sometimes also as 2008a and b.[1]

Listening to the system

First, John Pratt has essentially been on a guided research tour. He has listened too much to representatives of the system. This lies in his quotations, his summaries, his reading in general. There are numerous statements about the mildness of Scandinavian criminal policy which suggest this. I will give some examples.

Meetings in the mountains

In Part I, Pratt makes the following statement: 'In Norway, prisoners are included in the yearly "meeting in the mountains" where prison policy is *worked through and determined* by all interested parties. When it seemed likely that a proposal for a 1,000-bed prison in Oslo would go ahead in 2006, a meeting was held between senior civil servants, prison staff, academics and prisoners' groups, who successfully opposed it' (2008a: 120, my italics). The reference here is clearly the so-called Spåtind meetings, organized by KROM – the Norwegian Association for Penal Reform.

I wish this were true. I wish we had such an influence. I could well imagine this quote used in a propaganda folder. I wish we could just convene the right people, and prison policy would be changed through agreement. While I think we have had some influence, and I will return to that, KROM's work has nevertheless consisted of *continual sweat and tears, a continual struggle, for our whole life time*, 43 years to be exact (we started out as a pressure group in 1968). We have been completely unlike the streamlined ministerial image Pratt – at a distance – gives of our work. Prisoners 'are included', Pratt says, as if that has emanated from above as a benign and benevolent decision descending on the prisoners from senior civil servants and staff. Nothing could be further from the truth. The picture Pratt gives of KROM is like the picture he gives of Norwegian – and Scandinavian – criminal policy in general: decision makers are benevolent; harmony reigns.

Barometer of the times

KROM's struggles may serve as a barometer of the times. According to Pratt, the 1980s or 1990s are turning point years (Part II: 275, 277). During the decades before, the welfare state was running smoothly and the penal culture of the country was characterized by soft hearts, mellow attitudes and solidarity. The fact of the matter is that from 1968 and the early 1970s on, and at least until 1990, the atmosphere at least in Norway was not mild as Pratt suggests, but hard as stone. A few examples are in order:

- During all of the first years, prison staff and also higher-ranking people in the so-called criminal justice system, studiously avoided our mountain conferences and other types of meeting. They came only hesitantly in the first part of the 1970s. They came in their separate vans and left early. A single prison warden took actively part in the debate, against KROM. He was the warden of the Norwegian youth prison (years later, he gradually turned around and in fact became a partner).
- In 1968, right after we started, the Minister of Justice at the time informed Parliament in full session, as an answer to a left-wing parliament member, that 'the prison system has not barred inmates from becoming members'. The prison system 'has, however, not found it correct to contribute actively to such membership, and believes it not to be justifiable to let the inmates participate actively in [organizational] work along the lines presupposed by the regulations of the association'.[2] The tone was stiff to say the least.
- Prison officials censored our (and everybody else's) mail to inmates. They barred inmates from sending manuscripts to newspapers and, notably, to a book which KROM was going to publish. In 1969 to 1970 we had to muster the Parliamentary Ombudsman for Public Administration, an office established by Parliament a short while before, in a lengthy complaint over such censorship of manuscripts to our books.[3] The prison warden wrote to the university library, where we had found the articles which we wanted to reprint, requiring the prison newspaper to be sealed for 50 years pursuant to the Legal Deposit Act of 1939. Heavy media coverage followed. Eventually we won the case. But the sealing of the newspaper is still in force.[4]
- At the only meeting during all of the first years held between a couple of board member of KROM and the warden of Norway's main central prison at the time (the meeting was initiated by us), we were inter alia condescendingly refused to have any special arrangements set up for facilitating mail from prisoners to KROM (censorship was of course presupposed by us).
- Prison authorities refused to let us distribute a short folder on the Public Administration Act of 1967 (enforced 1970) as far as it pertained to inmates, written by a first-rate lawyer, to the prisoners. The folder was allowed in, but only after a battle.
- Prison authorities denied inmates to come to our meetings outside. For quite a few years, prisoners' participation at the mountain meetings mainly consisted of ex-convicts.

And so on and so forth. To be sure, we also won some battles. In the late 1960s Norway had plans for a detention centre, a 'short sharp shock' prison, which had to be called off when people in KROM found and made known British documentation (a White Paper) indicating that, in England, the detention centres for the youngest were to be dismantled. And we were part of a movement (where many others participated) having a major forced labour prison for alcoholic vagrants as well as the Norwegian youth prison closed down (1970 and 1975).

These victories were very important. But they did not follow from soft attitudes and social solidarity. *They had to be fought through when the time was ripe*, the institutions in question having proved to be complete failures. And our losses were also profound, and at times extremely hard to take. They took away our health as well as our marriages.

But the struggles were also interesting. They yielded a wealth of information on a major historical epoch which some of us analysed sociologically. In a sense, the struggles in which KROM was engaged[5] served as a barometer of the times. The temperature was icy.

This was exactly the time during which we supposedly were under the increasing and gradually more benevolent warming winds of John Pratt's welfare state.

Outside of KROM's orbit

However, there is a question. The question is essentially methodological. When you approach an organizational system such as the prison system with kindness and respect, or with neutrality, the approach elicits one kind of information. When you approach it with a fighting spirit, the approach elicits another kind of response. I can testify to this because I have been in both roles – the respectfully neutral and the fighting spirit, you might say – in relation to the prison system. In responding to the first spirit, the system often (but not always) reacts in a suave way and sometimes with limited openness (though not necessarily changing things for the better). In responding to the second spirit, the system often (not always) reacts with more or less deep-seated hostility. Both sets of response equally reflect *realities* embedded in the system.

Did our fighting spirit elicit the hostile response during these first decades? I think largely not. We began by approaching the prison system in a highly respectful, neutral spirit. The fighting variety of KROM's spirit came only gradually, as a reply to the completely negative responses from the prison authorities.

It may be, however, that the very existence of a prisoners' organization was understood as a provocation. To be on the safe side, therefore, I will now move onto several examples outside of KROM's orbit and experience, which testify that the attitudes of the prison authorities and people in the criminal justice system were not just a reaction to the prisoners' organization, but of a much more deep-seated kind, precisely at the time when the welfare state was blooming.

Relaxed conditions?

In Pratt's article Part I we read that 'Norwegian students often work as prison officers on a casual basis is indicative of the generally relaxed conditions to be found *in most prisons*' (121, my italics). True, one finds students working in prisons for example during vacations, but there are wide variations in what one would call 'generally relaxed conditions'. Some of my informants from some of the larger closed prisons such as Ila, Ullersmo or Ringerike prisons, tell a different story. Compared with the US, prison conditions are probably and generally more relaxed, 'objectively' and as an outsider would see it. I can testify to this from numerous visits in the larger European countries, the US and in South America. But prisoners who live in the Norwegian prisons I have mentioned, certainly have varying views. An ex-convict from Ila is currently developing an interesting thesis: the strong regimentation, cell controls including digital data controls, harassments and so on at Ila, a preventive detention prison, which according to him is engulfing not only prisoners but certainly also staff, is now becoming a general model (he calls it an 'experimental' model) for other closed prisons in Norway. Close to two-thirds of the Norwegian prisoners are, mind you, confined in closed prisons.[6] There are fairly benign prisons such as Bastøy prison, located on an island and therefore in fact closed (formally it counts as an open prison), but these are exceptional cases.

In another context Pratt refers to Norwegian 'trainee prison officers ... [as receiving] two years' training while on full salary'. About 150 officers are recruited from 2,000 applicants (Pratt I: 120–1). The formulations suggest that in Norwegian prisons staff is well trained for prison service. In reality, and for various reasons, from 2004 to 1 October 2009 at least 25 per cent of the workforce in Norwegian prisons were unskilled workers, meaning that they did not have the two years of prison officers' training within the prison service. During the summer the figure may reach 50 per cent. The training of stand-ins varies. The number of untrained officers is considered a major problem by staff organizations.[7]

Digital data processing and control

A few words specifically on digital data processing and control are in order.

Something like a paradigm shift seems to be coming up in Norwegian prisons. Physical control is of course still with us. But control is no longer just physical, it is also digital. It is based on categorizations and classifications of inmates, ending in predictive and risk-assessment devices suitable for control – for example of release time, leaves and furloughs, or what have you. OASys, a British invention, is one such system. OASys is a bit outdated in Norway, but similar systems follow in its wake. The predictive power of the instruments may vary and may be low, at least at present. But control is more than prediction of the future. Control is also a matter for the present: digital systems may also be used for extensive administrative control.

Digital control is silent, quiet, unnoticeable. You have to be very alert to discover it. Discovery is sometimes based on errors made by personnel. A prisoner at Ila Preventive Prison recently uncovered scandalous conditions concerning the spread of data. It turned out that sensitive information about prisoners was entirely unsecured. Not only could all prison officers see and read intimate details concerning all prisoners, they could also, unnoticed, introduce changes in the information. It turned out that an unofficial, uncontrolled and illegal database was in use which contained extensive personal information that could be read by large staff categories. Complaints from the prisoner uncovering this to higher authorities in the prison system were flatly rejected. But the prisoner went on to complain to the Norwegian Data Inspectorate, which scrutinized the case and criticized the prison system severely, demanding eight major changes in the prison's data systems. The scandal was extensively covered by the mass media.[8]

In other words, inmates won this case. This particular struggle of course took place after Pratt's research period. But the issue of digital control, for example based on OASys, has been widely discussed among Norwegian criminologists from the first part of the 2000s (see Giertsen 2006). And the development of the paradigm shift, with vast consequences for inmates, continues.

Work and education

Again Pratt tells his readers that 'Most prisoners work or receive full-time education well beyond remedial level – many are encouraged by the prison authorities to study for degrees by distance education' (Part I: 121). First: what kind of work? How many times have I heard prisoners refer to 'meaningless work'. In the early 1960s, when I did my research at Ila Preventive Prison, a main occupation was that of tying together small plastic bags to make envelopes for tobacco. The inmates never got to touch the tobacco (though smoking was allowed in the prison). The tobacco was sold at market price by outside companies. Similar meaningless work is referred to today, for example in Oslo prison, our largest prison.

And what about education? Yes, education in prison has grown since the early 1970s. Today there are educational facilities in all Norwegian prisons. This is one of the relatively few major real successes of the Norwegian prison system. Many prisoners follow educational courses. Education is apparently appreciated by prisoners.

But ask one of the earlier consultant secretaries at the Department of Criminology and Sociology of Law in Oslo about all of the difficulties she has had in getting inmates out to follow courses at the University of Oslo and in our department. She has written a telling article on her experiences on our website (kriminalpolitikk.uio.no). Unfortunately it is only available in Norwegian (Fjeldberg 2007). In general, prisoners testify to the fact that educational courses, which are important to them, in many places are disrupted and reorganized by sudden movements of prisoners to other sections of the prison or to other prisons, as well as by disciplinary measures. The various measures disrupt the courses, or at least makes teaching quite difficult and different from what the book says. Discipline and security frequently have an upper hand. Nothing of this is apparent from Pratt's account.

Pre-trial detention (remand)

Something specifically on pre-trial detention and related issues, which John Pratt hardly touches on (see Pratt I: 123–4), are in order. They present Norwegian (and Swedish) penal policy more or less at its worst, and are painfully embarrassing. The numbers of pre-trial detainees, the length of their detention and the use of isolation are old-timers as problems, and from as far back as the twentieth (or for that matter the nineteenth) century. They were relevant issues of debate even before the Criminal Procedure Act of 1887 (Bratholm 1958).

At any time a large proportion of Norwegian inmates are on pre-trial detention, often for very long periods of time. In 2004, the last year for which I have had access to official figures, there were on the average 618 individuals on pre-trial detention, which amounts to 20.4 per cent of the average prison population that year.[9] This is a very large proportion. Through the decades since 1960, the proportion has largely varied between 20 and 25 per cent. During 2004, 19.6 per cent of the 1,037 inmates who were transferred from pre-trial detention to serving a sentence had been kept from three to five months on pre-trial detention. Of this number, 13.5 per cent had spent six months to two years on pre-trial detention. One person had spent three years on pre-trial detention.[10] The last change in the relevant act (the Criminal Procedure Act) came in 2002, and was from before the figures given above were assembled and official. Inmates subject to pre-trial detention may not be detained for more than four weeks, but detention may normally be prolonged by court order for up to four weeks at a time (§185 of the Criminal Procedure Act). Rod Morgan, Professor of Criminal Justice at the University of Bristol and Director of the Centre for Criminal Justice there, has developed a lengthy and incisive critique based on first-hand knowledge of the Norwegian pre-trial detention system (see Peter Scharff Smith's contribution to this book, Chapter 3).

The main present regulation (§186 of the Act) gives the court very wide discretionary powers regarding isolation. The detainee may be *barred* from sending or reading letters or having visits, or he/she may be *controlled* by the police in these respects. The detainee may also be barred from having access to newspapers, radio, television, or may be barred from contact with specific other inmates (referred to as partial isolation). The latter formulations (partial rather than full isolation and isolation from specific other inmates rather than all other inmates) are considered as improvements (§186). But the court may leave it to the prosecuting authority to decide what inmates the detainee may be barred from contact with. Also, §186a stipulates that the court may decide that the detainee is to be barred from contact with the other inmates (full isolation).

Recent data provided in the International Covenant on Civil and Political Rights substantiate that total isolation is still used, and extensively so:[11]

During 2008:

> *404 individuals* in all were subject to total isolation, partly in combination with other restrictions.

64 individuals (15.8 per cent) were subject to total isolation not combined with any other restrictions.
24 individuals (5.9 per cent) were barred from access to letters, visits, radio, TV or newspapers.
258 individuals (63.9 per cent) were barred from access to letters and visits.
7 individuals (1.7 per cent) were subject to control of letters and visits, but barred from access to radio, TV, newspapers.
51 individuals (12.6 per cent) were subject to control of letters and visits.[12]

Being barred from contact in the form of letters and visits is possibly the toughest form of isolation, since it may involve breaking relationships with husbands, wives, children and other close relatives. From the information we may conclude that 346 individuals (85.6 per cent) of those subject to total isolation in 2008 were barred from such contact, often in addition to other restrictions. It should be added that 241 of these (69.7 per cent) were isolated for two to four weeks; 29 (8.4 per cent) for more than four weeks; 76 (22 per cent) for less than two weeks. *By far the largest category is that of being barred from letters and visits – including family – for two to four weeks. Some are even barred from such contact for longer periods of time: six individuals were barred for two to three months.*

The size of the prison population on pre-trial detention, the isolation and length and conditions of their stay are considered a major set of problems by alert audiences. We do not know how the figures compare with Anglo countries. At any rate, they may be viewed as significant and do not fit well with John Pratt's emphasis on humane Scandinavian prison conditions.

Police isolation cells

A person caught by the police may be kept in a police isolation cell (*glattcelle*, 'stripped cell', normally no furniture except a mattress and a toilet in the corner) for up to 48 hours, after which the rule says he must be transferred to an ordinary pre-trial detention prison cell, or released. Your wristwatch is taken away from you, so that you frequently lose sense of time, the cells are small, they may be extremely warm or extremely cold, the air is foul and the smell in the police cell has been called 'the smell of fear'.[13] Many spend longer than 48 hours there. Figures procured from the police by the Norwegian Bar Association show that in Oslo police district alone, there were 1,228 24-hour periods[14] exceeding the time limit during the first three-quarters of 2010.[15] This failure to meet the time limit is referred to as inhuman and degrading treatment by the European Committee for the Prevention of Torture (CPT). The number of incarcerations in stripped cells has been on the increase during the 2000s. According to the Ombudsman for Children, during all of 2009 and excepting two police districts including the capital city, *youths (aged 15 to 17) were placed in police isolation cells over 1,000 times.*[16] This is a formidable figure. We do not know how many individuals were involved, because an individual may have been placed in such a cell several times during a year. In addition comes the count for the capital city, Oslo, which according to the

Norwegian Bar Association was 680 for individuals in the 15 to 17-year-old age group in 2009.[17] Comparable information could easily have been obtained by Pratt during his period of research.

Until recently, a person who was caught by the police had to be brought before the courts within 24 hours for possible pre-trial detention, or released. This is now extended to 72 hours, on the grounds that it gives the police more time to evaluate the question of pre-trial detention, thus reducing the number of inmates on such detention. Provisional information (an evaluation is in progress) suggests that it increases the use of pre-trial detention.[18] Information on the reactions of the CPT on Norwegian practice may be found in Chapter 3 of this book. CPT has been very critical indeed.

Suicides. Mental illness?

We do not find information on prison suicides in Pratt's articles. But there are indeed suicides. The phenomenon of suicides among prisoners is well researched and readily available in Norway, and I therefore add some information on it.

Between 1990 and 2007, 59 suicides were registered in Norwegian prisons. Suicides predominantly take place in *closed prisons* and in *pre-trial detention*. During the period mentioned, 66 per cent took place in pre-trial detention, for the most part during periods of isolation. Almost three out of four suicides took place by hanging. Of these, 22 per cent of the individuals were aged 25 years or younger (Hammerlin 2009).[19] Suicides in prisons have apparently been on the rise. Yngve Hammerlin, a prominent expert on suicides in prison, has this to say:

> During 1956–1998 81 suicides were registered in Norwegian prisons; over 60% took place during the period 1980–1998. These are minimum figures. Largely and as a tendency we can say that during the 1960s one person on the average committed suicide per year in Norwegian prisons; during the 1970s two, during the 1980s three and during the 1990s between three and four. 1995 has the highest figure of registered suicides in the prisons, six persons.
> (2000: 29)

Note that the total number of prisoners has also increased.

The existence of mentally ill prisoners has been well known for a long time. Bloch and Mathisen have this to say:

> It also happens that some of those who are confined there are psychiatric cases [psykisk syke] who should have been in quite a different place. Nobody has general information on who as of today have psychiatric problems which are so great that they ought not to be in prison. The Ministry of Justice is today engaged in getting these figures on the table. The prison warden at Ila Preventive Prison has earlier come out with the information that in his prison alone, 6 to 9 prisoners are confined who are actually too ill to serve a sentence there.
> (2009: 24)

Pratt presents the policy of the Norwegian Labour Party (presently in a coalition government) on psychiatric health care services in the following words: 'Good psychiatric health care services and an active labour market policy are important for comprehensive crime fighting.' 'There is still the belief', he goes on to say, 'that state-provided welfare services and regulation can reduce crime problems and, in so doing, provide social solidarity, without recourse to exclusionary sanctions' (Pratt I: 134). True enough as belief and ideology. Here Pratt had a unique opportunity to look into the *actual* state of affairs concerning psychiatric health care and labour market policy in Norwegian criminal policy. He did not avail himself of that opportunity.

Psychiatric and other health care

The actual state of affairs concerning medical health has been known for a long time by people in and close to the prison system. It was certainly well known during Pratt's research period. Since 1987 the authority concerning the implementation of health care has been divided between municipal authorities, which employed medical personnel (and other specialists), and the prison authorities, which have been responsible inter alia for security. This division was introduced in order to increase the independence of medical personnel in prisons. Though an improvement, the difficulties of medical personnel did not vanish. The prison has had, inter alia, the final say concerning matters such as transfers to other institutions or shortening of sentences for medical reasons. In January 2010 a study of prisoners' opinion of health care conditions was made public (Bjørngaard *et al.* 2009). A total of 1,454 inmates in 29 prisons in southern and central Norway answered a questionnaire about experiences with health services (90 per cent response rate; 1,619 were eligible for inclusion in the sample and able to participate). The study followed a statistically sophisticated design. It revealed high levels of dissatisfaction with prison health services. There was a tendency toward general dissatisfaction; thus almost half, 41 per cent, reported 'very or quite dissatisfied' when answering a general question. This is interesting given the strong evidence of poor health among prisoners in general. Importantly, prison inmates' satisfaction with the health services provided were low compared with patient satisfaction measured in other health areas. Thus, the prisoners' mean satisfaction score was substantially lower compared with that of mental health patients.

Only 50 per cent of the prisons had a functioning contract with municipal authorities. In a radio programme on 29 January 2010 a high-ranking person in the Norwegian Directorate of Health, a state institution, in fact agreed with the prisoners that they had good reason to complain.

Prisonization?

Let me interject here that Pratt has referred to my early prison study (Mathiesen 1965) in his lecture notes for his Oslo talk in 2009. He refers to this study as one in which prisonization, significantly, did not occur. Prisoners held other, non-prison-like norms and values, very unlike prisoners in the US. He suggests that this is the situation also today. But he does not refer to Ulla Bondeson's classic study from almost the same time (Bondeson 1974), partly translated into English (Bondeson 1990): a large number of prisons and institutions in Sweden, 13 in all, showed prisoners with clear-cut signs of prisonization, drugification, neurotification, and so on. Bondeson's work includes a very skilled study of prisoners' language. Knowledge of argot language is seen as an operational criterion of degree of prisonization. My informal observations indicated that knowledge of prisoners' language was far less prevalent in my Norwegian prison at the time, though the prison had quite a few long-timers in custody. The Norwegian and the Swedish study, both from the growth period of the welfare state, testify to some significant differences between two Scandinavian countries at the time, and provide an explanation of why widespread prisoners' strikes got so great a momentum in Sweden during the early 1970s. I followed the Swedish prison developments closely at the time. Several hunger strikes took place, one of them counting 2,600 strikers out of Sweden's 4,800 prisoners (the count is KRUM's – a prisoners' organization parallel to KROM, which existed between 1966 and 1977; the prison authorities counted 1,889).[20] In addition, taking into account the great influx of prisoners from Eastern Europe and non-European countries to date,[21] I don't know from where Pratt got the suggestion that my 1965 study is representative, as far as prisoners' values go, also for Norwegian prisons today.

Conjugal relations

Pratt refers to conjugal relations (Part I: 122) which supposedly are 'encouraged and facilitated in Scandinavia', and the remarkable conditions under which the prisoner and his/her partner plus children meet during weekends. How many prisoners does Pratt think have conjugal visits under such conditions? My point would be that this generalization, as well as quite a few others, is characterized by an absence of qualifications, which gives much too positive a picture than warranted of Scandinavian conditions.

Solariums?

I could go on in this way. Also, Pratt refers to 'another illustration of the exceptional qualities of Scandinavian prisons, solarium facilities are provided *in a number of closed and open prisons*' (Part I: 122, my italics). He goes on to explain why – absence of sunlight during the Scandinavian winter and danger of vitamin D deficiency. He generalizes on Scandinavia – without qualifications. Where are the solariums in Norwegian prisons? A quick call to the Department of Prison and Probation revealed that offhand they knew of no place in Norway where they had solariums – not even in the newest large prison in the city of Halden, opened in 2010. They added that Finland, with its widespread tradition for saunas (steam baths), might have some. Further information concerning Norway revealed that in fact we have two prisons with solariums out of Norway's 49 prisons (2007)

– one small open prison and 'the shining jewel' among open prisons, Bastøy. According to the information I have obtained, there are no solariums in closed prisons. The prisoners in the two open prisons have to pay for using the facilities. They pay with the aid of a coin machine. The question of solariums is in a way a detail, but I have gone into it to illustrate Pratt's less than precise positive generalizations.[22]

One more point that Pratt makes: 'Many of those serving short sentences in open prisons are allowed to continue with their previous employment' (Part I: 122). How many prisoners are given this opportunity? We learn that 'Bastøy prison in Norway is the shining jewel in the Scandinavian open prison system'. Pratt goes into considerable detail about Bastøy (Part I: 123). I have already commented on it. While Bastøy is a relatively pleasant place (though there are differences of opinion about it among inmates, the prison being isolated on an island with open sea around it), it is hardly a shining jewel. And so on, and so forth.

Pratt referred to Bastøy as 'the shining jewel' in the system. For the sake of balance, why not also refer to the low point in the system? According to quite a few inmates, the low point is Ringerike prison. According to its own self-presentation on the Internet, '[w]ork at Ringerike is to be characterized by humane considerations, legal justice and a high professional standard. By supervision, the setting of limits and goal-orientation, the prison is to prepare the inmates for taking responsibility for their own lives.' I assume this is drafted by the Prison and Probation Department. Ringerike is designed for 160 prisoners and is considered as Norway's most secure prison. Though living conditions are modern and relatively high, many prisoners consider the institution as a 'brave new world'. It is an illustration of the fact that high living standards are certainly not enough to make prisons 'humane'.[23]

Some of the information about 'humane considerations' may be correct. But it is not contextualized by the rigours also characteristic of many Norwegian or Scandinavian prisons, and nowhere is the information balanced by the other side of the coin. Why has KROM kept struggling so hard for 43 years, and why go on with it? We should have retired long ago.

Other indications

Mention should be made of Norwegian legislation on drug crime (also noted by Pratt in Part II: 285–6). During a relatively short period of time, about 20 years, maximum punishment for drug-related crime has escalated sharply, from six months to 21 years. Here is a sample of legal provisions contained in the Norwegian Penal Code §162:

> illegal production, import, export, sending or transferring of substances defined as drugs, is punishable by fines or imprisonment up to two years;
> serious drug crime is punishable by imprisonment up to ten years. In deciding whether an offence is serious, particular emphasis should be placed on the kind of drug, the amount and the character of the offence;

offences dealing with very considerable amounts of drug are punishable by (a minimum) of three years to (a maximum) of fifteen years;

offences committed under particularly aggravating circumstances may lead to imprisonment of up to twenty-one years.[24]

The upper ends of these scales are approached relatively often, bringing a large number of individuals who have committed drug-related crimes to long-term imprisonment. But the 'war on drugs' has not been won: in the year 1980, 2,000 drug crimes were recorded by the police. In 2009 the figure was about 40,000. About one-third of the prison population are behind bars for drug-related crimes.[25] A retired Supreme Court judge publicly made the following statement about the situation in early 2010: 'It has been shocking to admit what I have actually taken part in, and I cannot, in contrast to those who only now understand the gigantic and useless costs of the drug war, excuse myself with not knowing better . . . It . . . has been a brutal and tragic error in relation to the goal: to fight the drug problem' (*Aftenposten*, 14 February 2010).

To this Pratt may answer that yes, Scandinavian exceptionalism *is* threatened, precisely now. But his study at this point has a problem: reality shows a mix of attitudes, especially in the 2000s, whereas Pratt presents an unequivocally positive Scandinavian *model* in the past, and the other trend towards penal populism in our own time as deviating from the model. The image of Scandinavian exceptionalism described in the first paper is actually *solidified* by indicating deviation and contrast in the second paper. Pratt is able to have his cake and eat it.

Why is this important?

The sum of what I have argued, inside and outside KROM's orbit, means that *Pratt's division of the development of criminal policy into historical periods is distorted as far as Norway goes.*

The period up to the 1980s or 1990s, which Pratt describes as benevolent due to egalitarianism and the growth of the welfare state (the two major underpinnings he outlines) were actually downright tough decades. I think it is to some extent true that KROM helped break the ice in Norway, so that Inger Louise Valle became our liberal minister of justice 1973 to 1979 (the story of how she got to that position is fascinating, but too long to be related here;[26] at any rate her journey to the top was, I think, influenced by KROM). But note that this quite successful minister was ousted – literally thrown out – in 1979[27] by the hardliners in her own Labour Party in government as well as by right-wing conservative lawyers and others. It was due in part to a liberal White Paper on criminal policy authorized by her in 1978.

Later decades, decades which Pratt in his second article (Part II) describes as invested with possible new tones of toughness, penal populism if you like, are in fact invested with such tones (see earlier), but have in important ways *also* been increasingly benevolent compared to earlier times.[28] There has been a mix; my experience is that during the 2000s, as opposed to the period from the 1960s,

Norway has had a certain touch of openness in the criminal justice system which we did not even see signs of in early decades. The relevant authorities come to our meetings, they debate and discuss with us. KROM, on the other hand, is a fairly constant variable – I don't think we have become much softer. The relevant authorities may have become wiser in terms of cooptation. They may also have discovered the importance of 'repressive tolerance', the famous concept coined by Herbert Marcuse in 1964. Several people inside KROM think so. The authorities may also have become more professional in relation to the media. They may have developed a media policy that does not always work as planned, but which presents penal policy in a favourable light. The present Minister of Justice is open and interested in exchange of opinion and debate. At the same time, he favours increased punishment scales concerning violent and sexual crimes (and favours them applied by the courts *before* they are to be legally enforced in 2012). He also favours hard measures in extraditing refugees who have been refused permission to remain in the country. But there also seems to be a measure of a wish for genuine dialogue. As an example, at our mountain meeting in 2009, the Minister of Justice came the long way on icy winter roads to give a lecture on a White Paper which his Ministry had issued. At our mountain meeting in 2010, two senior officials from the Prison and Probation Department and one State Secretary (next to the minister in political command), as well as a top lawyer in Politiets Utlendingsenhet (in English euphemistically called the National Police Immigration Service) came for discussions and confrontation. The two senior officials were to comment on papers given by one convict and one ex-convict.

In sum, these historical developments are more or less opposite of what Pratt describes: an early period, during 'the happy moment of the welfare state', Dalberg-Larsen's (1988) phrase, with harsh attitudes and tough politics; a later period with that, but also with benevolence and a certain measure of openness on the part of the prison system.[29]

Worse elsewhere?

At this point we should ask: are not the circumstances I have pointed to for Norway – suicides behind the walls, mental illness behind the walls, prisoners' dissatisfaction with medical care, the extensive use of police isolation cells, the extensive use of pre-trial detention and isolation in pre-trial detention, long sentences for drug offences (leading our prisons to become clogged up) – also present in other prison systems in the Anglo world which Pratt uses as comparison?

They most probably are, in many places. This should be kept in mind. But for several reasons these facts elsewhere do not excuse Pratt for omitting the same facts, even if on a lower scale, for Norway or Scandinavia. Because omitted they are. First, it is questionable, when a prison system is described as being of a positive, even exceptional kind, to *omit systematically* rather than carefully analyse features of the system which speak against the system. A macro-sociological approach, and perhaps also the study of culture 'at a distance', indeed allows for or even necessitates the omission of details. But the features I have pointed to are not details in the context of a prison system. On the contrary, they are salient facts.

Second, in terms of several of the negative features I have pointed to for Norway, the prison system of our country ranks quite high, though probably not among the highest in the Anglo world:

- Norwegian penal sanctions for drug crimes are on top internationally.
- So is the extensive use of long-term pre-trial detention and isolation.
- Prisonization certainly takes place. This is carefully documented for Sweden, and is likely to be present also for the other Scandinavian countries in view of the influx of prisoners from other countries.

John Pratt *idealizes the Scandinavian situation*. Through all of the trimmings with which he contextualizes shorter sentences and smaller prisons, he makes Scandinavian prisons look like a Christmas tree with all the decorations on display and a shining jewel (Bastøy) at the top. In effect, he makes an ideal type of 'Scandinavian exceptionalism' – not in a Weberian sense as a rigorous method of comparison, but in an idealistic sense, portraying it as the main reality, overlooking a very significant context of hardship and pain that has existed and continues to exist in Scandinavian prisons.

No reality? Only wishful thinking?

I am coming slowly to my conclusion. Is there nothing, then, in (or emanating from) Pratt's presentation which really warrants the term 'exception'? Yes, there is:

- Though many people are sentenced, sentences are shorter, leading to fewer prisoners per capita because of a more rapid circulation in the prisons. This is the main 'objective difference' between prisons in Norway and in the Anglo world.

There are also some other differences which are more subjective and more difficult to evaluate:

- Though increasingly being built larger by Norwegian standards, prisons are small relative to Anglo standards.
- Foreigners who do time in Norwegian prisons sometimes applaud conditions when they compare with prison life at home. This could be a criterion of humane conditions. But there are exceptions. Norwegian prison regimes, though based on such values as equality, are such that foreigners used to other contexts sometimes/often experience a lack of well-being.[30]

One major problem with Pratt's description and analysis of Norwegian and Scandinavian prison life is that it eventually may be used against both him and us.

This is always a danger with exaggeration and omission in research, at least in research which is controversial. Sooner or later someone with a conservative non-reformist stance will come around and say 'look, they are hiding the facts!'. That day will be a major setback to Scandinavian exceptionalism as an example for others, and even cast doubt on the three truths listed earlier.

Also, sooner or later, someone home based will come around and say 'look, you have nothing to worry about, you're the best in the world! Pack your bags and find something better to do than criticize.'

Is Norway/Scandinavia an example for others?

A hidden message in John Pratt's articles may be that others, presently bound to penal excess, may find an example of something different in Norway and Scandinavia. This is even more so a possible message in Pratt's recent article written with Anna Eriksson, 'Den skandinaviska exceptionalismen' (2009). As I have said, in terms of causation Pratt's two articles in 2008 concentrate on historical cultures of equality and the rise of a universal welfare state as major underpinnings of Scandinavian exceptionalism. Pratt and Eriksson (2009), which is a solid article having left out most of the exaggerations and omissions, develops this into four historical forces – the unique welfare state, the political economy, the political culture and the Scandinavian mass media.

I have spent good parts of my life advocating a combination of criminological analysis and action, and will continue to do so. But sometimes the two diverge. While interesting as a historical/sociological analysis, I fear that the reference to deep historical roots such as these does not help us much in finding concrete ways to a more enlightened and humane criminal and penal policy. Actually, the authors do not argue this, either. The reason is, of course, that these are major structural features coming up from the past. If they are basic root conditions for the fostering of a more enlightened criminal and penal policy in the present, my worry is that countries which are victims of penal excess have a long way to go. Basic structural features of the societies concerned would have to be altered first. This is no small order. Essentially, a revolution is necessary. To me, Rusche and Kirchheimer's (1939) classic study of the relationship between the labour market and punishment through history comes to mind. We have to be aware of the possibility that punishment and penality in phases are more independent of social structural features than we think. The possibility of a more or less reverse relationship in Norway between social structure and penal conditions and values, with harsh penal values and attitudes during the construction of the welfare state and more mixed (also benign) attitudes today, pointed out in my critique of Pratt, is a case in point.

Turning points

Let me present an alternative way of looking at it. There is a difference between explanations of growth and explanations of change. History does not always change through processes following from long-term and specific trends, but sometimes by *turning points* due to several or many intangible and interacting circumstances, notably including human action, which are difficult to unravel. 'The time is ripe', as the saying goes. The fall of the Roman empire (Scheerer 1986: 7), the end of witch hunting in the seventeenth-century Spanish empire (Henningsen 1984; Lea 1906/1966), and the fall of the Soviet empire in the late twentieth century are cases in point.

In penal policy, perhaps we are now moving towards such a turning point. There are signs, however modest, that things may be changing, just a little – in the midst of penal populism. In February 2009 a federal three-judge panel ruled that the California prison system, the largest prison system in the US with about 167,000 prisoners, could reduce its population by shortening sentences, give inmates good behaviour credits towards early release, reform parole (which they said would have no adverse effect on public safety), and the like. Without such a plan, the panel said, conditions inside the prisons would continue to deteriorate and inmates would simply die from suicide or lack of proper care.[31] As late as 2007 California's governor, Arnold Schwarzenegger, promised that there was no way any California convict was going to get a break on his prison term. Less than half a year later, he had turned completely around proposing to cut the prison population by a sizeable proportion to save the state from total bankruptcy due to the federal crisis. Federal courts had already ruled that the state's failure to provide medical and mental health care to prisoners had subjected them to cruel and unusual punishment, which is prohibited by the Constitution (Mathiesen 2010: 118).[32] In June 2010 Kenneth Clarke, newly appointed Secretary of State for Justice and Lord Chancellor in the new British government, signalled an end to short prison sentences after warning it was 'virtually impossible' to rehabilitate an inmate in less than 12 months. In this announcement he reminded one a little of Winston Churchill's famous speech on the same issue as Home Secretary in 1911 (Churchill's initiatives indeed lowered the prison population substantially at the time; Rutherford 1986: 123–6). In his first major speech since taking office,[33] Clarke indicated a major shift in penal policy by saying prison was not effective in many cases. This could result in more offenders being handed community punishments. Clarke, who described the current prison population of 85,000 as 'astonishing', faced immediate criticism from some colleagues in a party renowned for its tough stance on law and order. He signalled that fathers who fail to pay child maintenance, disqualified drivers and criminals fighting asylum refusals could be among the first to benefit and should not be in prison. Swede Johan Wennström, editorial writer in *Svenska Dagbladet* (liberal conservative), refers extensively to Kenneth Clarke in a major write-up, and claims that there is an increasing trend to criticize the prison for not functioning according to plan – though he (Wennström) personally defends the prison as our last resort for protecting the lower classes (Wennström 2010). During his visit to Norway in January 2010, the Russian Minister of Justice, Alexander Konovalëv, maintained that Russia is in its first phase of a reform plan towards 2020, by which the country wishes to introduce alternative penal measures.[34] On Norwegian radio (together with the Norwegian minister of justice, in English),[35] Konovalëv opened by saying that Bredtveit, a Norwegian prison for women which he had just visited, was 'quite a nice institution', but not of much use in relation to Russia's large number of prisoners. But several times he clearly stated that out of Russia's 900,000 prisoners, half could be punished in the outside community, with various types of community sentence (at one point he also mentioned one-third). He seemed to be looking for alternatives, his main point being that placing these prisoners in prison camps together with the hardened criminals would be counterproductive today. They would take on a criminal culture. The others, serious criminals who would have to remain inside walls, should be place in 'jails', not in prison camps of the old Stalinist type. He maintained that president Vladimir Putin, though viewed as a conservative in the Western mass media, was actually a pragmatist who understood that Russia needed change, and answered a straightforward 'yes' to the question of whether he had Putin's support for his liberal ideas.

We must seize the times. Though now coming from the top, the new signals are weak and may receive strong opposition. There will be setbacks and important strings attached. But the Scandinavian situation, with shorter sentences and thereby fewer prisoners per capita, and also smaller prisons by international standards and generally a more bearable life from a foreigner's, may be one departure. Indeed, the Norwegian Minister of Justice mentioned, in his radio talk with Konovalëv, that he had a dialogue developing with the latter, and that Russia's present course had global consequences (perhaps he tied him to it). Add a measure of abolitionism – such as getting the short-timers out of prison, as Winston Churchill and Kenneth Clarke suggested 100 years apart, or getting quite a few of those who have committed drugs crimes out – and you may have a package which is viable and not just spitting against the wind.

The danger, of course, is the effectiveness of alternative measures in terms of reducing recidivism, so typical an idea of Norwegian criminal policy of today. It is an argument as long as it works. But it may go wrong, which may lead to a counter-reaction. Another danger is what will happen to all of those who remain in prison. Issues such as these need careful thinking.

Sociological research is on our side in so far as prisons definitely do not function according to plan. We can show this empirically (Mathiesen 2006). Theoretically we also have much to draw on. Pierre Bourdieu, though in a way far from prison issues, is one source of ideas. His outline of public space contains three circles. It contains a *doxa* – opinions on which everyone agrees and takes for granted; the importance of 'motherhood and apple pie', to quote Daniel Hallin (1989). Second, doxa is in turn contextualized by *orthodox debates* – debates on the surface and on unimportant issues made to look important – which take place on the peripheries of *doxa*. Third, and finally, there are *heterodox debates*, which probe much deeper, but normally live in the dark corners of narrow publications (freely after Bourdieu 1977). But *doxa* may change, its defences may crumble, what is taken for granted today may no longer be taken so much for granted tomorrow. In fact, the *heterodox debate* may sometimes end up as *doxa*. It may take a long time, but sometimes it may be surprisingly short. Many historical examples testify to both. It is a matter of opinion formation, triggered by what we do in terms of opinion formation but also by basic conditions such as financial crises which make heterodox opinions important and interesting.

A part of the struggle is to unravel the mythology of doxa as it largely is today. A few years ago the Danish criminologist Flemming Balvig showed, in a large empirical study, that although public opinion about lawbreakers in Denmark generally is harsh, people become more lenient the closer they come to the issues. Concrete proposals regarding punishment stress far lower levels of punishment than those which are actually practised (Balvig 2006). Similar results are recently reported for Norway, Sweden and Denmark by Leif Petter Olaussen, Kristina Jerre and Henrik Tham, and Flemming Balvig respectively (2010). Two independent teams of trained judges fixed the *actual* punishment level in concrete and serious criminal cases. Samples of people were then asked what they *thought* would be the punishment level, and what punishment level they *proposed*, for a range of serious crimes. Both turned out far lower than the actual punishment levels decided by judges. The studies go against the premise, taken for granted, that people think courts are much too lenient. And it goes against the premise that the stiffening of sentencing level is necessary if we are to fall in line with public opinion.

It is as I have said, a question of triggering change, but it is also a question of giving change a direction so we do not go from bad to worse.

These are just examples. Resistance and action for change presupposes that among others, critical criminologists – and we are many – play an active part in reforming *doxa*. But the full story on how to do this belongs to a different book.

Notes

1 I should briefly mention my background for presenting these remarks. For 50 years – since 1960 – I have, among other professional matters, been preoccupied with and followed the development of criminal policy in my own country and abroad. I was first engaged in it through a long-term study of a major Norwegian prison (including two years of intensive observation) between 1960 and 1965 (*The Defences of the Weak*, Tavistock Publications, 1965). This was followed up by extensive participation in the Norwegian prisoners' organization KROM – the Norwegian Association for Penal Reform, which I took part in establishing in 1968. My participation, which has lasted until this day, for a long time took the form of a particular kind of 'action research', resulting in a string of books and papers in Norwegian, German, English and other languages, including *The Politics of Abolition*, Martin Robertson, 1974.
2 From a press release issued by the Norwegian News Agency.
3 The article which represented the core issue was signed 'Ho Chi Minh', the name of the revolutionary president of North Vietnam until he died in 1969. It was a completely harmless little piece about prison conditions, containing no names of inmates or other sensitive information whatsoever.
4 As of 29 January 2010, 41 years after the events, the sealing is still in force because no attempt has been made to overrule it. Source: National Library, same date.
5 I have described the early struggles in detail in several books, three of them in Norwegian and some of them also in a fourth collected volume in English. See Mathiesen 1974.
6 Of Norwegian prisons, 63 per cent are 'high security level' (closed institutions). Inmates there are generally allowed 20 minutes' telephone per week, and one hour of

visiting per week. Of placements, 37 per cent are 'low security level' or other types of placement (Bloch and Mathisen 2009).

7 Calculations by Kriminalomsorgens Yrkesforbund, a staff organization, reported in *Aftenposten*, 9 August 2010. The figures reported in *Aftenposten* have been corroborated by the head of the staff organization (same date). The basic idea of the head of the organization is that prison staff has ultimate power which they execute on behalf of society. Therefore, the high frequencies of unskilled staff according to him constitutes a major problem. Education specifically geared to prison staff is pinpointed to prison problems. His example is urine tests, which are frequently taken in prisons. Uncertainty often occurs when he interviews unskilled staff as to whether they have the right to take a given test. Reference to 'the others say so' is frequently heard. My remark is that this has nothing to do with 'generally relaxed conditions'.

8 Datatilsynet 2008. See also prisoner No. 03/43 at Ila Prison. The prisoner was not allowed a one-day leave to present the paper personally (see n. 29).

9 Statistics on Imprisonment 1960–2004, *Statistics Norway, Crime Statistics 2004*, Table 47.

10 Ibid. More recent unofficial figures, from 2005 on, bring even more disheartening news. The year 2005 saw an average of 586 inmates on pre-trial detention per day, a little lower than 2004. But by 2009 the figure had soared to 931 pre-trial detention inmates per day. In 2005 inmates on pre-trial detention spent on average 63 days behind bars before the case reached final judgment. In early 2010 the figure had reached 70 days.

A few days after a newspaper write-up had been published on the matter, the Ministry of Justice replied – not in the form of pointing out errors, but in the form of an advance opening of 56 cells for remand purposes in the new 251-man prison in Halden (source: press release from the Ministry, 1 March 2010), a large prison by Norwegian standards.

The size of prisons must be seen in relation to the size of the country and the prison population. A still newer prison sized 200, large by Norwegian standards, is currently being planned in the municipality of Sande, and may be ready by 2020. Municipal civil servants are excited because several hundred jobs may be generated (source: www.ha-halden.no/nyheter). See Berit Johnsen and Per Kristian Granheim's empirical contribution in this book (Chapter 11). One of her two major Norwegian empirical findings is that small prisons generate a better social atmosphere or climate than large ones.

11 United Nations, CCPR/C/NOR/2009/6; sixth periodic report October 2009, re Article 9, pp. 26–30, Table p. 28.

12 Since the fifty-one individuals were subject to *control* of letters and visits, they could well be characterized as subject to partial rather than total isolation. In general, the figures here are a bit uncertain/unclear.

13 Berit Reiss-Andersen and Merete Smith (2010). Reiss-Andersen and Smith are president and general secretary respectively of the Norwegian Bar Association.

14 A 24-hour-period is called one *døgn* in Norwegian.

15 Reiss-Andersen and Smith (2010).

16 Ibid.

17 Ibid.

18 Ibid.

19 This is the most recent publication I have found. Similar information has been available earlier.

20 For documentation, see Mathiesen (1974) and *Kriminalvården* 1970. How the prison authorities were able to specify the figure so accurately is unknown.

21 As of 26 January 2010, 29 per cent of the 3,499 inmates in Norwegian prisons are citizens of other countries than Norway. Ninety-three foreign countries were represented. The list of foreign nationalities in Norwegian prisons is topped by Lithuania (112), Poland (98), Nigeria (61), Iraq (57), Romania (53) and the Netherlands (46). Source: the Prison and Probation Department.

22 For Sweden, an e-mail question concerning solariums was answered by five prison regions. In one region, Stockholm (the capital city), there are solariums in eight out of ten prisons. In another region there are two solariums, in a third region two or three, in a fourth region two prisons out of the four replied they had solariums, in a fifth region they had some but were unable to provide a figure (source: Swedish Prison Department). As of January 2010, Sweden had six prison regions and 57 prisons. Leaving out Stockholm where special conditions may obtain, I would say that this amounts to 'some' prisons in Sweden with solariums, hardly solariums 'in a number of closed and open prisons'. But the choice of *language* ('in a number of closed and open prisons') gives important positive connotations of a general – you might even say sweeping – kind. The overall point is that Pratt as a rule chooses language which gives positive general connotations. His two articles could well have been analysed within a semiotic framework; see e.g. Janikowski and Milovanovic (1995).

23 An example: when back from furloughs, prisoners at Ringerike were to stand naked (or at least without trousers and underpants), on top of a large horizontally placed mirror, through which you clearly could observe the interior of the prisoner's rectum, making it easy for officers to inspect the rectum for contraband, especially drugs. In the early 2000s, an ex-prisoner from Ringerike illustrated this at one of KROM's mountain meetings. The illustration was performed in a very vivid way. The prison inspector (next in command in the prison) who was present was furious, to say the least.

Note that prisoners in Norwegian prisons as in other countries rank high on welfare problems such as lack of employment, lack of education, lack of housing, low income, drug addiction, and so forth. There are a number of studies on this, for example Skardhamar (2002).

24 § 162 in the Penal Code. For details see Christie, 2003: 113.

25 Data from the *Census Bureau*. Source: *Aftenposten*, 14 February 2010.

26 Some details are related in my *Invitasjon til kritisk sosiologi* ['Invitation to critical sociology'] (2011).

27 For a brief period she was given another ministry, while a right-wing Labour Party lawyer was given the Ministry of Justice.

28 In 2001, the Prison and Probation Department issued a regulation stating that inmates could 'be given up to 12 short time leaves per year over and above the ordinary quota of leaves, for participation at board meetings in KROM, provided the remainder of conditions for granting short terms leaves are present'. A similar stipulation was made for inmates' participation at our 'meetings in the mountains'. Compare this relative openness with the attitude of the Minister of Justice some 30 years earlier, in 1968, during 'the happy moment of the welfare state'.

29 Present-day *mix* or *ambivalence* within the prison system is testified by the fact there were actually two convicts and one ex-convict who were to speak at the mountain meeting in 2010. But two days before the conference started, one of the convicts was flatly denied a one-day leave to present an exciting and well-drafted paper on data control in prisons (see n. 8). It is also testified by the fact that in one major prison, discussions concerning criminal policy with a team of outsiders coming in were allowed in 2008, while denied in another prison in 2009. The denial was based on a refusal on the part of the staff organization. Overtones from the past are certainly still with us.

30 See Thomas Ugelvik's empirical contribution to this book (Chapter 7).

31 Source: *New York Times*, 9 February 2009 (at: www.nytimes.com/2009/02/10/us/10prison.html?_r=1).

32 See also *Los Angeles Times Local*, 2010 (at: http://latimesblogs. /lanow/2010/01/judges-approve-schwarzenegger-prison-plan).

33 30 June 2010, at the Centre for Crime and Justice Studies in London (at: www.justice.gov.uk/news/sp300610a.htm).

34 Source: press release from the Norwegian Ministry of Justice, 28 January 2010.

35 *Dagsnytt 18*, 29 January 2010. Cooperation between Norwegian prison authorities and British and Russian authorities has been going on from the middle of the decade, partly with formal agreements.

References

Austbø, Anne Marit (2000) 'Varetekt i Norge – i strid med internasjonal rett' ['Pre-trial detention in Norway – in conflict with international law'], *Amnesty International Norway*, 29 October.

Balvig, Flemming (2006) *Danskernes syn på straf* ['The Danes' view on punishment'], Advokatsamfundet 2006 (at: www.advokatsamfundet.dk).

—— (2010) *Danskernes retsfølelse og retsfornuft – et forspil* ['The Danes' legal sentiment and legal reasoning – a prelude'], Det juridiske fakultet, Københavns Universitet.

Bjørngaard, Johan Håkon et al. (2009) 'The prisoner as patient – a health services satisfaction survey', *BMC Health Services Research*, 28 September, 9: 176 (at: www.biomedcentral.com/1472-6963/9/176).

Bloch, Ann-Kristin and Helmers Bo Mathisen (2009) 'Psykisk syke bak murene' ['The psychiatrically ill behind walls'], *Sykepleien*, nr. 14 (October), pp. 22–30.

Bondeson, Ulla (1974) *Fången i fångsamhället* ['The prisoner in the prison society']. Stockholm: Norstedt.

—— (1990) *Prisoners in Prison Societies*. New Brunswick: Transaction Publishers.

Bourdieu, Pierre (1977) *Outline of a Theory of Practice*. Cambridge: Cambridge University Press.

Bratholm, Anders (1958) *Pågripelse og varetektsfengsel* ['Arrest and pre-trial detention'], Institutt for kriminologi og strafferett, Universitetet i Oslo.

Christie, Nils (2003) *Den gode fiende* ['The suitable enemy'] 3rd edn. Oslo: Universitetsforlaget.

Dalberg-Larsen, Jørgen (1988) 'Lige linjer, cirkler, trekanter eller spiraler i rettens og samfundets udvikling. En faseteori med kommentarer' ['Parallel lines, triangles or spirals in the development of law and society. A theory of phases with comments'], in Asmund Born (ed.), *Refleksiv ret* ['Reflexive law'] *Nyt fra Samfundsvidenskaberne*, pp. 175–95.

Datatilsynet (2008) *Endelig kontrollrapport etter tilsyn ved Ila landsfengsel* ['Final report on control after inspection at Ila prison'], Rapportdato (report date): 25.01.08. Saksnr.: 07/01455 (at: www.datatilsynet.no; in Norwegian only).

Fjeldberg, Nina Faye (2007) 'Rettighetsløse fangestudenter' ['Prisoner students without rights'] (at: kriminalpolitikk.uio.no, week 50).

Giertsen, Hedda (2006) 'Oppdelt i småbiter og satt sammen på nytt. OASys "Offender Assessment and Management System" – et lovbrytermålesystem' ['Split up in bits and pieces and put together again. OAsys "Offender Assessment and Management System" – a system for measuring offenders'], *Materialisten. Tidsskrift for forskning, fagkritikk og teoretisk debatt*.

Hallin, Daniel C. (1989) *The 'Uncensored War'. The Media and Vietnam*. Berkeley: University of California Press.

Hammerlin, Yngve (2000) 'Selvmord i norske fengsler: Part I' ['Suicides in Norwegian prisons: Part I'], *Suicidologi*, 5(1).

—— (2009) *Selvmord og selvmordsnærhet i norske fengsler* ['Suicides and suicide risk in Norwegian prisons']. Kriminalomsorgens utdanningssenter KRUS.

Henningsen, Gustav (1984) *Heksenes advokat* ['The witches' advocate'], Delta. Rev. edn of Gustav Henningsen (1980), *The Witches' Advocate. Basque Witchcraft and the Spanish Inquisition 1609–1614*. Reno: University of Nevada Press.

Janikowski, Richard and Dragan Milovanovic (eds) (1995) *Legality and Illegality: Semiotics, Postmodernism and Law*. New York: Peter Lang.

Jerre, Kristina and Henrik Tham (2010) *Svenskarnas syn på straff* ['The Swedes' view on punishment'], Report 2010: 1. Kriminologiska Institutionen, Stockholms universitet.

Lea, Henry Charles (1906) *A History of the Inquisition of Spain*, vol. IV (2nd edn, 1966). New York: AMS Press Inc.

Marcuse, Herbert (1964) *One-Dimensional Man*. Boston: Beacon.

Mathiesen, Thomas (1965) *The Defences of the Weak*. London: Tavistock Publications.

—— (1974) *The Politics of Abolition*. London: Martin Robertson.

—— (2006) *Prison on Trial* (3rd edn). Winchester: Waterside Press.

—— (2010) 'Ten reasons for not building more prisons', in Melissa McCarthy (ed.), *Incarceration and Human Rights. The Oxford Amnesty Lectures 2007*. Manchester: Manchester University Press.

—— (2011) *Kritisk sosiologi – en invitasjon* ['Critical sociology – an invitation'].

Mead, Margaret and Rhoda Métraux (eds) (1953) *The Study of Culture at a Distance*. Chicago: University of Chicago Press.

Merton, Robert K. (1968) *Social Theory and Social Structure*, enlarged edn. New York: Free Press.

Morgan, Rod (1999) 'Moderate psychological pressure – the Scandinavian way?', *Kritisk Juss*, 26(3): 201–204.

Olaussen, Leif Petter (2010) *Straffenivået og folks holdninger til straff i Norge* ['The punishment level and people's attitudes to punishment in Norway']. Oslo: Department of Criminology and Sociology of Law, University of Oslo.

Pratt, John (2008a) 'Scandinavian exceptionalism in an era of penal excess. Part I: The nature and roots of Scandinavian exceptionalism', *British Journal of Criminology*, 48(2): 119–37.

—— (2008b) 'Scandinavian exceptionalism in an era of penal excess. Part II: Does Scandinavian exceptionalism have a future?', *British Journal of Criminology*, 48(3): 275–92.

Pratt, John and Anna Eriksson (2009) 'Den skandinaviska exceptionalismen i kriminalpolitiken' ['The Scandinavian exceptionalism in penal policy'] *Nordisk tidsskrift for kriminalvidenskab*, 98(2): 135–51.

Prisoner No. 03/43 at Ila Prison (2010) 'Kontrollutviklingen i retning av forvaringsregimet. Dataskandalen, personvern og lærdommer' ['The development of control in the direction of the preventive prison regime. The data scandal, privacy and lessons to be learned']. Paper read at KROM's Spåtind Conference No. 40 (at: www.KROM.no; in Norwegian only).

Reiss-Andersen, Berit and Merete Smith (2010) 'Rettsstatens mørke rom' ['The dark rooms of a state governed by law']. *Aftenposten*.

Rusche, George and Otto Kirchheimer (1939) *Punishment and Social Structure*. New York: Columbia University Press.

Rutherford, Andrew (1986) *Prisons and the Process of Justice*. Oxford: Oxford University Press.

Scheerer, Sebastian (1986) 'Towards abolitionism', *Contemporary Crises*, 10: 5–20.

Skardhamar, Torbjørn (2002) *Levekår og livssituasjon blant innsatte i norske fengsler* ['Living conditions and life situation among inmates in Norwegian prisons']. University

of Oslo, Department of Criminology and Sociology of Law, K-serien nr.1 Unipub Forlag.
Statistics Norway, *Crime Statistics 2004*.
United Nations, CCPR/C/NOR/2009/6; sixth periodic report October 2009, re Article 9, pp. 26–30.
Wennström, Johan (2010) 'Fängelse är det bästa skyddet vi har' ['Prison is the best protection we have'], *Svenska Dagbladet*, 3 August 2010.

3 A critical look at Scandinavian exceptionalism
Welfare state theories, penal populism and prison conditions in Denmark and Scandinavia

Peter Scharff Smith

The thesis that Scandinavia exhibits an exceptionally humane penal culture in terms of both 'low rates of imprisonment and humane prison conditions' (Pratt 2008a) is interesting and clearly relevant for discussion. It is, for example, interesting as a piece of comparative penology – how can we analyse and compare different penal cultures, and what can we learn from such an exercise? One possible answer to the latter question, which also justifies looking into a possible Scandinavian penal exceptionalism, is the need to identify good prison practice across jurisdictions. Prison practices which, for example, can be promoted by international and national human rights-monitoring mechanisms.

There are however also reasons to discuss, question and analyse the idea of Scandinavian exceptionalism further. In this chapter I will do that by looking at Danish penal culture and Danish–Scandinavian prison practice, especially with regard to the influence of penal populism in Denmark, and the specific practice of pre-trial solitary confinement. The latter has been termed a 'peculiarly Scandinavian phenomenon' (Evans and Morgan 1998), and is highly relevant in terms of questioning and discussing to what degree not only Danish but also Swedish and Norwegian prison practice is generally lenient and humane. Looking at Denmark in particular is also relevant because this is the one Scandinavian country which so far has been left out of Pratt's analysis (2008a).

I begin by giving a few examples of Danish penal practices, which can be developed in order to support the existence of a so-called Scandinavian exceptionalism. Following that I will pose a number of questions of both a methodological and empirical nature, which I suggest need to be researched further in order to either strengthen, dismiss or nuance the thesis of Scandinavian exceptionalism. After that I will look into two of these issues through the use of two case studies: (a) the rise of penal populism in Denmark; and (b) the use of pre-trial solitary confinement in Denmark and Scandinavia. The first short case study will show us that penal populism has influenced policy debates and lawmaking quite heavily in Denmark during recent years – something which in my opinion needs to be reflected in discussions on penal culture in Scandinavia. The second case study is an example of an Old Danish penal practice, which is far from lenient and humane, but has nevertheless co-existed in apparent harmony with a Nordic welfare state model. The Danish and apparently partly Scandinavian history of using pre-trial solitary confinement could arguably be termed a significant example of an *inhuman* rather that a *humane* prison practice and is as such also clearly relevant to discuss in the present context.

Examples of liberal and humane prison conditions in Denmark

This contribution will concentrate on examples that question the thesis of Scandinavian exceptionalism. But there is no doubt that several examples of Danish penal practice could also be drawn forward in order to support the notion of Scandinavia as carrier of a humane penal culture. Below are a few important examples.

One of the characteristics of the Danish prison system is the extensive use of so-called 'open prisons', where the regime is relatively liberal (as prison regimes go). In Jyderup State Prison, for example, the prison gate is simply open and there is no physical barrier keeping you from actually walking in and out of the prison. An escape is still an escape, though, and will earn a (caught) prisoner a transfer to a closed facility. In Jyderup the entire prison grounds, featuring lawns and a small prison church, also function as a visiting area for visiting families, children, etc. Although this is not standard practice in all open prisons, they all feature regimes which make it much easier for inmates to keep in contact with the outside world. When coming from the outside and visiting Danish prisons, one is certainly struck by the very different atmosphere encountered in an open prison compared to the so-called closed prisons (i.e. maximum security). Out of the total Danish prison capacity of 4,116 spaces the open prisons take up more than a third – i.e. 1,421 spaces, compared to 1,749 remand and 946 closed facility spaces.[1] That said, open prisons are still in many ways similar to low/medium security prisons in other parts of Europe, and closed prisons in Denmark certainly resemble closed prisons in several western European countries.[2]

Another trademark of Danish prison practice, which often causes raised eyebrows from visitors from abroad, is the way that a self-catering regime is employed for sentenced prisoners throughout the prison system – including maximum security facilities. This was introduced in Denmark in the 1970s and requires shopping possibilities (a prison grocer) and kitchen facilities in all prison blocks as well as the accessibility of large kitchen knives (the latter have recently been attached to the walls by steel wires). This makes planning meals and cooking one of the most meaningful activities for many prisoners.

If comparing Danish prison practice with Anglo-Saxon jurisdictions one also needs to mention that conjugal visits are allowed throughout the prison system and that all visits can be carried out in private visiting rooms. The Danish prison system features few visiting rooms, where inmate and visitor are separated by a screen, and these are rarely used. One such room is located in Østjyllands Prison, which opened in 2006. When I visited the prison in the autumn of 2007 the visiting room with a screen was used for storage and had never been used for visits.

One could say that the philosophy supporting the above practices, and others, is the principle of normalization, which was officially introduced in Denmark in the early 1970s. When the UN Special Rapporteur on Torture, Manfred Nowak, visited Denmark in 2008 he considered the 'principle of normalization' to be a hallmark of the Danish prison system 'meaning that life behind bars reflects life outside to as great an extent as possible. Taken together with an attentive approach to the concerns of detainees by prison staff, the result is generally a high standard of conditions of detention inside Danish prisons, both in terms of infrastructure and day-to-day living standards' (Nowak 2009: 2). Nowak also had criticism, however, and I will return to one of those issues, namely the use of pre-trial solitary confinement, below. Furthermore, as I will touch upon later, there is also good reason to argue that the principle of normalization has been under attack during recent years through new legislation and certain administrative changes with regard to prison practices.

Scandinavian exceptionalism – a hypothesis in need of further empirical testing

While it is clearly relevant to discuss the thesis of Scandinavian exceptionalism, a number of important questions remain to be answered. Below I have listed four different issues, which in my opinion need to be addressed:

1. Is there a Scandinavian culture of equality which is embedded in the Scandinavian welfare state model, and, if so, to what degree is there causality between such a culture and penal policy/prison conditions?
2. Shouldn't the quality of prison conditions be compared primarily to the national quality of life and economic standard? That is, what do you lose by being imprisoned?
3. Is the Scandinavian debate on penal policy particularly humane and lenient?
4. What are the actual prison conditions/prison cultures in Scandinavian prisons and how do they compare to those in other European countries?

To my mind, each of these points deserves thorough studies and separate chapters. I will touch very briefly upon the first, and through my two case studies provide a more thorough discussion of some important issues relating to the third and fourth points.

Has a particular Scandinavian welfare state and ethos of equality produced a humane penality?

The practice of using welfare state models as an analytic tool in comparative criminology is very interesting but also somewhat under-researched and in need of more empirical testing. The attractiveness of employing the welfare state perspective undoubtedly has much to do with the very influential and much discussed theory by Gösta Esping-Andersen, in which he originally defined three types of capitalist welfare regime: the liberal welfare state, the corporatist welfare state, and the social-democratic welfare state (1995: 26 ff.). The three types of welfare state were characterized by, among other things, the degree of de-commodification, where social-democratic states scored high due to a wide range of substantial welfare benefits, etc., which lessened the individual citizen's need to rely on the forces of the free market. The degree of de-commodification was relatively low in liberal welfare states, and somewhere in between in corporatist welfare states. Esping-Andersen placed the Scandinavian states in the social-democratic category, Germany and France in the corporatist camp, and the US in the liberal system.

Esping-Andersen's typology was elegantly constructed and has since been used in an attempt to explain many different characteristics of different societies. The model has however been developed and in recent comparative criminology four different types of political economy/welfare state are used: neo-liberalism, conservative corporatism, social democratic corporatism, and oriental corporatism (Cavadino and Dignan 2006: 14ff.).[3] One of the perhaps most important reasons for using these models as a tool in comparative criminology is that rates of imprisonment seem to be associated with the political economy, with high rates in neo-liberal welfare states, lower in conservative corporate countries and the lowest in the remaining two types of state (Cavadino and Dignan 2006: 30). The Scandinavian so-called social-democratic welfare states have especially attracted attention in this regard (for example Pratt 2008a, b).[4] As pointed out by Cavadino and Dignan it is, however, 'not entirely clear' why the 'social democratic corporatist states' has a low rate of imprisonment and appear to have a rather distinctive type of penality' (Cavadino and Dignan 2006: 26). Cavadino and Dignan point to the 'strong emphasis on inclusiveness [and] the feeling that everyone is part of the same society', as well as 'the principle of egalitarianism' as possible explanations (Cavadino and Dignan 2006: 26).

A number of questions however remain to be answered. It is, for example, not clear to what degree a Scandinavian culture of equality – if we accept that such a thing exists – is the product of very homogenic societies rather than of the principle of inclusiveness as such (recent Danish debates on immigration and multiculturalism seems to suggest the former).[5] Similarly, the fact that Scandinavian welfare states are large, powerful and arguably often trusted by the public, can lead both towards humane policies on the one hand and effective social control on the other hand. The latter seems relevant to discuss for example in connection with the traditionally quite strong focus on rehabilitation in Scandinavian penal systems – a penal strategy which can produce empowerment of prisoners but has also been known to create disciplinary social control regimes. A Foucauldian analysis of the relatively uniform import of the Pennsylvania prison model (i.e. large-scale solitary confinement under strict discipline) in Denmark, Sweden and Norway during the nineteenth century illustrate the latter – i.e. how a rehabilitative prison policy supported a radical system of discipline and isolation. This practice continued well into the twentieth century in Norway, Sweden, and Denmark, and upheld a very disciplinarian and psychologically unhealthy prison regime with a strong focus on social control (Smith 2006b, c; Nilsson 2003).

Regardless of these issues, the fact remains that even if we accept the notion of a Nordic or Scandinavian culture of equality it has not necessarily led to the creation of a particularly humane penal culture and prison practice. To actually prove this one would have to – through empirically based historical studies – establish a link between such a culture and the formation of concrete humane penal policies and practices. The case study that follows, on the use of pre-trial solitary confinement, is arguably an example of the opposite, i.e. how originally humane intentions created a more or less inhuman prison practice – i.e. a mentally very unhealthy prison regime instead of a sound basis for moral reform.

Furthermore, if we take a closer look at some of the prominent examples of humane Danish practices mentioned earlier, they are not necessarily a direct product of a specific Danish/Scandinavian culture. If we look, for example, into the history behind the use of open prisons in Denmark, they seem to have a very coincidental rather than a well-planned and policy-led history. A thorough study of the creation of open prisons in Denmark still remains to be done, but the present evidence indicates that these facilities were never the result of long-term and thoroughly planned welfare state policies based on equalitarian principles, etc., but rather a direct result of the mass incarceration (in Danish terms), which took place immediately after the Second World War and the liberation of Denmark, when more than 40,000 alleged traitors and collaborators were detained, and which for a limited period raised the Danish prison population dramatically. This led to the use of barracks and summer-camp-like facilities, which ultimately revealed that prisons could actually be run with very liberal regimes and relatively low levels of security.

The introduction of self-catering regimes, which like the open prisons are often perceived as a humane and inclusive practice, was initially in the 1970s a rather coincidental product of the experiments in one new prison led by a controversial prison governor, and the practice was much fought by the prison directorate. One could of course still argue that the fact that these practices eventually became ingrained in the prison system still reflects a specific Scandinavian or Danish culture – but the actual empirical study and analysis remains to be carried out. More broadly speaking, history has taught us that we need to show caution in such questions. One example that springs to mind is the way that the famous rescue of the Danish Jews during the Second World War was initially explained as the product of an allegedly especially democratic culture among the Danes – a theory that has since been abandoned in light of empirically based studies (Christensen *et al.* 2003). Danish research has shown 'that foreign Jews [in Denmark] were treated with significantly less heartfelt warmth and suggests that anti-Semitism perhaps was not so uncommon in Denmark in the 1930s and 1940s' (Christensen *et al.* 2003: 63).

The rise of penal populism in Denmark

Historically speaking there have always been fluctuations in the way that punishment has been rationalized and legitimized. Retribution has been, and continues to be, a key rationale for punishment in many jurisdictions, and during the last 200 years the aim of rehabilitating offenders has also played a prominent role. When the so-called modern prison system broke through in the western world during the period from around the 1820s to the 1860s, for example, rehabilitation, deterrence and retribution figured prominently in the underlying ideology. In England during the latter half of the nineteenth century this rationale shifted towards a much more clearly punitive and retributive philosophy. As a result, treadmills were, for example, introduced in many prisons. From the 1890s onwards the focus on rehabilitation once again expanded in England. In that sense fluctuations either towards or away from more or less punitive and retributive prison and punishment practices are historically speaking a well-known phenomenon.

There is little doubt that recent years have witnessed an increased focus on retribution and the introduction of more punitive sentencing and penal practices. The US has for the last three or four decades inspired and led this international trend and in doing so reached an unprecedented level of imprisonment. During the early 1990s this wave of punitive policies reached Europe and prison populations grew significantly in, for example, England, Spain and Holland. This tendency, which has been termed a new 'culture of control', 'populist punitiveness' or 'penal populism' by criminologists (Garland 2001; Pratt 2007; Tonry 2004), has also influenced penal policy in Denmark (and Scandinavia) – but to what extent? This is clearly relevant to discuss in light of the notion of Scandinavian exceptionalism.

Penal populism and the new culture of control started to influence Danish penal policy during the 1990s. Under a coalition government led by the Social-Democrats laws introducing longer and stricter sentencing for violent crimes were passed in 1994 and 1997. In 2002 and 2004, under a coalition government led by the liberal party Venstre, tougher sentencing was once again introduced in the same area through new legislation. The arguments behind this legislation, as well as the public and political debate surrounding penal issues and punishment in general, clearly showed that penal populism had gained a foothold in Denmark. The overall political tendency was to constantly refer to and talk about the so-called public sentiments of justice (*retsfølelsen*), while showing increasing willingness to disregard expert advice and criminological knowledge. Here exemplified by the then Minister of Justice, Lene Espersen, from the Conservative People's Party, who in 2002 declared:

> Crimes committed against people are far more serious than crimes committed against money [sic]. Injustice against another human being is a crime against the most fundamental in our society: the respect for the individual human being. Therefore one of my first deeds as Minister of Justice was to put forward a bill, which contains several distinctive suggestions for tougher sentences against, for example, violent crimes and rape. By doing that we demonstrate that society will not tolerate crimes which injure and damage

individuals. This legislative initiative is in other words primarily motivated by considerations for the victims and the public sentiments of justice.[6]

In that manner longer and tougher sentencing policies were introduced despite criminologists and criminological evidence generally pointing in the exact opposite direction – i.e. advocating diversion and alternatives to imprisonment rather than an expanding approach to the use of imprisonment as a favourable policy in terms of preventing crime. Several politicians made it quite clear that they were well aware that they disregarded expert advice and similarly claimed allegiance to so-called public sentiments on crime and justice. Pia Kjærsgaard, the leader of the Danish Folk Party and part of the current governments parliamentary majority, for example concluded in 2003 that Denmark was 'a society breaking down' where 'gangs of immigrants and bikers' where producing 'uncertainty, violence, and terror'. The solution, according to Kjærsgaard, was to introduce harsher punishment and to help the victims. She made it quite clear, however, that the experts were of no use in these matters and she warned against their views: 'I'm sure that the usual group of criminological experts will soon be badgering us with their statistics – in an attempt to downplay the problems and lull the Minister of Justice to sleep. But many of us began to disregard the statistics a long time ago, we only need to look out of the window, walk the streets or read the papers and watch television in order to realize that things are getting out of hand. It cannot go on for any longer. We will simply not take it anymore.'[7] In a more or less similar vein the Minister of Justice dubbed the critics of much of the new and harsher legislation (on penal issues and antiterrorism) 'hylekoret', which translates into something like 'the whiners' or the 'wailing choir' (Greve 2010).

The public and political debate on penal issues and punishment in Denmark has not been subjected to a large-scale empirical research project, but has nevertheless been the subject of several scholarly articles (see for example Greve 2004, 2010; Nielsen 2006; Smith and Jakobsen 2010: Ch. 17). It seems that especially during the last decade the debate has shifted more and more towards penal populism, with discussions about zero-tolerance policies, punitive practices, three-strike laws, mandatory minimum sentencing, and longer sentences dominating the agenda. As illustrated above, the rationale for these policy suggestions has been emotional rather than rational in a traditional penal sense – meaning that politicians have not primarily argued that they want to rehabilitate criminals, prevent crime, etc., but have simply argued that they based their views and suggestions on the public sentiments on justice. In an interview in 2002 with the then Minister of Justice, Lene Espersen, she declared that she governed with her 'inner sense of justice', which she claimed to share with 'ordinary citizens' ('DJØF bladet' no. 7, 2002). The minister clearly regarded criminological advice and research as less important. In 2008 Brian Mikkelsen, also from the Conservative People's Party, replaced Lene Espersen as Minister of Justice and immediately speculated that he would probably become known as 'Tough Brian' ('Barske Brian') because 'I am very tough on crime. And I have been that throughout all my years in politics' (*Jyllandsposten*, 23 February 2010; http://jp.dk/indland/indland_politik/article1988

504.ece). Recently Brian Mikkelsen was replaced as Minister of Justice by Lars Barfoed, also from the same party, who has indicated that he will focus more on crime prevention. This could constitute a significant change but it remains to be seen, however, what this apparently new agenda will mean in practical terms. In reality one of the first acts of the new Minister of Justice was to get new 'tough on crime' legislation through parliament, which will, among other things, lower the minimum age for criminal responsibility in Denmark. This is truly populist and punitive legislation which has attracted very strong criticism from experts, practitioners, various NGOs, the National Council for Children and the Danish Institute for Human Rights.

There is in other words no doubt that Danish politicians from a wide range of political parties have embraced penal populism both in terms of general political rhetoric and also in terms of promoting and suggesting concrete policy changes. It is also, I think, fair to say that the general and politically broad character of this trend has made it more acceptable to propose even very radical 'tough on crime' suggestions also for prominent politicians from the big political parties. One such example is the 'three strikes' proposal made in September 2008 by the politician Søren Pind from the liberal Venstre Party. In light of gang trouble in Copenhagen, Pind suggested legislation, according to which gang members sentenced a third time would have to either be deported from Denmark (foreigners and immigrants without Danish citizenship) or simply locked up until 'society could be assured that they were no longer dangerous criminals' (*Politiken*, 17 September 2008; http://politiken.dk/politik/article568728.ece). Søren Pind was a prominent member of the governing party Venstre at the time, and although his (even in US terms) radical three-strike proposal was met with some criticism, it never became a political problem for Pind, who has continued moving up the political ladder. He is currently the government Minister of Development Cooperation.

But the question of course remains of how much actual impact penal populism has had in Denmark in terms of concrete legislation, penal policy initiatives and reforms? As previously mentioned, there is no large-scale empirical research covering this. There is, however, no doubt that penal populism has had a concrete and measurable impact. According to the prominent Danish law professor Vagn Greve, several new pieces of legislation and law amendments from the 1990s onwards has violated fundamental principles of criminal law and human rights (Greve 2010). Greve himself points to, for example: (a) an increased use of expulsion of immigrants without Danish citizenship (people who have lived almost their entire lives in Denmark can be deported if sentenced for certain criminal activities); (b) confiscations of assets (a citizen arrested with a few grams of hash can have his entire savings confiscated although this bears no relation to criminal activities); (c) the use of visitation zones, according to which the police can search everyone within certain allegedly dangerous zones, regardless of whether or not they act suspiciously or are accused of anything (according to the police the entire city of Copenhagen has been labelled such a zone); (d) the use of Kafkaesque confidential/secret proceedings, where the accused is not informed of what he or she is actually accused of.[8]

The last-mentioned practice has been introduced as part of anti-terrorism legislation, which has enabled PET (the secret service branch of the Danish police) to: (a) deny individuals entry to Denmark; (b) deny permits to stay in Denmark; and (c) to deny citizenship without disclosing a reason or evidence (Greve 2010). A somewhat similar procedure has since 2002 also been allowed in connection with transferring prison inmates from, for example, an open prison to a closed maximum security facility. The prison service can, for example, allege that a prisoner is a risk to other prisoners and remove him or her from an open prison to a much more restrictive environment without producing any evidence and without allowing the prisoner to see any of the relevant proceedings in that regard (Rentzmann *et al.* 2003: 59; Engbo 2005: 128). As a result prisoners have also been moved to isolation-type regimes without knowing why.

When looking at prisons and prison law in Denmark several other developments are equally or more problematic. One interesting example is the way that Danish inmates' freedom of speech can be limited to protect public sentiments of justice (the law on Execution of Punishment, §59 para. 2). This practice slowly and gradually emerged on an administrative level during the 1980s and 1990s and became law in 2001 (Smith 2007). A so-called 'zero-tolerance' policy against drugs in prison was also introduced in 2004 according to which the prison service routinely must demand urine samples from inmates regardless of whether or not they are suspected of taking drugs (Engbo 2005: 249). Together with the above-mentioned initiatives these are arguably examples of how the principle of normalization and inmate rights now have a lower priority. With reference to these and other new prison policies and practices a Danish prison governor in 2006 claimed that a regular 'change of regime' had taken place in Danish prisons during recent years (Smith 2006b).

Another central point in terms of discussing the possible impact of penal populism in Denmark is of course the fact that the prison population has risen during the last decade as a result of, among other things, legislation introducing longer sentences as well as a gradual but significant decline in the use of release on parole after serving two-thirds of a sentence (Smith 2009). Due to new constructions the prison capacity increased by almost 500 places during the first years of this millennium and was 4,149 in 2005. In 2001 the Danish prison population was on average 3,563 inmates, rising to 4,041 in 2005. The following years it dropped slightly (most likely due to a reform of the court and police system, which created a backlog of cases) but then rose again. On 12 March 2010 there were 4,005 inmates in the Danish prison system (Smith and Jakobsen 2010: 232). This means that the Danish prison population has risen by almost 15 per cent since 2000. This rise is very limited compared to developments in other European countries since the 1990s (Spain, Holland and England for example) but it is nevertheless there and it is at least partly produced by a form of penal populism.

The so-called 'scoundrel law' (*lømmelpakken*) is another recent example of a 'tough on crime' approach in Denmark. This legislation, despite broad criticism, was quickly passed by parliament in order to prepare the police for COP 15, the big international climate summit which took place in Copenhagen in 2009. The purpose was to introduce tougher punishment for disturbance of law and order, but more importantly the purpose was to allow the police to make preventive mass arrests of demonstrators and keep them detained for up to 12 hours without having to charge them with anything. The different pieces of legislation raised several human rights issues concerning both the rights to assembly, freedom of speech and detention without trial.[9] In connection with the actual summit the police constructed a new so-called 'climate prison' with big wire cages in which hundreds of demonstrators could be detained according to the new law. Almost 2,000 arrests were made during the summit and the prison was used quite extensively. On one occasion on 12 December almost 1,000 demonstrators were arrested. Around 900 of these were arrested on the Amagerbrogade Street where they were made to sit handcuffed in rows (each one between the legs of the one behind) several hours on a very cold day and some had to relieve themselves in their pants. This practice has since been labeled as degrading treatment according to Article 3 of the European Convention of Human Rights by the ombudsman and a Danish court.

Finally I will briefly point to the already-mentioned juvenile justice legislation, which among other things will lower the criminal minimum age from 15 to 14. The way that this law has been politically promoted against the advice of all relevant experts and organizations is also a clear example of penal populism in action. The political background of this law is the sad fact that the number of minors going to adult prisons has risen during recent years (although policy technically indicates that they should be placed in special institutions for young criminals and not in adult prisons). This is a practice which can violate Article 37 of the UN Convention on the Rights of the Child.

To sum up, there is no doubt that penal populism has had a significant impact in Denmark since the 1990s and arguably especially during the last decade. A fact which should be reflected in further discussions on (an alleged) Scandinavian exceptionalism.

The use of pre-trial solitary confinement

All prison systems have different ways of limiting the contact that remand prisoners may have with the outside world, the basic reason being a wish to keep them from interfering with police investigations. There are several variations on how to do this but they often include the possibility of restricting, disallowing or instigating surveillance of visits, limiting or disallowing phone calls, reading and screening correspondence, etc. It is however rare that such measures create conditions of outright solitary confinement of remand prisoners. In many jurisdictions the problem is often the opposite, that many remand prisoners are kept in very overcrowded conditions.

The use of solitary confinement during pre-trial detention has, however, been practised extensively in Norway, Denmark and Sweden for many years.[10] The official reason is the risk of collusion, i.e. the suspect interfering with the investigation. Since the late 1970s, this practice has been widely criticized within

Denmark, and especially since the 1990s, international criticism has been directed at Norway, Sweden and Denmark. This criticism has been voiced not least by the United Nations' and the Council of Europe's torture prevention committees, and furthermore, legal scholars abroad have termed the practice as a 'peculiarly Scandinavian phenomenon'.[11] Such international criticism is, however, in stark contrast to the traditional view of a humanistic Scandinavian liberal approach to punishment. Nor are the Scandinavian countries accustomed to being the subject of persistent human rights accusations, and many are perhaps of the opinion that this type of criticism is (or should be) restricted to countries abroad. It is therefore clearly relevant to look further into this matter, to which we now turn.

The European Commission for the Prevention of Torture (CPT), which periodically inspects prisons in the member states of the Council of Europe, has reported in detail on the problems of solitary confinement based on its visits in Norway, Sweden and Denmark between the years 1990 and 2010. It has visited Denmark and Norway four times, and Sweden received its fifth inspection in 2009. All visits to date have given rise to criticism about the use of solitary confinement of detainees (in Norway and Sweden, solitary confinement is used under the heading 'restrictions'). In 1990, for example, CPT delegates reported that the Danish detainees in Vestre Prison, who had spent between two and 21 months in solitary confinement, clearly presented symptoms of damaging effects. CPT recommended that solitary confinement during pre-trial detention should only be used 'in exceptional circumstances' (CPT, Visit Report, Denmark, 1990, section 13/65). Sweden was the subject of similar criticism in 1991, in which the Kronoberg Prison in Stockholm was reported as having 'wholly unacceptable conditions of detention for many of the prisoners held in the establishment'. A foreigner had been placed in solitary confinement for eight months with no visitation rights (with the exception of his lawyer) and without any association with the other inmates. These restrictions even continued after the court passed judgment, because the decision was appealed (CPT, Visit Report, Sweden, 1991, section 26/58). During a 1993 visit in Norway, one of the observations CPT reported was that a large number of pre-trial detainees were living 'in conditions of virtual solitary confinement', and they assessed this routine practice of isolation during the first four weeks of pre-trial detention as unacceptable (CPT, Visit Report, Norway, 1993, section 22/45). During subsequent visits, CPT has noted certain improvements: in Denmark, the number of detainees in solitary confinement has, for example, been reduced considerably, and in Oslo Prison, earmarked personnel try to keep the prisoners in isolation occupied. But criticism has not ceased. Following inspections in Norway (1999), Denmark (2002) and Sweden (2003), CPT again stressed the need for offering prisoners in solitary confinement improved opportunities for enhanced human contact (CPT, Visit Report, Sweden, 2003: 32; Visit Report, Denmark, 2002, section 19/44; Visit Report, Norway, 1999, section 18/39). Not only this fundamental problem, but also the legal conditions concerning the use of solitary confinement and 'restrictions' were criticized, as well as the extensiveness of the continued isolation practice. In 2003, CPT recorded that approximately two-thirds of all those in pre-trial detention in the

Swedish area of Gothenburg were subjected to 'restrictions', and of these, 93 per cent did not have access to telephone or visiting rights or any contact with other prisoners (CPT, Visit Report, Sweden, 2003: 27).

If we look at the most recent visits (Norway 2005, Denmark 2008 and Sweden 2009) criticism has continued. When the CPT visited Sweden in 2009 the delegation for example noted that although:

> efforts were being made at Gothenburg Remand Prison to partially or totally lift restrictions after a period of two to three months (. . .) a substantial proportion of remand prisoners at Gothenburg had restrictions, some being subjected to long periods of isolation (from 6 to 18 months). The management informed the delegation of a target of 7 hours of association per week for inmates under restrictions. While commending these efforts, on-site observations and interviews carried out by the delegation suggest that this target was far from being met and, in any case, appear to be rather low to counter the effects of isolation. The delegation gathered direct evidence – supported by the observations of health-care staff – of the damaging effects of isolation due to restrictions imposed on inmates. Significant periods of isolation induce disorientation in time, memory disturbance, and deterioration in communication skills, to name but three serious effects. Further, symptoms of anxiety disorder are commonly seen, post-traumatic stress disorder and depression develop, and there is agitation, self harm and a risk of suicide. The fact that juveniles as young as 15 are being subjected to restrictions akin to isolation is of particular concern to us.
>
> (CPT visit to Sweden 2009, prel. obs.)

When the UN Special Rapporteur on Torture, Manfred Nowak, visited Denmark in 2008, he praised the principle of normalization, as already mentioned, but he also voiced strong criticism of the continued use of pre-trial solitary confinement: 'Notwithstanding the Government's efforts to restrict the use of solitary confinement, the extensive recourse to this remains a major concern, particularly with respect to pre-trial detainees. Solitary confinement has a clearly documented negative impact on mental health, and therefore should be used only in exceptional circumstances or when absolutely necessary for criminal investigation purposes. In all cases, solitary confinement should be used for the shortest period of time' (Nowak 2009: 2ff.).

As a member of CPT, Rod Morgan, a British professor of criminal justice, has made visits to prisons in Denmark, Sweden and Norway as well as many other European countries, and he has compared the Scandinavian pre-trial detention practice with Israel's use of so-called 'moderate physical pressure' against terrorist suspects (which in 1999 was deemed illegal by the Supreme Court of Israel). The point is that in practical terms, solitary confinement of pre-trial detainees, regardless of what the authorities might or might not intend, constitutes, if not physical, then psychological pressure, in a situation wherein detainees can only escape isolation if they confess. Therefore, Morgan describes the Scandinavian discussion and criticism of Israel's practices as more or less hypocritical, because 'moderate psychological pressure' is employed in the Scandinavian countries in order to elicit a confession. 'This is the Scandinavian way. And can it always be said that the psychological pressure is moderate?', Morgan asks rhetorically, as he takes a strong opposition to both the methods used in Scandinavia and those previously used in Israel (Morgan 1999: 204). Others have made similar allegations, and numerous Danish attorneys have repeatedly stated that solitary confinement of Danish pre-trial detainees operates as a form of pressure.[12] This certainly makes sense, since as long as the reason for using solitary confinement is the fear of collusion, then both the legal reasons for using solitary confinement, and the psychological pressure, cease to exist once a confession is obtained. Pre-trial detention therefore easily turns into 'confessional detention' (Bratholm 1957: 150ff.). It is of course difficult to determine if the police consciously use restrictions and solitary confinement in this manner, but there is no doubt that the effect, i.e. the pressure, is real, regardless of the motive behind the use of isolation (Smith 2006a). In 1987, a Danish study concluded that confessions made during pre-trial detention were 'practically always' given while the detainee was in isolation, and many of them stated, 'that they did so to be released from solitary confinement' (Wilhjelm 1987: 21). Historically and in other parts of the world – in South Africa during the apartheid regime, in the former Soviet Union, as well as in the US so-called war on terrorism – isolation of detainees was (or is) consciously and deliberately used for precisely this reason (Smith 2006b).

The health effects of solitary confinement and the history of pre-trial isolation

The substantial criticism of Scandinavian practice in this area has led to a number of studies being conducted on the effects of solitary confinement, especially in Denmark, and conclusions have consistently shown that pre-trial detention in solitary confinement has detrimental effects, psychologically, and possibly physically as well, on a significant number of inmates. A large-scale official study on remand prisoners placed in and out of isolation was carried out in the 1990s, and following the study, in 1997, it was recommended both 'medically and psychologically (...) that the stress of pre-trial detention not be intensified by the use of solitary confinement' (Andersen et al. 1997: 59). Studies have also been conducted in Norway, which document the negative effects of pre-trial isolation (Gamman 1995, 2001). In addition, a broad consensus in international research further supports these studies on the negative effects of solitary confinement (Smith 2006a). Different conditions in different prisons can naturally give rise to different situations, but a certain 'quality' of solitary confinement regimes remains the same; a lack of psychological meaningful social contact, which will have negative effects on a number of prisoners in isolation regardless of whether one has access to TV and other materialistic goods. Many prisoners are affected by solitary confinement, and it can give rise to both minor and very serious problems (Koch 1983; Volkart 1983; Haney 2003; Andersen 2004: 42; Smith 2006a).

The facts surrounding the use of pre-trial solitary confinement therefore presents us with a number of important questions. Why do Scandinavian countries continue to employ a practice which is documented to be detrimental to prisoners' health? Why is a practice used in Scandinavia that is unnecessary in other countries with which Scandinavians normally compare themselves? In the Danish case we must go one and a half centuries back in time to explain this and the available evidence suggests that a similar historical explanation is relevant to examine in Norway and Sweden.

In Denmark the so-called Prison Commission of 1840, following their 1842 report on general prison reform and construction of penitentiaries, was also charged with reforming local Danish remand prisons. In 1846, their work formed the basis for new local prison and jail regulations, which in the spirit of the modern prison system prescribed the use of solitary confinement during pre-trial detention. These initiatives were motivated by both moral reasons and the desire to fight crime. The 1846 regulations stated explicitly that: (a) some detainees could obstruct the investigation if they were not placed in isolation; and (b) some detainees could demoralize other inmates if they were incarcerated together.[13]

By 1870, the reforms of 1846 had progressed to such an extent that the Danish local prisons and jails typically could – and did – hold most or all remand prisoners in solitary confinement. For example, in Odense, 32 pre-trial isolation cells were available to serve a daily average of 23 remand prisoners. In Copenhagen the reform process proceeded at a slightly slower pace. Here, only 88 isolation cells were available for an average of 160 detainees per day. However, Nørrebro, an area located just outside the Copenhagen city wall, held 30 isolation cells for an average of 25 remand prisoners (Bruun 1871: 2ff.). It is conceivable that Copenhagen's local prisons were not equipped with a sufficient number of isolation cells until Vestre Prison opened in 1895.

At any rate, pre-trial detention in solitary confinement had clearly become the main practice in Denmark around 1870 (presumably, even earlier). This practice continued into the twentieth century and was initially affirmed with the Amendment Act of 1916. According to the Act, solitary confinement of detainees was normal procedure, while communal confinement was permitted only in special circumstances, where particular considerations concerning age, health or lack of available cells gained priority. By 1916, the sole reason for using solitary confinement was fear of collusion, thus the moral argument and the idea of 'reform through isolation' was eliminated. The ideological framework had in other words changed, but the practice – the use of solitary confinement – continued without change (Danish Administration of Justice Act 1916, Ch. 72, § 784). Thus, it remained common practice to isolate remand prisoners, despite the adoption of the Penal Code of 1930, which officially relinquished the entire 'Pennsylvania' notion of 'reform through isolation'. The use of solitary confinement had thereby detached itself from the original idea of moral rehabilitation, and, as a result, it could continue to be practised undisputedly in Danish remand prisons.

As late as the 1960s, Danish pre-trial detainees were normally placed in solitary confinement. In 1969, however, new rules adopted by the prison administration made it possible for pre-trial detainees to gain access to communal confinement, following the initial 14 days of pre-trial confinement.[14] However, solitary confinement remained common practice, and contact with other detainees after 14 days of detention could easily be denied upon request from the police. Solitary confinement during pre-trial could therefore easily continue for long periods – up to more than a year. In Denmark, during the late 1970s, this practice became the focus of considerable public debate, which in waves of varying intensity has continued up until today. Since the 1990s the debate has been reinforced by the previously explained international awareness of this issue. With Amendment Acts of 1978, 1984, 2000 and 2006 various Danish governments have attempted to respond to this criticism, and the use of solitary confinement of remand prisoners has decreased significantly. In 1983, 1,936 cases of solitary confinement of pre-trial detainees were recorded, whereas in 2003, only 476 cases were noted. However, the average duration a prisoner is kept in solitary confinement has fluctuated somewhat during the same period and for example increased from 26.9 days in 1988 to 37 days in 2003.[15] Still, the most recent figures available covering 2007 and 2008 show a positive development with 273 cases of pre-trial solitary confinement in 2007 and 327 cases during 2008. This means that in 2008 5.3 per cent of all pre-trial detentions in Denmark were carried out in solitary confinement – for the entire period or part of the time spend in remand imprisonment (Statistik om isolationsfængsling, JM's Forskningskontor, June 2009). In terms of the health effect of solitary confinement, the medical and psychological recommendations, and the international human rights recommendations, this is still too high a percentage, but nevertheless a vast improvement compared to the situation a couple of decades ago. As late as 1980, 40 per cent of all pre-trial detentions took place in solitary confinement.

Unfortunately there has not been enough done to secure the health and well-being of those still subjected to pre-trial solitary confinement. In fact Denmark is the only one of the Council of Europe member countries which has made a reservation to the European Prison rules, and this relates directly to the use and health effects of solitary confinement. Rule no. 43, para. 2 of these prison rules thus require that 'The medical practitioner or a qualified nurse reporting to such a medical practitioner shall pay particular attention to the health of prisoners held under conditions of solitary confinement, shall visit such prisoners daily, and shall provide them with prompt medical assistance and treatment at the request of such prisoners or the prison staff.' For ethical reasons, Danish doctors have, however, refused to comply with this rule, which has resulted in the aforementioned reservation on the part of the Danish government. This arguably leaves pre-trial detainees in solitary confinement in Denmark in an even more vulnerable situation.

The development of the use of 'restrictions' and virtual pre-trial solitary confinement has not been studied in Norway and Sweden, but general studies of prison history suggest that it could make sense to go back to the breakthrough of the Pennsylvania system – just as in the Danish case. In 1857, Norway, for example, adopted a prison act, which provided that any 'prison district' should have at least one 'district prison'. In these prisons, inmates were subjected to isolation without any association with the other prisoners. Accordingly, 56 district prisons were constructed numbering more than 800 cells, of which 677 were isolation cells. These prisons were built throughout the 1860s and held both remand prisoners and criminals with short sentences. The use of solitary confinement during pre-trial detention in other words became normal procedure.[16] Isolation could, however, be avoided in some cases, and three- or four-men cells were arranged for those who could not endure solitary confinement (Isaksen 1998 :32). In 1934, solitary confinement was still practised in local district prisons, but it was possible to depart from this rule in exceptional cases concerning the prisoners' health or state of mind. Prison governor Hartvig Nissen specified that a prisoner was only permitted to work in an isolation cell for more than two years with the consent of a doctor, and a period of over four years required the prisoner's consent (Nissen 1934: 202–3). By doing so, Nissen illustrated that the solitary confinement system used in Norway more or less resembled the Danish model, but was quite special seen from a broader international perspective.

How custody practices in Norway developed during the 1930s and onwards to the current use of restrictions in Norwegian remand prisons has not yet been the focus of study. However, given the above it seems likely that current isolation practices were established in the 1800s, and persisted into the twentieth century – just as in Denmark. There are also similarities between developments in Denmark/Norway and Sweden. Pennsylvania-like isolation principles were in nineteenth-century Sweden not only adopted in penitentiaries for sentenced prisoners but also in numerous remand prisons (Nilsson 1999: 260). Around 50 prisons boasting approximately 2,500 single cells were constructed all over Sweden during the latter half of the nineteenth century, and existing prisons were reformed in order to produce around 500 additional single cells (Nilsson 1999: 241–2). This mass of available modernized prison space included single cells at a large number of local prisons and remand prisons (Nilsson 1999: 260, 362). A system capable of subjecting not only sentenced prisoners but also a large number of remand prisoners to solitary confinement was thereby created.

Conclusion

The idea of Scandinavian penal exceptionalism is well argued by Pratt and clearly relevant to discuss. It is however also in need of further theoretical and especially empirical testing. This chapter points to two important issues in that regard:

1   The rise of penal populism in Denmark (and Scandinavia).
2   The extensive and much criticized practice of pre-trial solitary confinement, which has been labelled a 'Scandinavian phenomenon'.

The case of penal populism should of course be analysed as part of an international wave of 'tough on crime' policies. In this context one of the important questions would be if, and to what extent, the Scandinavian welfare state and a possible egalitarian Scandinavian culture has influenced, and perhaps limited, the impact of penal populism. In the case of Denmark one could argue that penal populism has not been countered successfully by the existence of a so-called egalitarian welfare state. This is especially evident in the political debate on crime and penal issues, but is also reflected in several concrete policies, reforms and pieces of legislation.

The case of pre-trial solitary confinement could for analytical purposes be conceived as a different type of issue, which could perhaps be discussed as the result of some sort of systemic Nordic welfare state problem – i.e. the arguably anti-liberal social control tendencies, which are embedded in expansive more or less socialist types of state. This involves highlighting an aspect of the Nordic welfare state, which potentially has more to do with social control than egalitarianism and a humane penal culture.

Notes

1 According to a datasheet printed and e-mailed by the Directorate of the Danish Prison on 12 March 2010.
2 See also Crewe and Liebling (Chapter 10 in this book) and their brief discussion on differences and similarities between prison conditions in the Nordic countries and in the UK, as well as Johnsen and Granheim (Chapter 11 in this book) and their analysis of the morale performance of Norwegian prisons.
3 This expanded typology largely reflects that Esping-Andersen did not incorporate Asia into his theory.
4 It has, however, been argued by some that 'social-democratic' is an incorrect term for these welfare states. Peter Baldwin has, for example, argued that the liberal farmers and their politics played a major part in the creation of the Danish welfare state. See Baldwin (1990).
5 For a discussion on equality, 'likhet', and the welfare state in a Scandinavian country, see Ugelvik (Chapter 7 in this book).
6 Quoted from Smith 2009: 101 (translated from Danish by the author).
7 As above note.
8 Concerning the various bullet points, see Greve (2010).
9 The Danish Institute for Human Rights: 'Høring over udkast til forslag til lov om ændring af straffeloven og lov om politiets virksomhed', 3 November 2009, J.NR. 540.30/21868.
10 Regarding this practice in Norway, see also Mathiesen (Chapter 2 in this book).
11 Evans and Morgan (1998). The authors characterize pre-trial solitary confinement as a 'peculiarly Scandinavian phenomenon' (at 247). Iceland has also received the same criticism, see for e.g., CPT, Visit Report, Iceland. Visit 1998, section 15/49. See also report from the 1993 visit in Iceland. The official CPT reports are available at: www.cpt.coe.int/en.
12 See for example, Petersen (1998: 34), as well as Hatla Thelle and Anne-Marie Traeholt (2003: 772). In the Danish newspaper *Politiken* (8 January 1980), Erik Ninn-Hansen states that 'isolation is used to a lesser extent today as a means of disassociating prisoners from the outside world, and used to a greater extent to pressure them to confess', and he declares that: 'Isolation is a commodity.' See also Ninn-Hansen's comments in another Danish newspaper, *Information* (8 January 1980). A more detailed discussion of the question of solitary confinement and pressure is found in Smith 'The effects of solitary confinement on prison inmates: A brief history and review of the literature' in Michael Tonry (ed.), *Crime and Justice. A Review of Research*, 2006. Regarding CPT's reference to isolation as a means of pressure, see for e.g., CPT, Visit

Report, Denmark: Visit 2002, section 19/44, as well as Visit Report, Norway: Visit 1999, section 18/39, at www. cpt.coe.int/en.
13 Reglement for Arrestvæsenet i Danmark 1846, B Section 5. Isolation can be lifted due to health reasons, see C Section 6.
14 See notes from the Danish Minister of Justice to the Governor for Copenhagen's Prisons and others, 3 May 1969 (4. k. 950-0-6-3), as well as Erik Carlé *Københavns fængsler i 100 år*, 1995, p. 264 (Carlé quotes a source from 1970).
15 Report from *Arbejdsgruppen vedr. varetægtsarrestanters 'ulovlige' kommunikation*, January 2005, enclosure 4. See also statistics supplied in reports from Rigsadvokaten, at www.rigsadvokaten.dk.
16 Knut Even Isaksen, *Fengselsforhold og fangebehandling i Romsdal gjennom 250 år*, 1998, pp. 31, 35, Wister (1997, p. 29ff.), and Hauge (1996: 175). The 56 institutions, however, did number some older prisons, which were accepted according to the new rules. It is not known whether every district prison had solitary cells for all detainees and prisoners.

References

Andersen, Henrik Steen (2004) 'Mental health in prison populations. A review – with special emphasis on a study of Danish prisoners on remand', *Acta Psychiatrica Scandinavica Supplementum*, 110 (424): 5–59.
Andersen, Henrik Steen, Tommy Lillebæk and Dorte Sestoft (1997) *Efterundersøgelsen – en opfølgningsundersøgelse af danske varetægtsarrestanter* [The follow-up study – a study of Danish pre-trial detainees]. Copenhagen: Schultz.
Andersen, Henrik Steen, Tommy Lillebæk, Dorte Sestoft and Gorm Gabrielsen (1994) *Isolationsundersøgelsen. Varetægtsfængsling og psykisk helbred* [The solitary confinement study. Pre-trial detention and mental health], vols 1–2. Copenhagen: Schultz.
Baldwin, Peter (1990) *The Politics of Social Solidarity. Class Bases of the European Welfare State 1875–1975*. Cambridge: Cambridge University Press.
Bratholm, Anders (1957) *Pågripelse og varetektsfengsel* [Arrest and detention]. Oslo: Universitetsforlaget.
Bruun, Frederik (1871) *Beretning om tilstanden i landets samtlige arresthuse efter de ved Justitsministeriets Cirkulære af 19 Mai 1870 fremkomne oplysninger* [Report on the conditions of all remand prisons]. København.
Carlé, Erik (1995) *Københavns fængsler i 100 år* [Copenhagen's prisons through 100 years]. Copenhagen: Justisministeriet.
Cavadino, Michael and James Dignan (1996) *Penal systems. A comparative approach*. London: Sage.
Christensen, Claus Bundgård, Niels Bo Poulsen and Peter Scharff Smith (2003) 'The Danish volunteers in the Waffen SS and their contribution to the Holocaust and the Nazi war of extermination on the Eastern Front', in *Denmark and the Holocaust. Institute for International Studies, Department for Holocaust and Genocide Studies*, Copenhagen: Institute for International Studies, pp. 62–101.
Engbo, Hans Jørgen (2005) *Straffuldbyrdelsesret* [Enforcement of punishment]. Copenhagen: Jurist- og Økonomforbundets Forlag.
Esping-Andersen, Gøsta (1995) *The Three Worlds of Welfare Capitalism*. Cambridge: Polity Press.
Evans, Malcolm and Rod Morgan (1998) *Preventing Torture. A Study of the European Convention for the Prevention of Torture and Inhuman or Degrading Treatment or Punishment*. Oxford: Clarendon Press.

—— (1999) *Protecting Prisoners. The Standards of the European Committee for the Prevention of Torture in Context*. Oxford: Oxford University Press.

Gamman, Tor (1995) 'Uheldige helsemessige effekter av isolasjon. En klinisk studie av to grupper av varetektsinnsatte' [Negative health effects following isolation. A clinical study of two groups of remand prisoners], *Tidsskrift for den norske Lægeforening*, 115: 2243–6.

—— (2001) 'Om bruk av isolasjon under varetektsfengsling' [On the use of solitary confinement during pre-trial detention], *Nordisk Tidsskrift for Kriminalvidenskab*, 88.

Garland, David (2001) *The Culture of Control*. Oxford: Oxford University Press.

Greve, Vagn (2004) 'Får eller Ulve' [Sheep or wolf], *JTF*, 3–4, 2004.

—— (2010) 'Strøminger i Kriminalpolitikken'.

Grothe Nielsen, Beth (2006) *Straf. Hvad ellers?* [Punishment. What else?]. Copenhagen: Tiderne Skifter.

Haney, Craig (2003) 'Mental health issues in long-term solitary and "supermax" confinement', *Crime and Delinquency*, 49(1): 124–56.

Hauge, Ragnar (1996) *Straffens begrunnelser* [Reasons for punishment]. Oslo: Universitetsforlaget.

Isaksen, Knut Even (1998) *Fengselsforhold og fangebehandling i Romsdal gjennom 250 år* [Prison conditions and treatment of prisoners in Romsdal throughout 250 years]. Molde: Romsdal Sogelag.

'Istanbul statement on the use and effects of solitary confinement' (2008) *Journal on Rehabilitation of Torture Victims and Prevention of Torture*, 18(1): 63–6.

Morgan, Rod (1999) 'Moderate psychological pressure: the Scandinavian way?', *Kritisk Juss*, 3.

Nilsson, Roddy (1999) *En välbyggd maskin, en mardröm för själen. Det svenska fängelsesystemet under 1800-talet* [A well-built machine, a nightmare for the soul. The Swedish prison system during the nineteenth century]. Lund: Lund University Press.

—— (2003) 'The Swedish prison system in historical perspective: a story of successful failure?', *Journal of Scandinavian Studies in Criminology and Crime Prevention*, 4.

Nissen, Hartvig (1934) *Øie for øie, tann for tann? Skiftende syn på straff og fangebehandling* [An eye for an eye, a tooth for a tooth. Changing views of punishment and the treatment of prisoners]. Oslo: Cappelen.

Nowak, Manfred (2009) UN Special Rapporteur on torture, report on Denmark, A/HRC/10/44/Add.2, 18 February.

Petersen, Manfred W. (1998) 'Isolation – en illusion?' [Isolation – an illusion?], *Retspolitik*, 16(2).

Pratt, John (2007) *Penal Populism*. London: Routledge.

—— (2008a) 'Scandinavian exceptionalism in an era of penal excess. Part I: the nature and roots of Scandinavian exceptionalism', *British Journal of Criminology*, 48: 119–37.

—— (2008b) 'Scandinavian exceptionalism in an era of penal excess. Part II: does Scandinavian exceptionalism have a future?', *British Journal of Criminology*, 48: 275–92.

Rentzmann, William *et al.* (2003) *Straffuldbyrdelsesloven. Med kommentarer* [Enforcement of the Penal Code law. With comments]. Copenhagen: Jurist- og Økonomforbundets Forlag.

Smith, Peter Scharff (2004) 'A religious technology of the self. Rationality and religion in the rise of the modern penitentiary', *Punishment and Society*, 2.

—— (2006a) 'The effects of solitary confinement on prison inmates. A brief history and review of the literature', *Crime and Justice*, 34: 441–528.

—— (2006b) 'Når straffen rammer uskyldige. Deres problemer, behandling og menneskerettigheder' [When punishment strikes the innocent. Their problems, treatment and human rights], *Social Kritik*, 106.

—— (2006c) 'Prisons and human rights: The case of solitary confinement in Denmark and the US from the 1820s until today', in Stéphanie Lagoutte, Hans-Otto Sano and Peter Scharff Smith (eds), *Human Rights in Turmoil. Facing Threats, Consolidating Achievements*. Martinus Nijhoff.

—— (2007) 'Ytringsfrihed og følelser' [Freedom of speech and emotions], *Jyllands Posten*.

—— (2008) 'Solitary confinement: an introduction to the Istanbul Statement on the use and effects of solitary confinement', *Journal on Rehabilitation of Torture Victims and Prevention of Torture*, 18(1): 56–62.

—— (2009) 'Frihedsstraf og indespærring. Hensyn, formål og principper i et idehistorisk perspektiv' [Imprisonment and confinement. Considerations, purposes and principles in a perspective of history of ideas], *Slagmark*, 55: 89–120.

Smith, Peter Scharff and Janne Jakobsen (2010) *Når straffen rammer uskyldige. Børn af fængslede i Danmark* [When punishment strikes the innocent. Children of inmates in Denmark]. Copenhagen: Gyldendal.

Thelle, Hatla and Anne-Marie Traeholt (2003) 'Protection of suspects' rights versus investigation needs: the use of solitary confinement in Denmark', in Morten Kjærum, Xia Yong, Hatla Thelle and Bixiaoqing (eds), *How to Eradicate Torture: A Sino-Danish Joint Research on the Prevention of Torture*. Copenhagen: The Danish Institute for Human Rights.

Tonry, Michael (2004) *Thinking about Crime. Sense and Sensibility in American Penal Culture*. New York: Oxford University Press.

Wilhjelm, Preben (1987) *Dømte om retssystemet.* [The legal system according to sentenced criminals]. Holte: Socpol.

Wister, Ole A. (1997) *Enkelte trekk ved norsk Fengelshistorie* [Some characteristics of the history of Norwegian prisons]. Oslo: KRUS.

4 Media, crime and Nordic exceptionalism
The limits of convergence

David A. Green

Introduction

Two similar convergence debates have run in parallel in recent years. One's catalyst was David Garland's (2001) *The Culture of Control*, which outlines and attempts to account for the 'punitive turn' in Western penality, most evident in countries such as the United States and England and Wales but traceable elsewhere. The narrative of convergence elsewhere towards Anglo-American-style penal cultures has recently been contested by a number of comparative scholars (see Tonry 2007), as has the Anglo-American linkage itself. Franklin Zimring once remarked at an American Society of Criminology conference that Garland's comparison of English and American penal severity was like comparing 'a haircut to a beheading', so vast were the differences between them. Nordic countries' experience with penal harshening is similarly incomparable with American experience, or even that of England and Wales (Green 2008b), and John Pratt's (2008a, b) thesis of Nordic penal exceptionalism holds that the Nordic nations have been able to buck most of the more punitive trends experienced in high-imprisonment societies, or at least to withstand and accommodate them differently.

A parallel story of media convergence follows a similar narrative arch. Scholars in the communications fields are examining – and some are contesting – a comparable convergence thesis which holds that the world's media systems are converging towards a market-driven, American-style model. Few deny that some level of convergence has occurred and is continuing – as evidenced by the commercialization of newsgathering, the move from 'hard' to 'soft' news, and the elevation of entertainment over public service values – but as with the notion of penal convergence, debates have now shifted to the ways in which jurisdictions diverge from, modify and resist the forces converging towards what Hallin and Mancini (2004) call the 'liberal model' of media and politics.

It is probably fair to say that both convergence theses still retain considerable purchase among scholars who have qualified the influence of convergence rather than reject it outright, working to refine its contours, outline its limitations, and reveal where and how cultural attitudes, policies and practices have been tempered by more local, nation-specific contingencies. This chapter is an attempt to expand the scope of discussion about Nordic exceptionalism by drawing on comparative scholarship about media convergence. It first examines the utility of comparative frameworks that move the argument beyond *whether* the Nordic nations are somehow exceptional in the way they address crime and public concerns about it, and focuses discussion on and provides some conceptual tools for explaining *why* they are. The second section outlines the case for media convergence in the Nordic countries. It offers examples of how Nordic media practice and coverage of crime have come to reflect the Anglo-American trends that Nordic criminologists believe have helped usher in a harsher penal climate. The next section examines the structural and cultural limitations of convergence – the countervailing factors supporting the notion of Nordic exceptionalism. Finally, the conclusion offers some reflections on the future durability or longevity of Nordic resistance to the forces of media convergence.

The utility of comparative perspectives

Comparative scholarship 'can serve as an effective antidote to unwitting parochialism . . . [and] an essential antidote to naïve universalism' (Blumler and Gurevitch 1995: 75–6). Some even go so far as to suggest that 'an observation simply is insignificant without comparisons' (Strömbäck *et al.* 2008: 15). Questions of convergence can only be considered in comparative perspective, which also allows for a more rigorous assessment of putative explanations for social phenomena than can otherwise be achieved.

Comparing penal systems

The focus in comparative penology has recently centred on the role played by political culture and political economy in mediating and moderating late-modern pressures to respond punitively to perceived threats of crime and insecurity. For instance, Arend Lijphart's (1999) comparative typology of democratic systems has been employed to argue that in 'majoritarian democracies', such as the United States and England and Wales – with winner-take-all election systems, (usually) two dominant and opposing political parties that rarely compromise, and a free-for-all interest group pluralism – political actors are more strongly incentivized to respond to crime out of political expedience in ways that prioritize toughness and symbol over fairness and effectiveness, more so than do those in 'consensus democracies', such as the Nordic countries, where proportional election systems, multiparty coalitions and corporatist interest group access are the norm (Green 2007, 2008b; Lacey 2008; Lappi-Seppälä 2007, 2008).

Cavadino and Dignan (2006: 15) developed a broader typology of political economies to explain the 'penal tendencies' of a sample of a dozen countries grouped according to shared feature sets. Their four types include 'neo-liberalism' (United States, England and Wales, Australia, New Zealand, South Africa), 'conservative corporatism' (Germany, France, Italy, the Netherlands), 'social democratic corporatism' (Sweden, Finland), and 'oriental corporatism' (Japan). Appetites for and tendencies towards punitive responses to crime are highest in those countries where neo-liberalism dominates, particularly in the United States, and lowest among the Nordic countries with social democratic corporatist political economies, and Japan, with its oriental corporatism. Cavadino and Dignan found considerable evidence of penal convergence towards neo-liberal penality but are careful not to overstate its extent.

Comparing media systems

Hallin and Mancini (2004) accomplished for the comparative study of media systems what Cavadino and Dignan (2006) did for comparative penology. They identified three general models of media systems in 18 Western democracies whose groupings roughly correspond with the comparative–penological framework. Each of these models differs along four media-centred dimensions: (a) the *structure of media markets* and, particularly, the emergence and availability of a mass-circulation versus an elite-centred press; (b) the degree of *political parallelism* or political partisanship shown by media organizations; (c) the degree of journalistic *professionalism*, including the level of autonomy journalists have, their adherence to ethical standards and to notions of objectivity, and their commitment to public-service versus market-driven values; and (d) the degree of *state intervention* in the media system, including the extent of government subsidies, the regulations governing the provision of public service media, and the censorship of newsgathering and news presentation (Strömbäck *et al.* 2008).

In addition there are five dimensions characterizing the political context of media systems: (a) *the role of the state*: the distinction is between welfare state democracies systems – where the state maintains a strong role in ensuring citizen welfare, including intervention in the media systems – and liberal democracies – where a more laissez-faire, market-driven orientation obtains; (b) *consensus versus majoritarian democracy*: see Lijphart's distinction explained above; (c) *individual versus organized pluralism*: this distinction is between whether political representation is achieved via individual activism and a plurality of special interest groups or through the 'collective and highly organized social groups which enjoy advantaged positions in the relationship with the state' (Strömbäck *et al.* 2008: 17); (d) *the strength of rational–legal authority versus clientelism*: or whether a system has 'a form of rule based on adherence to formal and universalistic rules of procedure' (Hallin and Mancini 2004: 55) or whether 'patrons or powerholders' have the discretion to control access to resources for the benefit of 'clients in exchange for deference and/or different kinds of favours and services' (Strömbäck *et al.* 2008: 18); and (e) *moderate versus polarized pluralism*: or the extent to which the number and depth of political and social cleavages in a country generate conflict and politicization.

The Mediterranean or 'polarized pluralist model' is displayed in the southern European countries (France, Greece, Italy, Portugal and Spain), where the press developed relatively late, where newspapers retain allegiances to political parties, and where the professional autonomy of journalists is curtailed by political party and business interests. The 'democratic corporatist model', of which the Nordic countries are prototypes (including as well Austria, Belgium, Germany, the

Netherlands and Switzerland), characterizes those countries embodying three 'coexistences' that set them apart. These include the 'simultaneous development of strong mass-circulation commercial media and of media tied to political and civil groups; the coexistence of political parallelism and journalistic professionalism; and the coexistence of liberal traditions of press freedom and a tradition of strong state intervention in the media, which are a social institution and not a purely private business' (Hallin and Mancini 2004: 195–6). Although political affiliations have declined over recent decades, parallelism was historically strong but 'developed alongside a journalistic culture protecting journalistic independence and based on professional codes that transcended political affiliation' (Hardy 2008: 104). State intervention in media markets includes the limits placed on political advertising, subsidies to increase media pluralism, and regulation to preserve the media's public service mission in the face of market demands. Nations within this model have traditionally been consensus democracies and strong welfare states that retain systems of democratic corporatism, combining 'a diversity of parties and organised social interests with broad consensual agreement about the underlying political system, including processes and institutions of power sharing and decision-making' (Hardy 2008: 103–4).

Finally there is the 'liberal model', of which the United States is the exemplar (but also the UK, Ireland and Canada) and towards which the other models are said to be converging. These media systems are characterized by the early development of a mass-circulation press with a limited level of state intervention and firmly institutionalized norms of professionalism centred on the notion of journalistic objectivity. Party parallelism is comparatively low among liberal model countries, but with significant variations. For instance, the British newspapers, especially the tabloids, retain clear but shifting political affiliations (Hardy 2008). The British national newspaper market is both class stratified and segmented by 'political affinity', whereas the US markets are local, with each smaller market dominated by 'a single, monopoly newspaper with a catchall audience' (Hallin and Mancini 2004: 206–7). In the US, the commercialization of the press drove partisanship from the mainstream news market in the late nineteenth century. The need to raise advertising revenue produced an 'orientation toward the center and toward the political "mainstream"' (Hallin and Mancini 2004: 210), but commercialization has recently hastened the return of partisanship to some extent, with the deregulation of radio, the proliferation of new cable and satellite channels, and the arrival of outlets such as Fox News and MSNBC that are 'narrowcasting' their news and commentary to fragmented niche audiences.

These liberal model nations are predominantly majoritarian democracies, displaying individualized representation and moderate pluralism, with a limited state role both in subsidizing media and in the provision of welfare services – though more so in the US than elsewhere. American public service broadcasting survives but is 'marginal' (Hallin and Mancini 2004: 199) in comparison to Britain, retaining a low share of audiences, and market demands drive content more so than in Britain and much more so than in democratic corporatist countries where commitments to public service goals remain firmly established.

The media convergence thesis

In short, in the Nordic context, the media convergence thesis holds that democratic corporatist media systems are converging towards the liberal, Anglo-American model and that media systems and content are becoming homogenized. It is useful though to consider what convergence means in practical terms. What exactly is said to be converging? The most thorough approach would focus on three areas simultaneously: media production, media content and media audiences (Hardy 2008: xvi), and the question of convergence should be considered through these lenses. The production of media content has been shaped by a number of global forces and developments which can be traced both to changes in how content is produced and in what kinds of content are produced, but convergence in audience reception is obviously much harder empirically to pin down.

Proliferation, commercialization, secularization

Part of the convergence thesis concerns the proliferation of media technology which has placed severe pressures on news organizations to compete for the attention of increasingly fragmented news audiences with much more choice in what they consume. These are universal shifts in the direction of the liberal model, with consequential, though variable, impacts on the remaining media models. In the US in the 1970s the president of CBS News, Dick Salant, reportedly had misgivings the first time that the network's evening newscast made money. News had become a commodity rather than a public service and he feared that its quality would suffer (Goldberg 2002). The commercialization of news has since accelerated in an increasingly competitive marketplace.

In the field of broadcasting, the 'commercial deluge' of the 1980s to 1990s has displaced the public service monopolies of an earlier era in favour of mixed systems in which commercial media are increasingly dominant. Broadcasting has been transformed from a political and cultural institution in which market forces played a minimal role into an industry in which they are central, even for the remaining public broadcasters who must fight to maintain audience share (Hallin and Mancini 2004: 252)

These pressures naturally shape the kind of content the media produce, often in ways many scholars bemoan. Commercialization 'changes the social function of journalism, as the journalist's main objective is no longer to disseminate ideas and create social consensus around them, but to produce entertainment and information that can be sold to individual consumers' (Hallin and Mancini 2004: 277).

Commercial pressures also help explain the shift from hard news (topics of relevance to public policy) to soft news (human interest stories, entertainment and sport), impacting even public service broadcasters with a broader mission. Most crime news is considered soft news that usually offers only 'episodic frames' – treating events as one-offs without context and without connecting them to related events – and fails to provide the 'thematic frames' required for citizens, for instance, to place one-off crime stories in a broader context (Iyengar 1991).

From 1975 to 2001 in the UK, the BBC's coverage of crime rose from 4.5 to 19.1 per cent while its political coverage fell from 21.5 to 9.6 per cent (Winston 2002). These rises and falls were even more precipitous at ITN, the commercial broadcaster. Crime coverage tripled on American local news from 1992 to 1993, because it is cheap to produce, even though recorded crime had actually been declining. By 1994, 39 per cent of Americans polled rated crime as the most pressing issue, a number which had never been higher than 8 per cent in the previous decade (Patterson 2002). Findings such as these illustrate the fears of those warning of the dangers embedded in convergence.

In the Nordic newspaper markets, the traditional role of the politically aligned press has been eroded, due in part to 'secularization'. The mass media now serve much more of the socialization and political mobilization functions that the political parties, trade unions and churches once performed.

Party newspapers and other media connected to organized social groups – media whose primary purposes were to mobilize collective action and to intervene in the public sphere and that once played a central role in to the democratic corporatist and polarized pluralist systems – have declined in favour of commercial papers whose purpose is to make a profit by delivering information and entertainment to individual consumers and the attention of consumers to advertisers (Hallin and Mancini 2004: 252).

For instance, the market share of the party-aligned press in Finland declined from 70 per cent in 1950 to just 15 per cent in 1995. The contention, however, that Nordic nations are becoming more individualist and less collectivist must be placed, like similar contentions, in comparative context. Collectivism survives and still distinguishes Nordic countries from the USA and UK (Hofstede and Hofstede 2005).

Signs of convergence in crime news

Press and broadcast coverage of crime has increased in recent decades in the Nordic countries (Smolej and Kivivuori 2008), and the nature of that coverage has changed, too. In Sweden, for instance, media coverage of juvenile offending increased and shifted in the mid-1980s when 'descriptions of juvenile offending altered in character, becoming less understanding and more punitive. The juvenile offender has gone from being perceived as a victim of a poor upbringing and a difficult environment, to being a "super-predator" who assaults other people out of choice' (Estrada 2001: 653). The increase in both the salience of violent juvenile crime and the change in how it was explained were paralleled by an ideological shift in the official penal approach to such offending, from a treatment-based model to a retributive, just-deserts approach. Pollack (2002) has also noted changes in mass-mediated discussions of juvenile crime in Sweden since the 1970s, away from considerations of the offender's social circumstances to a more victim-centred discourse, a shift noted as well in Britain (Reiner *et al.* 2000).

The proliferation of cable and satellite channels in the 1990s has increased competition in the area of crime news, with political consequences. In Norway,

TV2, a hybrid channel combining a profit orientation with public-service obligations, became the country's second terrestrial television channel in 1992 (Østbye 2008), and NRK, the state-owned public broadcasting company equivalent to the BBC, launched a second channel in 1996, and a third in 2007 (Aalberg et al. 2010). TVNorge is a purely commercial station that has been on air since 1988, but it was initially available only on satellite and cable. 'The last two decades have . . . shown a wide acceptance among Norwegian media that crime should be covered quite extensively, also by media previously unlikely to carry much crime news', including the NRK stations (Røssland 2007b: 140). As one Norwegian media scholar explained, the tabloids *VG* and *Dagbladet* now might focus their attention on a crime problem which the remaining media outlets – including commercial and NRK stations, web-based and radio outlets – are now compelled to cover as never before. 'It's tougher today than just 10 years ago' (Allern 2007). Røssland (2007a) contends that in Norway an axis exists between TV2, *VG* and the populist Progress Party on crime issues and together they ratchet up public concern about crime and raise its profile. Other political parties have had to follow rhetorical suit when the Progress Party publicly responds to the front pages of the tabloids or agrees with TV2's talk-show moderator's emotive demands for swift and demonstrable action against crime (Dahl 2007; Røssland 2007a). Mathiesen (2003) traces a 'stiffening of the penal climate' in Norway to the high-profile escape of a well-known drug dealer from custody in July 1988. His account details how the news values of Oslo's media helped generate a moral panic about lax prison policy, and he links this episode to wider trends in media 'tabloidization'. Moreover, deference to experts in Norway appears to have weakened in recent decades, challenged by 'a very typically Norwegian *akademikerforakt* ("contempt for academicians"), which has been and is especially pronounced when it comes to questions of crime policy' (Dullum and Ugelvik 2010, personal communication).

Although fear of violent victimization in England and Wales is twice that of Norway (Green 2008b: 75–6), and victimization fears are generally much lower among Nordic citizens than their English or American counterparts (Bondeson 2003), there has been movement towards Anglo-American patterns. Clear causal linkages are hard to establish (Heath 1984; Smolej and Kivivuori 2008; Williams and Dickinson 1993), but victimization fears are correlated with media coverage. Smolej and Kivivuori (2008) found that the Finnish media's reporting of violent crime – among tabloid and broadsheet newspapers and in broadcast news – has increased significantly since the 1980s, as has fear of violent victimization, without any corresponding increase in victimization rates. Moreover, 'compared to the reporting in the 1980s there appears to be a shift to a more subjective perspective in the reporting at the beginning of the new millennium. Homicide reporting has become more sentimental, and it appeals more and more to the subjective experiences of lay people. Also the consequences of a homicide, such as grief and shock, are stressed in the reporting to a much larger extent than before' (Smolej and Kivivuori 2008: 208).

The story of the Norwegian tabloid *VG* provides a microcosmic overview of the fears about convergence towards market-driven content. *VG* was launched in 1945 with a journalistically high-minded mission that did not pay off (Eide 1997). It was the first to pursue news objectively, independently from political parties, and was dedicated to the ideals of the public sphere. Sales sunk, however, and only after it was taken over in 1966 with a new marketing strategy did sales rebound and double several times over. Eide (1997) believes *VG*'s success was tied more to its ability to target new consumers in a new economy, such as female readers at supermarkets, than to its treatment of news, but a soft-news popularization of the newspaper occurred as well. This included more celebrity news, more material related to radio and later to TV, more sports coverage, and the 'general prevailing melodramatic framework of the popular press, and its emphasis on drama, conflict, personalities and emotions' (Eide 1997: 178). Similarly, many of the quantitative and qualitative changes in the nature and style of Nordic crime coverage are driven by market factors. As links between the Nordic newspapers and the political parties have weakened, newspapers can no longer count on captive audiences and they face incentives to appeal to as many readers as possible. The change towards more sentimental coverage appears to be one result. American-style market influence is, however, much less apparent in the Nordic countries where there are clearly evident limits to media convergence.

Nordic exceptions and the limits of media convergence

Pratt summarizes the case for penal convergence: 'The decline of trust in government, discrediting of expertise, sensational rather than objective media reporting, the politicization of victimhood associated with such developments – the same forces that have contributed to penal excess elsewhere (Pratt 2007) – produce new forms of knowledge and understandings about crime and punishment, new power relations that determine policy' (Pratt 2008b: 277). Certainly, the recent accounts in the preceding section provide evidence of convergence in the Nordic countries, but they must be situated in comparative context, particularly alongside Anglo-American developments. Features of Nordic media culture and practice qualify if not fully undermine the convergence thesis, and the Nordic nations still manage to distinguish themselves comparatively, due in part to a number of peculiarities. Four of these include characteristics of their news markets, the relatively high level of confidence citizens retain in their institutions and in expertise, the relatively strong market position of public service broadcasting and the high level of hard news it produces, and the implications of their consensus-oriented political cultures.

Peculiarities of news markets

Regardless of convergence pressures, sensationalism or 'publishing whatever brings profit' (McChesney and Nichols 2010: 138) is far more common in the UK and USA than in the Nordic countries, where media have retained a more 'sober and reasonable attitude toward issues of criminal policy' (Lappi-Seppälä 2007: 243). In contrast, the dominance of the national newspaper market by the tabloids in England, for instance, means that the style and tone of dominant press discourses tend to reflect sensationalism, conflict, anti-elite bias, common-sense solutions and outrage. Newspapers in the Nordic nations display fewer of these characteristics.

Part of this is due to the heavy reliance on subscription-based newspaper sales in the Nordic countries, where a strong newspaper culture survives and newspaper readerships, with the exception of Japan, far exceed the rest of the world (Eide 1997). Lappi-Seppälä (2007: 243) explains that in Finland nearly:

> 90 percent of newspapers are sold by subscription, which means that the papers do not have to rely on dramatic events in order to draw the reader's attention each day. In short, in Finland, newspapers reach a large segment of the population, and the market leaders are quality papers that do not have to persuade the public to buy them every day. All this may affect both how crime is reported and how people think about these matters.

Sensationalism is further dampened by characteristics of the local newspaper market, which contrasts with England's highly competitive national market. Like the Finns, the majority of Norwegian readers read local or regional newspapers sold by subscription. Because these local papers serve relatively small audiences in smaller communities, they tend to be more careful in their reporting, lest they alienate their smaller customer base (Allern 2007). The two Norwegian tabloids, like the ten major newspapers in England, are sold in a national market and need not be so concerned about losing a few irritated readers.

Yet even tabloid readers are likely to encounter a very different level of analysis from the Norwegian newspapers than their English equivalents. The class divisions in the English press market reflect a much more distinct division between the quality or broadsheet press and the popular, tabloid press than exists in Norway. 'Norwegian newspapers may be termed "popular" but still contain many elements that can be considered as characteristic of the "quality" press. They have been termed schizophrenic (e.g. Gripsrud 1992: 85) because of this mixed profile' (Røssland 2007b: 140). This schizophrenia is evident in *VG* and *Dagbladet*, which combine some of the softest and sensationalistic content with some of the best investigative journalism and political analysis (Allern 2007; Egeland 2007; Røssland, 2007a). Moreover, the market presence of a tabloid such as Norway's *VG* does not mean other newspapers' readerships suffer. Rather, newspapers are so widely read that *VG* supplements rather than replaces quality titles (Eide 1997) and there is, then, no zero-sum game in the newspaper market. The schizoid 'combination strategy' of focusing on both hard and soft news is partially responsible for the national tabloids' commercial success. 'The Norwegian newspaper market as a whole was, and still is, too small for the one-sided cultivation of either an elite or a popular market' (Eide 1997: 181).

The English and Norwegian tabloids differ in another important way. Although Lappi-Seppälä (2007: 250) cites an example of a coordinated campaign by four Swedish newspapers to influence the direction of penal policy in the 1990s, such actions are much less common in the Nordic countries than in Britain. Tabloid-led campaigns in England to combat putative leniency in the criminal justice system are frequent. The *Sun*'s 'sack the softie' campaign in June 2006 published photographs of judges it deemed unduly lenient and the *News of the World* 'named and shamed' sex offenders by publishing their photographs as part of its campaign for a publicly accessible sex offender registry. Sigurd Allern (2007), a Norwegian media scholar and former newspaper editor, could not think of an instance when a Norwegian newspaper campaigned for a cause in the way that the English tabloids frequently do.

Hard news, public service broadcasting and public knowledge

An unresolved comparative question is whether some countries' mainstream media are better at providing the kind of thematic frames and context required for informed citizenship than media elsewhere. More comparative research is required to answer this question, but existing studies have compared the distribution of hard and soft news, which allows for some useful comparative analysis. Curran *et al.* (2009, 2010) found the share of soft news on Anglo-American television was twice that of Finland. They also compared Finnish and British news consumers' knowledge about a range of domestic and international issues and personalities, and patterns of media exposure predicted knowledge of hard news in both Finland and Britain. Finnish television provided more coverage of domestic hard news than British television did, and unsurprisingly, the Finnish viewers answered a significantly higher percentage of questions correctly (78 per cent) than their British counterparts (67 per cent) (Curran *et al.* 2010: 10). Americans perform much worse than the British or Scandinavians on indicators of hard-news knowledge and political knowledge, and the stark knowledge divide between Americans with low- and high-education levels is virtually absent in the Nordic countries (McChesney and Nichols 2010). The British perform much better overall than the Americans, but less-educated Britons perform significantly worse than the Scandinavians.

This higher prevalence of both hard news and public knowledge in Finland appears to be conditioned both by the media's public service mission and the way that broadcasting schedules increase the public's exposure to news. Both public and private media are legally required in Finland to serve the public interest, and 'this emphasis on the public purpose of Finnish television, underpinned by a regime of public ownership and regulation, thus derives from a political culture and way of doing politics that stresses the legitimacy of an active state, the importance of public deliberation, and a collective route to securing public well-being' (Curran *et al.* 2010: 7). Much more so than the Nordic media, the British media system reflects the liberalization of British politics since the 1980s, whereby the emergence of market forces weakened the media's public-service mission.

Moreover, whereas British broadcasters reserve primetime hours for entertainment programming, Finland's three main television channels broadcast news programming during peak periods, at 6.30 p.m., 7 p.m., 8.30 p.m. and 10 p.m. This provides 'a steady drip-feed of public information so that it requires an effort of will for a Finnish television viewer of a popular channel to avoid the news' (Curran *et al.* 2010: 13). This suggests 'that a critical difference between the public service and market models is the greater ability of the former to engage an "inadvertent" audience: people who might be generally disinclined to follow the course of public affairs, but who cannot help encountering news while awaiting delivery of their favourite entertainment programmes. The fact that public service television intersperses news with entertainment increases the size of the inadvertent audience' (Curran *et al.* 2009: 22).

These studies also show that it is not the case that Finns are necessarily more naturally civic-minded citizens. In fact, public interest in politics appears actually to be *lower* in Finland than it is in Britain, results consistent with 2001 World Values Survey, 'which reports that only 20 per cent in Finland said that politics is rather or very important in their lives compared with 34 per cent in Britain' (Curran *et al.* 2010: 6). This suggests that quality media are better able to reach and inform Finnish citizens, and that their media do a much better job serving democratic functions than American or British media. 'In other words, what the media report matters. One reason why Finns are better informed about hard news and European news is because they are better briefed by their media in these areas than British citizens' (Curran *et al.* 2010: 13).

Curran *et al.* (2010: 14) thus conclude the democratic corporatist media model 'best supports the functioning of democracy' because of the attention it gives to hard news. 'This is primarily because Finnish television is more subject to a public service regime of regulation, and the Finnish press is more influenced by professional journalistic norms, than the more market-driven media system in Britain' (Curran *et al.* 2010: 14), which still retains a much stronger public service commitment than the United States. This assures Finns are exposed to 'more substantive content, more educational–cultural content, higher quality, and less low-level populism' (Lappi-Seppälä 2007: 272).

Recently, on an influential American Sunday morning television news talk show, ABC's *This Week*, Roger Ailes, president of the conservative organ Fox News, currently the leading American cable TV news source, defended himself against criticism that his organization failed fully to cover an important policy speech by President Obama. He said, 'I'm not in politics, I'm in ratings. We're winning.' This kind of open embrace of market values over public service commitments by a news organization is a long way from either British or Nordic experience. These studies suggest a comparatively healthy public service media sector in the Nordic countries, and in Norway and Denmark, audience share of public service broadcasting actually increased between 1998 and 2005, in spite of the arrival of commercial stations (Esmark and Ørsten 2008; Hardy 2008). To offer another comparison, investment in public media is $101 per capita in Denmark and Finland, $80 in the UK, and a mere $1 in the USA (McChesney and Nichols 2010).

Confidence in expertise and institutions

The Nordic nations appear to differ from the USA and UK on another dimension, which is the extent to which their citizens retain confidence in expertise. There may be historical reasons for this, tied to the lack of a feudal history and a firm Nordic commitment to egalitarian values (Pratt 2008a: 126), but whatever its origins, this difference can have consequences for the quality of coverage the media produce. For one thing, expertise is required for the provision of thematic framing and contextual background about an issue.

Notwithstanding a rising *akademikerforakt* ('contempt for academicians'), my own comparative study of English and Norwegian responses to two child-on-child homicides, the killings of James Bulger and Silje Redergård (Green 2008b), found that the Norwegian press, both quality and tabloid titles, were much better than their English counterparts at providing context. English press accounts portrayed the killing of 2-year-old James Bulger by two young boys as both indicative of an increased prevalence of violent juvenile crime and as an act so unique as to be beyond compare, without providing substantive evidence for either notion. However, in its very first article on the Bulger case, the Norwegian tabloid *VG* provided the perspective the English papers did not: 'Every year the last ten years, between 39 and 73 children under the age of five have been murdered in Great Britain, according to public statistics . . . In nearly every incident, the murders have been committed by adults who were acquainted with the children' (*VG*, 18 February 1993). In addition, 'expert' views – those of psychologists and psychiatrists, medical doctors, social workers and researchers – appeared far more frequently in the Norwegian newspapers to contextualize the killing of Silje Redergård, with the Norwegian tabloid *VG* presenting them with a prevalence nearly twice that of *The Times,* the English broadsheet (39 per cent in *VG*, 22 per cent in *The Times*) (Green 2008b).

This kind of contextualization appears to be more common in the Nordic countries generally. In Finland, for example, 'the tone of Finnish [news] reports is less emotional, and reports – including when dealing with particular events – are usually accompanied with comments on research-based data on the development of crime' (Lappi-Seppälä, 2007: 243). Moreover, Nordic judges are much more insulated from media-generated 'public' concern and pressures from ministers than they are, for instance, in the UK, USA or Canada, where judges routinely acknowledge the influence of perceived public opinion when sentencing (Roberts *et al.* 2003). In Finland, 'for a judge, sentencing is an application of law according to the accepted sentencing principles, and appreciating the valid sources of sentencing law; the news media and opinion polls are not among these . . . [And] there are culturally accepted expectations that ministers do not interfere in the work of the judges and do not base their policy decisions on the changing results of superficial media polls' (Lappi-Seppälä 2007: 273). Of course, such a system would be untenable were there not relatively deep reservoirs of trust in expertise and in the courts in the Nordic countries.

Consensus democracy

Whereas the liberal model conceives of media as 'vertical channels of communication between private citizens and the government', and through which competing viewpoints of those who gain access compete for dominance, the more inclusive, consensus-oriented democratic corporatist notion is premised on the view that 'a democratic media system should represent all significant interests in society. It should facilitate their participation in the public domain, enable them to contribute to public debate and have an impact on framing policy . . . In short the central role of the media should be defined as *assisting in the equitable negotiation or articulation of competing interests through democratic processes* (Curran 1991: 30, original emphasis). Media content is shaped by these arrangements, with consequences for the public sphere, as 'a traditionally high prevalence of debate, commentary, and interpretation is connected with a political culture based on negotiation and discussion' (Hallin and Mancini 2004: 188).

Economists tell us that a citizen's ignorance of political affairs is rational when the likely return for one's significant investment of time and attention is likely to be low (Hamilton 2004). It follows that such 'rational ignorance' might be more prevalent in majoritarian democracies with winner-take-all election systems where the return on political engagement is lower than it is in concensus democracies, simply because one person's vote has less impact on the outcome of an election when representation is not proportional. I have argued elsewhere that Nordic-style consensus democracy – particularly the proportional representation and multiparty, power-sharing systems – generates a different style of political discourse than in the highly partisan majoritarian jurisdictions such as the United States and England and Wales (Green 2007, 2008a, b). Absent is the strong incentive to a zero-sum game style of politics, and this reduces, though does not remove, inclinations to oversimplify complex policy debates for pure political expediency. With reduced politicization of complex social issues such as crime and what should be done about it, the news discourse produced for public consumption is likely be very different in character and in quality than it would be if politically motivated claimsmakers were competing for attention in order to shape public debate in politically advantageous ways. We need more comparative research to test the hypothesis that the cognitive tools or ideational resources provided for Nordic news consumers differ from those encountered by American and British news consumers.

Conclusion

The notion of 'Scandinavian exceptionalism' (Pratt 2008a, b) in the face of penal and/or media convergence implies a dichotomy rather than a continuum, which might have more comparative utility. Pratt is right to point out that Nordic exceptionalism – particularly as a focal point of difference and opposition in 'the contemporary era of penal excess' – survives in part because 'mass media [are] largely controlled by public neo-corporate organizations rather than market forces which provided its already well informed public with objective rather than sensationalized crime knowledge' (Pratt 2008a: 135). That said, it is cold comfort to those in the Nordic countries with deep concerns to be told their experience with either kind of convergence is less acute and less consequential than that of the English or the Americans. Nonetheless, signs or symptoms of penal or media convergence are not evidence of equivalence of experience. What the comparative work reviewed in this chapter suggests is that considerable variations exist in responses to universal pressures, and the interplay of local cultures, structures and market peculiarities are consequential in explaining them.

Penal convergence is something like a prevailing westerly trade wind (Snare 1995), universally experienced but impacting nations in peculiar and particular ways that must be understood locally and comparatively to fully appreciate. It is likely the same westerly winds of Anglo-American penality are blowing in every place where crime and insecurity register high among public concerns, but that these winds impact each coastline and all geographical terrain differently, depending on the particular contours of the structures encountered locally. For all the demonstrable shifts towards greater Anglo-American penal severity in the Nordic countries (Pratt 2008b), a comparative perspective reveals just how well the Nordic nations have weathered the penal populist pressures that have pushed the United States and England and Wales to incarcerate so many more of their citizens than their neighbours (Pratt 2008a).

Just as the evidence suggests that the punitive turn evident in many countries has made significantly fewer inroads in Nordic penal practices, the trend towards the homogenization of media content and practice has been significantly tempered in Nordic jurisdictions, and for many of the same reasons. These reasons have much to do with differences in political culture and the structures and practices in place in each jurisdiction that sustain differences in cultural assumptions and values. For instance, even in Sweden, where Pratt (2008b: 14) argues the 'threat [to penal exceptionalism] is greatest' and where a number the pressures of convergence towards the liberal model of media systems have been experienced, its media system retains many of the characteristics of the democratic corporatist model. Although state intervention has become less important and parallelism has declined, the convergence that has occurred should not be viewed:

> as an absolute market-orientation towards full-scale commercialization and liberalization . . . The relative strength of newspapers as opposed to TV, the institutionalized systems for regulation of the media and the strong position of the public service media make Sweden stand out even in times of globalization, modernization and homogenization processes . . . Traditions and political culture matter, and this in combination with high public confidence in the historically most well known media institutions, as well as the institutionalized and corporative system for media ethical issues, may thus far have prevented a process where liberal market values turn the existing order upside down.
>
> (Strömbäck and Nord 2008: 116)

Just as Nordic penal exceptionalism has been jeopardized by converging pressures, so there are forces working to undermine Nordic exceptionalism in the media realm as well. Schmuhl and Picard (2005: 148) point out that the gaps between those with the requisite knowledge to participate meaningfully in democracy and those without it is 'compounded by problems of information "wants" and "want nots"', the latter of whom choose either to avoid sources of information, hard news and political commentary, or who choose from an increasingly broad range of news and information sources only those outlets whose views and politics confirm their own. Inadvertant exposure to hard news through primetime public service media might ensure that those in the Nordic countries, even for the information want nots, are better informed about the world than their American or British counterparts, but whether this is sustainable over the longer term is another question.

Manjoo (2008) warns of the dangers of niche-media proliferation which allows for an unprecedently high level of easy selectivity in news consumption. Although most of us might regularly engage in some level of daily selective attention, reception and retention – preferring consonant information confirming our worldviews and preferences – the explosion and fragmentation of media markets has made these psychological predelictions must easier to indulge. Nordic media systems have features that might lessen the impact of these universal niche-market pressures, though it is unclear how long this will continue. The internet has yet to emerge as a leading news source (Aalberg *et al.* 2010; Curran *et al.* 2010), but things could change considerably if or when it does. Moreover, the same menu-based media technology that allows viewers to avoid advertisements, to record only the programming they want to see, and to view it at a time of their choosing, is the same technology that works against the kind of inadvertent exposure to news content that appears to have rendered the Finns in Curran's studies more informed than their liberal model peers.

References

Aalberg, T., P. van Aelst and J. Curran (2010) 'Media Systems and the Political Information Environment: A Cross-National Comparison', *International Journal of Press/Politics*, 12: 255–71.

Allern, S. (2007) Interview. Oslo, Norway (8 March).

Blumler, J. G. and M. A. Gurevitch (1995) *The Crisis of Public Communication*. London: Routledge.

Bondeson, U. (2003) *Nordic Moral Climates: Value Continuities and Discontinuities in Denmark, Finland, Norway, and Sweden*. London: Transaction.

Cavadino, M. and J. Dignan (2006) *Penal Systems: A Comparative Approach*. London: Sage.

Curran, J. (1991) 'Rethinking the Media as a Public Sphere', in P. Dahlgren and C. Sparks (eds), *Communication and Citizenship: Journalism and the Public Sphere in the New Media Age*, pp. 27–57, London: Routledge.

Curran, J., S. Iyengar, A. B. Lund and I. Salovaara-Moring (2009) 'Media System, Public Knowledge and Democracy: A Comparative Study', *European Journal of Communication*, 24: 5–26.

Curran, J., I. Salovaara-Moring, S. Coen and S. Iyengar (2010) 'Crime, Foreigners and Hard News: A Cross-National Comparison of Reporting and Public Perception', *Journalism*, 11: 3–19.
Dahl, A. O. (2007) Interview. Oslo, Norway (8 March).
Egeland, J. O. (2007) Interview. Oslo, Norway (4 May).
Eide, M. (1997) 'A New Kind of Newspaper? Understanding a Popularization Process', *Media, Culture and Society*, 19: 173–82.
Esmark, A. and M. Ørsten (2008) 'Media and Politics in Denmark', in J. Strömbäck, M. Ørsten and T. Aalberg (eds), *Communicating Politics: Political Communication in the Nordic Countries*, pp. 25–43, Gothenburg, Sweden: Nordicom.
Estrada, F. (2001) 'Juvenile Violence as a Social Problem: Trends, Media Attention and Societal Response', *British Journal of Criminology*, 41: 639–55.
Garland, D. (2001) *The Culture of Control: Crime and Social Order in Contemporary Society*. Oxford: Clarendon Press.
Goldberg, B. (2002) *Bias: A CBS Insider Exposes How the Media Distorts the News*. Washington, DC: Regnery Publishing.
Green, D. A. (2007) 'Comparing Penal Cultures: Two Responses to Child-on-Child Homicide', *Crime and Justice: A Review of Research*, 36: 591–643.
—— (2008a) 'Political Culture and Incentives to Penal Populism', in H. Kury (ed.), *Fear of Crime – Punitivity: New Developments in Theory and Research*, pp. 251–76, Bochum, Germany: Universitätsverlag Brockmeyer.
—— (2008b) *When Children Kill Children: Penal Populism and Political Culture*. Oxford: Oxford University Press.
Gripsrud, J. (1992) 'The Aesthetics and Politics of Melodrama', in P. Dahlgren and C. Sparks (eds), *Journalism and Popular Culture*, pp. 84–112, London: Sage.
Hallin, D. C. and P. Mancini (2004) *Comparing Media Systems: Three Models of Media and Politics*. Cambridge: Cambridge University Press.
Hamilton, J.T. (2004) *All the News That's Fit to Sell: How the Market Transforms Information into News*. Princeton: Princeton University Press.
Hardy, J. (2008) *Western Media Systems*. New York: Routledge.
Heath, L. (1984) 'Impact of Newspaper Crime Reports on Fear of Crime: Multi-Methodological Investigation', *Journal of Personality and Social Psychology*, 47: 263–76.
Hofstede, G. H. and G. J. Hofstede (2005) *Cultures and Organizations: Software of the Mind*. London: McGraw-Hill.
Iyengar, S. (1991) *Is Anyone Responsible? How Television Frames Political Issues*. Chicago: University of Chicago Press.
Lacey, N. (2008) *The Prisoners' Dilemma: Political Economy and Punishment in Contemporary Democracies*. Cambridge: Cambridge University Press.
Lappi-Seppälä, T. (2007) 'Penal Policy in Scandinavia', in M. Tonry (ed.), *Crime, Punishment, and Politics in Comparative Perspective*, Chicago: University of Chicago Press.
—— (2008) 'Trust, Welfare, and Political Culture: Explaining Differences in National Penal Policies', *Crime and Justice: A Review of Research*, 37: 313–87.
Lijphart, A. (1999) *Patterns of Democracy: Government Forms and Performance in Thirty-six Countries*. London: Yale University Press.
Manjoo, F. (2008) *True Enough: Learning to Live in a Post-Fact Society*. Hoboken, NJ: Wiley.
Mathiesen, T. (2003) 'Contemporary Penal Policy: A Study in Moral Panics', paper

presented at the European Committee on Crime Problems 22nd Criminological Research Conference, Strasbourg, 20 October. (Online: www.coe.int/T/E/Legal_affairs/Legal_ co-operation/Crime_policy/ Conferences/PC-CRC(2003)8E-TMathiesen.pdf; accessed 9 February 2003.)

McChesney, R. W. and J. Nichols (2010) *The Death and Life of American Journalism: The Media Revolution That Will Begin the World Again*. Philadelphia: Nation Books.

Østbye, H. (2008) 'Media and Politics in Norway', in J. Strömbäck, M. Ørsten and T. Aalberg (eds), *Communicating Politics: Political Communication in the Nordic Countries*, pp. 83–102, Gothenburg, Sweden: Nordicom.

Patterson, T. E. (2002) *The Vanishing Voter: Public Involvement in an Age of Uncertainty*. New York: Knopf.

Pollack, E. (2002) 'Juvenile Crime and the Swedish Media in an Historical Perspective: A Series of Contextualised, Cross-Sectional Studies of the Years 1955, 1975 and 1995', paper presented at the IAMCR Conference and General Assembly, Barcelona, 21–6 July.

Pratt, J. (2007) *Penal Populism*. London: Routledge.

—— (2008a) 'Scandinavian Exceptionalism in an Era of Penal Excess: Part I: The Nature and Roots of Scandinavian Exceptionalism', *British Journal of Criminology*, 48: 119–37.

—— (2008b) 'Scandinavian Exceptionalism in an Era of Penal Excess: Part II: Does Scandinavian Exceptionalism Have a Future?', *British Journal of Criminology*, 48: 275–92.

Reiner, R., S. Livingstone and J. Allen (2000) 'No More Happy Endings? The Media and Popular Concern about Crime since the Second World War', in R. Sparks and T. Hope (eds), *Crime, Risk, and Insecurity: Law and Order in Everyday Life and Political Discourse*, pp. 107–25, London: Routledge.

Roberts, J. V., L. J. Stalans, D. Indermaur and M. Hough (2003) *Penal Populism and Public Opinion: Lessons from Five Countries*. New York: Oxford University Press.

Røssland, L. A. (2007a) Interview. Oslo, Norway (8 May).

—— (2007b) 'The Professionalization of the Intolerable: Popular Crime Journalism in Norway', *Journalism Studies*, 8: 137–52.

Schmuhl, R. and R. G. Picard (2005) 'The Marketplace of Ideas', in G. Overholser and K. H. Jamieson (eds), *The Press*, Institutions of American Democracy series, pp. 141–55, New York: Oxford University Press.

Smolej, M. and J. Kivivuori (2008) 'Crime News Trends in Finland: A Review of Recent Research', *Journal of Scandinavian Studies in Criminology and Crime Prevention*, 9: 202–19.

Snare, A. (ed.) (1995) *Beware of Punishment: On the Utility And Futility of Criminal Law*. Oslo: Pax.

Strömbäck, J. and L. W. Nord (2008) 'Media and Politics in Sweden', in J. Strömbäck, M. Ørsten and T. Aalberg (eds), *Communicating Politics: Political Communication in the Nordic Countries*, pp. 103–21, Gothenburg: Nordicom.

Strömbäck, J., M. Ørsten and T. Aalberg (2008) 'Political Communication in the Nordic Countries: An Introduction', in J. Strömbäck, M. Ørsten and T. Aalberg (eds), *Communicating Politics: Political Communication in the Nordic Countries*, pp. 11–24, Gothenburg: Nordicom.

Tonry, M. (Ed.) (2007) *Crime and Justice*, vol. 36: *Crime, Punishment, and Politics in a Comparative Perspective*, Chicago: University of Chicago Press.

Williams, P. and J. Dickinson (1993) 'Fear of Crime: Read All About It? The Relationship between Newspaper Crime Reporting and Fear of Crime', *British Journal of Criminology*, 33: 33–56.

Winston, B. (2002) 'Towards Tabloidization? Glasgow Revisited, 1975–2001', *Journalism Studies*, 3.

Part II
Commodification of exceptional penal systems

5 'The most progressive, effective correctional system in the world'

The Swedish prison system in the 1960s and 1970s

Roddy Nilsson

In this chapter, I am going to concentrate not so much on whether a Swedish (or Scandinavian) exceptionalism exists or not, but on the question of *how* such an image has been produced. In the 1960s and 1970s, Sweden was seen as *the* model when it came to prison systems. American scholars and students made study tours to Swedish prisons. In this chapter I am going to describe how the Swedish prison bureaucracy – in a very determined, and no doubt skilful, way – produced the idea of Swedish prison policy as progressive and humane – in one word, 'modern' – to the American audience.

I will argue that the image of Swedish prisons and criminal politics in general as humane, progressive and 'modern' at least to some degree was the result of a successful marketing campaign. The height of this campaign was the decade between 1965 and 1975, but the beginning could be traced back to the 1940s. At that time, the proliferating Swedish welfare state was already a source of inspiration for reform-oriented Americans. It should be noted that these generally favourable views about the Swedish prison system and criminal politics in the 1960s and 1970s stood in stark contrast to the strong criticism against the same system that dominated among Nordic scholars during this period. So at the same time as the Swedish Correctional Administration in the US was praised for its humanitarianism and progressiveness, it was under heavy attack at home.

Policy transfer and idea travelling

The political scientists Dolowitz and Marsh (2000; cf. Jones and Newburn 2007) have developed a model for studying what they call 'the policy transfer process'. The model contains a battery of questions with the ambition of a range that cannot be met in this short chapter. In the hope of inspiring further research, I will limit myself to a tentative discussion on two questions: what ideas and messages were transferred? What motivated these prison bureaucrats and scholars to engage in this process? For a more fully developed explanation of what this travelling of ideas meant, it would be necessary to broaden the scope and include a list of other questions. This means that what is discussed in this chapter concerns the symbolic and discursive level. Thus, I will avoid discussing the question of whether the idea of a Swedish prison model had any concrete influence over the correctional system in the US.

The process of 'idea travelling' concerning prison administration has a long history dating back at least to the beginning of the nineteenth century (Norris 1985; Nilsson 1999). An important role in this process was played by the international penal organizations that were founded in the latter half of the century (Henze 2007; Teeters 1949). The process described and analysed in this chapter is seen as a case of idea travelling, a process in which *knowledge*, i.e. a gathering of propositions and authoritative statements that are *held* to be true, is spread from one national or institutional context to another.

The Swedish welfare state and its American connections

The idea of a Swedish model in the area of criminal policy and prisons must be seen in the context of the Swedish welfare state. The research concerning the development and character of the Swedish welfare state has been considerable (Trägårdh 2007; Christiansen *et al.* 2006; Berman 2006; Baldwin 1990; Esping-Andersen 1990). It is not my intention to deal with this subject here. The rather limited aspect of this huge discussion I am interested in concerns the role the welfare state played in the construction of an extremely positive view of the Swedish prison system.

Even though the connections between Sweden and the US, foremost as a result of the large transatlantic emigration, had been strong since the middle of the nineteenth century, a new interest in Sweden began to develop in intellectual and political circles in the US from the 1930s (Ohlsson 1991, 2010; Blanck 1992; Alm 2004). When it came to the production of a positive image of Sweden, the publication of Marquis Childs' *Sweden: The Middle Way* (1936) played a pivotal role (Marklund 2009; Alm 2004; Ohlsson 1991). Childs portrayed Swedish society as built on compromise and adjustment, a society between capitalism and socialism. Sweden was seen as a modified capitalist economy where the excesses of capitalism had been curbed by a strong state and successful cooperative movements. In the US, a country with high unemployment rates still struggling to recover from the depression, the news that Sweden had managed to reconcile capitalism and socialism was met with great interest, not least in the Roosevelt administration (Ohlsson 2010). Childs' extremely positive account played an important role in creating a favourable view of Sweden and its welfare institutions (Geis 1979: 208). Childs also attracted followers such as the American author and literary professor Hudson Strode and former press attaché at the American embassy in Stockholm, Wilfrid Fleisher. In a 1949 publication, Strode, with direct reference to Childs, talked about the enlightened manner in which the Northern democracies handled their social problems (Strode 1949: xv). In contrast to Childs, Strode dedicated a couple of pages to a description of how Sweden treated its prisoners. He presented a rosy picture of Sweden as a country with no real crime problem and where 'personal decency, honesty, and law-abiding attitudes are in general high repute'. 'In Sweden', Strode wrote, 'they don't try to break a prisoner's spirit, but work to restore his self-confidence'. Referring to the key passage in the newly inaugurated penal law,[1] Strode told his American readers that in Sweden the basic principle was that the prisoner shall be treated with regard for his dignity as a human being, and that the idea of society taking revenge of the wrong-doer was a thing of the past (Strode 1949: 224f.). In his 1956 publication *Sweden: The Welfare State*, Fleisher dedicated a whole chapter to prison reform which he introduced by saying that 'Sweden is probably the world's most progressive country in prison care and reform' (1956: 205). Despite some resistance from conservatives, Fleisher told his readers, the progressives have the upper hand when it comes to prison policy. In the following, he spent some 20 pages presenting the Swedish prison system and penal law talking about the 'leniency shown to prisoners' as well as about the leave regularly given to prisoners and the shortenings of prison sentences (1956: 207ff.).

Once again: the Myrdal couple

The strong dependence on American social science is important for an understanding of how a specific form of thinking about society proliferated in Sweden (Björk 2008; Larsson 2001; Blanck 1992). Being the most famous of the intellectual architects behind the Swedish welfare state, Gunnar and Alva Myrdal from the late 1920s onwards spent periods studying and working in the US in contact with American scholars. The visits to the US made deep impressions, both scientifically and politically, on the Myrdals, who in turn played an important role in bringing American ideas to Sweden (Nilsson 1994: 138ff., 208ff.; Larsson 2001: 44–53; Blanck 2002; Vinterhed 2003: 94–126; Hirdman 2007: 153–62, 171ff.). Their views about the US were presented in the book *Kontakt med Amerika* (Myrdal and Myrdal 1941). Even though the dark sides of the American society were recognized, this book is foremost a celebration of American culture. Sweden, and Europe in general, had much to learn from America, argued the Myrdal couple, foremost its dynamism as well its optimism and idealism (Nilsson 1994: 285ff.). But, according to their experience, Americans admired Sweden, especially the popular movements and 'our ability to be rational and unbiased and to master the modern technology while keeping the inherited solidity in its forms' (Nilsson 1994: 286, my translation).

In the US, Gunnar Myrdal made his name as a prominent scholar by publishing the classic *An American Dilemma* (Myrdal 1944). Alva also published several important books and articles making her views known in the English-speaking world, most notably *Nation and Family* (1942) and *Women's Two Roles* (1956). Alva and Gunnar's writings and other activities played an important role in producing the image of Swedish social policy as modern, progressive and effective (Carlson 1990).

The Swedish penal reform drive

The Implementation of the Sentence Act of 1945 signalled a radical change in penal policy in Sweden. This act was part of a larger reform drive in the penal area that the Social Democrats had started immediately after coming to power in 1932, and was as such the result of several years of committee work and deliberations (Nilsson 2009; Petersson Hjelm 2002; Sundell 1998). The old system with solitary confinement was, at least in principle, abandoned as the standard form of punishment. Loss of liberty was in itself to constitute the only punishment, and no further deprivations, suffering or curtailment of rights other than those linked directly to the coercion of confinement were to be deliberately inflicted on the prisoners. The goal was that life inside the prisons was to resemble life on the outside as much as possible (Leander 1995; Sellin 1947). For the generation of post-war prison reformers in Sweden, the Implementation of Sentence Act of 1945 was seen as the starting point for a progressive penal policy in Sweden (Rudstedt 1994; Strahl 1970).

The three decades after the Second World War were the heyday of the treatment ideology. The idea of treatment and a welfare-oriented criminal policy was, of course, not restricted to Sweden and the other Scandinavian countries (cf. Garland 2001). But it could be argued that these ideas had a stronger and more long-lasting effect in these countries. The draft for a new criminal code in Sweden in 1956 went extremely far in this direction and among other things proposed a total abandoning of the concept of 'punishment' and its replacement with concepts such as 'protection' and 'sentence' (SOU 1956: 55). Although the most radical proposals fell when the new Criminal Code came into force in 1965, the idea of individual treatment was clearly in the foreground (Andersson 2002).

The most important salesmen: the two T(h)orstens

The single most important figure in the Swedish Correctional Administration during the post-war decades was undoubtedly Torsten Eriksson, a dedicated proponent of penal welfarism. Eriksson was a steadfast believer in individual prevention and differentiation of sanctioning. He often emphasized that the prisons ought to be more like healthcare institutions (Nilsson 2002: 16). He was also a Social Democrat and his wife represented the party in the Swedish parliament. Although educated in jurisprudence, Eriksson became a severe critic of this profession's rule-bound rigidity, conservatism and inability to depart from the punishment model. His own views could best be summarized as a mixture of medically and socially oriented views combined with a deep trust in the value of labour and the soundness of working-class culture (Eriksson 1967, 1976). From the 1930s to the 1950s, Eriksson took part in a series of committees dealing with questions of criminal policy besides holding posts in the Swedish National Social Board before subsequently becoming Director General of the Swedish Correctional Administration in 1960.

Right from the beginning, Eriksson was interested in the international development in the areas of prisons and the care for criminal and deviant youths. He read most of the important social scientists and early criminologists dealing with these problems and made several visits to prisons and other penal and treatment facilities in other countries. Throughout his career as a prison administrator, Eriksson kept in close contact with the developments in the US and also made several trips to the country. In order to learn more about the newest methods, Eriksson spent five months in the US in 1949 studying different models for the treatment of juvenile delinquents. He was critical of many features of the US correctional system, but saw with great interest on the experiments that were carried out with methods variably called 'group therapy' or 'group interaction' (Eriksson 1953). Other leading Swedish penal administrators visited the US for the same reasons (Rudstedt 1947a, 1947b, 1948, 1949).

Eriksson became a well-known figure on the international penological scene, writing reports and short articles for international meetings and conferences (see for example 1951, 1954). In the 1960s, as part of his growing international engagements, he travelled widely abroad delivering lectures on Swedish prison policy. In 1961 he was elected chairman of the United Nations consulting committee on criminal policy. He held the same position in the European Committee on Crime Problems (CEPC), a committee inside the European Council, from 1966 to 1969 (Eriksson 1967: 348ff.).

In a well-informed book published in 1967, Eriksson summarized his views on prison reform. It is an almost archetypical reform narrative, starting with the early correctional houses and finishing with the reforms of his own time. The English publication of the book pointed to the strong interest for prison reform. The Swedish title was *Kriminalvård. Idéer och experiment* but in the revised US version, the title was simply *The Reformers* (Eriksson 1967, 1976). As the title indicates, the book is about prison reform and reformers and a long parade of prisons and treatment experiments marches through the pages, from sixteenth-century bridewells and rasphouses to the therapeutic communities of the 1960s and 1970s. Most of the cases and examples are gathered from the European continent or from the US. Perhaps a little surprisingly, only one Swedish institution was given real space. This was the youth reformatory at Roxtuna, opened in 1955. Roxtuna, which in many ways must be seen as Eriksson's own 'baby' against the background of his pivotal role in its implementation, is described as 'a revolution in Swedish, as well as international institutional thinking' and further as 'a pattern and a source of ideas for therapeutic innovations in other countries' (Eriksson 1976: 208ff.). The picture material in *The Reformers*, however, included several photos taken inside the new Swedish treatment-oriented prisons, photos showing light and spatial living rooms with coffee tables and armchairs, as well as warm and cosy cells that looked like small hotel rooms.

After resigning as Director General of the Swedish Correctional Administration in 1970 Eriksson maintained his interest in international questions. In the first half of the 1970s he held the position of the United Nations interregional adviser on penal policy. His missions included work in small and relatively young nations such as Mauritania, Panama, Ceylon, the Philippines and Costa Rica. He also, for a time, was assigned guest professor at the United Nations institute for criminology in Tokyo (Eriksson 1976: 298).

The other Thorsten who played an extremely important role when it came to spreading the ideas about the progressive Swedish prison system was the well-known American criminologist Thorsten Sellin, himself of Swedish descent. Sellin had emigrated to Canada in 1913, before moving on to the US where he became one of the most distinguished criminologists of his generation. Sellin had perhaps the single most important role in spreading information about Swedish criminal policy to an American audience.

The interest for Sweden was boosted by the attention the country attracted at the 1939 World Exhibition in New York (Ohlsson 1991: 228). Besides industry, craftwork and culture, Sweden's social policy was presented in a special publication. The foreword was written by Sellin. From the beginning of the 1940s, information about Swedish penal policy and social policy produced by the Swedish state bureaucracy grew in availability. In 1945 the Swedish Institute, a quasi-official agency responsible for promoting information on Sweden abroad, foremost in the US, was established. It was openly stated that one main aim was to repair Sweden's tarnished reputation after the Second World War (Glover 2009; Colla 2002). The Swedish Institute published material dealing with social questions right from the start (Glover 2009: 251). Early examples were the publications *Social Welfare in Sweden* (Höjer 1947) and *Social Services for Children and Young People in Sweden* (1948). The Institute's first major publication, *Introduction to Sweden* from 1949, was a proud presentation of the country, its people and institutions (Glover 2009: 250).

As president of the International Society of Criminology (1956–65) and secretary general of the International Penal and Penitentiary Commission (1949–51), Sellin was clearly a criminological internationalist (Melossi 2010). He published a steady flow of articles and held numerous lectures presenting the penal reforms in Sweden over the course of his career. In 1946 to 1947, Sellin visited his native country. He gave lectures on criminology at the Swedish universities and worked as an adviser for the Swedish Penal Commission. After returning to the US, Sellin published several articles and gave several lectures in which he presented the penal reforms in Sweden (Sellin 1947, 1948a, b, c, 1948d, 1949).

Sellin presented the development in Sweden in an extremely positive way, finding much 'not only admirable but also imitable' (Sellin 1948a: 63). Special interest was given to the correctional system and the Implementation of Sentence Act of 1945 and the treatment programme it aimed at (Sellin 1947). Sellin gave special credit to the 'open' character of the prison system and its small institutions, and he did not hesitate to tell his readers and listeners that the institutional treatment in Sweden 'actually rehabilitates the offender, if he is reformable' (1948b: 3). Through explicitly articulating a 'middle way paradigm', Sellin saw the reform work as a part of expanding welfare provisions, the new laws promising to make Sweden an 'acknowledged leader in this field of social planning' (1948b: 1). He furthermore saw a clear connection between the welfare legislation in Sweden and the 'astonishingly low' crime and prison rates (1948b: 2). He also pointed to Sweden's progressive and humane treatment of juveniles (1948a, 1949). A few years later, Sellin published an appendix to a Swedish committee report in which he once again praised the 'strong and productive' reform work in Swedish penal policy spurred by 'dynamic leaders' with 'able collaborators' (1953: 91). In 1956, the much-discussed draft for a new penal code in Sweden was published. The following year, Sellin presented this to the American audience (1957).

It is clearly hard to overstate the role Sellin and Eriksson played when it came to establishing the image of the Swedish penal system as a model to follow for those seeing themselves as modern, progressive and concerned with the well-being of their fellow humans. With the risk of overstating the possibilities for individuals to influence the development in areas like criminal policy, the political context must be borne in mind. First, the penal elite was much smaller than today. At the same time, the agenda for national politics in general was set by the governing Social Democrats. These conditions made it possible for dedicated, able and strong-willed men such as Eriksson to gain such a dominant position. Second, the state bureaucracies were not only much smaller in number, but also more deferential and loyal to the political programmes that were launched. Third, penal policy in general was much more than today exclusively an affair for the experts. Before the end of the 1960s, the voices of the media and non-governmental organizations were weak and their possibilities to influence criminal policy small. When it came to Thorsten Sellin, his unique double cultural competence made him a fitting bridge between the two penal systems.

The 1960s and 1970s

For penal progressives in the US, Sweden in the 1960s and 1970s became the country known for its humane penal system. During these decades, the Swedes continued to publish presentations and translations of their new penal laws directed at an international, but foremost American, audience. In 1965, The Swedish Institute published a presentation of the Swedish correctional system written by Clas Amilon, a leading prison administrator (Amilon 1965). That year, the new Criminal Code had come into force, a code which confirmed that individual treatment (and to a lesser extent, deterrence) was the leading principle and that non-institutional care should be given priority. Although Amilon's article had the subtitle 'a survey', it was a combination of a description of the criminal justice organization and a normative account of the goals and intentions behind the code. The same year, Sellin, on behalf of the Swedish Ministry of Justice, translated the Child Welfare Act and the new penal code into English (Sellin 1965a, b). The translation of the penal code appeared in new editions in 1972 and 1974 (Sellin 1972, 1974).

An important event put the spotlight on Sweden and its criminal policy. The United Nations Congress for the Prevention of Crime and the Treatment of Offenders was held in Stockholm in 1965. It is not a wild guess that Torsten Eriksson's influential position on the international penological scene was a main reason for choosing Stockholm as host for the congress. The general theme of the congress was crime prevention. During the congress, the Swedes took the opportunity to show the 1,100 participants from 84 countries the best side of the Swedish Correctional Administration. The opening address was held by the Swedish

Minister of Justice and Social Democrat Herman Kling. He set the agenda by declaring that humanitarianism should be regarded as a fundamental obligation to mankind and that it was particularly important to be steadfast in our allegiance to this principle when it comes to criminal policy (1976: 249).

A series of visits to Swedish prisons was arranged and as Director General of the Swedish Correctional Administration, Torsten Eriksson delivered a keynote speech in which he presented the Swedish prison system as well as parts of the penal policy. He emphasized that Sweden now had introduced a new up-to-date Penal Code which aimed at a 'sensible, effective and humane treatment of all offenders' (1965: 53). He described the 'open' character of the Swedish system with a large number of prisons of a colony type, frequent use of furloughs, lack of censorship and generous opportunities to receive visits from relatives and friends. However, the real pride of the Swedish correctional system was the vocational training programme in which the goal was to adapt the working conditions in prison as closely as possible to conditions in civil society. When new institutions are built, the motto is, Eriksson told his listeners, 'first we build the factory, then we add the institution' (1965: 60).

From around 1970, the Swedes intensified their efforts to spread information about their prison system as a steady flow of articles, pamphlets and announcements were released by agencies such as the Swedish Institute in Stockholm and the Swedish Information Service in New York. In these publications intended exclusively for publication abroad, the Swedish prison authorities presented a picture of a humane, progressive and tolerant prison system. Titles such as *Prison Democracy*, *Opening up the Prisons*, *Labor-Market Wages for Prisoners*, *In for Repairs* and *Where Prisoners are People* signalled a clear message. Articles with the same message could also be found in *Sweden Now*, published by the Swedish Information Service in New York (Buss 1970; Link 1973). It is interesting that the name denoting the central prison bureaucracy in older publications, 'Swedish Correctional Administration', now was changed to 'Swedish Prison Service'. In 1971 Eriksson's successor as Director General, Bo Martinsson, wrote in *Prison Democracy in Sweden*:

> According to Swedish law there is nothing to prevent the inmates of penal institutions from forming their own organization. The general freedom of association applies to them. Likewise there is nothing to prevent them from electing bodies within the institutions to further their demands.
>
> (1971: 1)

Martinsson underlined that 'in the Swedish prison's advisory councils, the pros and cons of the prison system and correctional treatment are now being discussed rather than plans for new crimes after discharge'. According to Martinsson, the ongoing negotiations between the delegates representing all of Sweden's prisoners and the representatives of the correctional authorities and the personnel organizations were unique in placing the different parties on *equal* footing (1971: 3ff., my italics).

In 1974, a new Swedish Correctional Reform Act came into force. It launched a row of reforms and 'liberalizations'. The guiding principle was the creation of an 'open' correctional system which would make it possible for the prisoners to keep and extend contacts with the outside world. The possibilities for furloughs, visits, non-censured telephone calls and correspondence, etc. would be greatly enhanced. The Act explicitly underlined that non-institutional care should be the 'natural' form of penal treatment. The so-called 'principle of normalization', which meant that everyone sentenced to prison should have the same right to society's arrangements for social support and care as other members of society, was also established. The Act was immediately presented to a foreign audience (Smith 1974; Swedish Correctional Care Reform 1975).

In the article 'Probation – Not Prison', published in *Sweden Now* in 1976, the Social Democratic Minister of Justice, Lennart Geijer, gave his view on the reform work in the country. The article was a *plaidoyer* for a criminal politics with clear utopian features. Coming close to an abolitionist position, Geijer expressed a far-reaching reform agenda and stated that we, in order to form a better and more effective penal policy, must break loose from old well-worn paths and antiquated patterns of thought. Correctional work, where it was needed, should be the task of social service bodies. Prisons would be reserved, argued Geijer, for a few hundred people, a very small group of 'dangerous' people – 10–15 per cent of those held in prisons at the time (Geijer 1976, cited in Ward 1979: 142ff.). In hindsight, Geijer's article could be seen as a last effort to maintain Sweden's reputation as the leader of penal reform. It was clear for most observers that the winds had already begun to blow in other directions. Swedish penal policy and the prison system had lost a good deal of its credibility in the aftermath of prison unrest and several dramatic escapes by some of the country's most notorious criminals, as well as a rising problem with drugs in prisons. Later the same year, the Social Democrats lost the general election and Geijer was forced to leave his post.

American views and responses

During the period from the middle of the 1960s to the middle of the 1970s, the Swedish prison system attracted large interest in liberal and reform-oriented circles in the US. But the word about the 'advanced' and humane Swedish prisons had, as we have seen, already spread long before this period. Introductory books about Sweden often devoted at least a couple of pages to its progressive criminal policy and prison system. For example, in *The Scandinavians*, Donald Connery described Sweden's prisons as 'friendly' with homelike conditions and a 'good measure of privacy' for the prisoners (1966: 409f.). The Scandinavian treatment of lawbreakers was, Connery went on, 'far removed from traditional methods of imprisonment and punishment. It is enlightened – and successful' (Connery 1966: 152). Other writers sent the same message to American readers. In *Sweden and the Price of Progress*, David Jenkins stated that convicts in Sweden were considerably better off than in most countries, and that Swedish prisons are world famous for their explicit aim of reform, not punishment or vengeance (1968: 96). Paul Austin, in a book aiming at a broader presentation of the social and cultural structure of Sweden, pointed to the liberal regimes in Swedish prisons and noted that the 'humane, non-moralistic attitude is reflected in Sweden's prisons which, by comparison with most European or American prisons are almost homes away from home' (1970: 49f.). The works of Connery, Jenkins and Austin were part of a tendency to uphold Sweden as the modern and enlightened society, which attracted a large part of the liberal left in the US (Trägårdh 2007). This tendency perhaps got its most far-reaching expressions in the works of Frederic Fleisher (1967) and Richard Tomasson (1970).

American newspapers and magazines also picked up the thread. In a 1967 article *Time Magazine* wrote that 'prison reform must have gone further in Sweden than anywhere else in the world' (*Time Magazine* 1967). A few years later the *New York Times* also pointed to Sweden as the 'Leader in Prison Reform' and *Time Magazine* referred to the Swedish prison system as a 'fascinating model for the Americans to follow'. On another occasion the latter cited a press release with the heading 'A Prison in Sweden is more like a Hotel' (Ward 1972: 249). The well-known *New York Times* journalist Tom Wicker concluded that 'Sweden seems to have almost the best of everything, including a criminal justice system generally considered fair, humane and effective. Sweden's prisons are models of decency and humanity' (Pratt 2008a: 132). In some publications the authors were extremely enthusiastic and wrote about the hotel-like institutions, the restaurant quality of the prison food and happy prisoners going cross-country skiing (Ward 1979: 90f.). The hyperbole went even further when a 1972 article stated that:

> For the Swedes a prison sentence can be fun time: The nation's welfare system takes lawbreakers, too, under its permissive wing, giving them love, entertainment, even vacations.
>
> (Durham 1972: 46)

Durham talks about the 'overwhelming compassion' of the Swedish system in general and of the 'remarkably tolerant view' of outcasts held by the Swedes (1972: 49). The article was illustrated with several photos. One showed a man – apparently a prisoner – and a women sitting on a bed kissing. The caption said that the photo was taken in a prison 'love room'. A second photo showed what was said to be a prisoner couple bicycling in peaceful village of cottages and a third a group of people – of which one was said to be a prisoner on furlough – sitting in a train laughing, eating and drinking beer. Even though the article was written by a journalist with apparently limited knowledge of the Swedish correctional system, it nevertheless contributed to the image of the Swedish penal policy as one of humanity and progressiveness. At the same time, the article had a slightly ironic tone and anecdotal style, which gave room for different interpretations of the text, especially as the author also make some references to Roland Huntford's much-discussed *The New Totalitarians*, a book deeply critical of Swedish society. In his well-known critique of Sweden, Huntford wrote about the leniency and treatment orientation that characterized the Swedish prison system. For him, the

Swedish dedication to treatment became yet another proof of the welfare state as an instrument of control (1971: 194–203).

Along with the praise came a certain amount of exoticism (see de Maré 1952). It is clear that writers such as Connery, Jenkins and Austin, in the same way as their predecessors Strode and Fleisher in the 1940s and 1950s, looked at this peculiar little country at the northern fringes of Europe with a mix of admiration and surprise. The same goes for more critical or hesitant writers such as Durham and Huntford. For all these foreign writers, Sweden, for good or bad, was a country where special political, social and cultural conditions determined its role as a forerunner in modernity.

Also from a more professional view, the positive judgements began to increase. In 1965 an American criminological textbook described the Swedish Correctional Administration as 'the most progressive, effective correctional system in the world' (Berkley *et al.* 1965: 501). A favourable article published in 1966 in the journal *Federal Probation* by Norval Morris (1966) has been seen as especially influential in drawing attention to Swedish penal policy (Ward 1979: 97f.). These positive responses were part of an intellectual climate in the US where it still was possible to think of a future where prisons played a minor role (see Brown 2009: 156). When Morris together with Gordon Hawkins a few years later published what they called *The Honest Politician's Guide to Crime Control*, they once again picked out Sweden, foremost its prison industry, as the major foreign inspiration (1970: 130ff.). Four years later Morris repeated his positive views on Swedish and Scandinavian penal policy when he talked about the 'advanced' treatment institutions in this part of the world (1974: 14).

Swedish prisons also attracted academic visitors from the US. A sociologist who in 1971 had visited a number of Swedish prisons depicted them as 'probably the most advanced in the world' (Bultena, cited in Ward 1979: 97). The same year, another American sociologist, David Ward, undertook a visit to Swedish and Danish prisons. He generally paints a very positive picture, particularly in comparison with the situation in the state of New York where the big riot at Attica prison had recently taken place. Ward described how the Swedish inmates had the rights to conjugal visits, regular home leaves, communication by telephone and uncensored mail, to vote in national elections, and to bring complaints against prison officials to the national ombudsman. He also described the 'vacation institutions' and the system with inmate councils. The inmate council had regular meetings with the prison governor discussing a wide range of questions concerning the prisoners situation (Ward 1972: 241, 246f.). Ward also had a favourable view of the Swedish justice system in general reporting that 'compared to American prisoners few complaints are heard about harassment, deception, and discrimination by the police, prosecutors, and judges' (1972: 243). However, Ward was one of the few anglophone commentators who also had some doubts. This led him to warn his American readers about having too rosy a picture of the Swedish prison system. Ward emphasized that there were still large differences between different prisons and that much of the publicity was given to innovative aspects of Swedish penal policy that only applied to a small number of institutions. Ward also noticed the problems the reform movement had run into when the inmates, supported by the National Association for the Humanization of the Correctional System (KRUM), had presented their list of demands. The reaction from the authorities clearly showed that there were limits to prison reform also in Sweden (Ward 1972: 250ff.).

A psychologist visiting Swedish prisons in the middle of the 1970s described three 'special' prisons in Sweden, the educational facility in Uppsala named Studiegården, the modified 'therapeutic community' at Gävle prison and the 'prison factory' in Tillberga, outside the town of Västerås. In his discussion concerning the effectiveness of these prisons, he concluded that Studiegården and Tillberga appeared to 'be right on target' while concerning Gävle he was more ambiguous (Snortum 1976: 159). The most important factor behind the positive development was, according to him, of a cultural kind. He saw Sweden's prison system as having moved 'along a continuous trail of reform, supported by 42 consecutive years of control by the Social Democrats' (1976: 163). The reformist drive in Swedish prison policy was seen as 'an organic extension' of other, more fundamental, social systems. He summarized his views:

> There is a relatively stronger link between prisons and the general community in Sweden because of a broader base of citizen participation in post-release supervision of offenders; a longer tradition of adult education; a lower rate of unemployment; a lower level of protectionism among Swedish labor unions and private industry; and a broader and more stable base of political support for prison reform.
>
> (1976: 166)

The same positive correlation between the welfare state and a progressive prison policy was put forward by another visiting sociologist who concluded that Sweden's penal and legal philosophy had developed out of a general social welfare ideology. The result was a welfare policy built on the idea that society had a responsibility for the welfare of its members (Friday, cited in Ward 1979: 99). Yet another scholar coming to Sweden praised the successful way the prison population had been reduced and reported of a pro-prison stance in the mass media. In the same way as several other foreigners, he told the now well-known stories about the treatment-oriented attitude in the prisons and the experiment institutions (Salomon 1976). The readers of the American journal *Offender Rehabilitation* were told that Sweden's biggest prison Kumla had a swimming pool and a soccer field and that the atmosphere between the staff and the inmates was 'relaxed' (Siegel, cited in Ward 1979: 97).

It is interesting to contrast the image of the Swedish prison system produced by American scholars and journalists with the impressions of American penal policy at the same time by Gunnar Marnell, a leading prison reformer in Sweden (Marnell 1973). Based on visits to prisons and talks with prison officials as well as inmates, Marnell identified several 'promising developments', but he also saw environmental conditions which he thought 'no health official in Sweden would allow to exist'. He also saw the American system of keeping human beings behind iron bars – 'like animals in a zoo' – as very disturbing, 'not only for psychological reasons' but also because his view was that everybody should have the right to some quiet and rest behind closed doors (Marnell 1973, cited in Ward 1979: 100).

But at the same time as the word was spread in American liberal circles about the progressive Swedish prison system, the same system was under heavy fire from groups of academic scholars, social service professionals, liberal journalists and left-leaning activists at home. The years around 1970 were the most turbulent ever for the Swedish prison system. Even though what happened in Sweden could not be compared with the American prison revolts and the resulting violence and hatred, prisoners protests and strikes and outside prison activism was the order of the day. An important role in this was played by the prisoner support group KRUM (Mathiesen 1974). These radical critics in Sweden did not talk about the most progressive prison system in the world or about 'love rooms', happy prisoners in hotel-like institutions or vacations for cross-country skiing. Their talk was about inhumane, unjust, destructive, even sometimes cruel and brutal institutions, and about the prisoners being victims of an oppressive state power. The critique was very much directed at a penal policy associated with the Social Democrats. For the radical critics, Torsten Eriksson more than anyone came to symbolize this putatively unjust system and the years preceding his retirement in 1970 were filled with angry debates between him and his opponents. The irony was that Eriksson always had seen himself as a radical when it came to penal matters. It is clear that he experienced the assaults on 'his' prison policy as deeply unjust and ill-advised.

The latter half of the 1970s witnessed a declining enthusiasm for the Swedish prisons and the possibilities of prison reform in general. A 1977 article in the *Corrections Magazine* by sociologist Michael Sherill serves as an illustration. It was based on the impressions during a study trip to Swedish correctional institutions. He contended that Sweden by liberal American social critics had been held up 'as the country that has come closest to achieving the "perfect' society"' and as well as having a 'well-established reputation for [being] one of the most liberal and humane prison systems in the world'. It is nevertheless clear that this article is written in a more distanced style. Besides presenting figures and key data concerning the correctional system and the criminal justice process, Sherill also built his article on visits to correctional institutions and interviews with prisoners, staff and others, including some critical researchers. When Sherill relates his talks with the last category, it became apparent that the enthusiasm for the Swedish prison model had begun to weaken. This must be seen in the light of the growing critique of the treatment model that gradually had developed. A leading Swedish criminologist told Sherill that the idea of individual treatment as an antidote to criminality, was in large part abandoned as utter 'nonsense'. Another researcher working in the Swedish Correctional Service told the author bluntly that 'people could not be treated, as crime is a social, not an individual, problem' (1977: 21).

When sociologist Ward came back with another article seven years after his first publication on Swedish prisons, his tone had also changed (1979: 110). Ward now stated that he saw it as remarkable that Americans, including many scholars, had so uncritically accepted the official picture of the Swedish penal policy produced in government reports and by the prison administration. Ward was the American scholar who had the most direct experience of Swedish penal policy, as he spent time doing research in Sweden. He also seems to have made good contacts with Swedish criminologists and radical jurists, and it is not a wild guess that these contacts moved his views in a more sceptical direction.

Discussion

It is clear that many US criminologists, prison bureaucrats and radical journalists looked at the Swedish penal policy, especially its prisons, in an extremely positive way. For some years, references to the progressive Swedish penal policy became a stereotype in American discussions on penal matters. This image emerged almost in full bloom before the heydays of Swedish prison reform around 1970. How should this be explained? The thesis put forward in this chapter is that we must see this in part as a result of a quite successful and systematic marketing strategy. There is, however, both a longer and a shorter perspective in this story. When the more intensive phase began around 1965, the ground was already prepared. The Swedish welfare state was generally looked upon as a model to get inspiration from in liberal and radical circles in the US. Positive information about the development in the penal area in Sweden had been produced for the US audience ever since the 1940s. Furthermore, I think that the above-mentioned critique at home played an indirect role, making the Swedish prison authorities and foreign branch even more determined to spread their version of the state of Swedish prisons. The channels through which these messages were sent were controlled by the state bureaucracy. The image of a progressive Swedish prisons and penal policy had right from the beginning been an integrated part of Social Democratic welfare policy. Bo Martinsson, Torsten Eriksson's successor in 1970, was an experienced lawyer and member of the parliament for the Social Democrats. Hence, the marketing of the Swedish model was also part of a strategy to take control of the situation at home.

One should also not underestimate the tendency to self-righteousness that the story of the welfare state had produced among Swedes – a sort of 'welfare nationalism' (see Fleisher 1967: viii). Sweden's growing reputation for being the welfare state *par excellence* was accompanied by a certain proselytizing spirit. Swedes were, and with good reason, proud of how their society had developed, from a rather poor agrarian society to a highly productive, effective and democratic one. Sweden's rise to the top of the welfare league also created a feeling of being 'ahead' of other nations, at least in some areas. One of those areas was, no doubt, that of criminal policy. This, in turn, produced a desire – with the best of intentions – to 'export' the Swedish model to other parts of the world. It is, however, important not to see this effort as the marketing of any other form of goods. There is no reason to doubt that the administrators, politicians and scholars that took part in what I called the 'marketing' of Swedish penal policy, did this in good faith. They were convinced that the humane and progressive methods were something that could be of real use. However, Swedes never made claims to have discovered or invented these new ideas and methods. Rather, the Swedish contribution was the creation of conditions where these ideas and methods could be improved and redefined in a more rational and humane direction. A big advantage in this was the nation's limited size, as well as the dominant small group of experts who largely shared the same goals.

But there is the other side of the coin. There must have been a fertile ground in the US for these messages to be attractive; a will to search for solutions to the crime problem in the direction of what was seen as humane and progressive examples. Perhaps the panegyric praise that for a period accompanied the discussion about Swedish penal policy was especially attractive to Americans, a people often associated with strong affections for utopianism and idealistic hopes themselves (Roark 2001; Shor 1997; Fogarty 1972). Dating back to the 1930s, an image of Sweden as social science utopia, a laboratory for building a new and modern society, could be seen among the American left. Sweden stood out as a country that has shown that it was possible to deal with social problems and economic inequalities in a rational way (Larsson 2001; Musial 2002; Marklund 2009). The news of the Swedish penal policy came at the right time, offering reform-oriented groups in the US an alternative to a penal policy that seemed to have come to a dead end. It is also clear that the positive image of Swedish prisons was related to the hopes and aspirations about treatment in prisons in general. So, when the critique of the treatment model began to grow, most strongly in the US but also in Scandinavia, the Swedish prison model lost most of its attraction.

What we have seen is a case of 'discourse travelling' or travelling of ideas back and forth over the Atlantic which can be traced back at least to the time of the Second World War. The in many ways uncritical acceptance of the Swedish publications by American journalists, prisons officials and even scholars, helped the course in building a positive image. But the story dealt with here must also be seen as a reflexive process, where self-images meet the gaze of others in a mutually reinforcing way (see Andersson and Hilson 2009: 222). This was a process in which personal networks as well as more institutionalized contacts forged the links but in which media-driven campaigns also played a role.

Pratt makes his claim about a Scandinavian exceptionalism well aware of the fact that Swedish criminologists as well as journalists and others for several years have been talking about the growth of tough-on-crime policies in Sweden (von Hofer 2004; Tham 1996, 2001; Leander 1995). For Pratt, there still exists some preventive barriers against Sweden's falling into the penal excesses seen in the anglophone nations. His general argument is that the Scandinavian exceptionalism has to do with the Scandinavian culture of equality which, in turn, became embedded in the social fabric through the universalism of the welfare state (2008a: 124f.).

The discussion about Scandinavian exceptionalism could theoretically be seen as concerning two different problems: (a) *if* a Swedish (or Scandinavian) model really existed or exists; and (b) if, in such a case, the thesis put forward by Pratt gives the *best* explanation for this. Although there is a considerable amount of truth in what Pratt says, I nevertheless, at least when it comes to the inferences he draws from the historical material, find his thesis partly built on speculative reasoning and anecdotal evidence (2008a: 125) However, my aim in this chapter has not been to discuss Pratt's paper as such. I have concentrated my discussion not so much on whether a Swedish (or Scandinavian) model really existed (or exists), but on the question of *how* such an *image* has been produced. This image has been created in a tradition of discourse travelling in which also Pratt's papers could be placed.

The discussion brought about by Pratt shows that this image is a living one. American media continue to produce articles on the humane Scandinavian prisons. In language almost identical to that which was used in the 1960s, *Time Magazine* describes how present-day Norway is building the world's most humane prisons, and about prisoners being 'sentenced to the good life' (*Time Magazine* 2010b). Pratt has a long list of anglophone predecessors when it comes to looking at Scandinavian penal systems as a model to aspire to. Perhaps Sweden and the other Scandinavian countries are not depicted as a kind of social utopia any more. But they can still, albeit in more toned down or indirect ways, be looked at as alternative models when it comes to criminal policy (Reiner 2007; Cavadino and Dignan 2006; Currie 1998). Pratt is not alone in seeing Sweden in a slightly romantic way, perhaps overestimating the egalitarianism and harmony of Swedish society. In a recently published comparative study of national penal systems, British scholars Cavadino and Dignan depict Sweden as a 'peaceful place' with an 'extremely generous and egalitarian' welfare state (2006: 153). In the second part of his paper Pratt (2008b) discusses the risk that Sweden (as well Finland and Norway) might fall into what he calls a politics of 'penal excess'. His conclusion, however, is that the core values of egalitarianism and tolerance are so deeply imbedded in the social fabric that it still holds. Hence, and even though Scandinavian exceptionalism never could be exported, it *could*, as this chapter has shown, serve as a reminder that there are other penal policy choices available (Pratt 2008b: 289f.).

Notes

1 The law referred to was not the general penal law but the Implementation of Sentence Act of 1945.

References

Alm, M. (2004) 'The New Deal in Sweden', in K. W. Shands, R. Lundén and D. Blanck (eds), *Notions of America: Swedish Perspectives*. Stockholm: Södertörns högskola, pp. 75–94.

Amilon, C. (1965) *The Swedish Correctional System. A Survey*. Swedish Institute for Cultural Relations with Foreign Countries.

Andersson, J. and Hilson, M. (2009) 'Images of Sweden and the Nordic Countries', *Scandinavian Journal of History*, 34(3): 219–28.

Andersson, R. (2002) *Kriminalpolitikens väsen* [The nature of crime policy]. Stockholm: Kriminologiska institutionen, Stockholms universitet.
Austin, P. B. (1970) *The Swedes. How They Live and Work.* Newton Abbot: David & Charles.
Baldwin, P. (1990) *The Politics of Social Solidarity: Class Bases of the European Welfare State, 1875–1975.* Cambridge: Cambridge University Press.
Berkley, G. E., M. E. Gillis, J. F. Hackett and N. C. Kasoff (1965) *Introduction to Criminal Justice.* Berkeley: University of California Press.
Berman, S. (2006) *The Primacy of Politics: Social Democracy and the Making of Europe's Twentieth Century.* New York: Cambridge University Press.
Björk, H. (2008) *Folkhemsbyggare* [Builders of the people's home]. Stockholm: Atlantis.
Blanck, D. (1992) 'The Impact of American Academy', in R. Lundén and E. Åsard (eds), *Networks of Americanization: Aspects of the American Influence in Sweden.* Uppsala: Acta Universitatis Upsaliensis, pp. 80–93.
―― (2002) "We Have a Lot to Learn from America": The Myrdals and the Question of American Influences in Sweden', in C. Juncker and R. Duncan (eds), *Angles on the English-Speaking World. Trading Cultures. Nationalism and Globalization in American Studies,* 2. Copenhagen: Museum Tusculanum Press.
Brown, M. (2009) *The Culture of Punishment: Prison, Society, and Spectacle.* New York and London: New York University Press.
Buss, H. (1970) 'In for Repairs', *Sweden Now*, Swedish Information Service.
Carlson, A. (1990) *The Swedish Experiment in Family Politics: The Myrdals and the Interwar Population Crisis.* New Brunswick and London: Transaction Publishers.
Cavadino, M. and J. Dignan (2006) *Penal Systems: A Comparative Approach.* London, Thousand Oaks and New Delhi: Sage.
Childs, M. (1936) *Sweden: The Middle Way.* New Haven: Yale University Press.
Christiansen, N. F., K. Petersen and N. Edling (eds), (2006) *The Nordic Model of Welfare: A Historical Reappraisal* Copenhagen: Museum Tusculanum Press.
Colla, P. (2002) 'Race, Nation and Folk: On the Repressed Memory of World War II in Sweden and its Hidden Categories', in N. Witoszek and L. Trägårdh (eds), *Culture and Crisis: The Case of Germany and Sweden.* New York and Oxford: Berghahn Books, pp. 131–54.
Connery, D. S. (1966) *The Scandinavians.* London: Eyre & Spottiswoode.
Currie, E. (1998) *Crime and Punishment in America. Why the Solutions to America's Most Stubborn Social Crisis Have Not Worked – and What Will.* New York: Henry Holt & Company.
Dolowitz, D. P. and D. Marsh (2000) 'Learning from Abroad: The Role of Policy Transfer in Contemporary Policy-Making', *Governance: An International Journal of Policy and Administration,* 13(1): 5–24.
Durham, M. (1972) 'For the Swedes a Prison Sentence Can Be Fun Time', *Smithsonian,* 4.
Eriksson, T. (1951) 'Should the Protection of Neglected and Morally Abandoned Children Be Secured by Juridical Authority or by a Non-Juridical Body?', Report to the Twelfth International Penal and Penitentiary Congress 1950, *Proceedings,* pp. 147–52 (Berne).
―― (1953) 'Amerikanska erfarenheter' [American experiences], in *SOU,* 1953: 32 *Vårdorganisation för förvarade och internerade* [Care organization for detainees and inmates]. Stockholm: Justitiedepartementet.
―― (1954) 'Postwar Prison Reform in Sweden', *Annals,* May, pp. 152–62.
―― (1965) 'The Correctional System in Sweden', Third United Nations Congress on the Prevention of Crime and the Treatment of Offenders, Stockholm, 9–18 August.

—— (1967) *Kriminalvård. Idéer och experiment* [Correctional care. Ideas and experiments]. Stockholm: Norstedts.

—— (1976) *The Reformers. An Historical Survey of Pioneer Experiments in the Treatment of Criminals*. New York, Oxford and Amsterdam: Elsevier.

—— (1977) *Politik och kriminalpolitik* [Politics and crime politics]. Stockholm: Tiden.

Esping-Andersen, G. (1990) *Three Worlds of Welfare Capitalism*. Princeton: Princeton University Press.

Fleisher, F. (1967) *The New Sweden. The Challenge of a Disciplined Democracy*. New York: David McKay Company Inc.

Fleisher, W. (1956) *Sweden: The Welfare State*. New York: John Day Company.

Fogarty, R. S. (1972) *American Utopianism*. Itasca, Ill: F. E. Peacock.

Friday, P. (1976) 'Sanctioning Sweden: An Overview', *Federal Probation*, 40.

Garland, D. (2001) *The Culture of Control: Crime and Social Order in Contemporary Society*. Oxford: Oxford University Press.

Geijer, L. (1976) 'Probation – Not Prison', *Sweden Now*, 10.

Geis, G. (1979) 'Epilogue: On Imprisonment', in M. E. Wolfgang (ed.), *Prisons: Present and Possible*. Lexington, MA and Toronto: Lexington Books.

Glover, N. (2009) 'Imaging Community: Sweden in "Cultural Propaganda"' Then and Now', *Scandinavian Journal of History*, 34(3): 246–63.

Henze, M. (2007) 'Danmark og den internationale fængselreformbevægelse 1820–1950', [Denmark and the international prison reform movement 1820–1950] in *Fængelsehistorisk Selskab 2007*. Nyborg.

Hirdman, Y. (2007) *Det tänkande hjärtat. Boken om Alva Myrdal* [The rational heart: the book about Alva Myrdal]. Stockholm: Ordfront.

Holmwood, J. (2000) 'Three Pillars of Welfare State Theory: T. H. Marshall, Karl Polanyi and Alva Myrdal in Defense of the Nation Welfare State', *European Journal of Social Theory*, 3: 23–50.

Huntford, R. (1971) *The New Totalitarians*. Stein & Day: New York.

Höjer, K.-J. (1947) *Social Welfare in Sweden*. Swedish Institute.

Jenkins, D. (1968) *Sweden and the Price of Progress*. New York: Coward-McCann Inc.

Jones, T. and T. Newburn (2007) *Policy Transfer and Criminal Justice: Exploring US influence over British Control Policy*. Maidenhead: Open University Press.

Larsson, A. (2001) *Det moderna samhällets vetenskap. Om etableringen av sociologi i Sverige 1930–1955* [A science for the modern society: on the establishment of sociology in Sweden 1930–1955]. Umeå: Institutionen för historiska studier, Umeå universitet.

Leander, K. (1995) 'The Normalization of Swedish Prisons', in V. Ruggiero, M. Ryan and J. Sim (eds), *Western European Penal Systems: A Critical Anatomy*. London, Thousand Oaks and New Delhi: Sage, pp. 169–93.

Link, R. (1973) 'Where Prisoners are People', *Sweden Now*, Swedish Information Service.

Maré, de E. (1952) *Scandinavia: Sweden, Denmark and Norway*. London: Batsford.

Marklund, C. (2009) 'The Social Laboratory, The Middle Way and The Swedish Model', *Scandinavian Journal of History*, 34(3): 264–85.

Marnell, G. (1973) 'Comparative Correctional Systems: United States and Sweden', *Criminal Law Bulletin*, 8.

Martinsson, B. (1971) 'Prison Democracy in Sweden', *Swedish Information Service Release*, April.

Mathiesen, T. (1974) *The Politics of Abolition*. New York: John Wiley & Sons.

Melossi, D. (2010) 'Torsten Sellin', in K. Hayward, M. Shudd and J. Mooney, (eds), *Fifty Key Thinkers in Criminology*. London and New York: Routledge, pp. 76–82.

Morris, N. (1966) 'Lessons from the Adult Correctional System of Sweden', *Federal Probation*, 30: 3–13.
—— (1974) *The Future of Imprisonment*. Chicago and London: University of Chicago Press.
Morris, N. and G. Hawkins (1970) *The Honest Politician's Guide to Crime Control*. Chicago: University of Chicago Press.
Musial, K. (2002) *Roots of the Scandinavian Model: Images of Progress in the Era of Modernisation*. Baden-Baden: Nomos Verlagsgesellschaft.
Myrdal, A. (1941) *Nation and Family: The Swedish Experiment in Democratic Family and Population Policy*. New York: Harper.
Myrdal, A. and G. Myrdal (1934) *Kris i befolkningsfrågan* [Crisis in the population question]. Stockholm: Bonniers.
Myrdal, A. and G. Myrdal (1941) *Kontakt med Amerika* [Contact with America]. Stockholm: Bonniers.
Myrdal, A. and V. Klein (1956) *Women's Two Roles: Home and Work*. London: Routledge & Kegan Paul.
Myrdal, G. (1944) *An American Dilemma: The Negro Problem and Modern Democracy*. New York: Harper & Brothers.
Nilsson, J. O. (1994) *Alva Myrdal – en virvel i den moderna strömmen* [Alva Myrdal – a whirl in the stream of modernity]. Stockholm/Stehag: Symposion.
Nilsson, R. (1999) En välbyggd maskin, en mardröm för själen. Det svenska fängelsesystemet under 1800-talet ['A well-built machine, a nightmare for the soul. The Swedish Prison System during the nineteenth century']. Lund: Lund University Press.
—— (2002) 'A Well-Built Machine, A Night-Mare for the Soul': Swedish Prison System in Historical Perspective', *Journal of the Institute of Justice and International Studies*, 1: 11–22.
—— (2009) 'Creating the Swedish Juvenile Delinquent: Criminal Policy, Science and Institutionalization c. 1930–1070', *Scandinavian Journal of History*, 34(4): 354–75.
Norris, R. L. (1985) 'Prison reformers and penitential publicists in France, England and United States, 1774–1847'. Unpublished Ph.D. dissertation. Washington, DC: American University.
Ohlsson, P. T. (1991) *Over There. Banden over Atlanten*. Stockholm: Timbro.
—— P. T. (2010): 'Sweden: Still the Middle Way?' (at: www.google.com/search?client=safari&rls=sv-se&q=Sweden+the+Middle+way&ie=UTF-8&oe=UTF-8).
Petersson Hjelm, A.-C. (2002) *Fängelset som välfärdsbygge. Tre studier om behandlingstanken i svensk fångvård*. [The prison as a welfare project: three studies about the idea of treatment in Swedish corrections]. Uppsala: Universitetstryckeriet.
Pratt, J. (2008a) 'Scandinavian Exceptionalism in an Era of Penal Excess. Part I: The Nature and Roots of Scandinavian Exceptionalism', *British Journal of Criminology*, 48(2): 119–37.
—— (2008b) 'Scandinavian Exceptionalism in an Era of Penal Excess. Part II: Does Scandinavian Exceptionalism Have a Future?', *British Journal of Criminology*, 48(3): 275–92.
Reiner, R. (2007) *Law and Order: An Honest Citizen's Guide to Crime and Control*. Cambridge: Polity Press.
Roark, J. L. (2001) *The American Promise: A History of the United States*. Boston: Bedford/St Martin's.
Rudstedt, G. (1947a) 'Prisons without Bars', *American Swedish Monthly*, November.
—— (1947b): 'Amerikansk kriminalvård. Intryck från en studieresa', *Tidskrift för kriminalvård*, 4: 103–12;

—— (1948): 'Probation and Parole. Skyddsverksamhet i USA', *Tidskrift för kriminalvård*, 2: 33–9.

—— (1949) 'Svensk kriminalvård presenteras i USA' [Swedish corrections presented in the US], *Tidskrift för kriminalvård*, 4: 79.

Rudstedt, S. (1994) *I fängelse. Den svenska fångvårdens historia*. [In prison: the history of Swedish corrections]. Stockholm: Tiden.

Salomon, R. A. (1976) 'Lessons from the Swedish Correctional System: a Reappraisal', *Federal Probation*, 40: 40–8.

Sellin, T. (1947) *Recent Penal Legislation in Sweden*. Stockholm: Norstedts.

—— (1948a) 'Some Aspects of Prison Reform in Sweden', in *Philadelphia County Prison, Board of Inspectors, Annual Report 1947*. Philadelphia, pp. 53–82

—— (1948b) 'The Treatment of Offenders in Sweden', *Federal Probation*, June: 1–5.

—— (1948c) 'The Treatment of Adult Offenders in Sweden', *Federal Probation*, spring.

—— (1948d) 'Probation and Parole of Adult Offenders in Sweden', in *Yearbook of the National Probation and Parole Association*.

—— (1949) 'Sweden's Substitute for the Juvenile Court', *Annals of the American Academy of Political and Social Science*, 261(1): 137–49.

—— (1953) 'The Treatment of Mentally Abnormal Offenders in Sweden. A Blueprint of Reform', in *SOU 1953: 32 Vårdorganisation för förvarade och internerade*. Stockholm: Justitiedepartementet 1953.

—— (1957) *The Protection Code: A Swedish Proposal*. Stockholm: Norstedts 1957.

—— (1965a) *The Child Welfare Act of Sweden*. Trans. by Thorsten Sellin. Stockholm: Ministry of Justice.

—— (1965b) *The Penal Code of Sweden*. Trans. by Thorsten Sellin. Stockholm: Ministry of Justice.

—— (1972) *The Penal Code of Sweden, as Amended January 1972*. Trans. by Thorsten Sellin. Rotman.

—— (1974) *The Penal Code of Sweden*. Trans. by Thorsten Sellin. Stockholm: Ministry of Justice.

Sherill, M. S. (1977) 'Profile/Sweden', *Corrections Magazine*, June: 12–13.

Shor, F. S. (1997) *Utopianism and Radicalism in Reforming America.* Westport, CT: Greenwood Press.

Siegel, H. (1977) 'Criminal Justice – Swedish Style: A Humane Search for Answers', *Offender Rehabilitation*, 1.

Smith, D. (1974) 'Opening up the Prisons', *Current Sweden*, 53, November: 1–10.

Snortum, J. R. (1976) 'Sweden's "Special" Prisons: Correctional Trends and Cultural Traditions', *Criminal Justice and Behaviour*, 3.

Social Services for Children and Young People in Sweden (1948) Swedish Institute.

SOU (1956) 55 *Skyddslag* [The protection code].

Strahl, I. (1970) Den svenska kriminalpolitiken. En presentation av brottsbalken och en översikt över den svenska straffrättens utveckling från 1800-talet till våra dagar ['The Swedish criminal policy: a presentation of the penal code and an overview of the development of Swedish criminal law from the nineteenth century to the present']. Stockholm: Bonniers 1970.

Strode, H. (1949) *Sweden: Model for a World*. New York: Harcourt, Brace & Company.

Sundell, J.-.O (1998) *Karl Schlyter – en biografi* [Karl Schlyter – a biography]. Stockholm: Norstedts Juridik.

'Swedish Correctional Care Reform' (1975), *Current Sweden*, 87.

Teeters, N. K. (1949) *Deliberations of the International Penal and Penitentiary Congresses. Questions and Answers*. Philadelphia: Temple University Book Store.
Tham, H. (1996) 'From Treatment to Just Deserts in a Changing Welfare State'. Stockholm: Stockholm University: Department of Criminology, offprint, pp. 89–122.
—— (2001) 'Law and Order as a Leftist Project? The Case of Sweden'. Stockholm: Stockholm University: Department of Criminology, offprint, pp. 409–26.
Time Magazine (1967) 'Prisons: Living Out', 22 September.
—— (2010a) 'Norway Builds the World's Most Humane Prisons', 10 May.
—— (2010b) 'Sentenced to Serving the Good Life', 12 July.
Tomasson, R. (1970) *Sweden: Prototype of Modern Society*. New York: Random House.
Trägårdh, L. (ed.) (2007) *State and Civil Society in Northern Europe. The Swedish Model Reconsidered*. New York and Oxford: Berghahn Books.
Vinterhed, K. (2003) *Kärlek i tjugonde seklet. En biography över Alva och Gunnar Myrdal*. ['Love in the twentieth century. A biography of Alva and Gunnar Myrdal']. Stockholm: Atlas.
von Hofer, H. (2004) *Crime and Reactions to Crime in Scandinavia*. Stockholm: Stockholm University.
Ward, D. A. (1972) 'Inmate Rights and Prison Reform in Sweden and Denmark', *Journal of Criminal Law, Criminology, and Police Science*, 63.
—— (1979) 'Sweden: The Middle Way to Prison Reform?', in M. E. Wolfgang (ed.), *Prisons: Present and Possible*. Lexington, MA and Toronto: Lexington Books, pp. 89–169.

6 Comparisons at work
Exporting 'exceptional' norms

Andrew M. Jefferson[1]

> There do seem to be some 'essential similarities' between prisons.
> (Liebling and Arnold 2004: 168)
>
> So prisons differ, in significant and numerous ways.
> (*ibid.* 170)

Introduction

It was March 2010, and I'd just spilled Arabic coffee on the enormous desk of the Director of the Correction and Rehabilitation Centre known as Muwaqqar One. Forty minutes' drive from Jordan's capital, Amman, Muwaqqar One houses over 850 convicted prisoners with sentences ranging from less than 30 days to death. There were six people in the Director's office: the Director himself; the deputy head of the Prison Directorate's Training and Development Centre; a psychologist called in to share with me about prisoner entry and registration procedures; and a member of a unit known as the Prosecution Police – to my eyes he resembled an archetypal prison guard but he described himself as a kind of ombudsman for prisoners, making sure prison staff live up to norms and standards and follow procedures. Completing the group was the head of control and inspections and myself, a self-styled prisons researcher with a specific interest in prisons beyond the Euro-American sphere.

I'd just returned from a tour (is that the right word?) of the prison complex and I was filled with impressions of American-style visiting booths with glass dividers and telephones for communication – the kind I'd only seen before on TV; dormitory cells featuring around 25 prisoners, bunk beds and access to a sun yard and bathroom; school classes (computing and literacy) being taught by prisoners, swipe-card-controlled gates, a well-equipped snack shop and pharmacy; surveillance cameras, fences and exercise yards. Seated in the Director's office, I was conscious of having to create a decent impression and to carefully manage my presentation of self. The coffee spillage was not the ideal start.

Via the interpretive skills of the deputy head of the Training Centre I had been having a conversation with the psychologist and posing questions to the Director about his own career in the Public Security Directorate. I was ill-prepared for the all too predictable question he then posed about how I saw his prison. What did I think of the place? How did it compare to the other prisons around the world I had visited? These were not his exact words but that was the drift of what he meant and I understood instantly that this was the most obvious question that he could ask and also that I had no reasonable answer. The same question was posed to me the following day by the Director of the Jordanian Corrections and Rehabilitation Service and I was just as flummoxed. There was really no excuse. It is not even that I had never been put in a similar situation before. In Nigeria and Sierra Leone, where I have conducted lengthy periods of fieldwork, prison officers, be they trainees or experienced staff, have often asked me exactly the same question. I have often fobbed them off with a true but somewhat unsatisfactory answer that my interest is in how *they* see the prison and that my own view is not really important. This orientation left me ill-prepared to offer any kind of evaluation. I found myself mumbling something about how the prison resembled more the European prisons I had worked in and visited than the West African prisons I have studied.

In retrospect I wonder what kind of answer this was. I teach a class on human rights in Africa where one of the key analytical themes, inspired by work by Achille Mbembe, is the need to see Africa in its own terms, in and for itself. Mbembe's critical post-colonial scholarship polemically takes issue with the dominant scholarship on Africa which sees it in oppositional terms as an entity through which the West comes to define itself. No one, claims Mbembe, takes Africa seriously in its own terms. Describing my experience in Jordan to the class I suddenly realized that perhaps seeing people and practices in their own terms is easier said than done. My answer to the prison directors was certainly a direct contradiction of this ideal. Instead of reflecting on what I saw – in and for itself – I made a deliberate comparison; I reduced my observations of what was for me a strange, previously unknown reality to a version of what was familiar to me.

How might we make sense of this? Perhaps we truly and quite literally cannot *see* beyond the limits of our own experiences? There are undoubtedly hordes of mitigating circumstances for my own behaviour. I was feeling slightly out of place and vulnerable, keen to display my prison expertise, and present an image of myself as someone who knows about prisons, someone the Jordanian authorities might want to collaborate with. I was overwhelmed by impressions and quite self-conscious in that half-embarrassed way one sometimes can be in an unusual situation. I was also keen not to cause any offence or to jeopardize any future cooperation. So I was seeking some kind of innocuous neutral response. To compare was the closest strategy to hand.

This chapter has two key purposes: (a) to reflect on the work comparisons do, in this case, for Western anti-torture practitioners and justice sector professionals engaged in the export of values, norms, ideas and best practices to the Middle East; and (b) to propose an orientation to comparison which includes processes and relations as key dimensions or 'axes of variation' (Bowen 1999: 234). (I will approach the second part via a discussion of Pratt's (2008a, b) exceptionalism thesis with specific reference to the way he uses comparison.)

Comparison involves translation and vice versa (Fox and Gingrich 2002: 9; Melhuus in Gingrich and Fox 2002: 81) and the 'negotiation of unequal power relations' (Fox and Gingrich 2002: 9). The latter point, but also the former, will become important as I unpack the empirical world of an intercultural exchange programme aimed at justice sector and prison reform revealing how the negotiation of power relations lies implicit in practices of translation. But first a glance at the way comparison has been used in the social sciences, more specifically within anthropology.

Comparison in anthropology

Until the last couple of decades of the twentieth century anthropology was dominated by three competing approaches to comparison characterized by Fox and Gingrich (2002) as holocultural, structuralist and neo-evolutionist. Subsequently these approaches have been subject to much critique. Early cross-cultural comparisons, for example, have been criticized for reproducing a distinct order of separately existing cultures rather than a single system with quite particular relations of power and exploitation. The structuralists assumed a shared cognitive structure underplaying what they perceived as merely superficial diversity and the typological comparisons and stage theory models of the neo evolutionists reproduced difference along the dubious dimension of superiority–inferiority.

Anthropology and social science more generally have fortunately moved on. Yet new challenges have emerged. On the one hand there remains a temptation to try to live up to some kind of positivist, hard science ideal when thinking about the possibilities of comparison, exhibiting a strong commitment to *the* Comparative Method. On the other, the deconstructionist turn has questioned the very possibility of comparing. If social life has lost its substance, if subjectivity has myriad fluid identities and the world itself a mirage what is there to compare? Of what can we be certain? (See Melhuus 2002: 79–80.)

Anthropology and the ethnographic endeavour, today appropriated by scholars from many different backgrounds, is renowned for its intensive attention to the micro dynamics of everyday life, a common accusation being that it has no power to generalize. However, if this allegation is true we might as well forget about comparison. As Kuper puts it (in Gingrich and Fox 2002: 144): 'If there is no generalizing social science, if objectivity is an illusion, then comparison must be abandoned as a relic of obsolete positivism.' My contention would be that this is not the case. We can and do generalize from local particularistic studies and we utilize comparison to do so. As Strathern (in Gingrich and Fox 2002: xvii) has noted 'to speak of generalities is to speak of specificities and vice versa'. Indeed comparison is one way through which local descriptive analyses can contribute to theoretical work even as theory can also feature as a comparative dimension itself. For example we might ask what different empirical fields look like when examined from a particular theoretical vantage point, say Goffman's theory about the total institution. But as Herzfeld (2001: 260) points out comparison must be complemented by reflexivity. Indeed, 'reflexivity . . . is always-already entailed in the very act of comparison'. This means we must be explicit about our comparative endeavours and be sensitive to their 'context of production' (Herzfeld 2001: 261). Pratt's influential work (as I will argue later in this chapter), is an example of comparison without reflexivity. The exception – i.e. Scandinavian penal policy – is defined in terms of an absent other but there is no reflection on that other. It is taken for granted. Pratt, we might say, is insensitive to the context of production of his own categories of exception.

Comparison, I suggest, cannot be overlooked. It remains imperative to pay theoretical and empirical attention to comparison not simply because of the 'trivial' (Melhuus, in Gingrich and Fox 2002) truth that comparison is a ubiquitous human activity, nor because comparative methodologies are part of the stock in trade of social science (especially fieldwork where there is a conscious recognition of the importance of the researcher's own shifting position within and in and out of the field) but because comparisons perform – comparisons do work for us. They are productive. They are a fundamental implicit and explicit way in which we human beings and we scholars of social practice and sociality construct the world. In the case of this book's contributors comparison is an integral, though not always conscious, aspect of our readings of the prison. In the second part of this chapter I will return to this. The next part considers comparisons as they play out *in practice*.

On the export of ideas, norms, values and techniques

> [D]evelopments in penal ideas and practices are flitting ever faster around the globe
>
> (Cavadino and Dignan 2006: 3)

Nilsson (Chapter 5, this book) unpacks the *production and marketing* of the romanticized image of the Swedish penal system of the 1960s and 1970s, focusing particularly on the way in which ideas travelled.[2] He documents less the export of penal knowledge or the exchange of ideas about penality and more the deliberate, determined attempt by high-level bureaucrats to sell an image of the Swedish system and Sweden itself as a beacon of modernity, a state charting a successful middle way between capitalism and socialism. My own analysis considers the way 'ideas travel' even as they are *implicitly* located within practices and embodied in particular professionals, institutions and policies.

The analysis below features the Karama ('dignity') programme, a project aimed at preventing torture and cruel, inhuman and degrading treatment and improving conditions for prisoners in Jordan. The Karama programme is a deliberate and determined effort to shape judicial and penal policy in the direction of fewer incidents of torture and better conditions for prisoners. The programme is facilitated by the Rehabilitation and Research Centre for Torture Victims (RCT), funded by the Danish Foreign Ministry's Arabic Initiative and involves stakeholders representing the Prosecution, the Police and the Prisons in Denmark and in Jordan, as well as organizations from Jordanian civil society.

The discussion of the work comparison does in this interstate 'exchange' programme is guided by three critical questions, the first of which I will ultimately conclude is somewhat misguided:

- Is the choice to export penal, judicial and rights-oriented norms and values via exchange programmes evidence of Nordic exceptionalism, better knowledge or just knowing better?
- What assumptions about sameness and difference inform the programmes?
- What is the significance of sameness and difference in relation to the transfer from north to south of norms and values informing penal and judicial knowledge and practice?

The analysis is based on my own observations of and participation in programme activities, and interviews with key implementers from Denmark.[3] These were a representative of the Danish prosecution service, a representative of the Danish police and a representative of the Danish prisons and probation service. Each of these persons was actively involved in the design and implementation of elements of the programme in Jordan and in Denmark. Interviews were conducted in English and transcribed except the one with the prison officer. Translations in the latter instance are my own.[4]

The Karama Programme is a multi-stranded initiative drawing in state authorities and non-governmental organizations in Jordan and their counterparts in Denmark. On the surface it could be characterized as an exchange programme but it is arguably a mono-directional exchange programme primarily for the benefit of the Jordanian partners. It began with a 'high-level seminar' called 'Incorporating International Human Rights into the Criminal Justice Sector – Experiences and Challenges of Jordan and Denmark' held in Amman, Jordan, in November 2008. Arranged by the Public Security Directorate, in cooperation with the Ministry of Justice of Jordan, and the RCT the seminar gathered top officials from Jordan and Denmark's Police, Prosecution and Prison Service in order to exchange experiences and discuss the challenges of the criminal justice processes of the two countries. Four themes were addressed over the first two days, namely the history and the political and legal systems of Jordan and Denmark; international human rights standards; criminal procedures; and execution of sentences. Following the two-day seminar were workshops and another plenary event at which the issues were discussed in smaller groups.

One assumption underlying the high-level seminars was that the senior members of the Jordanian authorities were not in need of the kind of training that typically makes up human rights programmes. It was not basic capacity building they were in need of so much as a forum through which to engage in dialogue and be exposed to different ways of acting and thinking. This thread runs through the whole programme.

Each session of the initial two-day seminar featured presentations on the theme from Denmark and Jordan, a kind of parallel dance framed in the language of 'experiences and challenges'. Session II featured an extra input from an international perspective. In structure the programme was explicitly comparative, actually contrastive. Difference was deliberately emphasized, a difference the point of which was to encourage change, a directive difference. The assumption from the Danish side seems to be that confronted with a different way of doing criminal justice the Jordanians might be inspired to think anew. Indeed, the importance of being an inspiration was a dominant theme of my interview with the Danish representative of the Prosecution Service (henceforth the Prosecutor). She spoke with great conviction about the effectiveness and efficiency of the Danish system about how from such a privileged and respected position it is almost an obligation for Denmark to assist and help improve other countries' justice systems. Similarly, the representative of the Danish prison and probation service (henceforth the Prison Officer) frames the involvement of his agency in the exchange programme partly in terms of duty. Despite the fact that international exchange programmes are not 'an area to which much attention is paid by the Danish Prisons and Probation Service' he explained that '(W)e feel it is an important task to take on because we are part of the global community.' The task is to 'get them to be better in an area where we think we are good'.

Comparison is explicit in the Prosecutor's description of her work in the project. Denmark and Jordan are clearly different seen from her perspective. History has determined that the Danish Prosecution Service is efficient and admired and therefore can function as an appropriate model for inspiration for a country less privileged and less modern and with a poor human rights record:

> We feel that we are very privileged in that we have high standards in our prosecution service, and we want to share that, we want to inspire other countries, we feel an obligation to assist countries that are in some sort of transition, that want to improve.
>
> We have a very long history of democracy and civil rights, human rights and standards . . . we think that we uphold the international standards in Denmark, we are proud of the way our system works, we have no corruption, we have good governance . . . legal decisions made on a just basis, no undue influence from political parties. So we believe that we have a system that we can be really proud of.

It is Denmark's privileged and progressive position that forms the basis for trying to inspire the Jordanian authorities to act differently. Tropes of development are utilized. The Prosecutor assumes Jordanians would be motivated to try to imitate or learn from Danes because Denmark is so developed, and has a long stable history of democracy, civil rights and adherence to standards. The combination of self-belief (conviction), affirmation from outside and contrast creates a strong platform from which to export values and norms, in this case norms governing the very nature of the institution itself. The Danish Prosecutor's main activity during the first phase of the programme was to facilitate the development of a set of guidelines instructing Jordanian Prosecutors how they might act in situations in which a court case is dismissed because the accused person has been subject to torture.

The purpose of the guidelines could be characterized as to turn 'Is who are 'completely passive' into 'wes' who 'do something' and are part of something:

> My idea with the guidelines was that the prosecution should position itself in the fight against torture, and say we have an obligation as prosecutors . . . and that by issuing guide-lines we would sort of support the local prosecutors and make it easier for them to say 'it is not me, it is us as an institution, as a system, that has to do something' . . . So my whole idea was that the prosecution should start to look at itself as an institution.

It is about the creation of an institutional identity, not however, modelled literally on the Danish Prosecution which itself features some level of role confusion. At the local level, for example, in Denmark, prosecutors are aligned with the police and often feel more part of the police than part of the prosecution (personal communication). Nevertheless, from the perspective of the Danish Prosecution the apparently personal power of Jordanian officials seemed to cry out for institutionalization and regulation. The idea of the guidelines was 'based on an assessment that working with institutional identity could strengthen them generally – and hopefully make them react more appropriately when faced with cases of torture' (personal communication).

In its original manifestation the project assumed that the respective systems might resemble one another more than they in fact do. In Jordan, for example, clear lines of authority are not evident to outsiders. Seen with external eyes, the system is opaque, though enough is revealed to sense a difference. For example, professional identities are not fixed (prosecutors can also act as, and have the title of judges as is common in inquisitorial systems); neither are institutional identities (e.g. the judiciary and the executive are merged); and communication seems based on formal authority, rather than on consensus. The interaction between the two prosecution services has at its heart 'a lack of a common frame'. Indeed it is this absence of sameness which grants the exchange process momentum. If the two organizations were identical what could one learn from the other? What would Denmark have to share? Difference is necessary.

Looking back the Prosecutor says:

> I am not about changing the system. I'm about changing the way they see themselves, and the way they act. It is not the system we are changing with these guidelines, but hopefully getting prosecutors to think about their role, and by this hopefully realizing that they should do something, and then do it.

This pragmatic goal exhibits a modest desire to inspire by example, to model, to assist. This does not sound like empire building or imposition, though there are elements of a civilizing mission to be read between the lines. But as the Prosecutor herself acknowledged rights discourse is a civilizing discourse.

Like the Prosecutor, the Prison Officer does not see a huge exchange potential in programmes such as Karama (although he does accept that one success criterion is that they too get something out of it). The Danish Prison Service are in it to give of their best practice rather than to learn. The Prison Officer sees no real need to dress the export of good practice up in false humility. The primary aim is not to learn from them but to share with them:

> My point of departure is that we come down there because we think there is something we are good at that would be really good to spread, so that others can do the same.

At the same time he pragmatically resists the logic of 'knowing better' as a pedagogical strategy: 'Knowing better is not an ideal entry point.'[5]

In contrast to the Prosecutor and the Prison Officer, the Deputy Police Commissioner (henceforth DPC) sees the Karama programme as an opportunity to reflect on her own practice and that of the Danish police in general. As she teaches on investigative techniques she reflects on whether 'we are actually this good at doing it ourselves'. The DPC elaborated that introducing people in a different context to techniques of criminal investigation utilized in Denmark facilitates a process of critical self-reflection. It is as if a mirror is held up to the Danish practices which also provokes thoughts about the way the Danish Police Force has developed norms and a particular culture through time. Her choice of co-trainer is also informed by an idea of potential benefits in terms of the learning experience. Exposure to another culture is seen to have knock-on effects with benefits back home. So for the police, more than for the prosecution there is a real sense of exchange and of having a common (professional) language. This is also the case for the prison officer trainers. According to the Prosecutor the contrast between the police and prison service and the prosecution in this regard has more to do with the choice of activities and mandate of the programme than anything else. She emphasizes that had the focus been not on how Jordanian prosecutors should react to cases of torture – and how they should carry out inspections of places of detention but on more general prosecutorial tasks then they too would have a natural professional 'sharing'. She elaborates:

> It is my experience that no matter how different you see another country's prosecution service, you are often surprised that they actually have very similar challenges and experiences as yourself.

How do Danish police officers and Danish prison officers approach the encounter? Both the DPC and the Prison Officer emphasized the importance of professional identification. In contrast to the Prison Officer, the DPC does not have 'any form of police experience'. Like many senior police officers in the Danish system, police training is not a prerequisite. She is a lawyer. Nevertheless, bearing the trappings of the profession, simply being a police officer or a prison officer grants a certain degree of credibility in the eyes of those subject to training – 'I am able to speak to the Jordanian police in a way the RCT would never be able to.' The DPC emphasized the importance of the uniform (even of the military shoulder insignia), for forging alliances across countries, while the Prison Officer suggested that it was not necessary for him to expend the same amount of energy that his colleague (a civilian) and I used establishing our 'prison' credentials – his experience and professional identity spoke for itself. Indeed, the value of a common professional identity and a common field of work functioned to offset for the Prison Officer the fact that he has never been inside a Jordanian prison:

> I have actually never seen a Jordanian prison, it's embarrassing but I haven't. Nevertheless I believe I know more about a Jordanian prison than (my colleague) and I persuade myself that I know more things than you for example do . . . there are some (pre)understandings that sometimes mean you don't need to say very much to understand what we each respectively mean.

He sees his natural curiosity, his pedagogical training, and his experience as a prison officer as key to the potential success of the training. The DPC emphasized the extent to which she uses herself during training, drawing on personal experiences of frustration and doubt, trying 'to connect on an interpersonal level' based on an idea that policing worldwide is basically about 'catching criminals'. What differs are methods, logics and approaches to this. She and her co-trainer share the same aims as the Jordanian investigators and their task is to help them be more effective. Despite the common ground found in identifying as a police officer the DPC recognizes that the institutional policing context in Jordan is quite different from Denmark's. For example, to become a police officer in Jordan requires three months of 'intensive military training' and little more. Tasks seen as basic to a Danish police officer – interviewing a suspect, for example – are seen as specialized activities handled by a special unit in Jordan. Nevertheless she hopes to make a modest difference: 'success is if I can get some of the investigators, just one of them to change'. Change, as well as the process of training is seen in personal and practical terms ('I did not have a single illusion about changing their system') but also as a long-term 'long-haul' process ('you can't change overnight'). Similarly the Prison Officer's ambition is not to change the prison system in Jordan but to effect the people who participate in training and their near environments in the hope that as part of the whole Karama programme positive effects might spread 'like ripples in water':

> What I hope is that one time, say two months after we have left them, just as a riot is kicking off, that one of the officers will go to the bars and shout 'hey you come here' and ask 'what is happening here?' (instead of calling the riot squad or initiating a total lock down) – if that happens just a single time then I think we have changed the world.[6]

Phase I of the Karama programme also featured visits to Denmark, for example a five-day visit made by four representatives of the Jordanian Corrections and Rehabilitation Department (part of the Public Security Directorate). These were the Head of the Department, two prison governors and a representative from the

Training and Development Centre.[7] The visit included trips to: the Danish Prisons and Probation Service HQ; a state prison; RCT; the Service's training centre; a remand prison; and an open prison.[8] Themes addressed during these visits included an introduction to alternatives to custody (with which Denmark has relatively limited experience); an introduction to RCT; an experience based workshop 'Everyday Challenges and Dilemmas Facing Prison Directors and Officers'; a seminar on the physical and psychological effects of torture; an introduction to the basic training course for prison officers; conflict resolution in practice and theory and discussion of how best to use unallocated programme funds.

RCT staff, responsible for facilitating the Karama programme, report that the prison visits in Denmark were a frustrating exercise for the Jordanians because the realities they encountered there were so far removed from their own. Much was made of the Jordanians' surprise at the presence of knives in prisoner kitchens and the absence of armed officers. The visits paradoxically assumed sameness or a level of identification between the Probation Service, RCT and the Jordanians. Was this a denial of difference or was difference presupposed but ignored, silenced at the moment of its invocation?

An additional issue related to sameness and difference concerns the relationship between RCT as a non-governmental rights-based, development organization with a mandate to prevent torture and rehabilitate survivors and the prison and police services in both Jordan and Denmark. RCT's role has been primarily facilitative but also agenda setting. We might see the project as an encounter between Denmark and Jordan or as an encounter between non-state and state actors. One might ask whether the two prison services, for example, might have more ideologically in common than say RCT and the Danish Prisons Service. RCT's legal adviser and programme coordinator disagrees with this analysis pointing, like the Prosecutor, to Denmark's long tradition of democracy and human rights which she believes also infiltrates Danish state institutions making the rights-based agenda of RCT a common point of reference. The fact is however that the police and the prison service are professional state organizations dealing with criminal justice and hands-on operational issues related to crime, and the maintenance of social order is drawn upon by the Danish agencies to emphasize their credibility and legitimacy and to argue that they have more leverage with the Jordanian authorities than RCT could have alone. Along one dimension then RCT and the Danish police are seen as similar. Along another dimension RCT and the other civil society organizations are posed as different to the state authorities.

An interview with a representative of the Danish Institute for Human Rights also active in exchange programmes similar to the Karama programme sheds further light on their logic. She noted the value of bringing representatives of different institutions – judiciary, police, prisons, civil society – together 'out of context' as it were. Bringing them to Denmark 'gives them a chance to talk among themselves *outside their normal context*'. Here she points to a positive value for decontextualization. She was adamant that exchange visits are no longer about the transfer and imposition of a particular model, if they ever were. It is not about making *them* like *us*.

She utilized the metaphor of the mirror. Exchanges are an opportunity to facilitate reflection. The juxtaposition of different practices, exposure to alternative ways of arranging a police station, conducting prison visits, doing criminal justice allows delegates to recognize that one *can do things differently* – 'If you should change something, then you first have to have the hope that things can be different'. From this perspective exchanges are about combating prejudice, challenging assumptions and facilitating local inter-institutional reflections.

The Karama Programme clearly has practical value, especially when seen not as a set of isolated activities but more as a dynamic long-term relationship of exchange and learning within a framework of mutuality and not merely as being about values and norms but also about techniques and practices. This is not to say that we should hesitate in applying a critical lens[9] to the activities. The analysis here is confined to the views of the implementing agents and neglects those of the partner agencies, recipients and potential beneficiaries. I hope that I have shown that comparison plays an important animating role – be it explicitly or implicitly. It remains necessary to be alert to any tendencies to base interventions on dubious premises, for example, erroneous, reductionistic models of human being, naïve theories of change or theories of knowledge which posit knowledge as a mono-dimensional, packagable, standardized commodity to be simplistically delivered and implemented. The accusations made towards the early anthropological approaches to comparison could all too easily be relevant to ill-founded interventions. Interventionists should therefore be wary of reproducing a distinct order of separately existing cultures and recognize that in these globalized times the world is common and relationships entangled and interdependent. Intervening agencies, be they facilitators or service providers, should strain to be cognizant of the unequal distributions of power at work in interventions. And we (for I too am a 'kind of practitioner') should be careful not to underplay difference or dismiss it as superficial or renounce it as belonging to the realm of the unreasonable, or justify our difference and our endeavours to convert their difference along the dubious dimensions of superiority–inferiority or expertise–deviance (see Jefferson 2008).

I want to turn now to the second theme of this chapter, to propose an orientation to comparison which includes processes and relations as key dimensions, that is the kind of processes I have highlighted as significant above.

Revisiting comparison

The notion of exceptionalism – the theme of our volume – is itself a comparative notion. A state of affairs is only exceptional in relation to another state of affairs. Pratt's readings of Scandinavian penal policy as in some way exceptional – in terms of prison conditions and the relatively few persons incarcerated – is a reading that only makes sense against a backdrop understanding of prisons elsewhere as featuring harsh conditions which 'degrade and debase all within'[10] (2008a: 119) and high numbers of people incarcerated. An external norm or a neutral measure seems necessary to make a comparison (though neutrality here is often a myth in practice). In Part I of his paper Pratt engages in a within-region comparison based on similarities ('points of intersection and commonality' 2008a: 120) and a between-regions comparison based on postulated differences. Part II traces how countries in Scandinavia (Sweden, Norway and Finland) are becoming less like their immediate neighbours ('emerging differences') and more aligned with the rest of the western world (2008b: 277). Apart from the methodological weaknesses of Pratt's study – he seems to accept the word of the authorities a little too easily, reproducing official discourse on the prison without sufficient attention to potentially subaltern voices reflecting prisoner experiences[11] – his project would have benefited from a much more explicit reflection on the empty box up against which his claims of exceptionalism lean, a more 'contextualised contrast' (Bowen, in Bowen and Petersen 1999: 239). In Pratt's papers the norm against which the exception is posited is an understated Anglo-American form of penal policy and practice with the occasional glance toward New Zealand.[12]

The empty box is invoked through numerous rhetorical moves through which the reader is invited to identify with its non-disclosed content.[13] A common understanding of the box and its contents is assumed: 'Officers wear uniforms, *but* these have no military trappings or insignia' (121, my italics) for example invites the reader to identify with an idea that military trappings are equivalent to brutality and cruelty and that a lack of them indicates progress and humaneness. Is this true? The *but* indicates the extent to which empirical observations are here being used as tools in service of a *normative* comparative argument rather than as raw data in themselves. It is an interesting fact that insignia are not used but we are given no help in interpreting what that means in practice.[14] The earlier reference to the importance of military style insignia for forging alliances in exchange programmes suggests a variety of possible meanings attributed to uniforms.[15] Pratt's overall argument is that Scandinavian prisons are exceptional because the Scandinavian countries are exceptional, that is it is their socio-historical circumstances which make the difference. What are the implications of this thesis for exchange programmes such as the one discussed in the first part of this chapter? Does Nordic exceptionalism – presuming for the moment it is a valid thesis – create a good or bad case for export? He addresses the issue directly:

Scandinavian exceptionalism

> is a reminder to us that the penal excesses of other modern societies are not universal or hegemonic. Because of these *particular* social arrangements Scandinavian exceptionalism could never really be exported as a penal model beyond these boundaries, however wistfully reformers elsewhere might have looked to it.
>
> (2008b: 289)

Clearly the Middle East has had its own socio-historical trajectory which is not the same as the Scandinavian. Nevertheless Pratt does present some grounds for optimism about the possibilities of exchange and exposure across national boundaries:

even if it cannot be replicated outside this region, it still tells us that there are other choices available to us in how to respond to crime and manage prisons.
(2008b: 290)

This argument echoes that of my informants involved in export and exchange programmes. The positive value of revealing difference is not necessarily in demonstrating that another way is a better way, but in demonstrating that different ways under different circumstances are possible.

In the introduction to this chapter I raised the issue of the relationship between comparison and studying phenomena in and for themselves. Herzfeld and Barth separately suggest that comparison is one way through which to allow phenomena to speak for themselves. Herzfeld (2001: 266) notes that cultural translation should be viewed as an 'ongoing procedure leading us to a recognition of irreducible uniqueness that we can *initially only grasp* through what instead appear to be familiar or comparable features' (my italics). (This partially redeems my own clumsy attempts to respond to the Jordanian prison authorities when asked how I saw their prisons and relates directly to the question I raised in my introduction: Can we *see* beyond the limits of our own experiences?) Barth (in Bowen and Petersen 1999: 89) suggests that by bringing cases into dialogue with one another (in opposition to making static comparisons of separate cases) and by paying special attention to 'dimensions of variation' we might actually come 'closer to the empirical object(s)' (80) in and for itself.

I agree with Melhuus (2002: 80) when she claims both that 'we need more conscious reflection about comparison in order to access the potential of theory building' and that 'questions have to be posed concerning not only translation but also what properties, categories, institutions, practices etc. may be legitimately compared'. In our penological comparative endeavours we do not have to live up to the idealized standards of positivist science. We do not have to contribute to universalist, reductive theories or grand meta-narratives but this is not to say we cannot contribute to new knowledge and new ways of theorizing. Interpretive field-based studies with their deliberate self-conscious focus on *how* we come to know what we know shift emphasis from results to methods, from findings to processes of discovery. This explicit attention to these processes is part of the rhetorical power of ethnography. It is partially through self-conscious reflexivity that accounts attain legitimacy in the eyes of the reader. It is this same kind of reflection I am advocating in relation to acts of comparison. Not only for scholars but also for practitioners engaged in exchange and reform programmes.

Pratt's analysis raises the further issue of along what dimensions one might compare. How does one define the unit of comparison? (See Kuper 2002: 146.) Ultimately Pratt's papers might be read as advocacy (for more progressive penal policies), although the majority of the two papers are not about prison, but about historical and societal structures, and patterns and values, doing what much comparative penology does and looking at prisons in terms of socio-historical variables. Prison conditions and number of people incarcerated are relatively static dimensions of comparison.[16] Is it legitimate to reduce the social practice and hostile, conflictual realities of penal establishments to such arid categories? When Pratt writes that 'prisoners are still prisoners' and begins a sentence 'prisons being prisons' (123) he appeals to some kind of universal taken-for-granted understanding which a comparative project should surely attempt to counter. He implies a given static meaning for 'prison' and 'prisoner' but this is only so within a homogenizing discourse which reduces incidences of otherness to the same. Comparative discourse ought to lend itself more to the specification of difference, the identification of similarities and the definition of criteria. In addition, incidences of exceptionalism should be sought for within apparently dominant paradigms and not only posited as external to them as Mary Bosworth (2010) and others have recently pointed out. Penal populism is not quite as hegemonic as contemporary scholarship might lead us to believe, though this is no reason not to critique its pretensions.

Fox and Gingrich (2002: 19) suggest that units of comparison need not be considered as 'discrete, homogenous and stable entities' pointing rather to the necessity of 'understanding them as the differentiated, changing result of wider developments within their fuzzy boundaries'. Might we then be able to identify other (process-oriented or relational) dimensions of comparison worthy of exploration especially in the light of Melhuus's observation that:

> Because similarities or differences are not given in the things themselves but in the way they are contextualized, i.e. in the relations of which they form a part, we must compare frameworks, processes of meaning construction, structures of discourse.
>
> (2002: 82)

Indeed '"theorizing contexts" is indispensable for any explicit comparison' (Gingrich and Fox 2002: 21). Herzfeld (2001: 268) notes similarly that the comparative project 'is not about fixed entities, but about the contexts in which they acquire their significance'. This indicates quite starkly the need to attend to process. As he goes on to write 'the goal is to decipher, not an underlying code or structure, but the unstable play of power in social and cultural relations' (270).

These perspectives on comparison offer useful foils to Pratt's less reflexive comparative analysis. However, it must be said that by posing Scandinavian penal policy in an exceptional relation to that of Europe and America Pratt has succeeded in stimulating a potent debate about the significance of comparison, the importance of theorizing context and the relationship between sameness and difference. Even a not wholly accurate image of Scandinavian prisons raises important questions about the power to punish and forms of punishment and the societal conditions which give rise to particular versions of these.

Concluding thoughts on knowledge[17]

Earlier in this chapter I raised the question of whether the choice to export penal, judicial and rights-oriented norms and values via exchange programmes is evidence of Nordic exceptionalism, better knowledge or just knowing better. Through my interactions with professionals and my analysis of discussions with them I have come to see this question as somewhat misguided and it has given me cause to think differently about my own former critical analyses of interventionist practices.

How much must we know? I have repeatedly argued that only by getting to grips with the peculiarities and particularities of different prison institutions can we get to grips with how best to engage in transforming them. At the same time as I have advocated for greater attention to perspectives from within I have emphasized the need for understanding, suggesting that only when we truly understand will we have a chance at implementing anything other than 'imaginary reform'. The Prosecutor casts a different light on this issue implying that a perspective from within almost does away with the need for a perspective from without. *They* know, that is the targets of the programme. So *we* don't necessarily need to. She actually suspends any desire for knowledge and grants that they in and of themselves have the context well understood. They know it as 'habitus'. They own it and are possessed by it. The ignorance of the intervening agency is therefore less significant. We might say that by getting to grips with the peculiarities and particularities of different prison institutions we satiate our own desire to understand in terms of *our* rationality. Perhaps the suspension of that rationality, including our desire to document, measure and evaluate could open up a space for dialogue and transformation which remains closed by constant interrogations designed to elicit the truth, and reduce our ignorance, about a way of organizing which is alien to us. It is hoped that this is not to make redundant the kind of scientific analysis of processes and practices and relationships I am attempting here. But it is to be iconoclastic about knowledge as a dominant rationality. It is to shift attention from knowledge to practice, and to knowledge *as* practice, as one practice among many and to the situatedness of knowledge. In addition it is a reminder to pursue the allusive task of understanding practices *in their own terms*.

Knowledge is certainly not the primary animating factor for practitioners. Facts and interpretations of them, or meaning, is secondary to ideas, norms and values but also and to a greater degree to techniques and procedures. Values, ideas and norms are embedded in institutional practice rather than in facts and understandings. The professionals I interviewed and engaged with during phase I of the Karama programme did not think primarily in terms of knowledge, but utilized a much more practical action-oriented register. For professionals engaged in justice sector reform within the Karama programme the issue is simply not whether they know better or have better knowledge but whether they can share their expertise and experience to create an alternative set of professional practices.

In Nilsson's words the export process should be understood as a 'reflexive process, where self-images meet the gaze of others in a mutually reinforcing way' (p. 93, see the mirror metaphor evoked earlier).[18] Going in a slightly different direction, Weiss and South (1998) conclude their comparative study on penal systems with two alternative strategies for pursuing change: (a) human rights diplomacy; and (b) macroeconomic policy. The activities of the Karama programme would seem to fall somewhere else. Through high-level seminars and training activities a dialectical process is enacted where sameness and difference, proximity and distance are constantly brought into play as ideas are shared, activities discussed and local political significance negotiated. Change is sought through institutional encounters and 'entangled' relationships.

This chapter represents an attempt to see intervention practice 'on its own terms' in the same way in which I have advocated elsewhere that local (post-colonial) prison practices should be seen in their own terms (Jefferson 2007a, b, 2008). To effectively orient ourselves to entangled practices of penality, penal policy and penal reform the next step would be to pay attention to multiple stakeholders *as they come together* in 'entangled institutional complexes' (Jefferson 2010) recognizing unique trajectories of development, and diverse, competing and complementary standpoints. The work that comparisons do within such configurations would also be a fruitful subject of analysis.

Notes

1 Acknowledgement: I am grateful to my RCT colleagues working on the Karama programme for facilitating my access to and involvement in the programme. Similarly, I thank the Jordanian partners and most significantly the representatives of the Danish Police, Prosecution and Prison and Probation Service who have shared their thoughts with me. Thanks also to Morten Nissen and Ernst Schraube for valuable sparring.
2 Throughout the 1960s and 1970s potent voices sold an image of the Swedish system as progressive, humane, modern and effective (see Nilsson, Chapter 5 in this book) propagating a myth of advanced penality and moderate penal values, a myth belied by the voices of prisoners and progressive political voices echoing their protests but warmly received in America. Further, Nilsson mentions how one of the Swedish 'salesmen' was active within United Nations' bodies and within the European Council. Such bodies remain important sources of discourse about penological values – e.g. the standard minimum rules, the Optional Protocol to the Convention Against Torture – and are examples of sites where mainstreaming of penal values, norms and standards takes place. My examples are more local.
3 My own involvement included participation in planning meetings and various activities during exchange visits and missions. I also facilitated a session of prison officer training in Jordan. I toured Danish prisons with a Jordanian delegation and participated in their meetings with the Danish prisons service. I also conducted a focus group interview with my own colleagues about the history and the background for the programme. Subsequently I have been even more active in an advisory capacity in the development of phase II of the programme.
4 While it may be stylistically clumsy I have chosen not to use the names of the three representatives or to give them pseudonyms.
5 See Nilsson (Chapter 5, in this book) who is sensitive to 'a tendency to self-righteousness' in the Swedish penal system of the 1960s and 1970s: 'Sweden's growing reputation for being the welfare state *par excellence* was accompanied by a certain proselytizing spirit. The Swedes were – for good reasons – proud of how their society had developed'. It was this pride that produced the desire to export the Swedish model.
6 Thanks to Morten Nissen for pointing out the interesting way in which a single unique incident here comes to stand in for 'the world'.
7 Exchange visits might be seen as a form of incentive for Jordanian staff more than they are a form of strategic planning and institutional transformation, probably a good

incentive since it brings both foreign travel and escape from everyday realities. As one prisons director put it during the workshop at RCT 'if I open the prison gate, staff will escape before prisoners'.

8   At the Danish open prison the 'tour' was conducted by the head of education and at the state prison by the governor. This meant that operational details were only treated superficially. The governor's hesitation to get into discussions with delegation members demonstrated not merely his impatience to get the visit over with (he had another appointment) but also a relative lack of knowledge of operational details on the ground (he is a manager not a warder). To some extent they were exposed to the wrong people.
9   'Comparison is fundamental to the critical moment' (Strathern, in Gingrich and Fox 2002: xvi)
10 Is this exaggeration or rhetoric from Pratt? It is certainly not documented in his papers.
11 Pratt relates to the pains of imprisonment only in the abstract because he relies on official discourse; they are not demonstrated empirically either with reference to the 'non-exceptional' context of Anglo-American or the 'exceptional' Scandinavia. The contrast between stated intentions and experienced reality is an important dimension that seems to be gaining increased attention in prison studies.
12 That the point of comparison is the Anglo-American is revealed by the author's remark 'what strikes any visitor familiar with Anglo-American prisons is the personal space and relative material comfort of most prisoners' (2008a: 121).
13 For example, two references are made to a notion of shame associated with imprisonment outside Scandinavia. In one instance Pratt notes that prison officers 'need not feel shame' and in another it is noted that prisons in Norway are not too shameful that they should be shunned by representatives of the royal family. What, I wonder, is the source of the 'shame criteria' which is invoked to create an image of contrast? (2008a: 121).
14 The South African correctional services demilitarized their uniforms as a symbolic gesture in the post-apartheid regime, but did this make their prisons more humane?
15 In another attempt to demonstrate the exceptionalism of the Scandinavian context, Pratt quotes the Finnish Sentences Enforcement Act 2002: 'The enforcement of the sentence must be organized so that the sentence is *only* loss of liberty. Other restrictions can be used to the extent that the security of custody and the prison order require' (2008a: 120). The analysis over-emphasizes the perceived exceptionalism but does not note that the latter sentence in the quote has the potential to severely curtail the former as it does in so many jurisdictions where concerns of security and order are invoked to limit stated good intentions.
16 Although Pratt's comparative histories of welfare systems are much more dynamic.
17 These thoughts remain somewhat fragmentary, pointing in possible directions and inviting to further – it is hoped, collaborative – work unpacking them.
18 The substance of encounters and relationships is, of course, always transformed somewhat by its mediation. In Nilsson's Swedish case the image promoted abroad was lapped up in the USA. In Jordan the Karama programme receives a mixed reaction, intervening as it does in a somewhat incendiary political and institutional context where local, national and not least regional and international stakes are relatively high.

References

Barth, F. (1999) 'Comparative Methodologies in the Analysis of Anthropological Data', in R. Petersen and J. Bowen (eds), *Critical Comparisons in Politics and Culture*. Cambridge: Cambridge University Press, pp. 78–89.

Bosworth, M. (2010) 'Introduction: Reinventing Penal Parsimony', *Theoretical Criminology*, 14: 251–6.

Bowen, J. (1999) 'The Role of Microhistories in Comparative Studies', in R. Petersen and J. Bowen (eds), *Critical Comparisons in Politics and Culture*. Cambridge: Cambridge University Press, pp. 230–40.

Bowen, J. and R. Petersen (1999) *Critical Comparisons in Politics and Culture*. Cambridge: Cambridge University Press.

Cavadino, M. and Dignan, J. (2006) *Penal Systems. A Comparative Approach*. London: Sage.

Fox, R. G. and A. Gingrich (2002) 'Introduction', in Gingrich and R. G. Fox (eds), *Anthropology, by Comparison*. London: Routledge, pp. 1–21.

Gingrich, A. and R. G. Fox (2002) *Anthropology, by Comparison*. London: Routledge.

Herzfeld, M. (2001) 'Performing Comparisons: Ethnography, Globetrotting, and the Spaces of Social Knowledge', *Journal of Anthropological Research*, 57(3): 259–76.

Jefferson, A. M. (2007a) 'The Political Economy of Rights: Exporting Penal Norms to Africa', *Criminal Justice Matters, Politics, Economy and Crime*, 70.

—— (2007b) 'Prison Officer Training and Practice in Nigeria: Contention, Contradiction and Re-imagining Reform Strategies', *Punishment and Society: The International Journal of Penology*, 9(3).

—— (2008) 'Imaginary Reform: Changing the Postcolonial Prison', in Pat Carlen (ed.), *Imaginary Penalities*. Cullompton: Willan.

—— (2010) unpublished research programme application. Confinement Violence and Reform: Interrogating Institutional Agency.

Kuper, A. (2002) 'Comparison and Contextualisation: Reflections on South Africa', in A. Gingrich and R. G. Fox (eds), *Anthropology, by Comparison*. London: Routledge, pp. 143–63.

Liebling, A. and H. Arnold (2004) Prisons and Their Moral Performance: A Study of Values, Quality and Prison Life. Cambridge: Cambridge University Press.

Mbembe, A. (2001) *On the Postcolony*. Berkeley: University of California Press.

Melhuus, M. (2002) 'Issues of Relevance: Anthropology and the Challenges of Cross-cultural Comparison', in A. Gingrich and R. G. Fox (eds), *Anthropology, by Comparison*, London: Routledge, pp. 70–90.

Pratt, J. (2008a) 'Scandinavian Exceptionalism in an Era of Penal Excess. Part I: The Nature and Roots of Scandinavian Exceptionalism', *British Journal of Criminology*, 48(2): 119–37.

—— (2008b) 'Scandinavian Exceptionalism in an Era of Penal Excess. Part II: Does Scandinavian Exceptionalism Have a Future?', *British Journal of Criminology*, 48(3): 275–92.

Strathern, M. (2002) 'Foreword: Not Giving the Game Away', in A. Gingrich and R. G. Fox (eds), *Anthropology, by Comparison*, London: Routledge, pp. xiii–xvii.

Weiss, R. P. and South, N. (1998) *Comparing Prison Systems. Toward a Comparative and International Penology*. Amsterdam: Gordon and Breach Publishers.

Part III
Closing in on the Nordic I
Cultures of equality?

7 The dark side of a culture of equality

Reimagining communities in a Norwegian remand prison[1]

Thomas Ugelvik

> The evils that extreme equality may produce are slowly disclosed; they creep gradually into the social frame; they are seen only at intervals; and at the moment at which they become most violent, habit already causes them to be no longer felt.
>
> Alexis de Tocqueville

> Like Tocqueville pondering the future of America, a modern observer of the North surely will ask what values are being sacrificed by the passion for equality that governs these countries ... Can these countries, with their romantic notions of equal folk joined together in national communities, really cope with the pressure for pluralism in a modern industrial society, with its social conflicts and its free flow of communications?
>
> Hans Fredrik Dahl

According to John Pratt (2008a, b), one of the main causes of Scandinavian exceptionalism is a culture of equality typical of the Nordic countries and, related to this culture, homogeneous Nordic societies which historically have had few 'visible others'. With reference to Norway, the description seems correct; equality, or rather *likhet*, as a cultural value has been held in high esteem. Even today, after the advent of globalization has made the population more heterogeneous, the culture of *likhet* is still very much part of the Norwegian way of life. There is, however, a price to be paid. Equality as a general value may be commendable, but it also has a darker side: the related pressure to conform, to be like *vanlige folk* (regular people), 'one of us' and always on 'our' terms (Lacey 2008; Pratt and Eriksson, Chapter 13, this book). For those unwilling or unable to conform, this has consequences. In a context with a strong culture of *likhet*, the playing field is limited, the distance from centre to margins shortened. And margins and borders are, as always, key: any inside needs to be constituted in relation to its outsides (Norton 1988; Connolly 1991; Derrida 2006). Studying strategies of adaptation and resistance to exclusion or 'othering' (Jensen 2007) may thus give insights both into the constructions of the resulting Norwegian self, the placement of its margins, and the costs of pushing 'the others' to and beyond the margins in just such a way.

Likhet is put to work as an important part of the dual process where Norwegians collectively imagine themselves into being as Norwegians and Norway is recreated as an imagined community. Benedict Anderson's (1996) famous point is however only a place to start. The relevant follow-up questions are what the nation is made to be in a specific context, how it is put to use, and to what effect.

Liminal prisoners and the Norwegian culture of *likhet*

This chapter will consider the culture of *likhet*, a linchpin in Pratt's theory, from the point of view of some of the people who are seen as the opposite – as *ulike* – in Norwegian society. I will describe prisoners' strategies for adapting to and resisting the way they experience, *qua* prisoners, being positioned on or beyond the margins of the general society of equal Norwegians on the other side of the walls.[2]

In 2009, 28 per cent of prisoners serving time in Norwegian prisons were non-citizens (*Kriminalomsorgens årsstatistikk 2009*). Oslo Prison is Norway's largest, with a capacity of 392 prisoners, it is at any time housing over one-tenth of the total national prison population. Being in Oslo, it reflects the multiethnic society outside its walls. On a random day in December 2007, Oslo prison held prisoners from 54 different countries.

On the remand wings where I conducted most of my fieldwork, the national and ethnic diversity was even greater, since a foreign family connection increases the likelihood of a person being seen by the court as an escape risk.[3] This is one of the principal arguments for the use of pre-trial imprisonment in Norway. The less 'Western' this family connection is, the more likely it seems to be that you are held on remand. The number in Oslo Prison is even higher. Furthermore, a large but unknown number of those counted as Norwegian citizens (unknown, since official statistics do not register ethnicity) have a 'minority background'. Some of them, children of the first wave of immigration from Pakistan in the 1970s, have been citizens since birth. Others came as refugees in the 1990s after the break-up of Yugoslavia, and have been Norwegian citizens for years. Others still have come from Mediterranean Africa more recently and speak Norwegian with an accent. If they are not (yet) citizens, they have girlfriends and children who are. Some, from Rumania or sub-Sahara Africa do not speak Norwegian, but communicate well enough in English. The last group, from Russia or the Baltic states, have never really lived in Norway and only understand very basic English.

Take Fariz.[4] He was born in Norway and has lived here all his life. His parents came from Pakistan during the first major influx of non-Western immigrants to the country in the 1970s. The following excerpt is from him explaining his current situation to me:

> Well, I was running, a fugitive, before I turned myself in. That's why the police are so afraid that I might run again. I could've just gone underground, they would never have found me if I hadn't turned myself in. But I'm born and raised in Norway, I could never live in Pakistan, where I'm really from. I mean, hello, I don't even speak the language. What are they thinking?

Born and raised in Norway, the strictly Norwegian-speaking Fariz still feels that he's *really* from Pakistan, even though he would not manage to live there. One could say that he is in between statuses, put in what we might call, following Anne Norton (1988), a liminal position. He speaks the Norwegian language and is born and raised here, but he's *really* Pakistani. But he couldn't live in Pakistan; he is way too Norwegian for that.

Erol is another example. He came to Norway as a refugee from Kosovo in the early 1990s. He is a Norwegian citizen and has been for years, and is very well aware of the rights this status give him vis-à-vis the Norwegian state. He actively uses the various complaint and appeal channels that are open to him. At the same time, however, he wants to create a home environment for his children which would work as a sort of Albanian embassy in Norway, understood as a place where Albanian culture and customs trump the Norwegian alternative:

TU: You're describing a way to raise your kids that seems quite foreign from a Norwegian perspective, not many people would share your thoughts on this. It's something you have brought from Kosovo.
EROL: In my house, my rules apply. Those are Kosovo rules. As soon as I put my feet outside the door, I follow Norwegian rules.
TU: But inside the house?
EROL: Inside the house, my rules, no one can change that, no Norwegian system, no Norwegian culture, nothing. Between my four walls, well that's Albania.
TU: So the Norwegian culture won't change how you raise your kids?
EROL: Absolutely not. They will be raised like they would be in Kosovo. They won't get the opportunity, I mean, they will get the opportunity to learn to know the soft Norwegian society, but they will always have the strong feelings, well, wanting to take care of their parents, not like Norwegian people.

If Fariz is really Pakistani and Erol really Kosovar, what makes somebody Norwegian? Traditionally, this has been a fairly easy question to answer. If you own a Norwegian passport, you speak the Norwegian language and you feel part of a community of Norwegians, you are Norwegian. At least since the dissolution of the union between Norway and Sweden in 1905, Norway has been one of those rare so-called 'ethnic states' (Øverland 2003), where the twin levels of nation and state have a very large degree of overlap. In such countries, patriotism, understood as feelings of loyalty to the state, is difficult to separate from nationalism, understood as feelings of loyalty to the nation. When I say 'I am Norwegian', what am I saying? Am I referring to a relationship with the Norwegian state, or with a national and ethnic community of Norwegians? The answer is that I might be referring to any or all of the above, depending on the context. For me, this presents no problem; my feelings of nationalism and patriotism are in perfect harmony. Erol's relationship with Norway, however, is based on dissonance. He has a relationship with a *state* that gives him rights and also obligations. Norway as a *nation* of Norwegians is out there, beyond his threshold, and will not get past his front door.

Fariz and Erol both speak Norwegian fluently and they both own Norwegian passports. But they are not *really* Norwegian. Rather, they are what Georg Simmel has referred to as a 'strangers':

> The stranger will . . . not be considered here in the usual sense of the term, as the wanderer who comes today and goes tomorrow, but rather as the man who comes today and stays tomorrow – the potential wanderer, so to speak, who, although he has gone no further, has not quite got over the freedom of coming and going. He is fixed within a certain spatial circle . . . but his position within it is fundamentally affected by the fact that he does not belong in it initially and that he brings qualities into it that are not, and cannot be, indigenous to it.
> (1971: 143)

A stranger changes the place he moves into. He unites closeness and remoteness; he acts as one of us and not one of us simultaneously, blurring the difference. The traditional high degree of overlap between nationalism and patriotism is thus being put to the test through the figure of the stranger. Viewed like this, strangers represent challenges to the nation, challenges that must be met.

As in all modern societies, the collective imagining of community is an all-important part of the social glue binding Norwegians together as people of the same kind (Anderson 1996; Gullestad 2001). The continuous process of reimagining Norway as imagined community articulates a range of different elements. Take the national anthem:[5]

> Ja vi elsker dette landet,
> som det stiger frem,
> furet, værbitt over vannet,
> med de tusen hjem.
> Elsker, elsker det og tenker,
> på vår far og mor,
> og den saganatt som senker,
> drømme på vår jord.

> Yes, we love with fond devotion,
> this our land that looms,
> rugged, storm-scarred o'er the ocean,
> with her thousand homes.
> Love her, in our love recalling
> those who gave us birth,
> and old tales which night, in falling,
> brings as dreams to earth.

First performed publicly at the fiftieth anniversary of the Norwegian constitution in 1864, this first verse of *Ja, vi elsker* establishes a Norwegian 'we' comprising people who come together in their love for the country and its rugged nature. It further connects the 'we' to beloved ancestors and the long Norwegian history. Bearing the country's relatively short history in mind, this might be speculative history writing, but that is beside the point. The connection with nature and our forefathers are first and foremost symbols used in the re-articulation of Norway as imagined community.

Another such symbol frequently articulated is the value of *likhet*. As Marianne Gullestad (2002) has shown, this Norwegian concept is complex and difficult to translate, its meaning sliding between 'equality', 'similarity' and 'sameness'. *Likhet* may mean 'being of the same worth', 'having the same status' and 'looking alike'. The opposite of *likhet* may be such different concepts as *inequality*, *unfairness*, *diversity*, *difference* and *variation*.

A Norwegian culture of *likhet* is a social fact, and as such, it has effects. Essentializing representations of a nation do not become any less real for being imagined. The question is what *likhet* means in a Norwegian context and how this ideal is put to practical use. Certainly, the Norwegian population has never been completely homogeneous. Minorities have existed also in the past; the indigenous Sami population is one example, the Traveller community another. But these have been relatively small and the questionable techniques of assimilation and invisibilization have historically been quite effective. In fact, Norway has a long history of excluding and marginalizing the different. So Norwegians have for a large part looked the same, thought the same and felt the same, or so the story goes. Up until fairly recently, we have had one public broadcaster, one state-sponsored religion, one food tradition. There have been variations, of course, but these have been seen as just that; variations over the more fundamental common theme. In the following, I will adopt William E. Connolly's (1991) distinction between 'differences', describing the sort of variations between units which are in some way fundamentally similar, and more radical 'otherness', which can be used to cancel out differences and make them into similarities.

Nation building is a process of continuous retelling of the story of who fundamentally belongs among the different-but-equal on the inside, and, conversely, who 'the others' are. Such processes are a necessary part of the constitution of any group; feelings of in-group loyalty are based on a continuous objectification and expulsion of out-groups, of those deemed *ulike* ('un-*lik*'). The social use of difference is fundamental to any group. The problem in the Norwegian setting may be that when those on the inside are very similar, it takes very little to be put on the outside. For those deemed outsiders, their *ulikhet* is experienced through the sliding equality–similarity scale, where being *different* often will amount to also being *other*. This has been called the Nordic paradox of equality (Lien *et al.* 2001). It has consequences. On the positive side, Norway is one of the most gender-equal societies in the world. Historically, class differences have been relatively small, even compared to neighbouring Sweden and Denmark. These are both in part effects of the strong standing of the *likhet* ideal; being Norwegian is being of the same worth as other Norwegians. The darker side to this is that diversity and difference have been considered suspect. Norwegian people have felt a strong pressure to fit in, to conform. Because *likhet* is such a central value, demanding prestige and recognition is problematic (Gullestad 1989: 117). The ideal is being *vanlige folk*, meaning regular, ordinary, normal people, like most people. Being *vanlig* might sound somewhat dull, but there is also solidity to it, a 'salt of the earth' kind of quality highly valued in the Norwegian context. Aspiring to be something more or other than *vanlige folk* is in fact considered almost obscene (see: Dahl 1986; Lien *et al*. 2001; Gullestad 2002). The culture of *likhet* has been used in this way to gloss over profound differences between people, making them 'fellow Norwegians' in the process. The unwritten code[6] is this: keep your place. Don't think you are *somebody*. Be in control of yourself. Live as others do, think as others think. Be similar. Embrace equality. Pay your taxes. Belong. The Scandinavian culture of equality described by Pratt (2008a, b) has also been a powerful technique of social control.

Destabilizing *likhet* – a new multicultural reality

I have alluded to a possible discrepancy between the reality of equality and *likhet* as a cultural value. A little over 20 years ago, Stephen R. Graubard could write:

> The Nordic World is very protected, remote in wholly new ways . . . It knows so little of the social tensions and turmoil characteristic of much of the rest of the world. The Nordic countries are not obliged to integrate 'outsiders'; they have no need to create unity between diverse and disparate peoples and races; the larger questions of subordination and dominations are unknown.
>
> (1986: 14)

Today, much has changed. The remoteness may have been exaggerated somewhat by Graubard, but today, no such exaggerations are possible. The last 20 to 30 years have seen the Nordic countries becoming natural laboratories for students of rapid population change. The population of the capital is the most pronounced Norwegian case, and as such illustrative. Today, more than one in four people living in Oslo is an immigrant or a child of immigrants. Oslo has always been a city with an east–west divide, symbolically marked by the Akerselva river which crosses the city north to south. Today the river divides the population along ethnic as well as class lines. The population on the eastern side is more ethnically diverse, have a shorter life expectancy and report lower income, are more often unemployed, on welfare, have more serious health problems, and so on. Pratt observes that:

> The homogeneity of Scandinavian countries had played an important part in reaffirming egalitarian values, tolerance and trust; people who are similar to each other are more likely to be content with inclusionary rather than exclusionary punishments for lawbreakers, who are less likely to be understood as alien others. This . . . seems to be eroding to some degree.
>
> (2008b: 282)

The fact that 'homogeneous' no longer offers the best description is clearly visible when you walk around the city, as it is if you follow Norwegian public debate. What happens when an egalitarian society is replaced by a multicultural one? The category *innvandrer*, literally 's/he who wanders in', has a problematic permanence to it. Several theorists have remarked that the borders between countries no longer are physical spaces (Hudson 2006; Aas 2007). The border is everywhere; it can also be found wherever people are positioned as not quite insiders. The visibly different carry the border with them, the colour of their skin given precedence over the colour of their passport. Permanently on the border wherever they are, the *innvandrer* is given a painful 'not quite'-status, an indefinite stay in identity limbo vis-à-vis the 'real' Norwegians. You may be Norwegian, but you are still *innvandrer*, always different, and always being understood first and foremost on the basis of this difference (Alghasi 2006). The experience is captured by one of Gullestad's informants: 'I feel Norwegian, but I don't look the part' (2001, my translation).

Pratt's 'alien others' from the quote above have arrived. The political climate has become, as he observes, and is increasingly becoming, more 'tough on crime'; Pratt may even be understating it. He attributes this mostly to the rise of the right-wing Progress Party. However, even members of the current Labour Party dominated coalition administration campaigned on tough on crime policies; this has become the mainstream. Anderson (1996) sees the news media as an important part of the creation of a national community. If this is true, and I believe it is, I would say that the Norwegian nation today is, like many others, joined together in the belief that we live in a society where everything is worse than it used to be, that Oslo is a dangerous place, that evil predators might hide anywhere, and that these for a large part will be people who are categorized in Norwegian public debate as 'criminal immigrants'. The combination of youth, masculinity, immigrant status and crime virtually guarantees first-page headlines (Eide and Simonsen 2007).

People are no longer the same within the Norwegian borders. They do not look the same. They definitely do not act the same – tabloid headlines attest to that much. The proportion of people who want to make it more difficult for refugees and asylum seekers to obtain a residence permit is increasing rapidly (Blom 2009). In short, the xenophobic wave described by Loïc Wacquant (2002) seems to have reached the Nordic shores, creating a strong yet often implicit connection between immigration and crime. The exclusion of this favourite 'suitable enemy' (Christie and Bruun 1996) contributes in the construction of the equal–similar rest of the population as morally superior. The visibly different are, conversely, perceived as also culturally different, and, for many, this translates to morally different, or rather inferior; difference becomes otherness.

That category does two things. First, it puts together as a group of 'non-Norwegians' people with vastly different backgrounds and experiences from everywhere but Norway. Second, it places those thus positioned firmly outside 'our' Norwegian moral community. The *kriminell innvandrer* is the preferred 'ethnic folk devil' (Jensen 2007); such a status threatens to change the recipient from 'aliens' into 'monsters' in Barbara Hudson's (2006) terminology. In other words, it pushes the person from difference into otherness. No longer simply carrying the border, the *kriminell innvandrer* is a living, breathing example of the new, more dangerous Norwegian society, with all its new flaws.

Ulike prisoners of the welfare state

From being a marginal issue, the influx of the *innvandrere* has created a new political and administrative object. A large state apparatus has been charged with greeting, evaluating, classifying and ultimately either integrating or deporting the stream of potential strangers at the border. Integration is the name of a process, and also the desired end result.

In contemporary Norway, the subject is positioned vis-à-vis a social-democratic welfare state with a distinctly liberal flavour. The liberal subject is one who must be made accustomed to ruling himself – he is organically tied together with a specifically modern family of administrative and control technologies often called, with a term coined by Michel Foucault (2007), *governmentality*. The liberal subject is free to control himself and administer his own freedom. What Foucault (2000) called *pastoral power* is important in such systems. For the shepherd, the main goal is to give each member of the flock the best possible conditions to maximize the potential of the flock *in toto*, a direct analogue to the welfare state ideal of administrative care for each and everyone (or rather *omnes et singulatim*, see Foucault 2000) from cradle to grave. The demands of the individual to freely govern him- or herself according to the best of the flock (as seen from the perspective of the welfare state ideologues) is fundamental in such a system (Neumann 2003).

In this context, crime is understood as related to all kinds of problems on the individual level, problems that may or may not give individuals rights as state subjects. The individual criminal constitutes a direct challenge for the welfare state. In old pictures and dusty statuettes you may find the uncommon image of Lady Justice – *Justitia* – without her usual blindfold and with one breast bared. This is what the Norwegian *Justitia* should look like; assessing everyone according to need, working to find a balance (in practice always uneasy and deeply paradoxical) between that sharp blade in her hand and the nourishing milk from her bosom. This is the rational (no blindfold), humanitarian (bare-breasted) *Justitia* of the Nordic welfare states (cf. Zetterberg 1986).

When the liminal population is involved, crime is more than an individual flaw; it is also a sign of failed integration. Positioned as subject of the welfare state, always as a responsibility of some state agency or other, the poorly integrated *innvandrer* is as well-known cultural figure on the political scene, and as such has been the objective of a large number of state initiatives, programmes, and White Papers. And when integration fails, when the *innvandrere* turns out to be *kriminelle innvandrere*, that old liberal dilemma is given a new spin: how to control those who have shown that they are not among the 'us' who can control ourselves, and, given their liminal status to begin with, are thereby pushed firmly into otherness?

In recent history, the Norwegian state has tried several strategies. It has sterilized members of minority communities and outlawed the use of their native language. It put alcoholics and vagrants in institutions for years, not for committing crimes, but for their own benefit. These practices have, within the last 50 or 60 years or so, been thought of as part of the overall goal of creating a healthy, productive and happy flock. Norway may be a low imprisonment society (Pratt 2008a), but that it is a low control society is up for discussion. It may be this extreme possibility for explaining away atrocities as beneficial for one and all that prompts Foucault to state that societies with a highly developed pastoral apparatus has a demonic side (Foucault 2000; cf. Neumann 2006). In a culture of *likhet,* many things are possible when the minority of *ulike* are to be made to conform for the benefit of everyone.

Such a system is dependent on a very high degree of trust in the state. This is government at a distance (Rose 2000); the benevolent welfare shepherd quietly carries a briefcase and is trusted and relatively well liked by people he has never met. Norwegians take for granted that the authorities, wherever and whoever they are, are concerned with the good of all. As a Norwegian, you expect things to work (Alghasi 2006). The righteous anger stemming from the many examples of failure just proves the point: if you had lesser expectations, you would not be disappointed. The social-democratic credo *l'état, c'est nous* has been central for Norwegians' self-image; in fact, in the Scandinavian languages, the difference between 'society' and 'state' is often blurred (Enquist 1986). Norwegians are all children of the welfare state, part of the flock. And the bottom line is that most of us like it, even though we might be critical of the day to day (the growth of the Norwegian Progress Party might be seen as an anti-state control movement with an opposing ideal of the night watchman). Even with this in mind, there is a widespread absence of scepticism towards regulation, administration and control.

For prisoners, however, the welfare state shepherds are part of everyday life; they carry cell keys on sturdy chains, not briefcases. And, perhaps even more importantly, they represent a system that does not come across as particularly benign from their point of view. Being imprisoned as a *kriminell innvandrer* by the welfare state is being seen as a particular kind of problem, a failure of integration, a part of risk population of radical others. You are not like us. For the good of us all, the rational, humanitarian 'we' must protect ourselves from the likes of you.

Reacting to the ascription of otherness

Being made an *other* in this way (rather than merely different) may be seen as one of the central 'pains of imprisonment' (Sykes 1958). Moreover, for prisoners, it feels like something they must resist (Ugelvik 2010). Sometimes, making the ascribed otherness into a joke can do it. Like when Tarik proudly parades around the prison wing in his Moroccan national football uniform:

> He is grinning, like always. The uniform is green with red details. The coat of arms on the chest has two lions topped by a crown. I ask him what it means.

TARIK: The green, maybe because we are great at getting things to grow, tomatoes and things like that, what's the English word ... agriculture. Agriculture. We're just peasants, heh heh.

A fellow Moroccan gets involved, and they agree that the green colour must rather refer to the great Moroccan hashish:

TARIK: We are great peasants, yes, the best hashish, and the red colour is blood. Violence. Heh heh, hashish and violence, that's us from Morocco, yep, heh heh heh.

Playing with the prejudice and exaggerating it, Tarik tries to show its feeble foundation. Embracing the otherness and giving it new value is a well-known strategy for reinventing yourself and coming out on top. In general, exploring ways of challenging the undesirable status of *kriminell innvandrer* is a major project for liminal prisoners. I will describe some of the most common strategies at work.

The failed state

The prisoners describe a feeling of being positioned as the morally deficient enemies of a seemingly benign welfare state whose good intentions mask the reality they experience. In such a context, it is no surprise that the prisoners are preoccupied with showing that the state and its avatars are not perfect.

An expression of the Norwegian pride in the well-functioning state can be seen every year when the UN publishes its Human Development Index. Every year, this event gets a lot of press in Norway. The reason, of course, is that Norway since 2003 has ranked number one, spawning tabloid headlines such as 'Norway still best'[7] and non-ironic blog entries such as 'Congratulations! You're Norwegian'.[8] To put it mildly, the prisoners do not agree:

TARIK: I heard on TV that Norway is the best country to live in? I had to laugh! Morocco, where I'm from, is not the best, but much better than Norway! In Morocco, they can't just throw you in prison for 17 months without bringing your case before the courts. They may beat you up, but they can't just imprison you at will. And the weather is nice, also, not like here [Norwegian summer outside], just look outside, heh heh.
[...]
Norway is good, but the best country of all? Norway is rich. But Norway is poor, also. What about the old people? ... They all move to Spain. Why? Is Norway the best country to live in then? ... Everyone just say yes, yes, yes here. Expensive petrol? Yes. More taxes? Yes. There's no money left for regular people, like you and me. Still, no one will tell them no. In England, for instance, they would have said no. They tried to raise the tax on sugar there by one per cent, and riots almost broke out. But here, it's always yes, yes, yes. Sometimes you have to say no.

Tarik is critical of the high degree of trust in and tolerance for the power of the central state. The prisoners do not trust the Norwegian state; many remand prisoners in fact see their individual cases as examples of the state cheating and breaking the rules to get the not-quite Norwegian prisoners. Youssuf is an example:

> I'm ashamed to have the Norwegian passport, I'm going to change back. As fast as possible. What's happening, it is a very dangerous development. Very dangerous, Thomas. I have been proud to be Norwegian. When I've been travelling, in the US, one time, for instance, I have talked about my country, showed pictures of my wife and kids. And they have said to me, Youssuf, you're so lucky, living in Norway, with the best social system in the world, great nature, nice people, beautiful wife, wonderful kids. I've felt proud being Norwegian. But now, I just feel shame for the red passport. All foreigners talk about it now, how Norway treats people, foreigner they don't want, how they put people on remand for too long. The police only run after foreigners these days. Norway is not a good country any more.

The Norwegian citizen Youssuf slides between different levels of commitment to Norway and a community of Norwegians he may or may not be a part of. This is common among the liminal prisoners; they have a relationship with Norway and everything Norwegian which is unstable and ridden with conflicts. Furthermore, Youssuf sees his own situation as an example of how a state he used to trust, like any good Norwegian, is not trustworthy. In other conversations, he places himself firmly like a citizen of the Norwegian state. He is clearly aware of the rights this status offers him – sending letters of complaint to the state ombudsman, for instance. He is not disappointed when such actions get him nowhere, not really. He has gone through the welfare state looking glass, and knows the truth about the failed system. This kind of state-directed censoriousness (see Mathiesen 1965) is very common in Oslo prison.

Marginal Norway

Visibly different people in Norway often report that they see Norwegians as not particularly well informed of the world beyond Scandinavia. Norwegians are often seen as inhibiting a combination of arrogance and ignorance; remember, we are citizens of the worlds' best country to live in, a humanitarian superpower, and we know it (see Nilsson, Chapter 5). Norwegian-Iranian anthropologist Sharam Alghasi (2006), for instance, remembers being asked at a party whether there are any refrigerators in Iran. When I encounter Tarik one day, he is steaming after being asked about the status of Moroccan plumbing:

> Asking me if there are toilets inside the houses, shit! He is eighteen years old and drives a Ferrari around Oslo and thinks he owns the world, and he believes that there aren't any toilets in Moroccan houses? What is he thinking?

What can I say, Thomas? You can't do anything with such stupidity. You can only smile and shake your head, and say 'no, of course, no toilets in Moroccan houses, sure'. The fucking ignorance, what do they think, just cause it's in Africa, it's all fucking monkeys and fucking zebras and giraffes and that's that?

Partly as an answer to such ignorance, partly to further denounce the Norwegian state responsible for imprisoning them, many prisoners responds by placing Norway in its rightful place as a small, marginal country on the outskirts of everything important. Like Youssuf:

YOUSSUF: Norway is a small country, a very small country, it's not like France or anything like that, it's just a small country far, far away, few people, and we gotta say that Norway, it's not a country which colonized other countries, Norway never did that, like in Africa, where France colonized Morocco and Algeria, and, eh, Belgium, the Congo, Norwegian people have been isolated in a way, very isolated. I first knew the Norwegian people as Vikings from history, that's it. But in my childhood, when we talked about Scandinavia, we only knew about Sweden, beautiful girls, that's it. Never Norway, and to be honest, I couldn't even place Norway on a map. It's true! And it's just, I'm Norwegian now, I fight for this country now, I'm just telling you what it was like. Scandinavia, that was Sweden, that's it. . . . Norway, it's just a small country on the outside! It's full of paysants. I have called it paysants. Paysage, countryside. So, for instance the French, they call Norway le paysage de l'Europe.
TU: We're bønder.
YOUSSUF: The bønder of Europe. What I heard before I came, that's it. It's not critique, nothing like that, it's just the way people see it.

The yeoman farmer or *bønder* class Pratt describes as part of the historical foundation for the Norwegian culture of equality is here used to describe Norway's marginal status. As marginal, you should not try to look like you are in the centre. You should know you place, and act accordingly. Norwegians overplay their hand.

Soft Norwegian men

An important boundary marker used by the liminal prisoners to differentiate themselves from Norwegian men is that they are soft, weak and cowardly halfmen. The Norwegian softness is not always portrayed as utterly negative; prisoners acknowledge some positive aspects of the welfare state, for instance. But in most cases a hierarchy is established where whatever 'contrast culture' the prisoners articulate is seen as superior to the Norwegian one:

Later, I'm hanging out in the sofa with Amir and Naveed and some others. Amir is jokingly making fun of Bassim who sits across from us.

AMIR: You know, he isn't right, that one [smiles in Bassim's direction]. The doctor told me I shouldn't talk with him.
TU: Yeah? It's dangerous?
AMIR: Yep, he's wacko, you know, strange. He's been on remand here for two years.
TU: Two years! Shit...
NAVEED: Yeah, but it's OK. The police say that you foreigners, you have to be on remand. You can take it, not like the Norwegians, heh heh. The Norwegians can't take it. It is true, if you have tough experiences in your life, you manage better here.
AMIR: [smiles] That's why there are only foreigners here. Look around, how many Norwegians do you see? Two or three? The foreigners need to be here, the police think we are going to go underground or something. Norwegians are released.
NAVEED: But why would we run? Been living here for many years, speak Norwegian, we work here. We are not going anywhere.
AMIR: [more seriously] We are both Norwegian, man. He has a Norwegian passport, I have one. But we have to stay here just the same.
NAVEED: [leans back, relaxes] But it's OK. We can handle it. We are strong. One day, we'll get out and you'll see, we'll raise hell, heh heh.
AMIR: Revenge can be very sweet, they have to think about that [shakes his head]. The cultures are different. In our [Pakistani] culture, we keep thinking that revenge can be very sweet.

Even though both Amir and Naveed have Norwegian passports, they do not see themselves as fully Norwegian. Imprisoned by the cheating Norwegian state, which marks them as liminal, they respond by setting up a difference between themselves as strong non-Norwegians and the weak and wimpy Norwegians. Erol makes a similar point when he explains to me why it is so much easier to swindle Norwegians:

Well, it's because, you know we have had a difficult childhood, and we are used to the hard life, almost all the time, from the day we are born, and that's why it is so difficult, you would have to use tough methods to get close to us. And then you have a regular Norwegian, born in a hospital with flowers around him, from day one, the flowers, all the way up until he starts to get wise, and then they make the wrong choice, some of them, but then again they lack the, I dunno, honour, they lack what makes them strong as a person, to stand up for themselves, no matter what road they choose, the good road or the bad one.

The Norwegian citizen Erol has low regard for the Norwegian *vanlige folk*. The regular Norwegian male has grown up in a safe and sanitized environment within a culture lacking any focus on strength and honour. As a result, Norwegian men do not stand up for themselves, and they do not take responsibility for their own actions. They are not real men.

Cold and selfish Norwegians

The Norwegian man is not hard or tough enough. But he is also too cold; he lacks compassion, and does not accept responsibility for those who should be in his care. Many liminal prisoners, like Nadir below, are shocked by Norwegians' family affairs:

> I can't understand, I will never, never understand how it is possible to be like that with your family, the way you are in Norway. Why are you like that? I spoke with a Norwegian, I asked him when he last saw his parents. Not long ago, he answered, I saw them at Christmas. This was in May! I just don't get it, what a boring life! You have to see each other.
>
> ...
>
> My mum will never go to an old folks' home. Over my dead body. Either she dies, or I die. Up to that point, I will look after her. That's it.

The dysfunctional and immoral Norwegian family is also related to the general lack of honour among Norwegian men, but it also has to do with their cold and selfish nature. The Norwegian culture inhibits social life, Norwegians prefer to go to their beloved cabins in the weekends by themselves. This is problematic for Mehmet, also a Norwegian citizen, who cannot decide where his children should grow up:

> I just want to tell you, straight up, and don't take this as an insult, I don't think I want my children to grow up here. I want them to be social people. They can't become social in Norway. I mean if you see one of your neighbours in the street, you should greet him. And he should greet you. If you see an old man who needs help, you help him. It goes without saying! In the Qur'an, it says [quotes in Arabic], it means that if you go to bed with a full stomach, and your neighbours starve, you will be punished. That's it. It is just wrong. But Norwegian kids, they don't learn that. I don't think I want my kids to grow up in Norway.

Norwegians fail to take their individual responsibilities seriously. The Norwegian culture of *likhet* places too much trust in the welfare state, absolving the individual from contact with his fellow man. Norwegians are cold, introvert and selfish. Again, Norwegian men have no honour, and are, again, therefore not real men.

The dark side of a culture of *likhet*

The welfare state has had to adjust to the influx of a large number of visible strangers. For this to work seamlessly, for *vanlige folk* to coexist with ever-present strangers, a more definite and more radical other, demonstrating the rules of conduct between strangers and what happens to rule-breakers, might be needed. The radical strangers put behind the walls of the prison thus serve to symbolize that a society of strangers is possible after all, that everything will work out in the end. Dario Melossi (2003) sees the deviant immigrant other as part of the intra-European construction of a shared European identity. Following such an analysis, the role of the *kriminelle innvandrer* might be seen as vital for a society suddenly filled with large numbers of *ulike* citizens; faced with the prospects of controlling all these visible strangers, it is important to be able to divide between the good and the bad. The focus on radical otherness may have strengthened the egalitarian Norwegian culture of *likhet* in a time where it has been threatened. The otherness of the *kriminell innvandrer* has made it possible to live with those merely different.

At the national level, the prison is a vital part of this symbolic work. Anderson (1996) describes censuses, the production of maps and the construction of national museums as institutions of power put to use to reify the feeling of national loyalty and thus recreate the nation as imagined community. The prison also works as a carrier of symbolic power that demonstrates that a community of law-abiding citizens is possible. A community of stranger-citizens needs another kind of prison for this purpose, however, than a more ethnically homogeneous community. This new situation is part of the background for the current coupling of welfare-oriented sanction, with more tough on crime policies. This move is not, however, a simple move from A to B, but rather a movement where A and B coexist and are aimed at different kinds of people. Very roughly, one might say that following Garland's (2001) work, in a Scandinavian welfare state context, we might have three different criminologies working alongside one another: a criminology of the self, exemplified by the cognitive behavioural programmes put to work on those of us who are caught driving while intoxicated; a criminology of the poor and destitute other, the welfare client prisoners, who perhaps as a result of rising social differences may need a job and roof over his head; and a criminology of the dangerous, radical other who should not even have been here in the first place, and who should, if possible, be made an outsider once again.

One result is, of course, that some people have to fill the position of *kriminelle innvandrere*. Being put in prison as an example of radical otherness in a culture of *likhet* adds a specific flavour to the experience. After years in Norway, the prisoners quoted in this chapter know Norwegian society well. They know that many perceive them as *innvandrere* as subjects of the Norwegian welfare state, but not as 'real' Norwegians. As *kriminelle innvandrere*, the push from difference into otherness is completed.

The liminal prisoners lack the characteristically Norwegian trust of the state. Their ties with Norway are shifting and filled with conflicts. Positioned as ethnic folk devils, the resulting negative relationship vis-à-vis the state makes identification with anything Norwegian difficult. In a Norwegian context where the difference between nation and state can be hard to spot, the negative evaluation rubs off on national symbols in general. Rejecting their rejecters (see McCorkle and Korn 1954), the prisoners may feel connected to the Norwegian state as subjects of rights – even though they often just emphasize ownership of a particular passport, nothing more – but they do not feel like they are members of a nation of weak, dull, cold, *vanlige* Norwegians without honour, easy to trick and so selfish that they put their loved ones in homes to be cared for by strangers.

How does all this fit with the Scandinavian exceptionalism thesis? The darker side of the Scandinavian culture of *likhet* is barely a theme in Pratt's original two-part article. Pratt and Eriksson's contribution in this book (Chapter 13) however goes a long way to correct this. They conclude that '[T]he presence of both oppressive conformity and an overpowerful state does not undermine the Scandinavian exceptionalism thesis: what it reflects, instead, is the social costs associated with this' (p. 254). The question then, is of course whether this is a necessary cost. Is it possible for a human collective to be able to hold the value of *likhet* high, while avoiding making difference into otherness? Would it be possible to ease the pressure to conform and the tough sanctions imposed on some of those who do not, without losing the positive effects of *likhet* as a value? How may equality best be combined with a high degree of tolerance for the different? Scandinavian societies have a lot going for them. That they are perfect in this or any other regard does however seem unlikely.

Notes

1 I would like to thank and Katja Franko Aas, Nina Jon, Thomas Mathiesen, Iver B. Neumann and Synnøve Ugelvik for valuable comments on earlier versions of this chapter.
2 As part of a larger ethnographic study of power relations and identity work in prison, I collected interview and observation data on two connected wings over a period of one year. The majority of the prisoners on these wings were remand prisoners, at any time between 80 and 90 per cent. Those who had received a final verdict were with a few exceptions in the process of being transferred to other prisons better suited for prisoners with longer sentences. I was given free access to the two wings, could come and go as I pleased, and talk to any prisoner without going through the officers first. Observation notes were written on the same or following day, with an effort to reflect meaning, language tone and style, as well as the relevant context.
3 In 2010, 60 per cent of the prisoners being held on remand were non-citizens.
4 All names are of course pseudonyms. Excerpts from field diaries are translated from the Norwegian by me.
5 There are several unofficial English translations of the Norwegian national anthem. This seems to be the most common one.
6 Well, not quite unwritten. It was formally codified as the Law of Jante in Axel Sandemoses's 1933 novel *En flyktning krysser sitt spor* ('A fugitive crosses his tracks'). The Law of Jante has been seen as a powerful metaphor for the Scandinavian obsession with *likhet* (Dahl 1986).
7 www.aftenposten.no/nyheter/iriks/article1526606.ece
8 http://shiva82.blogspot.com/2009/10/gratulerer-du-er-norsk.html

References

Aas, Katja Franko (2007) 'Analysing a World in Motion. Global Flows Meet "Criminology of the Other"', *Punishment and Society*, 11(2): 283–303.
Alghasi, Sharam (2006) 'Innvandreren. Jeg er fortsatt inne, og jeg vandrer fortsatt' ['The in-wanderer/immigrant: I am still inside, and still wandering'], in Sharam Alghasi, Katrine Fangen and Ivar Frønes (eds), *Mellom to kulturer*. Oslo: Gyldendal Akademisk.

Anderson, Benedict (1996) *Forestilte fellesskap. Refleksjoner omkring nasjonalismens opprinnelse og spredning* [Imagined communities. Reflections on the origin and spread of nationalism]. Oslo: Spartacus.
Blom, Svein (2009) *Holdninger til innvandrere og innvandring 2009* [Attitudes towards immigrants and immigration 2009]. Oslo: Statistics Norway.
Christie, Nils and Kettil Bruun (1996) *Den gode fiende. Narkotikapolitikk i Norden* [The good enemy. Drug policies in the Nordic countries]. Oslo: Universitetsforlaget.
Connolly, William E. (1991) *Identity/Difference. Democratic Negotiations of Political Paradox.* Ithaca, NY: Cornell University Press.
Dahl, Hans Fredrik (1986) 'Those equal folk', in Stephen R. Graubard (ed.), *Norden. The Passion for Equality.* Oslo: Norwegian University Press, pp. 97–111.
Derrida, Jacques (2006) 'Différance', in Karin Gundersen (ed.), *Dekonstruksjon: klassiske tekster i utvalg.* Oslo: Spartacus.
Eide, Elisabeth and Anne Hege Simonsen (2007) *Mistenkelige utlendinger. Minoriteter i norsk presse gjennom hundre år* [Suspicious foreigners. Minorities in Norwegian press through a hundred years]. Kristiansand: Høyskoleforlaget.
Enquist, Per Olov (1986) 'On the Art of Flying Backward with Dignity', in Stephen R. Graubard (ed.), *Norden: The Passion for Equality.* Oslo: Norwegian University Press.
Foucault, Michel (2000) '"Omnes et singulatim". Toward a Critique of Political Reason', in James D. Faubion (ed.), *Power: Essential Works of Foucault 1954–1984 III.* New York: New Press.
—— (2007) *Security, Territory, Population. Lectures at the Collège de France 1977–1978.* Basingstoke, New York: Palgrave Macmillan.
Garland, David (2001) *The Culture of Control. Crime and Social Order in Contemporary Society.* Chicago: University of Chicago Press.
Graubard, Stephen R. (1986) 'Introduction', in Stephen R. Graubard (ed.) *Norden. The Passion for Equality.* Oslo: Norwegian University Press.
Gullestad, Marianne (1989) *Kultur og hverdagsliv. På sporet av det moderne Norge* [Culture and everyday life. In search of the modern Norway]. Oslo: Universitetsforlaget.
—— (2001) 'Likhetens grenser' ['Limits to Equality'], in Marianne E. Lien, Hilde Lidén and Halvard Vike (eds), *Likhetens paradokser. Antropologiske undersøkelser i Norge.* Oslo: Universitetsforlaget.
—— (2002) 'Invisible Fences. Egalitarianism, Nationalism and Racism', in *Journal of the Royal Anthropological Institute*, 8(1): 45–63.
Hudson, Barbara (2006) 'Punishing Monsters, Judging Aliens. Justice at the Borders of Community', in *Australian and New Zealand Journal of Criminology*, 39(2): 232–47.
Jensen, Sune Qvotrup (2007) *Fremmed, farlig og fræk. Unge mænd og etnisk/racial andenhed – mellom modstand og stilisering* [Foreign, dangerous and cheeky. Young men and ethnic/racial otherness – between resistance and stylization]. Aalborg: Aalborg Universitet.
Kriminalomsorgens årsstatistikk 2009 (2010) [Correctional services year statistics 2009] Oslo: Kriminalomsorgens sentrale forvaltning.
Lacey, Nicola (2008) *The Prisoners' Dilemma. Political Economy and Punishment in Contemporary Democracies.* Cambridge: Cambridge University Press.
Lien, Marianne, Hilde Lidén and Halvard Vike (2001) *Likhetens paradokser. Antropologiske undersøkelser i det moderne Norge* [Paradoxes of equality: anthropological studies in Norway]. Oslo: Universitetsforlaget.
McCorkle, Lloyd W. and Richard Korn (1954) 'Resocialization within Walls', *Annals of the American Academy of political and Social Science.* 293 (nummer ikke oppgitt), 88–98.

Melossi, Dario (2003) '"In a Peaceful Life". Migration and the Crime of Modernity in Europe/Italy', *Punishment and Society*, 5(4): 371–97.
Neumann, Iver B. (2003) 'Innledning. Regjeringsbegrepet og regjeringens historiske fremvekst' ['Introduction. Governmentality – the concept and the historical emergence'], in Iver B. Neumann and Ole Jacob Sending (eds), *Regjering i Norge*. Oslo: Pax.
—— (2006) 'Å studere den (post)moderne staten. Epistemologiske forutsetninger' ['Studying the (post)modern state. Epistemological assumptions'], *Norsk antropologisk tidsskrift*, 17 (3–4): 214–25.
Norton, Anne (1988) *Reflections on Political Identity*. Baltimore: Johns Hopkins University Press.
Øverland, Indra (2003) 'Regjering av liminaritet. Urfolk, minoriteter og innvandrere' ['Governing liminarity. Indigenous populations, minorities and immigrants'], in Iver B. Neumann and Ole Jacob Sending (eds.), *Regjering i Norge*. Oslo: Pax.
Pratt, John (2008a) 'Scandinavian Exceptionalism in an Era of Penal Excess. Part I: The Nature and Roots of Scandinavian Exceptionalism', *British Journal of Criminology*, 48(2): 119–37.
—— (2008b) 'Scandinavian Exceptionalism in an Era of Penal Excess. Part II: Does Scandinavian Exceptionalism Have a Future?', *British Journal of Criminology*, 48(3): 275–92.
Rose, Nikolas (2000) 'Government and Control', in David Garland and Richard Sparks (eds), *Criminology and Social Theory*. Oxford: Oxford University Press.
Simmel, Georg (1971) *On Individuality and Social Forms. Selected Writings*. Chicago and London: University of Chicago Press.
Sykes, Gresham M. (1958) *The Society of Captives. A Study of a Maximum Security Prison*. Princeton: Princeton University Press.
Ugelvik, Thomas (2010) *Å være eller ikke være fange. Frihet som praksis i et norsk mannsfengsel* [To be or not to be a prisoner. Freedom as practice in a Norwegian men's prison]. Oslo: Institutt for kriminologi og rettssosiologi, UiO.
Wacquant, Loïc J. D. (2002) 'The Curious Eclipse of Prison Ethnography in the Age of Mass Incarceration', *Ethnography*, 3(4): 371–97.
Zetterberg, Hans L. (1986) 'The Rational Humanitarians', in Stephen R. Graubard (ed.), *Norden. The Passion for Equality*. Oslo: Norwegian University Press.

8 Imprisoning the soul

Cecilie Basberg Neumann

In 1988, the prisoners at Bredtveit Prison for women initiated a two-day hunger strike because of inadequate kitchen facilities in one of the common rooms in the high-security department. They had applied for a new waffle iron for several months, and were denied a replacement due to ill treatment of the old one; they had been using it as a frying pan for steaks, hamburgers, etc. Around the same time, the world press reported about hunger strikes in prisons in different countries due to terrible hygiene conditions, overpopulation and malnutrition.[1]

The prisoners' different reasons for hunger strikes refer to very different prison situations, materially speaking, and one may argue: (a) that the prisoners at Bredtveit Prison had no (morally) legitimate reason to hunger strike; and (b) that the hunger strike at Bredtveit Prison is a reflection of Norwegian prison authorities and Norwegian prisons in general. If prisoners do not have more important things to complain about, they must live rather good lives in prison.

This is, however, a simplistic and materialistic way of understanding imprisonment and its probable effects on prisoners, ignoring not only the specific knowledge of a given culture in a given country, but also the particular discourses and practices in which the prisoners are situated; discourses and practices that have moulded their frames of references, life choices and life expectations. Such an understanding is also ignoring methodological and theoretical challenges when comparing prisoners' experiences and the effects of imprisonment in different countries. In this chapter, my point of departure is that what the context-sensitive frame of reference cross-cultural comparison calls for is something John Pratt (2008 a, b) seems to overlook when he claims that Scandinavian prisons, and Norwegian ones in particular, are more humane, than prisons elsewhere.

In a passage in which Pratt discusses the UN criticism of Norway's use of prisoners on remand, he nonetheless claims:

> However, on the basis of what I *did* see and experience, then, despite some warning signs and qualifications, the exceptional conditions in most Scandinavian prisons, while not eliminating the pains of imprisonment, must surely ease them.
>
> (2008a: 124)

This evaluation should, however, be based on answers to the following questions: how materially different are the prisons in Britain and Norway? How would these material differences constitute the prisoners in the two countries? What is the relationship between the material differences and the experience of being imprisoned? Given that the researchers are usually part of the community they study, what is the impact of their social and cultural background on the phenomena they study? And finally: if one agrees with Pratt that the material conditions in British and Norwegian prisons are different, is this difference equal to the differences between other institutions in the two countries? Such as the differences between Norwegian and British schools, hospitals and medical care centres? This points to the importance of the material and social context for incarceration and suffering, something I suppose will be relative to the experiences of pain felt by prisoners in different countries.

Basically, I work from the assumption that the individual prisoner's experience of the 'totality' of pain infliction is relative to the specific material conditions which one is accustomed to, bearing in mind the ethnic[2] Norwegian prison population and the (foreign) researcher's eye. I use the term deprivation synonymously with marginalization (see Cloke *et al.* 1997), and as a sensitizing concept embedded in a Bourdieu-inspired understanding of class and class divisions, and his inquiries into how social structures are reproducing themselves (Bourdieu 1995, 1996, 1999). On the level of individual meaning, I furthermore understand relative deprivation as a concept referring to the condition of comparison; the individual evaluates her economic and overall situation relative to her peers or significant others (see Eibner and Evans 2001).[3]

My frame of reference in the following will be the Norwegian prison system in general,[4] and Bredtveit Prison for women in particular. The open prison, also discussed by Pratt (2008a), will be my case. I will juxtapose Pratt's views with my own prison work and research (Basberg 1999), and with the small comparative research I did on Norwegian and British health visiting practices in 2005 (Neumann 2009). Finally, I will discuss some of the methodological issues that in my opinion seems to be of great importance if cross-cultural research and comparisons is to reach its potential. I will particularly discuss the importance of the gaze of the foreign researcher.

According to theorists as different as Gadamer (2004) and Haraway (1991), all knowledge, and all knowledge production, is positioned and situated. I will reflect upon the question of how material conditions matters across different cultural and societal arrangements – using reflections of the researcher's situatedness as social scientists when evaluating pain infliction and practices of punishment in different cultures, as my main frame of reference. More specifically, I will foreground the meaning of the material conditions in prisons and its probable impacts on prisoners as well as on the gaze of the researcher, specifically the foreign researcher, evaluating prisons. These would be gazes I assume to be locally situated within theoretical and empirical bodies of knowledge and expectations embedded in a particular cultural and ethnical situation (Haraway 1991; Bourdieu 1999; Basberg Neumann 2009).

Letting Pratt's cultural and societal analyses of Scandinavia in general and Norway in particular as historically egalitarian and consensus oriented societies stand uncontested,[5] I will see his analyses as rooted in a general impression[6] of Norwegian prisons and present-day society and culture.

The empirical background from which I am theorizing, is my experiences as a prison officer at Bredtveit Prison for women from 1987 to 1992, the only state prison for female prisoners in Norway then and now, and my subsequent research on prison officers in 1994 to 1997. I worked part time in the high-security departments from 1987 to 1990, and as a full-time employee from 1990 to 1992 at Bredtveit's minimum security wing. Later, I held a position as a probation officer in Oslo from 1997 to 2000. This included a position as a supervisor for prison officers at Oslo Prison (a men's prison) and probation officers from the Correctional Service in Oslo in 2000 and 2001, who collaborated on a project aiming at helping prisoners to find work and places to live after having served their sentences (see Ødegaardshaugen 2005, for an evaluation of this project). Working on this chapter, I revisited Bredtveit's open prison in June 2010 and interviewed the prison manager and a prisoner during my visit.

Do exceptional material conditions equal humane treatment of prisoners?

According to Pratt, Scandinavian prisons are treating their prisoners more respectfully, more like fellow human beings, than their British counterparts. In particular, Pratt emphasizes certain Scandinavian prison practices, such as assigning only one prisoner to each cell, giving them sufficient and healthy food, sufficient medical assistance and recreational facilities. In addition, prisoners in open prisons are 'free to walk around the prison grounds and sometimes into local communities' (2008 a: 122). Pratt not only focuses on the material dimension in his evaluation of the Scandinavian prison system, but he also seems to understand good or excellent material conditions as an important part of a humane prison. Whether this is how the prisoners experience the imprisonment themselves is not part of his research agenda. Materiality is, however, only one aspect of imprisonment (and only one aspect of life in general), and good material conditions are, as I will turn to later, only one aspect of a respectful and humane institution.

There *are* differences between the two countries. But the differences are not necessarily greater than differences between prisons and other institutions in Norway, and between prisons and other institutions in Britain. I assume this will be an important frame of reference for how the prisoners experience imprisonment. If prisoners in Norway and Britain face material conditions that are rather similar to the material conditions in other institutions in their respective societies, the relative difference in the two countries will not be that noticeable. This is important if we are going to discuss humane treatment of prisoners and the pains of imprisonment.

Prison research, cross-cultural comparisons and the meaning of materialism

How do researchers view, thematize and theorize the relationship between material conditions and the effects and experience of deprivation of freedom? According to Weiss and South:

> The most serious shortcoming [in comparative prison research] is that we have little cross-cultural knowledge, and the few comparative studies are regional or ahistorical.
>
> (1998: 4)

Even if more recent prison research has dealt with topics on comparing levels of national security, law enforcement and incarceration rates in relation to democracy and globalization in different countries (Lacey 2008), and have offered insightful views on methodological and theoretical challenges in cross-cultural research and comparisons (Nelken 2010), it still seems fair to say that prison research has had little to say about the relationship between, and the meaning of, differences in material prison conditions, both on national and cross-national levels. This, I believe is partly due to the dominant prison discourses in critical criminology, and partly due to the lack of ethnographical prison studies in Norway as well as in other European countries (cf. Ugelvik 2010a: 34). Critical criminologists, whether Scandinavian, European or American, will, when they discuss the causes, effects and pains of imprisonment target what they perceive to be the policy makers' misguided concepts and beliefs in prisons as an important instrument of crime prevention, the belief that rehabilitation of prisoners in prison is possible at all, or the supposed preventive effects of prisons on the general population. Instead these researchers focus their gazes on more latent functions such as renovation and control of the poor classes (e.g. Mathiesen 1965; Christie 2007 [1981]; Feely and Simon 1992; Irwin 2005; see also Ugelvik 2010a: ch. 1, for a similar analysis). Their analyses of the effects of imprisonment shows that prisoners are further marginalized and stigmatized, and they document the losses and fears experienced by prisoners: being deprived of a private life and a sexual life, having to adjust to rules, regulations and restrictions they perceive as humiliating and illegitimate. Finally, such research has focused on prisoners' creative adjustments to the prison system, their resistance, learning and coping strategies (cf. Mathiesen 1965; Sykes 1958, Foucault 1986; Finstad and Gjetvik 1990; Vegheim 1995; Irwin 2005; Ugelvik 2010a).

To the extent that material conditions such as food supplies, health facilities, the space and inventories of the inmates cells, the overall quality and look of the prison buildings are problematized, they are related to the context they provide as the scene and the background of imprisonment, fortifying the main figure in prison inquiries: the pains of incarceration, loss of freedom and prisoners' experience of imprisonment.

When prison researchers draw on studies conducted in other countries, similarities rather than differences will be emphasized, addressing the overall and

Imprisoning the soul 143

common logics of punishment – and culturally specific traits and material conditions will remain unthematized. According to Liebling:

> Theories about the nature of prison have been concerned with their essential similarities.
>
> (2004: 53)

And even if literature on differences has focused on material differences between prisons with different prison regimes in the same countries (see Kruttschnitt *et al.* 2000), it has not considered more closely the relative aspects of material conditions within a framework of cross-cultural comparisons.

From this perspective, Pratt's observations and analyses of and claims about the Scandinavian prison systems as exceptionally humane, provides an excellent opportunity to start reflecting on how and why material conditions matters, and, when considering the forms of power structures at work, why different material conditions in open prisons perhaps do not matter that much after all. Before I continue, let me first have a look at the concept of *humane prison conditions*.

Humanity

What exactly is meant by humane prison conditions? According to Liebling (2004) humanity is linked to respect. Humane treatment is based on the acknowledgement of the other, of the recognition of him or her as a person:

> It [humane treatment] acts as a constraint against cruelty and as the root of compassionate action [. . .] To 'treat with humanity', then, means to treat someone as an individual and as a person [. . .]In the modern prison, considerable effort is expended in trying to expel 'distasteful' and violent punishment [. . .] Civility is part of humanity to the extent that it recognizes and is sensitive to the unintended suffering of the individual person.
>
> (2004: 218–19)

Prisoners obviously respond positively to being treated with respect and humanity (Basberg 1999; Liebling and Price 2001; Johnsen and Granheim, Chapter 11, this book). Liebling's inmate informants who elaborate on the importance of being treated humanely by prison officers, also include the material dimension such as 'great food, good lay out, clean and comfortable accommodation etc' (Liebling 2004: 223). Thus, Liebling's findings point to the fact that some British prisoners also feel they are treated humanely and respectfully by their prison officers, even if the prison conditions under which they serve may be, materially speaking, far more scarce than in Scandinavia.

In addition, Liebling's findings correspond well with my own research on prison officers at Bredtveit Prison in 1995/96. My project was to analyse the conditions for care in prison; what the concept meant to individual prison officers, their thoughts on how they practised care, the tensions and dilemmas between tasks of care and control, and the challenging moralities embedded in having a 'caring approach' towards prisoners, in contrast to the repressive prison structures and systems based on a strict regime of rules and regulations. One of my central findings was that the quality of the care and acts of care provided by the prison officers depended on the prison officer's willingness to see the other (see Levinas 1996), to relate to her as a person, and to be flexible about the prison rules. I also emphasized that the caring acts of the prison officers were easier to perform in less restrictive departments (Basberg 1999).[7]

Two questions come to mind. First: how come Liebling's and my own research on prison officers correspond so well in this respect, considering Pratt's exceptionalism thesis? Obviously, prison conditions can be experienced as humane by British prisoners. Second: would this emphasis on humane treatment of prisoners, a form of treatment also perceived to be at least partly humane by at least some prisoners themselves (see Skardhamar 2002; Lerdal 2005), be enough to characterize the whole prison system in Norway as humane?

Norwegian prisons are – materially speaking – well equipped and relatively comfortable. This is as should be expected in a wealthy society with a humanitarian self-image and internationally acknowledged as a peace builder and peacekeeper (see Sending and Andersen 2010). Humane prison conditions are however not a logical consequence of a wealthy society. In more elitist and non-democratic, but wealthy societies, the opposite situation is easily imaginable. A list of the top ten richest counties in the world based on GDP per capita in 2007, placed Norway as number four, Kuwait as number five and the United Arab emirates as number six. Luxemburg, Qatar and Bermuda held the three top places.[8] The prisons in a rich country such as Kuwait seem to be not nearly as well organized and respectful towards their inmates, even if material conditions in themselves would not reveal this at first glance.[9] A US official paper states that the prison conditions in Kuwait are up to international standards, yet the same paper also states that there are severe problems with overcrowded prisons; it is not unusual for 13 to 15 prisoners to share the same cell in Kuwaiti prisons. No doubt, part of the explanation for the – materially speaking – humane conditions in Norwegian prisons would be cultural values, cultural identity and a social-democratic political system.

But, saying that prisons in Norway are *more* humane than prisons in other countries – something that might well be true when considering the material conditions in prisons in other countries – is also to imply that being imprisoned in a Norwegian prison is not only less painful, but also less stigmatizing, and does not have severe consequences for the rest of the lives of the inmates. This is most certainly wrong, and, I would suggest, due not only to the experience of deprivation and loss of freedom when imprisoned, but empirically true when considering the lives of the criminals – before and after imprisonment (see Skardhamar 2002; Helgeland 2009). Being a convicted person in Norway normally means being at the very margins of Norwegian society. What then would be the mechanisms at work?

Foucault on discipline and governmentality

Even if several logics of policy making and moral beliefs on prisons – such as the logics of discipline and punishment, focus on rehabilitation, and risk and group security thinking – are directed towards different criminal groups and prisoners in different countries, and also come in different mixes, I understand the overall perspective of Foucault (1986 [1977], 1980, 2002) on crime, punishment and discipline to be valid. To Foucault, the aim of punishment, as is the aim of much social policy governance,[10] is the emphasis on prisoners' prospects of adaption and 'change' through prison *discipline*, and the more generalized form of power Foucault called *governmentality*. The change in the prison population is supposed to be caused by the individual prisoner's internalization of not only law-abiding norms and the wish to comply with prison rules, but also of an internalization of 'new' life perspectives, projects and suitable patterns of behaviour. This is supposed to translate into both collaboration with authorities, and more specifically a new form of self-control (see Rose 1999 for a general analysis)

The prisoner I interviewed in June 2010 at Bredtveit's open prison made this remark:

> This really is a beautiful prison and I am grateful to be here, not in a high security department. I can work. I have this lovely room, spacious, delicate and tidy, with my own bathroom and my own balcony. Yet, I am still in prison. I have to follow the rules [. . .] It takes a lot of patience and a lot of self-discipline.

The prison system is based on two major power strategies, according to Foucault. The *direct* form of power, discipline, works through the maze of micro power technologies controlling the prisoners and making them compliant; making their bodies 'docile' (1986: 163). The *indirect* form of power, governmentality, works through expectations of future conducts, communicated through the normalizing discourses of authorities (authoritative bodies of knowledge, truths and practices) internalized though self-discipline and self-government (1980: 131). Governmentality is, however, a form of power not only directed at prisoners, but at all members of society (see also Dean 1999; Rose 1999). Foucault sees the new prison regimen where: 'the soul is the prison of the body' (1986: 30) as opposed to the old regime declining in the eighteenth and nineteenth centuries, with its direct and brutal forms of punishment directed at the body, not the soul.

However, when Foucault introduces the development of the modern prison as a new form of power technology directed towards the criminal, aiming at rehabilitating or changing the criminal person himself, as something profoundly different from the medieval practices of punishing the criminal act by punishing the criminal's body, he comments on the material aspects of – and the contemporary criticism of the 'humane' aspects of the new punishment – as follows:

> The criticism that was often levelled at the penitentiary system in the early nineteenth century (imprisonment is not a sufficient punishment: prisoners are

less hungry, less cold, less deprived in general than many poor people or even workers) suggests a postulate that was never explicitly denied: it is just that a condemned man should suffer physically more than other men. It is difficult to dissociate punishment from additional physical pain. What would a non-corporal punishment be? There remains, therefore, a trace of 'torture' in the modern mechanisms of criminal justice – a trace that has not been entirely overcome, but which is enveloped, increasingly, by the non-corporal nature of the penal system.

(1986: 16)

By quoting this passage, my intention is not to say that good material conditions are not important in themselves, also as a part of humane treatment of prisoners, but to pay attention to the cruelty lying at the outskirts of the discussion of (too good) material conditions as opposed to prison as a pain-inflicting institution meant to be exactly that (see Christie 2007). As Ugelvik has shown (2010b), many Norwegians have voiced moral indignation at the fact that Norway's newest high-security prison in Halden is up to modern standards, materially speaking, comparing the prison with a hotel. What interests me most in this context, though, is how the concept of governmentality intersects with the experience of material conditions. I will approach this complex cluster of power, materiality and meaning (see Neumann 2001a) by reflecting on my experiences as a prison officer at Bredtveit's open prison.

Bredtveit's open prison

As already mentioned, I worked at Bredtveit Prison for women from 1987 to 1992, part time at the high-security prison from 1987 to 1990, and full time at the open prison from August 1990 to November 1992. As a relatively young prison officer (I was 24 when I started working in the prison), I was struck by two contradictory observations: one was the fact that the cells of the inmates were about the same size (about 8 square metres) as the room I rented from an old lady at the time. Working in that prison over some years, I observed that the prisoners got plenty of food; many in fact gained a lot of weight during their incarceration. They had enough clothes, a sparse but sufficient supply of beauty products, library facilities, school, options to work, and, to some extent, work-out possibilities. My observation was one of, and a reaction to, material conditions, resembling the Foucauldian quotation earlier.

The other observation was the habit of newly arrived prisoners trying the doorknobs when being followed from one part of the prison to another. The experienced prisoners would just stand waiting by the door, not even bothering to check if it was open (it seldom was). This was an observation of the effects of being institutionalized, and the loss of freedom forcing itself on prisoner subjectivity and agency (see Goffman 1990; and also Ugelvik 2010a).

I had many thoughts on how it must have felt to live under such a strict prison regimen; never knowing when you would be awakened by an officer with a urine test specimen jar, having to apply in writing to take a shower, the lack of privacy, and being with persons not of your own choosing. I gradually developed from thoughts and judgements made in the context of my own present experience (compared to my rented room, the cell didn't seem too bad) over to an understanding of the pains of imprisonment; the deprivation of agency and loss of freedom were not due to material conditions in themselves, but to the very imprisonment and its internal and external structures, imposing themselves on the prisoners as a body–soul experience. Still, I was not sure if I thought like this because of what I had seen in the high-security prison. Maybe this would be radically different in the open prison.

In 1990, I was thrilled to be removed from the high-security departments of the main prison building, to the open prison. The open prison was located in a picturesque house being the temporary home of the inmates serving the last months of their sentences. The house was situated at the outskirts of central Oslo, in an industrial era with residential houses as its closest neighbours. About ten inmates were living in the house, with two or three prison officers on duty in the daytime, and one working during nightshifts. The prisoners had regular day jobs, or went to ordinary schools and had to be back in the prison house at fixed hours in the afternoon. The legitimizing idea of the open department was, in line with official Norwegian prison policy, firmly rooted in the idea of rehabilitation; serving the last part of their sentences in this house was supposed to make the prisoners' transition back to a 'normal' life easier for them. Thrilled as I was by this situation, which implied a downscaling of my control tasks and the possibility of more personal relationships with the inmates, I was puzzled by the fact that they were all complaining about the lack of visible signs of imprisonment.

Seen from the perspective of a care-oriented prison officer, this could seem contradictory. In the high-security prison building, the same prisoners would complain about the food, about their isolation and loneliness, about the prison smell, about not being allowed to cook their own food, about not being able to call their friends and families whenever they wanted, about the continuous control routines of being counted, having their clothes, cells and bodies checked for weapon, drugs or contraband, and, when being transported around the prison from their cell to the school building or to the dining room or the workplace, waiting for the constant opening and locking of all the doors.

The open prison house, on the other hand, would remedy a lot of these control routines, allowing for what resembles normal life, not having to ask permission to take a shower, to eat, to watch TV, to buy your own food.

Except for the urine tests and the counting – as a rule done in ways that the inmates would not be offended by, and not counting in a militaristic manner – most of the security routines were abolished. The routines of the open prison house were based and organized on trust. We all knew – prisoners and guards – that the prisoners could just walk out of the house if they wanted to, whenever they wanted, and not return.

I doubt that the consequences of this kind of regiment had been thoroughly analysed with regard to the ideological assumptions about the rehabilitating and normalizing effects on the inmates.

What gradually became clear to me, was the fact that this kind of incarceration implied the ultimate version of the Foucauldian governmentality. The inmates would verbalize the extreme stress they experienced by the fact that they had the freedom to potentially leave the prison in the morning never to return. In order to return every day, they would have to build inner bars – some said they actually had to visualize the picturesque house with physical bars in front of the windows – constantly reminding themselves of the consequences of leaving the prison never to return. 'The police would just find me after a couple of days' 'Where would I hide?' 'I don't want a life on the run', 'You know, I really don't have a place to stay'.

This experience made me seriously reflect not only on the limitations of central aspects of the belief in rehabilitation as such, but also on the intersection between material conditions and punishment, the effects of imprisonment on future stigma, as well as the effects of upbringing, class background and life chances. As such, the prison house could indeed be viewed as a project facilitating a move towards normalization for the prisoners, made possible by the humane Norwegian criminal justice authorities – as Pratt points out. When considering the intentions of the authorities, there is nothing wrong with such an analysis. It is difficult to build an argument saying that harsh prison conditions are better than good prison conditions because harsh conditions makes the prison experience more congruent for the prisoners; when their life is in a ruin, it is better to live in a place that truly mirrors this fact.

However, when analysing the consequences of imprisonment, the good intentions fall prey to two important situations: first, you cannot remedy the loss of freedom by producing a material situation – covering up the fact that freedom is actually lost. This is the kind of euphemizing power both Foucault and Bourdieu are referring to when analysing how different modes of power work, something that is in fact also acknowledged by prison officers at Bredtveit open prison today. Second, you cannot remedy the stigmatizing effects of imprisonment by offering offenders progressive prison conditions due to good behaviour in prison. This is due to a number of reasons, most importantly the lack of education, lack of work experience, drug addiction, histories of abuse, etc. – having been in prison does not look good on your CV.[11]

Let me return to my initial question on how material conditions relate to the experience of pain and approach the question from a methodological angle: is it the gaze of an outsider coloured by the impression of material conditions in one country that produces Pratt's evaluation of the differences between Scandinavia and the UK? How can we unpack the layers of meaning connected to material conditions and at the same time consider words describing similar structures, but materially referring to very different situations? I will turn to an empirically different, but methodologically relevant case, to help clarify my points.

The gaze of the foreign researcher

In the spring of 2005 I was in Camden, London, doing research on the health-visiting service. My research task was to get some impressions from the British health-visiting system in order to compare it with its Norwegian equivalent, about which I wrote my dissertation. I interviewed three health visitors – two practitioners and a leading officer in the state bureaucracy – and also Jane Lewis, professor of sociology at the London School of Economics, who had done some research on the health-visiting service ten years prior to my own.

Entering one of the medical centres where the service was located, I met with a very aggressive and stressed female health visitor. She was not only overworked – she appeared as if she came right out of a Charles Dickens novel. Her clothes were dirty, as were her hands and hair. She sneered at me, and told me she did not have time to talk to me, not then, not ever. I sat in the reception room in two medical centres for a while and observed – as I did in Norway – and was puzzled by the huge material differences between what I had seen in Norway and what I saw here. In Norway, even in the traditional working-class parts of Oslo, where large groups of marginalized ethnic Norwegians and large groups of non-ethnic Norwegians live, the health-visiting centres looked – again, materially speaking – the same as they did in the posh upper-middle-class areas of Oslo.

What did mark class differences between the different centres, was the way the health visitors talked about problems in their populations and the information material made available to parents in the waiting rooms. In the working-class areas, there were visible anti-smoking brochures on the walls, healthy food recommendations, breast-feeding recommendations, etc. In the posh areas, no such information material was available, instead there were stacks of exclusive lifestyle magazines, filled with tips on how to make your holiday relaxing with your newborn baby, good sex during pregnancy, how to care for your relationship with a newborn, etc. But the locations – the material layout – were more or less the same: clean, tidy, professional, hospital like, with white or pastel colours on the walls.

In the Camden district, the centres gave the impression of being less organized, less spacious, less hospital like, less tidy, and not very clean. One of the health visitors I interviewed invited me into her office. It was tiny, about 5 square metres, had no windows, with barely enough room for both of us. This experience taught me several things. To see class differences in Norway – when doing research on professions – you have to be sensitive to the subtle differences. The professionals as well as the researchers will normally represent the middle classes themselves, and they will create surroundings according to class specific as well as professional standards. To be able to spot class differences in the population through the material structure of the centres, subtle differences in communication have to be focused – I am thinking of the messages communicated through information brochures as mentioned above, what is actually said and done to the parents and how. In the UK, material standards may be set at different professional standards, due to a more relaxed attitude towards dirt and of giving an impression of tidiness, etc. This does not, however, mean that professional qualifications will be better or worse than in Norway, only that standards are different. We know that class divisions are more pronounced in Britain compared to Scandinavia – meaning they would probably be easier to spot, also for people unfamiliar with British culture, where material conditions more obviously signify class differences (see Skeggs 2002).

Another observation from the same study was that the professional language among the health visitors was quite similar in Norway and the UK. In both countries, they spoke of the challenges of communicating the importance of a healthy lifestyle to their populations, and of empowering the mothers in particular. In both countries, this was seen as a prerequisite for confidence and therefore good parenting; the empowered parent would be in charge not only of a healthy lifestyle, she would also be knowledgeable of the value of firm boundaries – not only to secure good manners, but to avoid stress and conflicts in the family. The unknowledgeable parent who does not set firm boundaries, including a restricted sweets regimen, regular sleeping hours, teaching the child how to wait in order to grow out of the 'instant gratification phase', will be a less efficient and loving parent, compared to the one who manages to do this (see Skeggs 2002). This would be the messages from a professional discourse shared by nurses and health visitors in the two countries.

On the level of practice one may, however, expect differences including parental behaviour and how health visitors talk to parents and children, also coinciding with material conditions. Jane Lewis exclaimed, as did the UK health visitors themselves, that Camden district, however posh looking to the foreign researcher's eye, is in certain areas affected by poverty, overcrowded houses, domestic violence and alcohol and substance abuse – to an extent beyond belief. This does not mean that domestic violence and substance abuse among parents do not occur in the middle and upper-middle classes, but this would be a lot more difficult to detect in both of the countries, due to, again, the material and educational advantages of the middle and upper-middle classes and how they present themselves through codes of language and dress.

What does this have to do with foreign researchers' evaluations of prisons? The example points to the different intersections of culture and class, and how different levels of material conditions have relative meaning to the specific class structure and general material conditions in a specific society. Seen from a point of reflexivity, growing up in and living on the privileged side of the Norwegian society will give me certain expectations about preferred living conditions, valuable life projects and valuable knowledge in general. As a privileged Norwegian and a sociologist, I have specific expectations about what a good and valuable life is like, and many times when travelling, I have been confronted with my ethnocentric and biased views of people who lead very different lives under very different material conditions to my own.

For me, this would involve reflections on several issues. From the British practice of having carpets instead of tiles on the bathroom floors, to me, an example of matter out of place, to quote Mary Douglas (1996), to the poor hygienic conditions in an Egyptian hotel with polluted tap water, and to the overly strict, organized and expensive Geneva. All these evaluations and judgements are firmly located within the context of my own class-specific cultural upbringing and a life within a specific context equipping me with specific classification tools and schemas. To me, it is surprising that Pratt seems to neglect insights like these when he ventures abroad and attempts to size up Scandinavian prisons.

Concluding remarks

To sum up, and given the general differences between Britain and Norway, it is not at all certain that observable differences in material standards between the two countries have an effect on how prisoners experience being imprisoned.

Both my research findings and experience as a prison officer points towards the insight that good material conditions are not necessarily essential to how prisoners experience the pains of imprisonment. In Bredtveit open prison, the beautiful surroundings, the big garden, the light and spacious rooms with their own balconies, do not cover up the fact that the inmates are indeed incarcerated. When they use the beautiful garden, they must not venture out of the part visible to the guards. They cannot receive visitors whenever they like, and they have to ask permission to leave the prison days in advance. In short, prisoners have to cooperate with prison officers and prison authorities by following all kinds of rules and regulations. This does not mean, however, that beautiful surroundings are not important, and may be experienced as rewarding both by prisoners and prison officers. An open prison, however, challenges both prisoners and prison officers in ways totally overlooked by Pratt. The prisoners are forced to impose on themselves the image of prison discipline and to conduct a self-control that can be extremely challenging. The prison officers, on the other hand, have to acknowledge the fact that these prisoners, to a much larger extent that prisoners in high-security departments, experience the imprisoning of the soul. Whether they suffer more or less than their fellow inmates in similar (open) British prisons, is hard to say, as long as we have no cross-cultural and context-sensitive prison research to support such claims. John Pratt has done us all a favour by opening up the prison research field to future inquires.

Notes

1 For a recent example in Louisiana in 2009, see: www.southernstudies.org/2009/08/immigrant-detainees-hunger-strike-over-conditions-in-la-detention-facility.html. For political prisoners on hunger strikes in Iran, see: http://en.wikipedia.org/wiki/1988_executions_of_Iranian_political_prisoners#Isolation_of_the_prisoners; and for comments on hunger strikes, see: www.globallawyersandphysicians.org/storage/JAMA%20Hunger%20Strikes.pdf
2 By emphasizing ethnicity, I refer to material standards in Norwegian prisons set within the frame of the Norwegian welfare state.
3 The perspective of relative deprivation, however, may imply a methodological nationalism. In a globalized world, we are no longer formed solely by standards in our 'own' culture, as norms and values are distributed globally through travelling patterns, media, and cultural exchange on the level of individuals and groups emigrating

throughout the world (Scholte 2000; McRobbie 2009). Even though the ethnic diversity in Norwegian prisons has increased over the past twenty years, I still think that material standards are set within the frame of the ethnic Norwegian welfare state.

4 For the Norwegian case, see Mathiesen (1965), Vegheim (1995); Finstad and Gjetvik (1985), Skardhamar (2002), Ericsson (2002), Grøvdal (2001), Lerdal (2005), Hammerlin and Larsen (2000) and Ugelvik (2010a).
5 Other chapters in this volume will contest Pratt's analysis of the Norwegian culture as egalitarian and consensus oriented. I would like to emphasize though, that the Norwegian society is indeed class diverted (see Hennum 2002; Skilbrei 2003; Basberg Neumann 2009), and has been so historically (for a historical analysis of Norwegian nobilities, its elite and bourgeoisie, see Neumann 2001).
6 I use the term 'general impression' for a particular reason. Pratt has interviewed prison directors and elite bureaucrats. He has not been inside Norwegian prisons for a longer time studying the interaction between prisoners and prison officers, or interviewed prisoners. In this respect his knowledge of the Norwegian prison system stems from the policy discourse on good intentions for crime prevention, not from the level of practice. Furthermore, Pratt has interviewed a highly profiled Norwegian sociologist such as Ottar Hellevik. This esteemed scholar and others have however been criticized for not allowing perspectives of, and the challenges to, marginalization in their analyses of the Norwegian welfare state (Fossestøl 2010, Basberg Neumann and Egeland 2010 b), and Hellevik in particular for being universalistic and totalizing in scope when analysing Norwegian happiness (Døving 2010).
7 The book evoked strong reactions among criminological colleges in Norway. Leif Petter Olaussen, who reviewed the book in 2000, suggested that the least restrictive department that I had named 'The care department' instead should be called 'Department for particular pain infliction'. Olaussen was critical of the system of progressive sentencing, as were others such as my colleagues Hedda Giertsen and Kjersti Ericsson at IKRS/UIO, seeing this reward system as a creator of internal injustice and conflicts between the inmates, and as a system bringing further deprivation and experiences of loss to prisoners who did not manage to, or did not want to, behave in a disciplined way while imprisoned. This system is in other words denying the inmates the rights and possibilities to resist the prison system, rules and regulations.
8 www.mapsofworld.com/world-top-ten/world-top-ten-richest-countries-map.html
9 www.state.gov/g/drl/rls/hrrpt/2002/18280.htm. On capital punishment in Kuwait, and for a list of people who have been hanged, see: www.capitalpunishmentuk.org/kuwait.html
10 For two recent examples, see Basberg Neumann (2009) on the health-visiting service in Norway, and Basberg Neumann (2010a) for a recent example on child services in Norway.
11 The Norwegian government is trying to remedy this situation by several programmes and services offered to ex-prisoners and the marginalized population in Norway through KVP – programmes aiming at reintegrating people to ordinary work life, education or other kinds of meaningful conduct (see Legard 2010; Hansen 2010).

References

Basberg, Cecilie (1999) *Omsorg i fengsel?* [Care in prison?]. Oslo: Pax forlag.
Bourdieu, Pierre (1995) *Distinksjonen. En sosiologisk kritikk av dømmekraften* [Distinction: A Social Critique of the Judgement of Taste]. Pax Forlag: Oslo.
—— (1996) *Symbolsk makt* [Symbolic power]. Pax Forlag: Oslo.
—— (1999) *Meditasjoner*. [Pascalian Meditations]. Pax Forlag: Oslo.
Christie, Nils (2007 [1981]) *Limits to Pain*. Eugene, OR: Wipf & Stock.

—— (2004) *A Suitable Amount of Crime.* London: Routledge.
Cloke, Paul, Paul Milbourne and Chris Thomas (1997) 'Living in Different Ways? Deprivation, Marginalization and Changing Lifestyles in Rural England', *Transactions of the Institute of British Geographers.* New Series, 22(2): 210–30.
Dean, Mitchell (1999) *Governmentality: Power and Rule in Modern Society.* Sage: London.
Douglas, Mary (1996 [1966]) *Purity and Danger.* Pax Forlag: Oslo.
Døving, Runar (2009) Bokessay: 'Ottar Hellevik: "Jakten på den norske lykken.1"' [Book essay: 'Ottar Hellevik: "The quest for the Norwegian happiness"'], *Sosiologi I dag*, 3: 94–104.
Eibner, Christine and William N. Evans (2001) 'Relative Deprivation, Poor Health Habits and Mortality', *Journal of Human Resources*, 40(3): 591–620.
Ericsson, Kjersti (2002) 'Fengselets tid – og livets' [The prisons time – and the time of life], in Barbro Sætesdal and Kristin Heggen (eds), *I den beste hensikt?* Oslo: Akribe.
Feely, Malcom and Jonathan Simon (1992) 'The New Penology: Notes on the Emerging Strategy of Corrections and Its Implications', *Criminology*, 30: 449–74.
Finstad, Liv and Anne Lise Gjetvik 1990 *Varetektsfanger forteller.* [The storys of prisoners in custody]. In: *KS-serien* nr 3-90. Institutt for kriminologi og strafferett. Universitetet i Oslo.
Fossestøl, Knut (2010) 'The Norwegian model of corporation', unpublished manuscript. Oslo: Work Research Institute.
Foucault, Michel (1986 [1977]) *Discipline and Punish: The Birth of the Prison.* London: Penguin.
—— (1980) *Power/Knowledge.* London: Longman.
—— (2002) *Forelesninger om regjering og styringskunst.*[Lectures on governmentality and the art of governance]. Translated by Iver B. Neumann. Oslo: Cappelen Akademisk Forlag.
Gadamer, Hans Georg (2004) *Truth and Method.* London: Continuum.
Goffman, Erving (1990 [1961]) *Asylums.* New York: Doubleday.
Gordon, Colin (ed.) (1980) *Michel Foucault. Power/Knowledge.* London: Harvester Press.
Grøvdal, Yngvil (2001) *Sånn er det bare!: En kvalitativ studie av fengselsbetjenters arbeid.* [That's just how it is! A qualitative study of prison officers' work]. Oslo: IKRS, University of Oslo.
Hammerlin, Yngve and Egil Larsen (2000) 'Tungtsonende': forsknings-/evalueringsrapport for TFP (tverrfaglig fengselsprosjekt) i Oslo kretsfengsel.
Hansen, H. et al. (2010) *Helhetlig oppfølging av brukere med behov for tettere oppfølging i Kvalifiseringsprogrammet. Sluttrapport om opplæringspilot* [End evaluation of a training programme for therapists in the social services in Norway]. Oslo: Høgskolen i Oslo.
Haraway, Donna (1991) *Simians, Cyborgs and Women.* London: Free Association Books.
Helgeland, Ingeborg Marie (2009) *Ungdom i alvorlig trøbbel.* [Youth in serious trouble]. Oslo: Universitetsforlaget.
Hennum, Nicole (2002) *Kjærlighetens og autoritetens kulturelle koder. Om å være mor og far for norsk ungdom.* [The cultural codes of love and authority. Mothering and fathering Norwegian youths].Oslo: NOVA Rapport 19/02.
Irwin, John (2005) *The Warehouse Prison: Disposal of the New Dangerous Class.* Los Angeles: Roxbury.
Kruttschnitt, Candace, Rosemary Gartner and Amy Miller (2000) 'Doing Her Own Time? Women's Responses to Prison in the Context of the Old and the New Penology', *Criminology*, (38): 681–717.

Lacey, Nicola (2008) *The Prisoner's Dilemma: Political Economy and Punishment in Contemporary Democracies*. Cambridge: Cambridge University Press.

Legård, Sveinung (2010) 'Pathways from Education to Work for Young People with Impairments and Learning Difficulties in Norway', AFI-Rapportsamarbeid, Paris: OECD.

Lerdal, Synnøve (2005) *Ditt eget ansvar!: Om rehabilitering og makt ved Bastøy fengsel* [Your own responsibility!: On rehabilitation and power on Bastøy prison]. Oslo: IKRS, University of Oslo.

Levinas, Emmanuel (1996) [1972]: *Den annens humanisme*. [The humanism of the other]. Oslo: Aschehoug Forlag.

Liebling, Alison (2004) *Prisons and Their Moral Performance*. Oxford: Oxford University Press.

Liebling, Alison and David Price (2001) *The Prison Officer*, Prison Service Journal.

Mathiesen, Thomas (1965) *The Defenses of the Weak: A Sociological Study of a Norwegian Correctional Institution*. London: Tavistock Publications.

McRobbie, Angela (2009) *The Aftermath of Feminism*. Los Angeles: Sage.

Nelken, David (2010) *Comparative Criminal Justice: Making Sense of Difference*. Los Angeles: Sage.

Neumann, Cecilie E. Basberg (2009) *Det bekymrede blikket. En studie av helsesøstres handlingsbetingelser.*[The worried gaze. A study of the conditions for action in the health visiting service]. Oslo: Novus.

—— (2010a) 'Ille, men ikke for ille' [Difficult, but not too difficult], *Norges Barnevern* (87)4: 244–55.

Neumann, Cecilie E. Basberg and Cathrine Egeland (2010b) 'The Watch Dog that Turned Silent? A Discourse Analysis of the Equality and Anti-discrimination Ombud', *Nordisk organisasjons tidsskrift*, (12)3, 50–72.

Neumann, Iver B. (2001a) *Mening, makt, materialitet*. [Meaning, power, materiality]. Bergen: Fagbokforlaget.

—— (2001b) *Norge – en kritikk*. [Norway – a critical approach to the concept of Norway]. Oslo: Pax forlag.

Ødegaardshaugen, Ann-Karin (2005) 'Løslatelse fra fengsel: om hvordan det mulige kan bli umulig' [Prison release: on how the possible may be impossible], master's thesis. Oslo: Institute of criminology/University of Oslo.

Olaussen, Leif Petter (2000) 'Cecilie E. Basberg: Omsorg i fengsel?' [Care in prison?] Book review *Nordisk tidskrift for kriminalvidenskap*, 87(2): 170–3.

Pratt, John (2008a) 'Scandinavian Exceptionalism in an Era of Penal Excess. Part I: The Nature and Roots of Scandinavian Exceptionalism', *British Journal of Criminology*, 48(2): 119–37.

—— (2008b) 'Scandinavian Exceptionalism in an Era of Penal Excess. Part II: Does Scandinavian Exceptionalism Have a Future?', *British Journal of Criminology*, 48(3): 275–92.

Rose, Nicolas (1999) *Governing the Soul*. London: Free Association books.

Scholte, Jan Aart (2000) *Globalization. A Critical Introduction*. New York: St. Martin's Press.

Sending, Ole Jacob and Skumsrud Andersen, Morten (2010) 'Liberia og fredsbygging: en institusjonell forskningsagenda' [Liberia and peacebuilding: an institutional agenda for research] *Internasjonal Politikk*, 4: 261–73.

Skardhamar, Thorbjørn (2002) *Levekår og livssituasjon blan innsatte i norske fengsler*.

[Living conditions and life situations among Norwegian inmates]. Oslo: IKRS, University of Oslo.
Skeggs, Beverley (2002) *Formations of Class and Gender*. London: Sage.
Skilbrei, May-Len (2003) 'Dette er jo bare en husmorjobb. Ufaglærte kvinner i arbeidslivet' [This is only the job of a housewife. Unskilled female workers in working life]. Oslo: *NOVA Rapport* 17/2003.
Sykes, Gresham (1958) *The Society of Captives: A Study of a Maximum Security Prison*. Princeton: Princeton University Press.
Ugelvik, Thomas (2010a) 'Å være eller ikke være fange' [To be or not to be a prisoner], Ph.D. thesis. Oslo: IKRS, University of Oslo.
—— (2010b) 'Når er et fengsel som et hotell?' [When is a prison like a hotel?], Retfierd, 1, vol. 34, pp. 85–100.
Vegheim, Berit (1995) *Kvinners møte med straffeapparatet. Del II. Det uforutsigbare systemet og det sårbare fellesskapet*. K-serien nr. 1. Institutt for kriminologi, Universitetet i Oslo.
Weiss, Robert P and Nigel South (eds) (1998) *Comparing Prison Systems: Toward a Comparative and International Penology*. Amsterdam: Gordon and Breach Publishers.

9 A blessing in disguise

Attention deficit hyperactivity disorder diagnosis and Swedish correctional treatment policy in the twenty-first century

Robert Andersson[1]

John Pratt claims that the roots of Scandinavian exceptionalism 'are to be found in the highly egalitarian cultural values and social structures of these societies' (Pratt 2008: 120), central components being a strong welfare state built on belief in social engineering and expert rule. My argument in this chapter is rather the opposite – Scandinavian exceptionalism consists not in egalitarian values but rather in a 'culture of intervention', and that this 'culture' is a requirement for the development of a strong welfare state built on social engineering and expert rule. When the prison was introduced in the Scandinavian countries during the nineteenth century the main ambitions and arguments were social reform, the betterment of the prisoners and prevention (Lundgren 2003; Nilsson 1999; Smith 2003; Schaanning 2007). The prison was a pedagogical project brought on to educate the lower classes morally. The hopes and expectations were big and the prison was seen as something utterly modern (Nilsson 2001; Lundgren 2003: 79). It was a way, as Schaanning (2007) put it, not of punishing less but of punishing more efficiently. The prison, alongside public schooling and problems such as pauperism, was the beginning of a government revolving round and directed at the population and above all the betterment of the same. It was a government built on a rationale that equalized the wealth of the nation to the health of the population, thus making the 'care of' the population into the principle question of government.

As Pratt points out, social engineering and scientific optimism would become the basis of Scandinavian exceptionalism. It was especially one voice of reason that permeated both the process of establishing the cell prison (Lundgren 2003; Nilsson 1999; Smith 2003; Schaanning 2007) and the establishing of a Scandinavian-type of rehabilitative ideal figure (Börjesson 1994; Qvarsell 1993) – the physician. For the physician, above all in the form of the psychiatrist, the prison played a large part in establishing the profession. Nonetheless, the downfall of the rehabilitative ideal in the 1960s and 1970s would come to mean the eviction of the physician as chief scientific expert of crime policy. My hypothesis in this chapter is that we are now witnessing a return of medical science in the prison and that the medical profession is reclaiming its lost position. Still further, this is possible because of a rearticulation of 'the culture of interventionism'. I will also claim that this (re)medicalization of penal policy coincides with, as did the original one, a governmentality permeating the prison as well a society in general. The purpose of this chapter is thus to analyse a return of Scandinavian exceptionalism in terms of moral engineering, expert rule and medical knowledge within the prison. This is to be done by analysing a medical conceptualization of the prisoner in terms of the attention deficit hyperactivity disorder diagnosis (ADHD).

In the first part of this chapter my focus is on the knowledge process. What recurring themes are there in the knowledge making up the ADHD condition? Knowledge is something that is produced rather than uncovered, and knowledge-production produces a subject turning it into something knowable as well as something governable. Drawing on Foucault's conceptualization of power/knowledge, I proceed from the assumption that the will to knowledge cannot be separated from power aspects. To know is to impose power, although what we know cannot be separated from prevailing power structures. Looking at the ADHD-condition as knowledge production is thus to uncover the assembling of a governable subject.

In the second part of the chapter I will try to exemplify what I see as a Swedish culture on intervention. I will also try to paint a trajectory of Swedish penal policy by discussing the differentiation question. Finally I will try to show how the ADHD condition as technology of self is part of an advanced liberal governmentality. I will start, however, with a presentation of the theoretical point of departure.

A way of governing – theoretical point of departure

The governmental state referred to by Foucault's concept of governmentality has the population as its target, political economy as its source of knowledge and the security apparatus as its central technical means (Foucault 1991: 102–4). It builds on a triangle of power comprising the sovereign, discipline and governance. It involves a governance society focused on transforming and optimizing the utilization and training of the population. The style of governance central in this context is a way of thinking about government that Foucault designates as liberalism (Foucault 1991: 102–4). When liberalism became established as a style of governance during the nineteenth century, it became so as *the natural solution* to the question of governing the life of society and the economy. The answer provided involved governing as little as possible – governance was to be restricted and to proceed from and to be organized so as to fit the natural processes of social life, but first and foremost those of the economy (Gordon 1991). Liberalism was framed as the natural answer to the extensive and invasive governance associated with mercantilism. My analysis draws especially on three aspects of the governmentality perspective, *biopolitics*, *advanced liberalism* and *technologies of self*.

Biopolitics is a way of managing people as a group or a population that emerged alongside the establishing of the modern nation-state. In an era where power must be warranted rationally, biopolitics builds on an emphasis on the maintenance and protection of life rather than the right to end life. Through the regulation of the body, and the production of a power formation that has the enhancement of life as its primary focus, biopolitics frames itself as a politics of life. By regulating customs, habits, health, reproductive practices, family, and well-being biopolitics conceptualize the state as a 'body' and the use of state power as essential to life of the social body.

My claim is that what we are witnessing in the Scandinavian societies, as well as the western world, is a form of governance that is part of advanced liberalism (Rose 1999). By that I mean a society where power is de-centred and where the population is expected as well as required to play a most active role through self-government. What is required is a subject able to regulate himself from within. Advanced liberalism is based on giving predominance to market mechanisms and of the restriction of the action of the state, thus acquiring a knowledge production that enables the assembling of self-regulated and self-correcting subjects.

These self-regulating and self-correcting subjects need technologies of self. Governmentality can, as power in general for Foucault, also be defined as a form of conduct of conduct. The regulation of conduct depends on technologies produced by expertise. Expert-produced technologies turn governing into something that is grounded in the authority of science and objectivity, creating a distance between self-regulation and the state (Rose 1996: 156). The technologies of self functions by a logic of choice, by transforming individuals' construction of themselves, thus 'inculcating desires for self-development that expertise itself can guide and through claims to be able to allay the anxieties generated when the actuality of life fails to live up to its image' (Rose 1999: 88).

Advanced liberalism also contains a claim to reduce the scope of government. A central means to do this is through responsibilization. Responsibilization amounts to making the populace conceive of risks such as illness, unemployment, poverty, not as the responsibility of the state, but as part of a domain for which the individual is responsible, thus transforming what used to be welfare state problems into a problem of self-care (Lemke 2001: 201).

ADHD as knowledge production

The central aspect here is: what type of scientific claims-making does the ADHD condition build on and necessitate? It is not just any ordinary psychological claims-making, what we have in the ADHD condition is a claim that we are talking about something inherently biological, a genetic defect. This entails a comeback of a reductive psychiatry with the ambitions to explain and thus colonialize all statements concerning deviant behaviour. Especially noteworthy is the fact that the criminal and the prison as parts of a system of governance build on a certain way of making the object of governance knowable, thus enabling a knowledge production that presupposes as well as produces that which is to be known and governed. It also entails the reoccurrence of the degeneracy theme, a persistent theme since the establishing of a criminological knowledge during the nineteenth century.

What I want to propose is thus that we understand ADHD as part of what Ian Hacking (2001) calls *the degeneracy research programme*. Hacking's argument

ADHD diagnosis and current Swedish correctional policy 159

builds on an analysis of degeneracy research as a *research programme* in the sense intended by Imre Lakatos. The primary reason for Hacking's choice of Lakatos's concept, is that Lakatos insisted that research programmes could go on and on despite repeated failure. Lakatos's argument builds on dividing progress in research programmes into two: (a) *empirical*; and (b) *conceptual* progress. The vitality of the degeneracy programme is not empirical. Over time it has been proved wrong. Yet it has been conceptually productive: 'The degeneracy program has been extraordinarily fertile [. . .] Its hypotheses have usually not panned out, but it regularly adds new hypotheses and new directions of research' (ibid.: 147). The degeneracy programme's hard core consists of two parts:

> First, there is a group of interconnected types of deviancy that are profoundly antisocial, possibly threatening to society itself; these types of deviancy are forms of degeneracy or innate defects in individuals. Second, degeneracy (as the word implies) is intergenerational; it is inherited, or when it is a novel defect, it is the result of throwback or mutation.
>
> (Ibid.: 145)

Hacking (146) points to what he calls allotropic degeneracy. Instead of the direct lineage of inheritance, i.e. that criminal beget criminals and alcoholics beget alcoholics, allotropic degeneracy entail that what appears as alcoholism in one generation can appear as criminality in the next evolving into epilepsy in a third.[2] Subsequently, my argument is that ADHD is part of this allotropic degeneracy research programme. Hacking himself cites an article where researchers announced the discovery of a possible link between a gene named the D2 dopamine receptor gene (DRD2) and autism, drug abuse, ADHD, pathological gambling, alcoholism and Tourette's syndrome.[3] Understanding the ADHD condition, and the research conducted about it, as part of the degeneracy research programme helps us to comprehend how a condition can live on, despite constant empirical failure. The vigorousness of the condition does not stem from empirical progress, but through conceptual growth.

The degeneracy research programme has been part of criminological knowledge production a long time and according to Nicole Rafter (2009: 87–8) the idea of degeneration affected criminological thinking in four important ways. First, it offered an aetiology, and '[d]egeneration is a condition, a state that pre-exists criminal behaviour and somehow cause it' (ibid.). The theorists of degeneracy also identified the aetiology of degeneracy – degeneration was brought on due to 'alcohol abuse, egotism, unhealthy environments, and general immorality' (ibid.). Thus criminality was seen as both *causing* degeneration and being *caused* by degeneration.

Second, the conceptualization of degeneration framed criminological understanding in such a way that association between social ills such as insanity and pauperism and crime became meaningful: 'All of these problems flowed from the underlying condition of degeneration; what mattered was the condition itself, not its external manifestations' (ibid.). The accumulation of social ills in certain circumstances thus got its explanation from the fact that degeneration breeds degeneration. From a degenerations perspective, it is obvious that criminal parents would produce criminal children. This kind of reasoning has been common in the Swedish debate and the fact that that condition mainly has been 'found' in boys from poorer conditions, both economically and socially, has been explained by the fact that the condition is heritable, making social difference and class division biologically given and thus natural (Kärfve 2001).

Third, degeneration theory paved the way for criminal anthropology. If criminals are degenerates, they must also be low on the ladder of evolution. In the same way, ADHD, together with psychopathy research, seems to have the potential to make neuropsychiatry into the new criminal anthropology which can explain everything about crime while at the same time exclude all competing explanations.

Fourth, degeneration mixed well with evolutionism: 'The "fit" evolve, and the degenerate "unfit" devolve. Good people inherit good qualities, bad people a tendency to degenerate' (Rafter 2009: 88). What this amounts to is a moral theory of merit. The emergence of degeneration theory coincided with the growth of the bourgeoisie as the dominant social group, a stratum of society that acquired its rightful status as the leading group in society via a conception of merit. The bourgeoisie's right to govern society was acquired on the basis of personal competence, high moral standards, reason and effectiveness – they deserved to be the ruling class due to their industry and ability. Degeneration theory became part of a form of governance guided by compassion, reason, virtue and efficacy. My argument is subsequently that degeneration theory, as a moral theory of merit, underpinned and rationalized the right to intervene in the lives of those deemed to be degenerates, and that the ADHD condition seems a likely candidate to provide a similar rationale for present-day use. Framing deviant behaviour in this way sustains prevailing social circumstances, making crime fighting into a question of protecting society against social harm. Further, a biologization of inabilities, poor results, and bad grades, make class-specific variations of school results disappear. Working-class boys, overrepresented among those who get the diagnosis, thus belong where they belong as a result of biological inferiority.

The primary 'knowledge' regarding the ADHD condition is not empirical but builds on a diagnostics manual that defines it. The *Diagnostic and Statistical Manual of Mental Disorders* (DSM) is published by the American Psychiatric Association (APA) and is designed to provide a common language and standard criteria for the classification of mental disorders.[4] The DSM has been revised five times since its first publication in 1952. The most important revision of the DSM so far, was DSM III in 1980. This revision meant that the manual left its original foundation in Freudian psychology and turned instead to classifying mental disorders in terms of symptoms, thus abandoning all claims concerning aetiology. It also meant abandoning an understanding of normal/abnormal as something continues and with the same basic causation for an understanding that place normal–abnormal in a dichotomous relationship (Brante 2006: 73). However, reading those who advocate the condition and its treatment, what emerges is a cumulative positivistic history telling a story about scientific exploration towards completion – it is a voyage uncovering both the extent of the problem and its cause.

The idea that children with behavioural problems have an impairment caused by brain problems occurred for the first time in the 1920s. Hyperactivity, antisocial behaviour and emotional instability were thought to be caused by meningitis in children. The same phenomena were thought to be observed where other brain damage was present. In 1937, Bradley reported that hyperactive children responded to treatment with amphetamine (Kärfve 2001: 35). In the 1950s the first form of the condition emerged in the terms of *minimal brain damage* (MBD), *hyperactive syndrome*, *hyperkinesias* and *hyperactive disorder of childhood* (Conrad 2007: 49). In the second version of the DSM, in the late 1960s, MBD and hyperkinetic reaction came to be understood primarily as childhood disorders, even though the DSM II opened up for the possibility that the condition could persist into adulthood (Conrad 2007: 49). The year 1980 saw the new DSM III, being a manual based on symptoms it included more behaviours in the diagnosis making it more wide ranging and '[t]hese changes in the diagnostics category meant that individuals who may not have 'qualified' for a diagnosis of hyperkinetic reaction or minimal brain damage under DSM-II could now be thought of as having *attention-deficit disorder* (ADD) under DSM-III' (ibid.: 51). In 1987, with the revised DSM III-R, ADD was renamed *attention deficit hyperactivity disorder* (ADHD). Merging hyperactivity and inattentiveness into one diagnosis made it possible to increase the number of children being diagnosed by 50 per cent (ibid.).

MBD is an interesting diagnosis and looking it up in a Swedish psychology encyclopaedia, it is presented as the forerunner to ADHD, and as more or less equivalent to this diagnosis. This cumulative explanation is given elsewhere as well, and appears to have become the generally accepted history of the condition. This implies an empirical knowledge progress; the movement from the MBD diagnosis was brought on by knowledge enhancement, hence the ADHD diagnosis is based on more knowledge than the MBD diagnosis. Accordingly we now know more about the condition. But this is far from the truth, since the ADHD condition is not defined by scientific means but by definition only. MBD had an aetiology, but having an aetiology made it open to empirical falsification, and the diagnosis met its permanent death[5] around 1987, being lifted out of DSM IV (Kärfve 2001: 41).

In the American setting, MBD slowly mutated first into ADD and thereafter into ADHD. In Sweden, MBD was replaced by the diagnosis *deficits in attention, motor control and perception* (DAMP). Mainly the work of one physician, DAMP was, according to sociologist Kärfve, nothing more than a renaming of MBD. Writing a book scrutinizing the DAMP diagnosis, Kärfve caused such great disturbance that it all ended up in court. When the court decided in favour of Kärfve, she wanted to review the empirical material that researchers made their claims on, the psychiatrists decided on destroying the material instead.[6] This 'science war', waged in the first years of the twenty-first century, appears to have left little traces of itself since neuropsychiatric research in Sweden is back in business again.

MBD–DAMP has merged nicely with ADHD making it hard to tell them apart, except for the claim that DAMP is actually a severe form of ADHD.[7]

Turning ADHD into a diagnosis for adults started with follow-up studies done in the late 1970s, on children diagnosed as hyperactive a decade earlier, studies that claimed that some of the symptoms persisted into adolescences and even into adulthood (Conrad 2007: 50).[8] Yet, all adults with ADHD had had the condition as children and adults whose diagnosis had been missed in childhood or adult onset was not yet in the discussion. Nonetheless, it was to be layperson publications that gave adult ADHD the means to really spread its wings as a diagnosis.[9] Typically in these publications, the authors confessed their disabilities, the problem the disabilities had caused them, and related the relief felt once the epiphany of the diagnosis had come to them. Together with other stakeholders such as patients' interest groups, these confessions brought personal suffering to the surface, putting adult ADHD on the scene.

Turning instead to the question of aetiology, the material ontology of neuropsychiatry becomes apparent. Since ontologically there is no room for non-material things such as concepts, feelings, culture and the like – what we must be observing when we observe behaviour is brain/mental reactions to stimuli. The inability to sit still is thus not a cultural understanding of behaviour, but a brain–body reaction to stimuli. The latest aetiology stand is that ADHD has an epigenetic causation (Smith *et al.* 2009). Epigenetics is the study of inherited changes in gene expression caused by mechanisms other than changes in the underlying DNA sequence, hence the prefix *epi-*, meaning over, above *genetics*.[10] Thus, non-genetic factors cause the organism's genes to behave differently, hence facilitating the reappearance of several classical 'causes', causes that all correspond to the behaviour of mothers during pregnancy, such as smoking, drinking or taking drugs. This also means that the epigenetic standpoint carries a potential for solving another recurring problem; the 5:1 overrepresentation of boys over girls being diagnosed with the condition (ibid.: 146). Overrepresentation as a problem arose when the genetic aetiology was launched. When hyperactivity was caused by brain damage, overrepresentation caused no problem since it could be claimed to be due to chance. With the epigenetic turn, overrepresentation can once again be explained in terms of chance and the behaviour of the mother during pregnancy. Opening up for external factors causing genetic changes as well as protecting the claim that ADHD is a neurological condition the epigenetic stand appears to be the ideal aetiology for neuropsychiatry for a while to come.[11]

Looking at the prevalence question it becomes apparent that the uncertainty surrounding ADHD breeds certainty; diverging results are always summarized into certainty. Every brochure or pamphlet informing the general public, medical practitioners or politicians, give certain answers to the prevalence question. Of children up to the age of 19 years, 3 to 7 per cent are afflicted by the condition, and 2 to 5 per cent of the adult population.[12] Nonetheless, voices are raised claiming that the DSM is too strict because of the early-onset criteria (Bitter *et al.* 2010). Drop the criterion, i.e. that at least one of the symptoms most have been present before the age of 7, and the number diagnosed with adult ADHD would greatly expand.[13] Thus, proponents for losing the criterion claim that, since likeliness of being diagnosed relates to age, what is happening is that people are *outgrowing the diagnosis – not outgrowing the condition* (ibid.).

Interestingly enough, prevalence studies on prisoners seems to have its roots in Sweden. The 'groundbreaking' study, conducted at the prison in Visby, Gotland, claimed that 25 per cent of the Swedish prison population had ADHD (Dalteg *et al.* 1998). A recurring feature in many prevalence studies is the fact that they are cross-sectional studies. In studies of that type, the selection criteria should be well grounded if one wants to infer anything about the population in general.[14] Dalteg *et al* (1998)[15] thus seem to make a rather weighty assumption when they claim that the subjects making up their study 'can be assumed to be representative of a normal Swedish prison clientele'.[16]

But claims are also made that 55 per cent of violent offenders are inflicted (Swedish Correctional Service 2005). The pedigree of these figures is an unpublished report, and 55 is actually 51.6, or 145 out of 281 inmates sentenced to long sentences.[17] The figures as such stem from the National Reception Unit (NRU) at the Kumla correctional facility; where all prisoners sentenced to four years or more are sent for a psychiatric screening and a risk evaluation. The opening of the NRU in 1997 was based on a belief that the number of prison escapes had risen dramatically in Sweden (Andersson and Nilsson 2009). The opening of and operations at the NRU also visualize the Swedish 'culture of intervention'. With its steady flow of empirical material, NRU has turned Sweden into one of the leading nations in psychopathy research (Hörnqvist 2007).

The return of the culture of intervention and re-enactment of a new governmentality

With the proposal for a new penal code in 1956 the 'culture of intervention' reached a zenith (SOU 1956: 59). The proposal was for a protective code where the criminals should as far as possible be turned over to psychiatric care. The proposal was egalitarian in the sense that sane or insane was to be treated as the same before the law and sanctions were adapted to suit the ailment of the offender (Qvarsell 1993: 330). Even though the entire proposal was not enacted, it is a telling example of the culture of intervention, a culture that has also produced ideas such as turning a middle-sized Swedish town into a laboratory for crime prevention, prevention based on mental hygiene and individual prevention (SOU 1964: 59). The overly interventionist fosterage mission assigned to Swedish schools during the twentieth century led one researcher to call it 'a nationalization of the soul of the children' (Broady: 131).

The culture of intervention can be interpreted as a major factor in installing the Swedish welfare state – a state that in the name of public good took upon itself to enhance its citizenry through medicine. Institutes such as the National Institute for Racial Biology (established 1922 on a social-democratic proposal and renamed in 1958 as the Institute for Medical Genetics) and laws such as the sterilization law (1934–76) illustrate that the pedigree of the welfare state sees eugenics and evolutionism in its 'ancestry'. The Swedish welfare state can thus be seen as biopolitics par excellence. The will to knowledge and the care of the population that underpinned the Swedish welfare state was primarily a medical knowledge that placed itself above individual considerations. Deviation in any way was an indicator of something being wrong, and if something was wrong, it was up to the state and its officials and civil servants to find a cure or remedy; preferably through expert-led interventions. It's a culture where the civil servant, the administrator and the physician 'make up the rules', the rights of individuals and the rule of law is overridden by administrative decision.[18] It was governance based on social engineering, which intervened in the name of public good. Nevertheless, the downfall of the rehabilitative ideal in the 1960 and 1970s can in many ways also be seen as the abandonment of the culture of invention.

Knowledge and differentiation

My hypotheses, that we are witnessing a return of medical science in the prison wherein the medical profession is reclaiming its lost position, can also be exemplified by the setting up of a scientific council in the prison services, a council primarily manned by physicians.[19] The council's task is to scientifically certify treatment programmes. Furthermore Sweden has come to see the opening of the Centre for Violence Prevention (CPV).[20] Manned by psychiatrists the centre is part of the biggest Swedish university hospital. The rationale of the council as well as the centre seem to be 'what works', framing research as assessment and evaluation based on risk analysis. In many ways, what is happening in the Swedish prison today could be seen as a continuation of the benevolent welfare state. The strong belief in reform and the reliance upon the medical profession (see Nilsson 1999; Schaanning 2007) seem to be the same. Nevertheless, this (re)medicalization of prison policy, sides with a new way of governing permeating the prison as well as society in general – a governmentality best visualized by its conceptualization of liberty.

Present-day conceptualization of liberty is in terms of the free market and the ability to make rational choices on this market, freedom is thus to make use of the faculty of reason in a situation based on choice. Liberty is freedom to choose. Looking at the changes in Swedish penal policy since the 1990s, we see that governing through the instating of individualized choices has been a guiding principle, hence the introduction of treatment programmes assuming a free will (Andersson 2004; Petersson 2003), the ambitions, still unaffected, to reinstall a facultative release on probation or the introduction of conditional release by means of electronic surveillance. The question of differentiation, i.e. on what grounds inmates should be sorted according to their need for treatment, is the key in understanding Swedish penal policy during the twentieth and twenty-first centuries. Differentiation is the essence of the rehabilitative ideal in both practice and theory. The differentiation of the 'clientele' was essential to the application of the correct, individualized, treatment. But differentiation was also the number-one enemy of the critics of the rehabilitative ideal; it was the inability to correctly differentiate, combined with sanctions such as the undetermined sentencing, which made the rehabilitative ideal both implausible and unsound. In Sweden, the critique resulted in a major penal reform in 1989, whereby prevention, and especially individual preventive reasoning, came to be replaced by a retributive rationale in adjudication (Andersson 2002).

The downfall of the rehabilitative ideal also brought on a legitimization of the prison claiming that, even though the prison was in itself something bad to be used only as a last resort due to its overwhelmingly negative effects, it was unavoidable due to its general deterrent effects (ibid.). Nevertheless, during the late 1980s and beginning of the 1990s, narcotics, framed as the main problem for the correctional service, became an argument for differentiation. Thus both prison and differentiation as inherently bad got outweighed by something essentially even worse – narcotics. The innately negative effects of narcotics turned into an argument for both a harsher and stricter prison regime and a need to differentiate resulting in special narcotics wings.[21]

Swedish penal policy has also come to see a leaner regime. With the use of alternative sanctions, as well as different therapeutic programmes based on cognitive behavioural therapy, the rationale of correctional treatment seems to be split in half. A harsher policy, directed at 'serious' crime, i.e. sentenced to more than two years' imprisonment, coexist with a lenient policy set to deal with 'everyday' crime (Andersson and Nilsson 2009). In this we see a decisive change: during the welfare state crime policy was part of a governance aiming at installing a good work ethics, making subjects know their station in life, and enabling citizens to contribute to the general good of society, hence institutions, such as the school and the prison, where there to implement a form of governance turning the population into a useful asset. The hidden curriculum of the present-day rehabilitative ideal is not to counteract laziness and install a healthy work ethics. The Swedish prison of today and its reform programmes are all about teaching freedom of choice and making one assume responsibility for one's choices (Andersson 2004). The goal is a form of self-knowledge, available through the confession of one's faults, which is to be realized through the care of oneself and successful self-management (Petersson 2003). The goal of this process is the production of a prudent citizen capable of constituting part of the governmental visions of advanced liberalism (Andersson 2002, 2004; Petersson 2003). It is a government aiming at stimulating a personal responsibility that should manifest itself in actively taking charge over and managing one's own punishment, schooling or personal growth, sought after is thus an active subject made accountable for his or her choice.

ADHD as part of a (neo-)liberal governmentality

If, as is claimed, something like 25 to 55 per cent of the Swedish prison population have an epigenetically caused impairment, an impairment that can be treated with good results in terms of recidivism, then we should be on the verge of the biggest breakthrough in correctional treatment ever.

There are at the moment two ADHD projects in the Swedish correctional service. Both of these build on the premise that recidivism can be prevented by medicating inmates with amphetamine. The projects originate from the National Psychiatric Coordination (NPC). NPC was set to evaluate as well as support and initiate research projects concerning psychiatric health.[22] The projects, both allegedly very successful, entail both a moral engineering assembling the subject to be corrected and a biopolitics aimed at utilizing the population.

As moral engineering, ADHD is about the inability to control oneself in a morally correct fashion, it's a moral pathology. The moral absolution brought on by the pathology associated with social engineering is replaced by a moral responsibilization – offenders are imprisoned not, as genetic threat to the national stock, but 'as intractable individuals unable to govern themselves according to the civilized norms of a liberal society of freedom' (Rose 2000: 22). As opposed to the biological determinism of the eugenics movement, we now face a governance in which people are expected to know, and hence can be held responsible for, their genetic constitution (Rose 2007).

Furthermore, ADHD as moral engineering becomes a re-instating of the bourgeoisie self-image. It is by applying control over oneself one begets the faculty of reason. Through the curbing of one's impulses, one might reach the high moral standards, reason and effectiveness that make one into a pillar of society. Imprisonment, on the other hand, depicts the opposite – an inability to curb one's impulses and control oneself; thus lacking the moral fibre of the prudent citizen. As a pathologization of the lack of self-control the ADHD condition also merges with the dominant crime prevention model – the control model (Andersson and Nilsson 2009; Garland 2001; Sahlin 2000). Since crime in every form stems from a lack of control, whether this is lack of control over situations or individuals, producing control becomes the preferred solution.

Based on a utilitarian logic of intervention the projects echo the rationale of social engineering. Nonetheless, what underpins the projects is a rationale of risk; it's not about the betterment of the stock, rather it's about screening and thus countering risks within the population. As biopolitical tool, the ADHD condition builds on framing the untreated condition as a potent and potential risk factor. Left untreated the condition can turn into high leave of absence due to sickness, unemployment, drug abuse and criminality. The remedy ordered is early screening and early intervention (Rodriguez et al. 2007). Based on assumptions of great societal costs,[23] a biopolitics of risk, i.e. intervening into people's lives to insure against misfortunes via neuropsychiatric knowledge becomes framed as something economically sound as well as ethically reasonable. Especially so, since, otherwise imprisoned and unlucky souls are given a life worth living.

The effects of the projects are not yet fully evaluated – they are to end during 2010 – still the Swedish correctional service has had an evaluation done (Swedish Correctional Service 2010). The reasoning in the study builds entirely on biopolitics of risk – the main argument being that programmes such as these can, and probably will, facilitate great cuts in costs for authorities. Just by preventing recidivism among the 30 inmates constituting one of the projects would in itself reduce costs by round about 800 million Swedish kronor!

Concluding remarks

I am inclined to accept a notion of Scandinavian exceptionalism. However, instead of interpreting it as something normatively positive, my argument is that the exceptionalism is rather a case of being good at enforcing policy by means of a culture of intervention. A strong belief in what is perceived as a benevolent government makes for expertise, as well as professionals, trusted to do good and thus being entrusted with the lives of the populace. I have long nourished the idea to explore what I perceive as the total incarceration level, i.e. incarcerated in both the prison and mental hospitals. In Sweden the abandonment of the mental asylum has come to result in a growing number of prisoners with psychiatric problem, something also witnessed in Norway (Dullum 2009). Stumbling onto Harcourt's (2010) article on neo-liberal penality, I found that what, among other things, Harcourt was presenting figures of the total incarceration level in the USA. As I see it Harcourt (ibid.: 76) shows three things; first, that the overall incarceration rate has gone down since a peak in the mid-1960s; second, that that the prison has come to replace the mental hospitals as the main means of incarceration; and, third, that the period from the late 1960s to the early 1970s should be conceived as an anomaly – a temporary dip in the incarceration level.

As I interpret Harcourt, the question concerning American exceptionalism might be wrongly put since the total incarceration level seems to have gone down at the same time as the numbers imprisoned has risen. What the total incarceration level has looked like historically in the Scandinavian countries, I do not know. Nevertheless, since the 1990s, Sweden has seen an ongoing debate based on the assumptions that sentencing criminals to psychiatric care is too lenient as punishment and that they, once they're declared sane, should be turned over to the prison to serve out whatever is left of the punishment meted out. Even opening up mental hospital wings has been proposed. To summarize: as the ADHD research shows, no one doubts that the psychiatric health of our prisoners is a deteriorating problem. Nonetheless there seems to be no debate about turning these prisoners over to psychiatric care. The general assumption is that they still deserve to be imprisoned – they are still responsible for their crimes. A responsibilization reinforced by the CBT reform programmes used in prison – programmes that builds on making the prisoner take responsibility for his actions, thus also contribute in the making of imprisonment into a reasonable answer to former actions (Andersson 2004).

If, as I now assume, the prison has taken over from the mental asylum as primary incarceration facility, this signals a biopolitics based on a corrective punishment in which a personal responsibility, manifesting itself in actively taking charge over and managing one´s own punishment, producing an active subject accountable for his choices. The ADHD condition enables this kind of subject since it absolves from neither responsibility nor moral blame – rather the 'curability' of the condition builds on a subject taking accountability over medicating himself.

As part of a reformulation of the culture of intervention the two ADHD projects are extremely interesting: once again the voice of the expert seems to stand unchallenged in Swedish correctional treatment. As such, the projects are initiated, governed and to be evaluated by experts. Nowhere is there anything implying that this is a question of policy, there is no opposition to be heard – this is not penal policy, this is just science being applied.

Notes

1. The initial research done for this chapter was financed by the Scandinavian Research Council for Criminology.
2. In an information sheet concerning crime and ADHD published by the Swedish patient interest group, Attention, it is claimed that 'You do not inherit criminality, what you inherit is personal properties or capacities that in an unfavourable interplay increase the risks.'
3. Concerning the question of 'culture of intervention': Hacking (2001) points to the fact that the rather integrity-violating methods used to collect the empirical material for the study would hardly be permitted in Anglo-Saxon countries. I don't know whether this is so or not, but the study Hacking refers to was carried out in Finland, and I know that questions concerning integrity play a rather minor role in Sweden if any preventive measures seem to be within reach.
4. http://en.wikipedia.org/wiki/Diagnostic_and_Statistical_Manual_of_Mental_Disorders
5. The vitality of these concepts is striking, even if formally dead they can come to life in different settings. Thus MBD appears in a report from the Swedish crime prevention council in 2001, *Kriminell utveckling: tidiga riskfaktorer och förebyggande insatser*, Brå 2001: 15, 34.
6. This affair has been seen as the worst 'science battle' in Sweden, with professors in psychiatry demanding that Kärfve should be made to leave her position at Lunds University (www.dn.se/nyheter/vetenskap/hjarnkampen-1.187302).
7. http://user.tninet.se/~fxg297r/diagnos_damp.htm
8. The prevalence numbers given in one of the studies, 66 per cent, have become one of those magical numbers that float around in the generalized descriptions of adult ADHD. See for example www.lul.se/templates/page_3647.aspx. What's interesting is the small number making up the study; a more than common theme is this research programme. Out of 75 test subjects in the initial study only 60 per cent took part in the follow-up (Conrad 2007: 50).
9. Frank Wolkenberg got his diagnosis when, seeking help for depression and suicidal ideation, he received treatment from a psychologist *who specialized in learning disorders* (ibid.: 52).
10. There is, however, no change in the underlying DNA sequence of the organism.
11. Recall Hacking's words on the causes of degeneracy: 'or when it is a novel defect, it is the result of throwback or mutation' (2001: 145).
12. The difference between having 3 or 7 per cent of the population under 19 years inflicted would in Sweden amount to having either 65,070 or 152,830 children with ADHD. The higher percentage would increase the prevalence by 2.33. In the adult population the figures are 144,340 or 360,850, an increase of 2.5.
13. On important factor in establishing the adult condition is recollection of childhood behaviour. Interviewing parents or siblings is the common procedure in establishing the existence of early onset.
14. Appelbaum (2008: 1521) concludes his overview of prevalence studies in prisons by stating that the studies often 'rely on limited sources of information, retrospective reviews of symptoms [. . .] or small and nonrepresentative inmate samples'.
15. One argument for choosing the Visby correctional facility might have been the fact that

the main author of the article at the time was a resident at Visby psychiatric clinic and probably had easy access to the inmates.
16 My translation. The cormorbidity of this section of the Swedish prison population appears rather heavy since 75 per cent had personality disorders and drug abuse, 25 per cent were psychopaths, 33 per cent hade life-long prevalence diagnosis in anxiety disorders (ibid.: 3079).
17 The source given in the report is Peter Johansson, one of the psychologists who do the assessing at the NRU. To the best of my knowledge, these figures cannot be found anywhere else.
18 For a telling example concerning the powers of psychiatric care in Sweden, see Qvarsell (1993: 303).
19 www.kriminalvarden.se/sv/Om-Kriminalvarden/Forskning-och-utveckling-i-Kriminalvarden/Vetenskapliga-radet/
20 www.cvp.se/about/index.html
21 The culture of interventionism shows itself in the Swedish narcotics code, wherein use is penalized. This goes against the classical liberal argument, promoted among other by J. S Mill, that what you do to yourself and your body is no one's business but your own. Having western Europe's highest mortality rates as a consequence is seen as acceptable due to assumed societal gains.
22 As part of the abandonment of the culture of intervention due to the downfall of the rehabilitative ideal a reform was enacted in 1994 that consisted in closing the big psychiatric asylums. The homelessness problem witnessed in Swedish today is partly due to the reform, since subjects who had spent the greater part of their lives inside these asylums were given flats to live in on their own, soon to be evicted. In consequence the number of persons with psychiatric problems visible on city streets increased and at the beginning of the twenty-first century, a few so-called nutcase accidents involving persons with psychiatric disorders made the reform into a problem. NPC was to evaluate the reform.
23 This line of reasoning was present already in Richard Dygdales's study on the Jukes. One of Dygdales's main arguments was the costs to be saved by intervening in the lives of the unfit.

References

Andersson, R. (2002) *Kriminalpolitikens väsen* [The essence of crime policy], Avhandlingsserie nr. 10, Kriminologiska institutionen, Stockholms universitet 2002.

—— (2004) 'Behandlingstankens återkomst – från psykoanalys till kognitiv beteendeterapi [The reappearing rehabilitative ideal – from psychoanalysis to CBT], *Nordisk tidskrift for kriminalvidenskab*, 91(5): 384–403.

Andersson, R. and R. Nilsson (2009) *Svensk kriminalpolitik* [Swedish crime policy], Liber: Malmö.

Appelbaum, K. L. (2008) 'Assessment and Treatment of Correctional Inmates with ADHD', *American journal of Psychiatry*, 165(12): 1520–4.

Bitter, I., V. Simon, S. Bálint, Á Mészaros and P. Czobor (2010) 'How Do Different Diagnostic Criteria, Age and Gender Affect the Prevalence of Attention Deficit Hyperactivity Disorder in Adults? An Epidemiological Study in a Hungarian Community Sample', *European Archives of Psychiatry and Clinical Neuroscience*, 260(4): 287–96.

Börjesson, M. (1994) *Sanningen om brottsligen: Rättspsykiatrin som kartläggning av livsöden* [The truth concerning criminal: forensic psychiatry as charting destiny] Stockholm: Carlssons.

Brante, T. (2006) 'Den nya psykiatrin: exemplet ADHD' [The new psychiatry: ADHD as an example] in G. Hallerstedt (ed.), *Diagnosens makt: Om kunskap, pengar och lidande*. Göteborg: Diadalos.
Burchell, G., C. Gordon and P. Miller (eds) (1991) *The Foucault Effect: Studies in Governmentality*. Chicago: University of Chicago Press.
Conrad, P. (2007) *The Medicalization of Society: On the Transformation of Human Conditions into Treatable Disorders*. Baltimore: Johns Hopkins University Press.
Dalteg, A., P. Gustafsson and S. Levander (1998) 'Hyperaktivitetssyndrom vanligt bland interner' [Hyperactivity syndrome is common among interns] *Läkartidningen*, 95(26–27): 3078–80.
Dullum, J. (2009) 'Fengslene og de psykiatriske institusjonene' [Prisons and psychiatric institutions] *Nordisk tidsskrift for kriminalvidenskab*, 96(1): 35–53.
Foucault, M. (1991) 'Governmentality', in G. Burchell, C. Gordon and P. Miller (eds), *The Foucault Effect: Studies in Governmentality*. Chicago: University of Chicago Press.
Garland, D. (2001) *Culture of Control: Crime and Social Order in Contemporary Society*. Oxford: Oxford University Press.
Hacking, I. (2001) 'Degeneracy, Criminal Behavior and Looping', in D. Wasserman and R. Wachbroit (eds), *Genetics and Criminal Behaviour*. Cambridge: Cambridge University Press.
Hallerstedt, G. (ed.) (2006), *Diagnosens makt: Om kunskap, pengar och lidande* [The Power of the diagnosis: Concerning knowledge, money and suffering] Göteborg: Diadalos.
Harcourt, B. (2010) 'Neoliberal Penality: A Brief Genealogy', *Theoretical Criminology*, 14(1): 74–92.
Hörnqvist, M. (2007) 'Psykopatfabriken. Det olyckliga äktenskapet mellan kriminalvård och psykopatforsning' [The psychopath factory. The unfortunate marriage of correctional service and psychopath research] in A. Nilsson and H. von Hofer (eds), *Brott i välfärden*. Stockholm: Kriminologiska institutionen.
Kärfve, E. (2001) *Hjärnspöken: DAMP och hotet mot folkhälsan* [Figments of the mind: DAMP as a public health problem] Symposion: Stockholm.
Lemke, T. (2001) 'The Birth of Bio-Politics: Michael Foucault's Lectures at the Collège de France on Neo-liberal Governmentality', *Economy and Society*, 30(2): 190–207.
Lundgren, F. (2003) *Den isolerade medborgaren: liberalt styre och uppkomsten av det sociala vid 1800-talets mitt* [The isolated citizen: liberal government and the origins of the social question in mid-19th century] Hedemora: Gidlunds.
Nilsson, A. and H. von Hofer (eds) (2007) *Brott i välfärden* [Crimes in the welfare], Stockholm: Kriminologiska institutionen.
Nilsson, R. (1999) *En välbyggd maskin, en mardröm för själen. Det svenska fängelsesystemet under 1800-talet* [A Well-Built Machine, A Nightmare For The Soul. The Swedish prison system during the 19th century], Lund: Lund University Press.
Petersson, K. (2003) *Fängelset och den liberala fantasin: en studie om rekonstruktionen av det moraliska subjektet inom svensk kriminalvård* [The prison and the liberal imagination: a study concerning the re-construction of a moral subject with in Swedish correctional care], Norrköping: Kriminalvårdsstyrerelsen.
Pratt, J. (2008). 'Scandinavian Exceptionalism in an Era of Penal Excess: Part I: The Nature and Roots of Scandinavian Exceptionalism', *British Journal of Criminology*, 48(2): 119–37.
Qvarsell, R. (1993) *Utan vett och vilja: om synen på brottslighet och sinnesjukdom* [Without intent: concerning criminality and mental illness], Stockholm: Carlssons.

Rafter, N (ed.) (2009) *The Origins of Criminology: A Reader*. Routledge: New York.
Rodriguez, A., Järvelin, M. R. *et al.* (2007) 'Do Inattention and Hyperactivity Symptoms Equal Scholastic Impairment? Evidence from Three European Cohorts', *British Journal of Criminology*, 7(1): 327–36.
Rose, N. (1996) *Inventing Our Selves*. Cambridge: Cambridge University Press.
—— (1999) *Powers of Freedom: Reframing Political Thought*. Cambridge: Cambridge University Press.
—— (2000) 'The Biology of Culpability: Pathological Identity and Crime Control in a Biological Culture', *Theoretical Criminology*, 4(1): 5–34.
—— (2007) *The Politics of Life Itself: Biomedicine, Power, and Subjectivity in the Twenty-First Century*. Princeton: Princeton University Press.
Sahlin, I. (2000) *Brottsprevention som begrepp och samhällsfenomen* [Crime prevention as concept and social phenomenon], Lund: Arkiv.
Schaanning, E. (2007) *Menneskelaboratoriet: Botsfengelsets historie* [A laboratory on humanity: the history of the penitentiary]. Oslo: Scandinavian Academic Press.
Swedish Crime Prevention Council (2001) *Kriminell utveckling: tidiga riskfaktorer och förebyggande insatser* [Deliquent development: early risk factors and preventive measures]. Bråraport 2001: 15.
Swedish Correctional Service (SCS) (2005) 'Final report concerning inmates with neuropsychiatric disabilities', 2003-12-11.
—— (2005) *Unga män i anstalt och häkte* [Young men in prison and remand prison]. Slutrapport, February.
—— (2010) 'Bättre sent än aldrig: utvärdering av ADHD-projektet på Norrtäljeanstalten' [Better late than never: an evaluation of the ADHD project at Norrtälje prison], 15 February.
SOU (1956) *Skyddslag* [A Societal protection law].
—— (1964) 'Aktion mot ungdomsbrott' [Drive against juvenile delinquency].
Smith, A. K., E. Mick and S. V. Faraone (2009) 'Advances in Genetic Studies of Attention-Deficit/Hyperactivity Disorder', *Current Psychiatry Reports*, 11: 143–8.
Smith, P. Scharff (2003) *Moraliske hospitaler – Det modern fængselvæsens gennembrud 1770–1870* [Moral hospitals – the breakthrough of the modern prison 1770–1870], Forum: Köpenhamn.
Wasserman, D. and R. Wachbroit (eds) (2001) *Genetics and Criminal Behaviour*. Cambridge: Cambridge University Press.

Part IV
Closing in on the Nordic II
Prison management and prison cultures

10 Are liberal-humanitarian penal values and practices exceptional?

Ben Crewe and Alison Liebling

In this chapter we present some of the findings from a recent interview-based study of the professional biographies and values of a very large sample of senior managers currently working in prisons in England and Wales. Some of the questions we are asking ourselves are: can correctional senior managers be decent, liberal, humanitarian professionals 'doing justice'? Under what circumstances, and at what points in history, has this been more or less the case? How are the tasks of punishing and 'being humanitarian' reconciled in a management role? The task we have set ourselves is not an easy one.

Some scholars (e.g. Gallo and Ruggiero 1991) have argued that a liberal-humanitarian prison is a contradiction in terms, given the inherently punitive nature of penal institutions. However, some prison systems appear considerably less severe and more humane than others (Pratt 2008a) and attempts have been made, usually in the margins of more traditional containment functions, to experiment with liberal and humanitarian or progressive versions of confinement: in Britain, for example, the Borstal system, open prisons, regimes for long-term prisoners, and within the long-term system, small units for difficult and challenging prisoners (Bottoms and McClintock 1973; Jones and Cornes 1977; Advisory Council on the Penal System 1968; Bottomley and Hay 1991). David Garland goes so far as to describe an entire historical phase in criminal justice (1914–1980s) as welfare oriented in its values, during which a combination of humanitarian and 'corrective' or remedial impulses dominated official thinking (Garland 1985). Our understanding of this so-called penal-welfare phase, shaped by a kind of oral history of those who worked in it, is that its scope was limited in practice and that the official penal rhetoric espoused by policy elites was resisted or regarded as irrelevant by most prison officers at the time.

Our main task in this chapter, which is the first step in a more detailed analysis we are working on, is to reflect on the extent to which liberal-humanitarian values in particular are present today among senior prison managers in the United Kingdom or whether they are, and always have been, exceptional.[1] Senior practitioner ideologies receive fairly scant attention in most accounts of penal culture. In his analysis of Scandinavian exceptionalism, Pratt (2008a) refers to a culture of 'expert-dominated' policymaking, historically 'well insulated' from the drivers of punitive excess (see also Warner 2009). His direct references to the influence of prison authorities come in his pessimistic prognosis of future penal trends, where they strike a comparatively optimistic tone: 'liberal opinion [. . .] seems deeply embedded in penal thinking and administration in Norway and would likely provide significant resistance' to penal populism (Pratt 2008b: 284). In Norway and Finland, at least, Pratt argues that prison officials seem committed to maintaining 'exceptional' (by which we assume he means liberal-humanitarian) prison conditions (see for example, Norwegian Ministry of Justice 2010). Meanwhile, Lacey (2008) argues that in coordinated market economies (such as the Nordic nations) there is greater deference to the professional bureaucracy, including policy advisers and prison officials, than in liberal market economies (such as the UK), with less expectation that bureaucrats exhibit political neutrality. Both authors suggest that these characteristics are important contributors to penal tolerance.

The orientations and ideologies of practitioners and policymakers merit greater consideration because these figures play a role both in shaping penal policy and in its implementation.[2] A 'bottom-up' professional and organizational description helps us to understand penal cultures in the two senses in which Pratt and others (see, for example, Cavadino and Dignan 2006) use the term: in relation to imprisonment rates and other aspects of policy, and in relation to everyday prison conditions. An analysis of this kind can provide insight into the professional cultures that reflect and refract wider cultural discourses about offenders, and which in turn relate to broader social and institutional arrangements (Cavadino and Dignan 2006; Pratt 2008a; Lacey 2008). If the United Kingdom represents a 'neo-liberal' society, in terms of its political economy, then we would expect to find the idioms of neo-liberalism in the views and values of significant sub-groups of its senior correctional managers (professional ideologies may vary by, for example, age group, gender, and social class as well as over time). The testimonies of professional insiders are also useful in identifying the disparities between what is said at the highest levels of an organization and what is translated into practice on the ground. This discrepancy between official ideology and the reality of the prison experience may help explain some of the differences between outsider and insider accounts of Nordic penality (see Chapter 1 in this book, by Dullum and Ugelvik).

A brief history of liberal-humanitarian penality in England and Wales

Alexander Paterson is credited with 'placing the liberalising stamp upon our penal system' during his reign as a member of the Prison Commission between 1922 and 1947 (Jones and Cornes 1977: 5; Thomas 1972). He famously argued that 'a man is sent to prison *as* punishment and not for punishment', attempting to set limits to the role of retribution in prisons, and to make room for 'training'. His belief that 'you cannot train a man for freedom in conditions of captivity' led to the opening of the first open prison in Britain. Largely as a result of the flourishing Borstal system, England became 'a world centre of the prison reform movement' (Thomas 1972: 156).[3] There were anti-liberal currents throughout this period, some of which were expressed by the Prison Officers' Association (POA), but from 1922 to sometime in the 1980s there existed an identifiable body of liberal-humanitarian governors who found their ideals affirmed and supported in the field, in government, and elsewhere.

Borstals were abolished in 1988, the last remaining open prisons are currently under review, and regimes for long-term prisoners, who now serve extremely long sentences with highly demanding sentence conditions, must meet stringent new tests of 'public acceptability' for all aspects of their regimes. It is possible that local prisons for remand and shorter sentence prisoners, once considered the least 'humane' portion of the British penal estate, now constitute the most reformed and humanitarian part of the system. Most prisoners now face a deeper, heavier, 'tighter' and less liberal version of imprisonment than their predecessors, with some Victorian notions of individual responsibility and less eligibility returning in new guises. The contemporary policy and political context shaping late modern penality is somewhat punitive and austere.

The research process

We are interested in what these developments mean in practice, including to those operating at senior levels in the prison service, and have been interrogating the relationship between professional ideologies and prison cultures as part of a wider study of values, practices and outcomes in public and private corrections.[4] In this chapter, we focus on two questions: first, what are the main sources and characteristics of the contemporary penal value base in England and Wales? Second, is there an identifiable 'liberal' and/or 'humanitarian' position in contemporary penal practice?

Our account draws primarily on findings from 80 long, biographical interviews with prison governors and directors, area managers, Prisons Board members, and some of the chief executives and operational directors of the private companies currently running prisons in England and Wales. These include a number of individuals with whom we have had contact during the course of other research projects, or on courses that we teach. We are aware that we are, to a minor extent, part of the network of players whose world we are investigating. But we also remain outsiders, and because of this have found ourselves being told versions of events that our interviewees would not talk to each other about, for all sorts of cultural and professional reasons. Our interviews, the majority of which were conducted jointly, took place between 2007 and 2009, mainly in Cambridge. In them, we asked about a range of topics, including family backgrounds, professional histories and motivations, views about the prison service and various aspects of penal policy. Due to the currency of the term within British penal culture (and to some degree building on Rutherford 1994; see also Bryans 2007), we asked interviewees whether they would consider themselves 'liberal humanitarians', and, if so, what this entailed. To explore this area, we asked for views about whether prisons could be 'benign, constructive places', about human nature (whether people were 'fundamentally good or bad'), and about issues such as prisoner voting rights and conjugal visits.[5] Responses to these questions, alongside wide-ranging discussions of career experiences, form the core of our analysis.

Some conceptual issues

In order to explore the liberal-humanitarian theme further, we need to elaborate on two contextual issues. The first of these is conceptual: how we are using the concepts of 'security' and 'harmony' values; the second is descriptive and introductory: a sketch of what senior prison managers were like in general.

First, then, we want to outline a distinction we have drawn in previous work between 'good' and 'right' relationships (Liebling and Price 2001: 75–84), or between a theory of the moral and a theory of 'being nice' (Thomas *et al.* 2003; Liebling 2004). This is best expressed by drawing on the work of Valerie Braithwaite. In her studies of political values in the general population, Braithwaite argues that two relatively independent value orientations – security and harmony – tend to be prioritized by different individuals (with security favoured by conservatives and harmony favoured by liberals). These value orientations bring together personal and social goals and modes of conduct (Braithwaite 1998b) and can be characterized as follows:

Security values	*Harmony values*
Self-protection	Peaceful coexistence
Rule of law	Mutual respect, human dignity
Authority	Sharing of resources
Competitiveness	The development of individual potential
Tough law enforcement	Wealth redistribution

Most people favour either security or harmony values, and these preferences are linked to their voting behaviour. According to Braithwaite, each value orientation implies a conception of the 'other' (for example, as a competitor or as an equal, worthy of respect). In general, and at a personal rather than organizational level, harmony values are 'other oriented' and security values are 'self-protective' (Braithwaite 1994).[6] Braithwaite also found two additional 'types' of people – dualists, who favoured *both* 'security' and 'harmony' as ideals or goals, and moral relativists, who had a weaker commitment to either (Braithwaite 1998a, 1994). Dualists have high commitment and balanced values, and must engage in complex moral reasoning in order to 'solve the value balance dilemma' (Braithwaite 1998a: 227; see also Abbey 2000: 130).[7]

Applied to the prison, 'security values' might include order, stability (including resistance to change), security procedures, and the 'rule of rules'. 'Harmony values' include attention to human dignity, respect, relationships, cooperation, equality, opportunity and progress. This conceptual distinction between value orientations usefully reflects the oscillating organizational priorities outlined in many histories of penal policy (the liberal penal project versus security and control), as well as the institutional-level differences in 'ethos' found in studies of particular establishments. Prisons tend to lean in one direction or the other, towards 'security' or 'harmony' priorities, just as people do. The most complex position of all is the dualist position, where strong adherence to apparently conflicting values often results in an ongoing value balance dilemma.

An outline of a senior management typology

This concept of value dualism is highly relevant to the typology of professional styles that we have discerned through our interviews. These styles encompass strengths, weaknesses, distinct approaches to the task of governing, and different forms of moral vision. They are linked to personal and biographical characteristics, as well as formative experiences during careers. Underlying them are distinctive visions of the moral status of offenders, and different conceptions of the means and ends of prison work. Briefly, the types are set out below:[8]

1. *Operators*: these managers are strong, experienced and highly skilled in operational terms, with forceful personalities, often found in poorly performing prisons, where they are tasked with challenging difficult staff cultures.
2. *Managerialists*: a younger generation, who tend to simplify the management task, focusing mainly on targets and smooth administration. This group includes some 'technicists' who are particularly focused on the technical tasks of the job, at which they are highly adept. They are driven by 'performance' but are also committed to due process and decency, albeit defined quite narrowly.
3. *Entrepreneurs*: these are energetic, innovative, 'ideas men'. They are often confident, powerful and effective. They can also be risk takers, impulsive and sometimes over optimistic. Some, but by no means all, are working the private sector. A very small number are women.
4. *Moral dualists* are highly competent and balanced both in terms of their value priorities and their management means. They are sensitive to the dynamics of power and to the plight of the individual. They are intelligent and operationally astute, almost always with a clear focus on performance, but alongside a broader grasp of the wider purpose of performance targets. They have a clear moral direction but it is not 'one sided'. They see order and targets as *for other things*; and security and relationships as mutually reinforcing rather than in conflict.
5. *Idealists* are thinker speakers or value intellectuals. They tend to be less pragmatic than their peers. Some are uncomfortable wielding power and with their own position in the punishment enterprise. But there appears to be a new style of idealism, about which we will say more shortly, which differs from a previous style and is unapologetic about using 'hard means' in order to try to achieve liberal-humanitarian ends.
6. *The alienated* – some of this group are approaching pensionable retirement, and have lost interest in the job. Some constitute a more toxic 'traditional–resistant' sub-group – governors who embody indifferent or disparaging

orientations towards prisoners. Others are disillusioned liberals who have become alienated from the service, and are leaving it, because they feel out of sympathy with the current organizational culture.

These are 'ideal types' in the sense that individuals may be on the edges of a group, while some types merge into others. Practitioners in the first three categories tend to be more managerialist, and more security than harmony oriented. Moral dualists and liberal idealists are more comfortable with harmony values, with some practitioners in both categories labelling themselves liberals, albeit with some unease (as we describe later). The last type might be Valerie Braithwaite's moral relativists or William Muir's (1977) 'cynics' (see Liebling, in press). None of our interviewees promoted what Rutherford (1994) labelled a 'punishment credo', involving 'a powerfully held dislike and moral condemnation of offenders', although some came close. The majority fitted into Rutherford's second credo, in which the primary goals were smooth management and efficiency.[9] As has been widely noted (e.g., Liebling 2004), this credo can be combined with either a punitive, liberal or 'just deserts' orientation to penal issues. It is an ideology of management without a further ideology, and is 'concerned with the rationality not of individual behaviour or even community organization, but of managerial processes' (Feeley and Simon 1992: 455). In the light of this, we have identified two key axes that emerge from the typology: *values* and *style*, as shown in Figure 1.

Values range from social justice to punishment-as-deterrence, but since few individuals can be located near the latter, we have placed 'internal order' at the opposite end of the spectrum from social justice, reflecting a different scope of moral vision. *Style* ranges from soft or consensual means to a harder, more robust approach. We have found it possible to place most individuals in fairly precise places in the four quadrants of this table, and have also found that we can impose Braithwaite's analysis of harmony and security orientations onto our framework (as shown). We propose that these orientations operate as follows: managers who believe in social justice and consensual management approaches are generally 'harmony oriented'; those who prioritize internal order and use tougher management styles are generally 'security oriented'.

In general, the balance within the prison service seems to have shifted towards the bottom right quadrant – the security, order and tough management end of the diagram – without becoming explicitly punitive. Almost all governors are more liberal than their predecessors in terms of their views about equal opportunities, sexuality and race relations. At the same time, there seems to be widespread unease with some harmony values – such as care and compassion – and with harmony-based orientations which make issues of social justice explicit in professional discussions about imprisonment (on the ascendancy of managerial values over those of justice in criminal justice more generally, see, e.g., Sanders 1998). The main question we seek to address in this chapter is why this has occurred – why have softer means and liberal-humanitarian moral positions become less prevalent (or discredited), and why has internal order become a more significant motivator than social justice at senior levels in criminal justice?

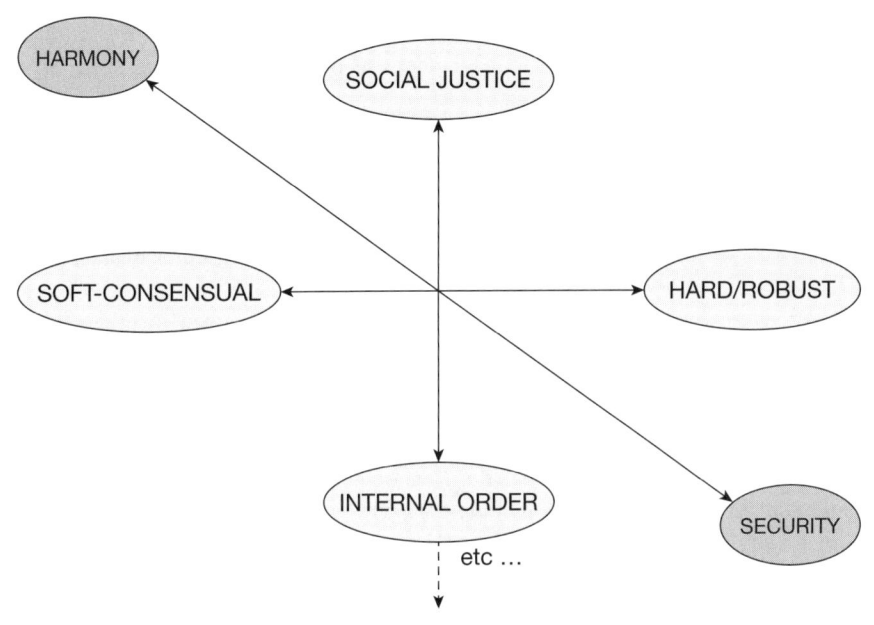

Figure 10.1 Values and style among senior correctional managers

The decline of penal liberalism

> [T]he penal landscape in this period was much bleaker than the reformers would have had us believe [. . .] Prison reform belonged more to the world of official discourse than reality.
>
> (Ryan 2003: 40–1)

For practitioners who worked inside prisons from the 1970s to the early 90s, the liberal rhetoric of those who made policy outside it felt rather empty. It may have made a difference in some establishments, but – as Mick Ryan has argued – there was a huge gap between the official discourse of the small, liberal post-war policymaking elite and the realities of the prison landings (for critical accounts of these realities, see Caird 1974; Stern 1987; McDermott and King 1988; King and McDermott 1990; Scraton *et al.* 1991; Sim 1990; Jameson and Allison 1995). In recalling their early career experiences, our interviewees consistently recounted dishonest staff practices, abuse of prisoners and an organization that lacked managerial competence. Officers in most prisons never signed up to the liberal agenda, and neither did many governors. Some who did, entering the service with a commitment to 'changing people', found themselves posted to decrepit local prisons like HMP Strangeways, where there was little possibility of rehabilitating prisoners. Phil Wheatley, chief executive of the National Offender Management Service from 2001 to 2010, recalled a highly disorganized and 'slightly corrupt' organization, with almost no systems of accountability, and claimed that he met only one 'really good governor' in his first 17 years as a uniformed officer in service. More recent recruits also reported finding themselves in a highly delinquent service, where poor management was pervasive:

> I would look round the table and think that the governor's secretary was about the only competent person there and it was really rather scary. [It was] amazing that the place got by on a day-to-day basis. [It was] Firstly disorganised, and [there was] an inability to deliver anything to any kind of timeframe.
>
> (Senior manager 66)

Power was over-used in some establishments and under-used in others, discrediting official visions of penal liberalism in two different ways. In at least one high-security prison in the 1980s and 90s attempting to run 'a liberal regime within a secure perimeter' (Advisory Council on the Penal System, 1968), staff under-policed the wings, abdicating power to prisoners, and creating an environment that was out of control and highly unsafe. In another, in the early 1990s, the under-enforcement of rules contributed to the escape of several IRA prisoners from what was meant to be an escape-proof unit (Home Office 1994; 1995). Several interviewees recalled prisons of this kind with dismay: managers 'being truly, genuinely frightened in situations where [control] hasn't existed' (senior manager 67), and prisoners having 'a massive amount of inappropriate authority' (senior manager 42).

In other establishments – mainly local prisons holding people on remand or short sentences – the problem was the over-use of authority. Officers were under-policed by their managers, allowing them to assault and abuse prisoners. This 'dark side' of staff power, and the dangers of managers abdicating their authority, was described by a large proportion of our interviewees. For example:

> The Governor, whenever he had a problem, he'd leave the prison and have a cup of coffee because he was scared of the POA [...] He was completely impotent [...] prisoners just weren't unlocked. Prisoners were being assaulted in the Seg[regation] unit when they were being restrained. Use of force was massively higher than it should have been.
>
> (Senior manager 58)

As described in the accounts we were given, governors of the penal-welfare era fitted into two (rather broad) categories: *cynics* and *romantics*. The former were themselves punitive and indifferent – one interviewee recalled working for a governor who, in a meeting with union committee members, referred to prisoners as 'bastards' (senior manager 66); others described senior management teams turning a blind eye to staff brutality.[10] *Romantics* were liberal-idealists, who were intellectually thoughtful, value driven and well intentioned. They often wrote for the *Prison Service Journal* – a practitioner-oriented publication – reinforcing a relatively progressive public image of the Service. According to our interviewees, however, they were rarely capable of translating these ideals into practice:

> Let's face it, the liberals of the past were not realistic and bad things happened, you know, really, really bad things. They were incompetent and they had their utopian visions in their offices but there was a kind of dystopian reality out there in the Segregation units.
>
> (Senior manager 67)

As described to us, Romantics were often unable to communicate with or control officers, and were weak in the face of staff cultures that were brutal, apathetic or resistant to reform. Their benign intentions and disorganized methods did not produce benign prisons, and their preference for making decisions on a case-by-case basis – 'to do good as individuals to individuals' (senior manager 12) – antagonized prisoners and staff by being inconsistent and unsystematic.[11]

The organizational behaviour of the Prison Service has been deeply inscribed by these collective experiences. They do not on their own account for the rise of managerialist practices, but they have certainly played a part in institutionalizing a performance culture that values effective management, 'delivery' and pragmatism above loftier priorities or penal utopianism. Senior managers recognized the chasm between progressive ideologies and the actual prisoner experience, and concluded that prisons required firm leadership, 'systems' and management grip – a form of 'benign Stalinism', in the words of one interviewee (senior manager 16). The aims of such developments were to introduce an element of fairness, due process and objectivity to the system (rather than rely on individual beneficence), and to control two inherent dangers: first, the tendency for staff to use their power abusively (Haney *et al.* 1973); second, the danger of staff slipping into compromise and collusion with prisoners (Sykes 1958). Liberalism became associated with both hazards: a management style that was naïve and ineffective ('sprinkling gold dust around the place' as one interviewee (senior manager 12) described it disparagingly); or regimes that were under-controlled and permissive, i.e. excessively harmony oriented. One of our more liberal interviewees summarized the prevailing wisdom that has resulted as follows:

> What you can't have these days, I think, is the old fashioned governor who, sort of, understands, the moral and philosophical framework in which a prison exists but doesn't have a handle on performance. [We] can't afford that. I think there were lots of people like that running prisons a while ago and some of them probably presiding over the worst Segregation Units, because the Governor's office could be a bit of an ivory tower, [just] full of interesting books.
>
> (Senior manager 2)

The key contemporary narrative was one of sound management, with much less room for *romantics* or liberal idealism.

Liberal-humanitarianism in the contemporary prison service

These developments do not mean that there are no liberal-humanitarians within the England and Wales Prison Service. However, the way that these terms are understood has changed and the nature of the governing task has shifted. When asked directly if they would define themselves as liberals or liberal-humanitarians, few of our interviewees said that they would, and most of those who did sought to qualify the label. Several said that being known as a 'liberal', or speaking out as one, would not be a good career move. Some said that they might be liberal in principle, but added that they had become 'managerialists with knobs on' (senior manager 67) in the current operating climate. Many identified themselves as 'humanitarian' or 'progressive', but the term 'liberal' generated considerable discomfort. It signified 'do-gooding', having a 'soft' stance towards prisoners or failing to have a grip on the institution. Some felt that it connoted the traditional Probation Service ethos of 'advising, assisting and befriending' which was at odds with the organizational emphasis on compliance and control. Even among those practitioners who spoke a language of care and welfare, there was a concern not to be perceived as 'soft' – the implication being that this implied a weak or un-disciplined approach to managing staff.[12]

The interviewees who were willing to describe themselves, however tentatively, as liberal-humanitarians had a number of distinctive characteristics, which can be illustrated by comparing them first with the new-generation *managerialists* who now predominate within the Prison Service (in the first three categories of our typology, and in the bottom right quadrant of Figure 10.1), and with the older generation of liberal *romantics* (in the top left quadrant of Figure 10.1). First, modern liberals recognized that prisons are what David Garland (1990) and others call 'tragic institutions'. Whereas most interviewees displayed a kind of penal optimism, in which they did not hesitate to say that prisons could be benign, constructive environments, the starting point of liberals was the opposite. They were pessimistic (or circumspect) about the impact of imprisonment, arguing that while prisons should aspire to be as positive and constructive as possible, they were almost always harmful:

I: Do you think prisons can be constructive places to send people?
R: No, I think the best that can be hoped for is to make them less damaging than they would otherwise be, and less intrinsically destructive, because the purpose is a negative one.

(Senior manager 67)

I: So do you think prisons can be constructive places?
R: [Pause] Not more constructive than *not* prisons, but more than 'not constructive'. [. . .] I would never say 'actually, what you need is [a spell] in prison!'. I suppose there are certain kinds of emergency things where it's almost a place of safety, but in terms of long-term mental health, I wouldn't recommend it.

(Senior manager 32)

Liberal-humanitarian penal values and practices 185

I: In such responses, modern liberals showed an awareness of the prison's exterior functions and consequences that many of their colleagues lacked.

R: Second, modern liberals had a particular 'criminology' and view of human nature. They believed that people were born as blank slates, or were fundamentally good until corrupted by life events:

> I have a view of human nature that you start by trusting people and then instinctively I think – and this includes pretty much all the prisoners I've ever met – you like to think that people are inherently good and that there are all sorts of reasons why they behave in other ways. I do not believe, for example, in evil.
>
> (Senior manager 66)

Linked to such views, modern liberals advanced sociological or psycho-social theories of criminality, regarding offending as an outcome of social deprivation and family breakdown, and seeing imprisonment principally as an indication of the failings of society. These views were often informed by backgrounds in social work or degrees in the social sciences, which had generated explicitly reformist career motivations: 'I was very excited about the Woolf Report and that agenda, and felt that I could play my part' (senior manager 69); 'When I joined the Prison Service, I did it for what I could bring to it [. . .] things about wanting to make a difference' (senior manager 32). Liberals were less likely than other interviewees to have fallen into prison work 'by accident' or for the pragmatic reasons that the majority of managers provided (a safe job and a decent pension). In contrast, many managerialists had been attracted and recruited to the service primarily because it offered interesting opportunities *to manage*:

R: I didn't come in to this job because I thought I would be doing a public service necessarily, so I don't know that that is why I do it, or why I would stay doing it.

I: Why do you do it, do you think?

R: Why do I do it? Because I do enjoy the challenge [. . .] I like the challenge, because I think you can make a difference in the place that you're at. I do genuinely believe that you dictate the tone of your establishment, and so even if you're not stopping people from going out there and committing further crimes, if you're making sure they're safe while they're in here, that they're being educated if they can, they gain skills, that's no bad thing, is it?

(Senior manager 84)

As suggested here, managerialists were by no means indifferent to the plight of prisoners. However – as is consistent with the terms of 'new penology' (Feeley and Simon 1992) – they were more concerned with the general art of management than with the lot of the individual. For these practitioners, despite their commitment to the job, prison work was not 'labour of love type stuff' (senior manager 41).

These differences in background and motivation mapped onto other professional attitudes and orientations. Modern liberals were committed to a position that saw prisoners as redeemable, almost as a matter of principle. In contrast to their pessimistic beliefs about imprisonment, their views of prisoners were relatively optimistic. Most other senior managers did not share this position. Their criminology was in part sociological, in that they were committed to forms of 'social rehabilitation' (Robinson and Crow 2010), but their language was neo-liberal, emphasizing choice, responsibility, and a just deserts notion of punishment:

> The vast majority have made the wrong choices along the way and that maybe because they haven't had much choice, or because they haven't learnt to make those choices ... haven't learnt to assess risk, haven't learnt what is acceptable with everyone else. So I don't excuse the offending, I think one has to take personal responsibility.
> (Senior manager 65)

> People are adults, and they have that choice [to offend or not]. So in that sense I am fairly hardnosed I guess, but once they're in we have a duty of care for them.
> (Senior manager 71)

In Muir's (1977) terms, while modern liberals held a 'tragic' view of offenders, 'one that sees individuals as essentially alike', managerialists presented a more 'cynical', dualistic attitude. They divided offenders into the reformable and the incurable, often describing the latter in terms of fundamental 'badness' or, occasionally, 'evil'. Sympathy and compassion were limited and conditional:

> I: Do you feel sympathy and compassion for prisoners?
> R: I feel some sympathy towards some people, not prisoners in general, and I don't feel compassion towards prisoners in general. I do with individuals, some individuals.
> (Senior manager 48)

> There's individual prisoners who I've got a great deal of sympathy for, because of what's happened to them for them to end up where they are, you know, but I don't view them as victims unless they are a victim of abuse.
> (Senior manager 41)

Modern liberals had fewer reservations about expressing compassion for prisoners, signalling a more 'inclusionary' (Cavadino and Dignan 2006) attitude towards offenders. They were acutely aware of the essential painfulness of imprisonment: 'There always has to be something going on at the back of your head that says: "this is bloody awful, thank God it isn't me", and make sure that other people are remembering that as well' (senior manager 61). For this reason among others, liberals were committed to normalizing the prison environment. They were more likely than most of their colleagues to be in favour of prisoners being granted voting rights, family or conjugal visits, and a wide range of material goods. In contrast, most managerialists believed that material benefits should be available chiefly as incentives, to 'responsibilize' prisoners and ensure their compliance. Their agenda was 'correctional' and operational, and although they were committed to civilizing the prison environment, their thinking betrayed a discourse of 'less eligibility' (see Sparks 1996); prisons should be '[genuinely] decent but reasonably austere' (senior manager 37). Managerialists were opposed to the introduction of conjugal visits and voting rights either because they believed that these would be too difficult to organize practically or because of a relatively punitive and exclusionary view of what the deprivation of liberty should entail. Losing certain rights and material provisions was 'part of the punishment' (senior manager 83):

> I: Are you in favour of things like prisoners having voting rights and conjugal visits?
> R: No.
> I: No to both?
> R: No to both. I think on the grounds that incarceration should mean the loss of certain liberties and luxuries, even something as basic as voting rights really.
>
> (Senior manager 65)

Here, as in recent political discourse, Paterson's historically embedded distinction between using imprisonment *as* but not *for* punishment was at risk of being collapsed.[13]

Modern liberals also differed in some important respects from their *romantic* predecessors. Both groups were 'other oriented' and expressed considerable empathy for prisoners. However, modern liberals were less comfortable with notions of 'sympathy', which they associated with the top-down, pastoral style of a more paternalistic era. Typified by Alexander Paterson, and institutionalized through the Borstal system, the spirit of this period had been one of 'benign authority' (Papps 1972; and see De Frisching 1975) or liberal paternalism, changing people by 'good example' or through social work techniques. *Romantics* had generally entered the service as assistant governors, where they had been trained in individual casework and 'treatment', and encouraged to think of themselves as 'caseworkers firstly and managers secondly' (Ainsworth 1971).[14] Some used a quasi-religious language of suffering, and were openly driven by religious faith or a sense of *noblesse oblige*.

Modern liberals saw themselves slightly differently: they were first and foremost managers; they considered 'kindness' and humanity to be ends in themselves, but did not see them as solutions to offending; and they were unsentimental in their view of prisoners:

> I don't think kindness is the route to salvation . . . no [. . .] It won't affect whether [someone] re-offends or not, unless it's backed up by a whole load of other things.
>
> (Senior manager 24)

> [Governor X] was a very moral man and [believed], 'if you treat them well they would become better'. I'm not saying that for one moment; I'm saying they're so damaged <sighs> [. . .] they have self-destructive tendencies which could destroy and damage others. We know this because they've done really, really bad stuff.
>
> (Senior manager 67)

Finally, although modern liberals were more sensitive than most managers about the essential power disparities that characterized prison life, they were unapologetic about using power and about 'security' values in general. In this respect, there were more 'hard' than 'soft' liberals, pursuing humanitarian ends through robust means and prioritizing order and safety over almost all other operational aims. They had no nostalgia for 'liberal' regimes, did not see decency as synonymous with 'niceness' or under-using power, and saw little trade-off between the goals of harmony and security:

> Duty number one is to keep them and others safe and so you create an ordered community and that means you've got to exercise controls over that community in a way in which means that it's safe and that can sometimes [mean] using force with them [. . .] So it is really, really difficult but I do feel comfortable with that approach. These are big establishments [. . .] they can go wrong and when they go wrong it is no life for anyone.
>
> (Senior manager 67)

They were also unembarrassed by the prison's custodial functions. As one liberal (moral dualist) declared: 'security isn't the only thing we do, it's not the only important thing we do, but it's the single most important thing we do' (Senior Manager 27). It was crucial, he argued, to be honest and pragmatic about the core penal task:

> Let's not somehow try and dress that up, or be apologetic for it [. . .] I think I joined an organisation that probably was a bit apologetic about it, and wanted to present what we were doing as if it was something somehow noble and separate from that rather dirty business of incarcerating people.
>
> (Senior manager 27)

In Figure 10.2, the liberal branch of the service like senior prison managers in general has moved towards the right and lower quadrants.

The silencing of the liberal voice

While liberal-humanitarian governors have not disappeared, their voices have been silenced considerably. They do not represent a coherent group, and there are few forums in which they can reinforce each other's ideals or promote a liberal agenda. They are often unaware of which colleagues share their views. One reason for this

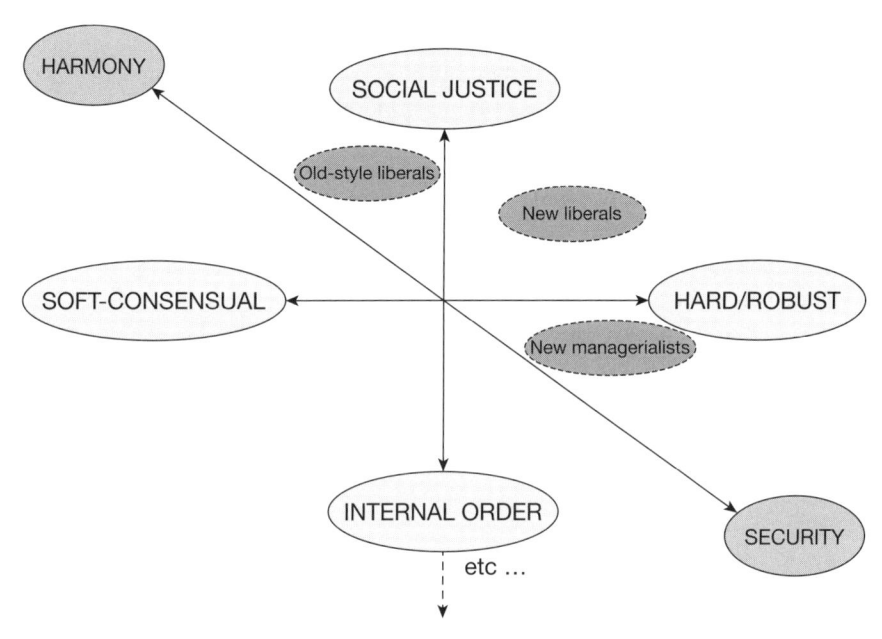

Figure 10.2 Values and style among senior correctional managers

is that practitioners do not talk to each other about their motivations. At area meetings, they stay 'in role' (senior manager 67), discussing operational and resource issues, much more than policy matters or moral questions. As one interviewee noted, intellectualism is 'not held in particularly high regard, because we're a delivery organisation' (senior manager 66). Performance culture has relegated care and criticism beneath other priorities:

> There's less mavericks than there used to be and with that I think you do lose some of the custodial care element. That doesn't mean Governors don't care, they do care a lot. [But] I think there's a tendency for them to value performance a bit higher than other things, which is a worry. [And] You've got more 'yes men' and women, so in open forum there's not much questioning of people.
> (Senior manager 75)

Most senior managers are compliant and unquestioning. Many young governors believe that careers can be scuppered or accelerated depending on how they are viewed by a small number of senior figures within the National Offender Management Service (NOMS) – the organization which encompasses the prison and probation services. These senior figures say that they do not want their governors to be meek or deferential, indeed, they worry that too many of them would be willing to 'lock prisoners up all day and poke them with sticks' (senior manager 14) were they told to do so. But the cadre of highly compliant managerialists is a product of professional socialization in an era during which the top-down grip on managers has become increasingly tight and the organizational emphasis has been on 'delivery' and 'performance' above all else. As a result, while some governors suppress any critical feelings about the organization, the majority are not especially exercised by moral and political questions about the wider functions of the prison. They are *'willing Jonahs'* (Le Grand 2003) – content to be 'inside the whale', and internally focused. Asked whether they worried about the expanding prison population, a significant number – even those with strong personal views on this matter – said that such issues did not feel relevant to their work, except in purely operational terms. The following response was typical:

> I: Do you worry at all about the broader context, things like the expanding prison population, the number of people that we lock up?
> R: No. No, is the short answer to that.
> I: Is that because you see that as a separate issue from what you do, or because...
> R: Yeah, probably because I see it as a separate issue [...] certainly the Ministry of Justice needs to get its act together in terms of who it sends to prison and why, and about how big a prison population they can manage, but day-to-day, if I'm full to operational capacity, that's as far as I have to think about really.
> I: Do you have personal views about the number of people we're locking up?
> R: We send far too many people to prison, would be my view.
> I: But you don't see those views as being all that relevant to what you do day-to-day?
> R: No.
>
> (Senior manager 84)

Many other managerialists were agnostic about wider penal questions:

> Would you happily describe yourself as a liberal or a liberal-humanitarian in terms of your views about prison and imprisonment?
> I wouldn't describe myself as anything really.
>
> (Senior manager 65)

Their primary concerns were managerial rather than social (Feeley and Simon 1992), and although they were highly cynical about politics and politicians (often as a result of having contact with ministers through jobs at Prison Service headquarters), they tended to bracket off politics from the daily demands of managing prisons.

The dwindling presence of liberal-humanitarians, and the declining currency of their values, has important consequences for the Service. Many of the older generation of liberal romantics spoke out at conferences and in other public forums about matters of penal policy. And while widely criticized for their management skills and styles, they played a significant role in demonstrating and infusing moral qualities to the governors who are most highly valued by the service. Many *moral dualists* said that it was through these liberal-romantics that they had learnt about care, about 'what prison was for and what could be achieved' (senior manager 83). As one interviewee noted, romantics were important 'for their moral compass as much as their ability to make things happen' (senior manager 66). Not least, they had helped persuade young, reformist governors that there was space for progressive thinking and practice:

> I didn't think that this was going to be a life for me, [but] we talked about the death penalty [. . .] and I remember thinking that if somebody like [him] can decide [that] this was a thing worth spending his life on, then maybe it is.
> (Senior manager 66)

> [Governors Smith and White] influenced and shaped my idea of what being a prison governor could be, and I would not have joined if it hadn't been for them. They were caring, compassionate, staff orientated, prisoner orientated, would breach and break rules where they felt it was important [. . .] They would appear on a wing: 'oh, let's make it better'.
> (Senior manager 15)

It was not only more liberal governors who expressed concern that certain kinds of values and personalities are no longer so visible within the Service. Even senior practitioners who were not themselves especially liberal acknowledged that the organization had been depleted in terms of characteristics such as care and intellectualism:

> I think what we look for in governors is different now, we look for people who can manage and sometimes we get that at the expense of people who have got the sort of moral dimension. A really good example of that was [governor X] who actually was fantastic in terms of caring and being really good at the moral stuff, but couldn't manage their way out of a paper bag in terms of performance targets and systems. If you walked round prisons that [he] governed there were no systems in place, but they were fantastic places in terms of the decency and the caring.
> (Senior manager 37)

> I think a lot of prison governors will manage whatever situation is thrown at them. They're very practical people, very delivery focused people, very task orientated people [. . .] I'm not sure how many of them I would describe as thinkers of real depth.
> (Senior manager 24)

Conclusions and implications

We have argued that the period of UK imprisonment that is conventionally seen as one of penal welfarism was far from being liberal and humane on the ground and that this disparity has impacted significantly on the development of the Prison Service's current management culture. The relationship between official rhetoric and practice is now much closer than it was. Managerialist reforms, particularly in the context of a new emphasis on public protection and individual responsibility, have narrowed the range of professional orientations, purging the service of mavericks at both extremes: there are fewer rogue and incompetent governors (although we are noticing a rather brutal form of managerialism that is preoccupied with targets to an amoral degree), but also fewer who are risk taking and innovative. There is little space for ideologies that are 'tragic', romantic, or even 'utopian realist'. The new generation of managerialist governors has been recruited and trained in a particular era which narrows its field of penal vision. These practitioners have been recruited primarily for their skills and capabilities rather than their values; they have never undertaken 'casework' with individual offenders; and many have not been through the kind of organizational self-questioning that follows large-scale disturbances or spectacular escapes. Arguably, they have been socialized in a period where the most fundamental questions about what prisons are for have become subordinate to questions about how best to manage them.

In the context of the United Kingdom, it could be argued that this 'new penology' framework – process driven and pragmatic – delivers better 'interior' outcomes for prisoners than an old penological vision which declared its liberal-humanitarianism ideals loudly without putting them systematically into practice. It could also be argued that with systems in place that ensure a certain quality of treatment and provision, there is less need for 'bleeding heart liberals'. At the same time, there are limitations and blind spots within the current framework: very few managers speak a language of empathy or compassion, and few have the resources to discuss penal issues and practices with theoretical depth. Criminological, legal and philosophical thinking has to a large degree been hollowed out from such debates, replaced by the neutral language of management speak. Most governors are politically unengaged, trained to be managers rather than critical thinkers. There is little protest about the extraordinary lengthening of prison sentences, the painful constraints on prisoners trying to work their way out, or the massive increase in the size of the prison population. We are concerned that the Service has been disciplined too far, that governors have been made too acquiescent and that, inasmuch as dissenting voices exist, they have become inaudible.

We have grounds to believe that these developments are shaping prison policy and the experience of imprisonment in some significant ways. In terms of the latter, we are convinced that a prison's value culture percolates down from its management team, setting the tone for staff behaviour, albeit in competition with other value frameworks (such as those provided by the Prison Officers' Association). In terms of the former, the insulation of policymaking from professional expertise has been a two-sided process. Senior managers believe that they are constitutionally disqualified from speaking out on prison issues – they understand their role as one of advising on policy but not commenting on it publicly.[15] Collectively, their views get little public expression. In recent years, the Prison Governors' Association which represents them has become more of a trade union, negotiating pay and conditions, than a professional association.[16] At a more senior level within NOMS, officials listen to academic expertise and warn ministers of the risks of pursuing populist strategies (while laying an audit trail to prove that they have done so), but ministerial ears have tended to swivel to the siren song of the tabloid and mid-market press. Lacey's (2008: 72–3) description of the tendency in liberal market economies for politicians to 'ignore the advice of technically neutral civil servants wherever this is judged to interfere with the chances of electoral success of political expediency' is borne out. As Lacey also suggests, this tendency is self-reinforcing, dissolving the buffer from populist currents that an influential and independent bureaucracy can provide. As a result, prisons have become highly politicized environments, subject to a 'public acceptability' test that is driven by media outrage: it certainly cannot be said, as it was in the 1960s, that ministers and MPs 'place trust in civil servants and do not interfere politically in their work' (Hayner 1962).

Up to a point, our findings support the argument found in recent work by Pratt (2008a, b) and others (Cavadino and Dignan 2006; Lacey 2008) that cultures of penality relate to a nation's cultural values, social structures and institutional arrangements. In such work, the United Kingdom is placed alongside nations such as Australia, New Zealand and the United States and is commonly described as 'neo-liberal' (or similar). The tropes of neo-liberalism, particularly the discourse of individual responsibility, are certainly present in many of the accounts we have provided and we do not find it hard to identify links between what appear to be decreasing levels of professional (and public) sympathy for offenders and wider socio-political developments in which levels of inequality have risen and the welfare state has been attacked as a source of rather than a solution to social problems.

At the same time, we suspect that differences in penal conditions *within* the country-types groupings that are typically presented in such work are enormous. To give just one example – it is hard to find many interior descriptions nowadays – Wacquant's (2002) description of LA county jail as a kind of human zoo is far more disturbing than anything an objective observer of prisons in the UK would produce. We also think it important to emphasize that differences in penal sensibilities between Nordic and other Western nations are a matter of degree. There are still some liberals within the prison system of England and Wales who hold the kinds of progressive, inclusionary and highly compassionate attitudes that are generally identified with Scandinavia. Furthermore, many of the kinds of prison conditions that Pratt observes – the lack of a 'prison smell' (Pratt 2008a: 121), and the 'relative material comfort' (ibid.), including internal sanitation – do not sound so different from those that could be found in many of the better prisons in the United Kingdom. While convincing accounts exist of senior practitioners in several Nordic countries quietly softening apparently increasingly punitive promises in practice (see, e.g. Lappi-Seppala 2007), there are many reasons to believe that any conception of Scandinavian penal cultures as 'simply and similarly liberal-humanitarian' are naïve and utopian (see rest of this volume).

Commentators on Nordic penality glance nervously across the North Sea or the Atlantic Ocean. They worry that they may be glimpsing an image of their futures and wonder whether their liberal-humanitarian exceptionalism is as real as it seems, and is at risk. We are in no position to gauge whether the developments that we have charted in this chapter resonate beyond the United Kingdom. Indeed, an implicit thread in our argument is that, to understand the character of national penal systems, it is important to take seriously the professional motivations and orientations of senior correctional managers, and to explore how these are shaped locally as well as globally, by organizational contingencies and histories, as well as wider trends. It seems unlikely that Nordic penality will simply follow the path of its neo-liberal cousins, for all of the reasons that have been articulated in recent analysis (Cavadino and Dignan 2006; Lacey 2008; Pratt 2008a, b), but it is also the case that we know too little about apparently 'liberal-humanitarian' penal systems, and that both carefully operationalized empirical studies and cross-time analyses in these locations are badly needed. Given our interest in penal dynamics, we have a few further observations about the future of Nordic exceptionalism.

First, prison systems seem particularly vulnerable to the impact of certain kinds of signal events, such as riots or escapes. In the UK, the escape of the spy George Blake from HMP Wormwood Scrubs in 1966 represented a defining moment of this kind. As one old-generation liberal explained, after this event, the 'the curtains of liberalism closed', initiating the shift towards a more security-oriented era.[17] The recent high-profile prison escapes in Sweden are therefore interesting and concerning, for they may provide a penal bellwether of developments to follow. Second, it is possible that the growth of drugs economies within Nordic societies will not only push politicians and sentencers towards more punitive policies, but might also make it harder for some practitioners to maintain an inclusive criminological worldview. A number of our interviewees noted the difficulties of 'seeing the good in everyone' when confronted with a brutal criminal subculture based around drugs, both within and beyond the prison.

More optimistically, a factor that might protect Nordic societies from the worst excesses of the trends we have outlined relates to the size of prison systems and individual prisons. Large systems require more management 'grip', and this might in itself account for some of the tendencies towards managerial compliance that we have documented. Likewise, large prisons lead to certain kinds of managerial attributes being valued above others. In England and Wales, it is no longer uncommon for establishments to hold over 800 prisoners, and several accommodate well over 1,000. Prisons of this size and complexity cannot be run on charismatic authority alone, requiring some generic management skills (although these do not, in themselves, ensure that they are humane). But large prisons create distance between managers and prisoners, making it harder for those in charge to maintain inclusionary and empathic attitudes towards those in their care. To quote one interviewee, 'I don't want to get involved in individual cases because I just haven't got the time to be involved' (senior manager 24). The smaller size of Nordic prison systems and establishments may serve as a protective force against the tendency for the needs and identity of the individual prisoner to become lost in the bureaucratic mire.

Finally, we want to sound a note of caution about accounts of penality that do not look beneath penal rhetoric in order to understand the true nature of the prison experience. Perhaps one reason why native researchers in Nordic states have been less sanguine about their prison systems than outsiders – who are generally reliant on official data and brief visits – is that, even if imprisonment is officially more humane in these countries than in western Europe and North America, the realities of prison life for prisoners (and sometimes for staff) fail to match the positive aspirations of official pronouncements.

Notes

1 We are reflecting in our more detailed analysis on what these important terms mean in practice: so, for example, one colleague has suggested that the relative 'humanitarianism' of penal systems in Scandinavian countries reflects a less 'self-contained' vision of penality, or a view of rehabilitation and reform as necessarily taking place in the community. 'The exceptionalism lies *outside* the prison', thus limiting its use (Coyle, pers. comm. 2010).
2 Publications such as Bryans and Wilson (1998) and Bryans (2000, 2007) cover some of this ground, but these studies focus on the competences of prison governors rather than their professional values and orientations.
3 Although there were Borstals that, in practice, were brutally paternalistic.
4 ESRC award RES-062-23-0212.
5 Prisoners in the United Kingdom are currently unable to vote and cannot receive conjugal visits.
6 'Materialist values are the concern of those who have experienced economic or physical insecurity: They give priority to order and stability, and to economic and military strength. In contrast post-materialists [who in this part of Braithwaite's analysis represent those with higher harmony values] have been exposed to greater security and are likely to place a higher value on ideas, brotherhood, greater citizen involvement in decision-making at government and community levels, and environmental protection' (Braithwaite 1994: 84, referring to work by Inglehart 1971). This account suggests that security values must be satisfied before harmony values will be prioritized, an observation that may be highly pertinent to prison life.
7 Jacobs points out that historically, when traditional authoritarian prison regimes were 'liberalized', the 'harmony' or rehabilitation role was given to civilian staff such as counsellors (and psychologists; see also Thomas 1972). This resulted in a new moral division of labour. Previously, there had been some 'moral balance' to the prison officer's role (Jacobs 1977: 96–7).
8 We will expand on this typology, on the analysis that led to it, and on the distribution of individuals by gender, sector, age and so on, in future publications.
9 Despite focusing mainly on credo three, interviewees, i.e. those with more liberal views, Rutherford (1994) reported that credo two was dominant among criminal justice practitioners at the time of his study.
10 'And you can imagine my jaw just hit the floor and I didn't know where to put myself and thought "what on earth...?" And I just didn't understand why he didn't get it, that if the governor is calling prisoners bastards to the POA Chair and Secretary, firstly every member of staff in the jail is going to hear that's been said. [And secondly] If the governor's calling them bastards in his office then in the Seg[regation Unit] the staff are kicking them'.

11 We are aware of the danger of oversimplifying what was almost certainly a more complex and varied picture. The aim here is to provide a descriptive sketch that is sufficient to help us contrast current with past orientations.
12 There is a longer story to be told about the impact of the POA on management styles, i.e. the difficulty of having a softer, more consensual management approach when faced with a highly traditional and often combative union culture.
13 In a speech in June 2008, the British government's Secretary of State for Justice, Jack Straw, argued that the purpose of prison should be 'punishment and reform', and that prisons not only are but should be 'first and foremost places of punishment, primarily through the deprivation of liberty but also through a regime behind bars which is tough and fair' (www.hmprisonservice.gov.uk/news/index.asp?id=8569,22,6,22,0,0).
14 'To be competent in these areas demands a knowledge of general theories relating to human growth and development (the individual), group dynamics and role theory (the group), and the sociology of institutions (the community)' (Ainsworth 1971).
15 This feeling has been reinforced by a recent decision to reactivate a ruling that NOMS employees who publish research or articles in the public sphere must not be critical of government policy. All *Prison Service Journal* articles written by NOMS employees have to be cleared by a central authority.
16 'It worries me that they spend all their time dealing with pay and conditions issues, and not enough time talking about moral legitimacy' (senior manager 2).
17 One article in the *Prison Service Journal* put it as follows: 'the [Mountbatten] report, whilst not denying the humanitarian aims, gave a reminder that we were also in the law and order business. The Prison Service was forced rudely to adjust to the post-war world' (Uzzell 1974: 7).

References

Abbey, R. (2000) *Charles Taylor*. Teddington: Acumen.
Advisory Council on the Penal System (1968) *The Regime for Long-term Prisoners in Conditions of Maximum Security*. London: HMSO.
Ainsworth, F. (1971) 'Making of Assistant Governors', *Prison Service Journal*, 1: 7–9.
Bottomley, K. and W. Hay (eds) (1991) *Special Units for Difficult Prisoners*. Hull: Centre for Criminology and Criminal Justice.
Bottoms, A. and F. H. McClintock (1973) *Criminals Coming of Age: A Study of Institutional Adaptation in the Treatment of Adolescent Offenders*. London: Heinemann Educational.
Braithwaite, V. (1994) 'Beyond Rokeach's Equality–Freedom Model: Two-dimensional Values in a One-dimensional World', *Journal of Social Issues*, 50(4): 67–94.
—— (1998a) 'The Value Balance of Political Evaluations', *British Journal of Psychology*, 89: 223–47.
—— (1998b) 'Communal and Exchange Trust Norms: Their value base and relevance to institutional trust', in V. Braithwaite and M. Levi (eds), *Trust and Governance*. New York: Russell Sage Foundation.
Bryans, S. (2000) 'Governing Prisons: An Analysis of Who Is Governing Prisons and the Competencies Which They Require to Govern Effectively', *Howard Journal of Criminal Justice*, 39(1): 14–29.
—— (2007) *Prison Governors: Managing Prisons in a Time of Change*. Cullompton: Willan.
Bryans, S. and D. Wilson (1998) *The Prison Governor: Theory and Practice*. Leyhill: Prison Service Journal Publications.
Caird, R. (1974) *Good and Useful Life: Imprisonment in Britain Today*. London: Hart-Davis.

Cavadino, M. and J. Dignan (2006) 'Penal Policy and Political Economy', *Journal of Criminology and Criminal Justice*, 6(4): 435–56.
De Frisching, A. (1975) 'The Prison Service – 10 Years On', *Prison Service Journal*, 18: 2–7.
Feeley, M. and J. Simon (1992) 'The New Penology: Notes on the Emerging Strategy of Corrections and Its Implications', *Criminology*, 30: 449–74.
Gallo, E. and V. Ruggiero (1991) 'The "Immaterial" Prison: Custody as a Factory for the Manufacture of Handicaps', *International Journal of the Sociology of Law*, 19(3): 273–91.
Garland, D. (1985) *Punishment and Modern Society*. Oxford: Clarendon Press.
—— (1990) *Punishment and Welfare: A History of Penal Strategies*. Aldershot: Gower.
Haney, C., W. C. Banks and P. G. Zimbardo (1973) 'Interpersonal Dynamics in a Simulated Prison', *International Journal of Criminology and Penology*, 1: 69–97.
Hayner, N. (1962) 'Research and Methodology: Correctional Systems and National Values', *British Journal of Criminology*, 3: 163–70.
Jacobs, J. (1977) *Stateville: The Penitentiary in Mass Society*. Chicago: University of Chicago Press.
Jameson, N. and E. Allison (1995) *Strangeways 1990: A Serious Disturbance*. London: Larkin.
Jones, H. and P. Cornes (assisted by R. Stockford) (1977) *Open Prisons*. London: Routledge & Kegan Paul.
King, R. D. and K. McDermott (1990) '"My Geranium is Subversive": Some Notes on the Management of Trouble in Prisons', *British Journal of Sociology*, 41(4): 445–71.
Lacey, N. (2008) *The Prisoners' Dilemma: Political Economy and Punishment in Contemporary Democracies*. Cambridge: Cambridge University Press.
Lappi-Seppala, T. (2007) 'Penal Policy in Scandinavia', in M. Tonry (ed.) *Crime, Punishment and Politics in Comparative Perspective. Crime and Justice: A Review of Research*, vol. 36, Chicago: Chicago University Press.
Le Grand, J. (2003) *Motivation, Agency and Public Policy: Of Knights, and Knaves, Pawns and Queens*. Oxford: Oxford University Press.
Liebling, A. (assisted by H. Arnold) (2004) *Prisons and their Moral Performance: A Study of Values, Quality and Prison Life*. Oxford: Clarendon Press.
—— (in press) 'Legitimacy and Authority Revisited: Important Distinctions in the Work of Prison Officers', *European Journal of Criminology*.
Liebling, A. and D. Price (2001) *The Prison Officer*. Leyhill: Prison Service and Waterside Press.
McDermott, K. and R. D. King (1988) 'Mind Games: Where the Action Is in Prisons', *British Journal of Criminology*, 28(3): 357–75.
Muir, W. (1977) *Police: Streetcorner Politicians*. Chicago: University of Chicago Press.
Norwegian Ministry of Justice (2010) *Punishment that Works – Less Crime – A Safer Society*. Report to the Storting on the Norwegian Correctional Services Oslo: Norwegian Ministry of Justice and the Police.
Papps, A. (1972) 'Control and Treatment: With Particular Reference to Long-term Maximum Security Establishments', *Prison Service Journal*, 8: 6–8.
Pratt, J. (2008a) 'Scandinavian Exceptionalism in an Era of Penal Excess: Part I: The Nature and Roots of Scandinavian Exceptionalism', *British Journal of Criminology*, 48(2): 119–37.
—— (2008b) 'Scandinavian Exceptionalism in an Era of Penal Excess: Part II: Does Scandinavian Exceptionalism Have a Future?', *British Journal of Criminology*, 48(3): 275–92.

Robinson, G. and I. Crow (2010) *Offender Rehabilitation: Theory, Research and Practice.* London: Sage.

Rutherford, A. (1994) *Criminal Justice and the Pursuit of Decency.* Winchester: Waterside Press.

Ryan, M. (2003) *Penal Policy and Political Culture in England and Wales.* Winchester: Waterside Press.

Sanders, A. (1998) 'What Principles Underlie Criminal Justice Policy in the 1990s?', *Oxford Journal of Legal Studies*, 18 (3): 533–42.

Scraton, P., J. Sim and P. Skidmore (1991) *Prisons Under Protest.* Milton Keynes: Open University Press.

Sim, J. (1990) *Medical Power in Prisons: The Prison Medical Service in England and Wales 1774-1989.* Buckingham: Open University Press.

Sparks, R. (1996) 'Penal Austerity: The Doctrine of Less Eligibility Reborn?', in R. Matthews and P. Francis (eds), *Prisons 2000.* London: Macmillan.

Stern, V. (1987) *Bricks of Shame: Britain's Prisons.* London: Penguin Books.

Sykes, G. (1958) *The Society of Captives: A Study of a Maximum-Security Prison.* Princeton: Princeton University Press.

Thomas, J. E. (1972) *The English Prison Officer since 1850: A Study in Conflict.* London and Boston: Routledge and Kegan Paul.

Thomas, J. *et al.* (2003) 'Critiquing the Critics of Peacemaking Criminology: Some Rather Ambivalent Reflections on the Theory of "Being Nice"', in K. McEvoy and T. Newburn (eds), *Criminology, Conflict Resolution and Restorative Justice*, Basingstoke: Palgrave Macmillan, pp. 101–30.

Uzzell, J. (1974) 'What Is Happening to the Prison Service', *Prison Service Journal*, 13: 6–8.

Wacquant, L. (2002) 'The Curious Eclipse of Prison Ethnography in the Age of Mass Incarceration', *Ethnography*, 1 December, 3(4): 371–97.

Warner, K. (2009) 'Resisting the new punitiveness: penal policy in Denmark, Finland and Norway', paper presented at Fifth Irish Criminology Conference, University College Dublin.

11 Prison size and quality of life in Norwegian closed prisons in late modernity

Berit Johnsen and Per Kristian Granheim

In light of John Pratt's description of Nordic prisons as having exceptional prison conditions when it comes to the high standards of material comfort, the relaxed prison atmosphere, the prison sentence being only the loss of liberty, and the principle of normalization (Pratt 2008a, b; Pratt and Ericksson 2009), it would be interesting to take a closer look at how prisoners experience their quality of life within them. In this chapter we will present a study of the quality of life in Norwegian closed prisons. The study is based on Alison Liebling's concept of the prisons' *moral performance* (Liebling 2006, 2004a, b). Central issues in our discussion are prison size and the influence of international discourses, such as penal excess and the new penology, on Norwegian crime policy.

The penal excess

The significant growth in the prison populations in many Western countries over the last three or four decades has been much discussed and analysed by criminologists and sociologists (e.g. Christie 2000; Garland 2001a; Gottschalk 2006; Hough *et al.* 2008). In what has been called an era of penal excess, Pratt (2008a, b) has pointed to the Scandinavian countries as exceptions. Even so and also acknowledged by Pratt, the prison populations in the Scandinavian countries have grown extensively over the last decades. In Norway, the daily average prison population increased from 1,828 to 3,480 prisoners from 1982 to 2007, i.e. an increase of 90.4 per cent (Statistics Norway).[1] This increase has resulted in a continuous need for increased prison capacity and a call for the building of new prisons or the expansion of those already existing. The prison capacity has increased from 2,334 places in 1990 to 3,574 places in 2008, i.e. an increase of 53. 1 per cent (Kristoffersen 2010). In spite of an official aim of using alternative forms of punishments (community service, drug courts, etc.) to increase the total system capacity, estimates show that 4,125 prison places will be needed by 2014 (Kriminalomsorgens kapasitetsplan 2010).

Strategic planning of future prison capacity and the location of prisons are predominantly discussed in public reports, rather than in the academic literature (Marianov and Fresard 2005). Like other reports – such as *Prison Costs* (1991) in the US, *Scottish Prison Service Estates Review* (2002) in Scotland, *Securing the*

Future (2007) in England and Wales, *Thornton Hall Prison* (2008) in Ireland – the *Storfengselsutredning* (2006) in Norway tends first of all to focus on costs; how to get the best value for taxpayers' money. Security for the public, efficiency, management and consequences for staff are central issues in this discussion, besides the issue of prison size. An exception is Baroness Corston's report (2007) discussing imprisonment for women. When considering size and location for female prisons, the cost effectiveness and efficiency are de-emphasized, and the focus is rather on the link between criminal justice and social (together with health) policy. Attempts to estimate the optimal size of a prison vary, e. g. in Scotland, the *Estates Review* (2002: 15) concluded that 'the optimum size for any new prison at the current time is around 700 cells or places'. In Scandinavia, the optimal prison size is estimated lower than in many other countries. According to *Lokalförsörjningsplan för platsutbyggnad åren 2005–8* the Swedish estimate is 250 places.

Pratt (2008a) underlines the importance of the large proportion of small prisons in the Nordic countries. In Norway, the average prison size is 79 places. Fifteen out of 48 prisons have fewer than 30 places. As Pratt rightly comments, Norway is sparsely populated. Although one-third of the population live in the greater Oslo area, people as well as prisons are spread almost all over the country. The settlement in the districts, mainly due to industrial and military purposes, has resulted in a decentralization of services such as health care, education, police and criminal justice, based on the principle of egalitarianism. In relation to prisons, the policy is that 'Convicted persons should as far as is practically possible and appropriate be committed to a prison in the vicinity of their home district' (Execution of Sentences Act § 11).

There is, as in many other countries, a tendency in Norway to build new prisons rather large in comparison with those already existing. An example is the newly opened Halden Prison with a capacity of 252 prisoners. This tendency is the context for our discussion of prison size in relation to the quality of prison life. The basis of the discussion is, in addition to Pratt's notion of Scandinavian exceptionalism, the influence of the so-called new penology (Feeley and Simon 1992, 1994) in Norwegian crime policy.

The new penology – a Norwegian perspective

In the late 1980s, some specific incidents marked a change in direction for Norwegian crime policy. These incidents involved several escapes, one of them resulting in the killing of a prison officer. The incidences were broadly referred to in the media, and sensational headlines and critical focus on the prison service made it necessary to built trust by convincing the public that punishment is carried out in a responsible manner. It became essential to shape a policy with broad political agreement, and in 1989, new restrictive rules were introduced in order to protect society from 'dangerous criminals'. The forces which according to Pratt (2008b) contribute to penal excess – such as a decline of trust in government, discrediting of expertise and sensational media reporting – seems to be present in

Norway as well. According to Pratt, one of the strongest indicators is a growing prison population combined with stable or declining crime rates. In Norway, crime rates have been stable since the 1990s, and declining in the period between 2002 and 2006. In the estimates of the prison capacity for 2014, an increased use of custody (1,100 places) and, according to new criminal code, more severe punishment for serious crimes, are taken into account (Kriminalomsorgens kapasitetsplan 2010).

However, as also noted by Pratt (2008a), the prison population in Norway has since 1980 been kept *artificially* low, because prisons are hardly overcrowded. In lack of prison places, convicts are placed on a waiting list (this system is hardly in accordance with the new penology). In the beginning of the 1990s, the waiting list reached almost 7,000 sentences. In 2005 the waiting list had been reduced to about 2,500 sentences. Since then, the top priority for the Correctional Service has been to remove it, and this was – at least temporarily – achieved in 2009. Politically this issue creates an untenable situation and draws a lot of attention, raising questions about the governance of the system and its ability to manage people that are sentenced to imprisonment.

The change in direction can also be traced back to the change of primary objectives for the prison service. The definition of punishment in Norway is to inflict an evil that is supposed to be experienced as an evil (Andenæs 2004), or in Christie's words: to inflict pain (Christie 1981). One of the primary objectives for the prison service, stated in the Prison Act of 1958 (§14), has been to minimize the harms of confinement. In the Execution of Sentences Act, which in 2001 replaced the Prison Act, this aim is stated explicitly for remand prisoners only. Besides, attitudes towards the infliction of pain have changed, and the awareness of the harms of confinement seems at present to be weak or almost non-existent. As Pratt (2008b) also notices, according to a traditional welfare model, where crime is regarded as a social problem which calls for social reforms and the improvement of living conditions for vulnerable groups in the society (see e.g. St.meld. 104 [1977–8]), there has been a shift towards a more neo-liberal way of considering crime. Crime is now perceived primarily as an individual problem; as a result of bad choices, and 'the blame is placed firmly at the door of the individual' (Estrada 2004: 440). In this context the Correctional Service aims to prevent recidivism by enabling the offenders, through their own initiatives, to change their criminal behaviour. An overall utilitarian purpose of the punishment is reflected in the title of a White Paper about the Correctional Service: *A Punishment that Works – Less Crime – A Safer Society* (St.meld. 37 [2007–8]), which was presented in parliament in 2008.

Critics of the new penology

According to Liebling (2008: 71), a central criticism against the new penology, is that efficiency is 'ethically blind', and that '[a]ctuarial models of justice risk neglecting the moral agency of persons'. Besides, Liebling says, new penology 'emphasises utilitarian purposes over moral considerations' (ibid.) (cf. Feeley and Simon 1994, 1992). According to Feeley and Simon, actuarial justice prefers quantitative over qualitative analyses, and there is a focus on the performance of the criminal process as a system, 'in which the effects of various stages have implications for each other and for the overall operation of the criminal law' (1994: 188).

Traditionally, Norwegian criminological research has been dominated by a qualitative approach. The focus has in general been critical to the system of criminal justice. Prison research has been dominated by sociological studies where 'the voice' of the prisoners has been prominent in order to describe and analyse prison life (in English, see e.g. Mathiesen 1965). But as in other countries, such studies have declined in recent years. In the wake of 'what-works' – an evidence-based rehabilitation and risk-management technology for efficiency in the Correctional Service (Strand 2006) – which principles and efforts were imported to Norway in the 1990, the research focus has changed. The public research funding agencies seem to be especially interested in effect studies of different efforts, as well as studies of recidivism rates.

As a reaction to the biased focus on system performance criteria in the prison service in England and Wales, Liebling (2006, 2004a, b) has identified what matters the most for prisoners and staff in prisons, and developed two questionnaires – MQPL (measuring the quality of prison life) for prisoners, and SQL (staff quality of life) for staff. The purpose of the project was to 'explore whether it is possible to develop well grounded survey measures of prison life and quality, which can provide an additional operationally useful measure to those already in place (such as Key Performance Indicators and standard Audits)' (Liebling and Arnold 2002: 1). In their study, Liebling and her colleagues identified important values for the legitimacy of prison in late modernity, and translated a distinctly qualitative issue – the quality of prison life – into specific dimensions suitable for quantitative analysis. Three of the five Nordic countries (Sweden, Finland and Norway) have taken an interest in Liebling's study (for Sweden, see Danielsson *et al.* 2006).[2]

The quality of prison life

According to Liebling (2004a: 461) '[p]risons are special moral environments in which *how people feel treated* (i.e. how prisoners *and staff* feel treated) has serious consequences, first, for what happens in them, and secondly, for the claims that can be made about them'. It is reasonable, though, to ask if prisons can be moral places at all. In Norway, the most severe punishment is the loss of liberty and the task of the prison is to accomplish it. Imprisonment causes an evil or pain, and the morality of this can undoubtedly be discussed. However, Liebling's studies (2004a, 2006) have shown that prisoners experience pain differently. In this context, the question of morality makes sense, because for prisoners as well as staff, regardless of which prison they represented, what mattered for the prison experience was 'a set of values which are essentially *interpersonal* and *civic*' (Liebling 2004a: 454).

The values identified in Liebling's studies (2004a, 2006) constitute a framework of dimensions such as prisoner–staff relationships, respect and order (see Table

11.1). Liebling (2004a: 236) defines staff–prisoner relationships as '[t]he manner in, and extent to which, staff and prisoners interact during rule-enforcing and non-rule-enforcing transactions'. The power-laden relationship between officers and prisoners can be difficult to balance in order to get it 'right' or 'good' (Liebling and Price 2001), but it is nevertheless identified as a key component for the experience of prison life. The performance of interaction, involvement and care have a great impact on the quality of these relationships. Respect in the sense of '[a]n attitude of consideration; to pay proper attention to and not violate. Regard for the inherent dignity and value of the human person' (Liebling 2004a: 212) is also important for the quality of the prisoner–staff relationships, but it also has a broader meaning by respecting the prisoners' rights and paying them attention. Order in the meaning of '[t]he degree to which the prison environment is structured, predictable and acceptable' (Liebling 2004a: 291) expresses predictability and is crucial for how the prisoners experience their safety in prison. The dimensions are indicators of the prisons' 'moral performance' or 'moral climate', where moral performance means 'those aspects of a prisoner's mainly *interpersonal* and material treatment that render a term of imprisonment more or less dehumanizing and/or painful' (Liebling 2004a: 473).

Our study

Our study of the quality of life in prisons concentrates on closed prisons, i.e. prisons that are physically separated from the surroundings with concrete walls and/or fences, of which there were 32 in Norway when the study was conducted in 2007. One of them is a prison for women only, but several of the others have small units for women. The reason for this is to allow women, as well as men, to serve their sentences close to home. The smallest prison in our study has only 12 prisoners and 19 employees, while the largest has 392 prisoners and 565 employees. Because our experiences told us that the prisons show rather great cultural differences, we decided to include them all.

The questionnaires (MQPL and SQL) were translated into Norwegian (the versions used in this study are from 2006), and the modified version of the MQPL questionnaire was later retranslated back to English and to German, French, Spanish, Polish and Russian in order to include as many foreign-speaking prisoners as possible. The questionnaires are divided into three parts. Part one collects demographic data, and part two consists of statements in which the respondents are supposed to agree or disagree on a scale from one to five (1–5 Likert scale). Scores higher than three reflect positive views and lower than three negative views on given dimensions. In our version of the MQPL questionnaire, there are 98 statements forming 16 dimensions of the quality of prison life (see Table 11.1).[3] In SQL, 117 form 17 dimensions. Part three consists of two open questions where respondents were asked to list the three most stressful and three most satisfying aspects of their lives in prison.

From June to September 2007 we visited all 32 closed prisons.[4] Before our visits, posters were sent to the prisons along with a request to put them up in units

Table 11.1 Reliability results

Dimensions	Cronbach Alpha
Relationships with staff	.95
Overall treatment	.88
Well being	.87
Personal safety	.71
Personal development	.88
Respect	.87
Order and organization	.83
Race equality	.85
Family contact	.76
Support for personal safety	.78
OB courses	.93
Specialist care/care for those at risk	.79
Healthcare	.94
Decency	.67
Entry into custody	.61
Fairness	.68

and wings to announce the forthcoming study. At the visits, we met the prisoners individually and/or in groups, depending on the most practical arrangement at each prison. Information was given and surveys handed out to all prisoners who wanted to participate in the study. The prisoners were expected to fill in the questionnaire by themselves. Depending on the arrangement, we came back later the same day or the day after to collect the questionnaires. If some prisoners needed more time, they could return the questionnaire in a pre-paid addressed envelope.

The sample consists of all prisoners present at each prison on the day of our visit. 2,050 questionnaires were handed out, and 1,132 were returned, which is a response rate of 55 per cent. The prison with the highest participation had a response rate of 100 per cent, while the lowest had 31 per cent. Of the returned questionnaires 148 (or 13 per cent) were in a language other than Norwegian.

The overall picture

Looking at the total score of all prisons, the only dimensions that have positive scores are 'Personal safety' and 'Race equality'. The rest of the dimensions scores negatively. Compared with results from England and Wales (Liebling 2004a, 2006; Liebling and Arnold 2002), there is not much difference – the scores are actually quite similar between the countries. Given Pratt's (2008a, b; Pratt and Ericksson 2009) notion of relatively humane conditions in Norwegian prisons – e.g. the high standards of material comfort, the relaxed prison atmosphere, the prison sentence being only the loss of liberty, and the principle of normalization – it would have been reasonable to expect a more positive quality of life in Norwegian prisons. Also taking into account that Norwegian prisons are less overcrowded than in England and Wales, that the prison–staff ratio is higher and the education or training of staff is longer and more elaborate, one should believe that Pratt is correct when speculating that 'the exceptional conditions in most Scandinavian prisons, while not eliminating the pains of imprisonment, must surely ease them' (2008a: 124).

Our study shows that this is hardly so, and for Norway – with a self-image of being a leading country in corrections[5] – the MQPL results from our study were disappointing according to the reactions of the Ministry of Justice. The results show, however, that prisoners who have filled out the questionnaire in other languages than Norwegian, seem to be more satisfied with their life in prison, perhaps reflecting a different expectation level.[6]

As in Liebling's study (2004a), we found that the 13 dimensions measured were highly correlated in general. A factor analysis showed that the 13 dimensions yielded one factor which explained more than half (52 per cent) of the variations in the dimensions. This indicates a more general or gestalt experience rather than the unique experience of every dimension of prison life by prisoners. According to Liebling (2004a), the dimension that matters most for prisoners, and could be the main underlying factor, is their relationship with staff. The quality of this relationship influences the other dimensions. The following comment in the open question may illustrate this:

> The officers who use their judgement and tries to help you a bit further with the few possibilities there is, they are worth their weight in gold and make you feel like a human being. By their attitudes and good behaviour, they create calmness and a good atmosphere at the wing.

The importance of staff for the prisoners' experience of prison life is illustrated in the answers to the open questions, as most of the prisoners' comments concern their relationship with first-line staff. The officers tended to evaluate their relationships with prisoners more positively than the prisoners did (see also Liebling and Price 2001), *except* in some of the small prisons where the prisoner actually rated their relationships with staff higher than vice versa. Our most striking finding, however, was how the scores differed in relation to prison size.

Differences related to prison size

In Norway, 20 out of 32 closed prisons have fewer than 50 prisoners, and in our study we have categorized these prisons as small. Five of the closed prisons have between 51 and 100 prisoners, and in the Norwegian context, these prisons are considered to be medium sized. Prisons that have more than 101 prisoners are considered to be large, of which five are closed.[7] Of the 1,132 questionnaires returned, 274 were from prisoners in small prisons, 194 from medium-sized and 664 from large prisons. When dividing the prisons into these categories, our analysis shows that the prisoners' scores differed significantly on several of the dimensions measured. Table 11.2 shows how the scores differed, and if these differences are significant.

As Table 11.2 shows, there are significant differences on 11 of the dimensions

Table 11.2 Results of prisoners split into small, medium and large prison sizes

	Prisons							
	Small		Medium		Large			
Dimensions	M	SD	M	SD	M	SD	F-ratio	Probability
Relationships with staff	3.47**	.96	2.89	.99	2.82	.98	42.14	0.000
Overall treatment	3.31**	.93	2.88	.88	2.72	.91	37.78	0.000
Well being	3.15**	.91	2.77	.89	2.62	.89	32.74	0.000
Personal safety	3.70**	.81	3.47*	.90	3.30	.90	17.25	0.000
Personal development	2.71**	.97	2.36	1.00	2.29	.93	19.50	0.000
Respect	3.01**	.89	2.55	.86	2.46	.88	35.58	0.000
Order and organization	3.34**	.88	2.95	.84	2.85	.85	29.77	0.000
Race equality	3.52**	.68	3.18	.63	3.19	.64	25.77	0.000
Family contact	2.79**	1.10	2.35	.99	2.37	1.02	9.12	0.000
Support for personal safety	3.25**	.81	2.93	.79	2.87	.83	19.40	0.000
Specialist care/care for those at risk	2.68*	.85	2.51	.78	2.35	.86	13.30	0.000
OB courses	2.99	1.12	3.08	1.11	2.83	1.11	0.46	0.635
Healthcare	2.71	1.15	2.61	1.09	2.72	1.12	0.16	0.848

Note: Dimensions with white background have significantly different scores among the different prison sizes. *Significant mean difference from large prisons. **Significant mean difference from both large and medium prisons.

measured ($p < .001$). 'OB courses'[8] and 'Healthcare' are the only two dimensions where prisoners from the different prison sizes do not appear to have significant different opinion of the quality of these aspects. Further analysis show that the dimension 'Personal safety', both in medium-sized (M = 3.47, $p < .05$) and small prisons (M = 3.70, $p < .001$), have significantly higher scores than large prisons. Small prisons have more positive scores than both large and medium-sized prisons on ten dimensions, and have a higher score on 'Specialist care/care for those at risk' than large prisons. On six dimensions, small prisons have a higher score than the middle value 3, while as medium-sized and large prisons have scores lower than 3.

These findings have been presented for prison staff and managers, and several of them have explained the results by referring to the differences in the composition of the prison populations in these three categories of prison size. According to our demographic data, however, the mix of prisoners in small, medium-sized and large prisons is quite similar, although small prisons have a higher portion of prisoners that serve shorter sentences (less than one year). However, all three categories of prisons have a majority of prisoners serving sentences of less than one year due to the fact that most sentences in Norway are short. The average sentence in 2007, when the study was carried out, was 162 days, and two-thirds of all sentences were less than 90 days (Kriminalomsorges årsstatistikk 2007). Our analysis shows that the length of sentence does not have any influence on the results of the dimensions measured. Small prisons also have a slightly higher proportion of remand prisoners. Because of the intense pressure to remove the waiting lists at the time of our data collection, the prisons had to keep a high occupancy rate. Most likely, this caused less flexibility in selecting prisoners to different prisons and created more similar populations in small, medium-sized and large prisons than anticipated by staff and managers at our presentations. However, there might be profile differences that are not seen in the background information. Prisoners considered to be 'difficult' are most likely to be held in large prisons, but sometimes these prisoners can be transferred to smaller prisons where they might be experienced as less troublesome. According to Baldursson (2000), in Iceland a general rule is to transfer 'difficult' prisoners to smaller prisons because of the positive staff–prisoner relationship in these prisons.

The more positive scores in small prisons than in medium-sized and large prisons, are supported by the qualitative data. The prisoners' comments on staff are mostly positive in small prisons, while in the medium-sized and large prisons, comments are mostly negative. In general, prisoners' negative comments on staff–prisoner relationships are about a lack of respect and individual care and concern, such as 'Not being treated with respect and civility' and 'The staff show me very little care'. Likewise, positive comments are about staff paying respect and showing care. Prisoners in small prisons have to a larger extent than prisoners in medium-sized and large prisons positive comments on social contact with officers, such as: 'The social association between me and the staff is very good', and 'Staff who takes part in social activities, is something that I appreciate very much'. This issue was also commented on by the officers in the small prisons: '[We] participate in the community at the unit and in activities together with the prisoners'. Also among the officers, positive relationships with the prisoners were mostly commented on by officers in small prisons (30 per cent, while approximately 15 per cent in medium-sized and large prisons shared this view).

When analysing the data concerning the prison officers in relation to prison size, we find the same pattern as in the prisoners' data, with more positive scores in small prisons. On the two dimensions concerning relationship with prisoners ('Relationships with prisoners' and 'Social distance'), the staff's scores were significantly higher in small prisons than in medium-sized and large prisons. In a paper in which we present findings on the prison officers (Johnsen et al. submitted), we discuss possible reasons why staff–prisoner relationships seem to be of a better quality in small prisons than in medium-sized and large ones. It seems that the decentralized and less hierarchical structure in small prisons make it natural for governors to have direct contact with prisoners. In these meetings, the manager gains first-hand insight into the prisoners' situation, and problems can be discussed and perhaps solved right away. In this way the stressful aspect of waiting for answers which causes a lot of frustration among prisoners, can be removed. Besides, as the quotations earlier show, there seems to be a lot of informal and less strained day-to-day contact between the parties involved in small prisons. In such a rather relaxed atmosphere, it becomes easier to relate to each other as individuals and not merely as prisoners and officers. Likewise, there is a long tradition of staff-prisoner interaction in small prisons. Social work as a part of the prison officer profession has existed in small prisons before it was formalized by the personal contact officer arrangement. Small institutions also mean more visibility and transparency. The prison officers may thus be more sensitive to changes in attitudes among the prisoners. This in turn makes them capable to react more quickly when a prisoner is experiencing problems. Moreover, the fewer opportunities for activities in most small prisons compared to the larger ones require cooperation between prisoners and staff in order to get prison life to run smoothly. Under such circumstances, the prison officers' discretion and underuse of power become pivotal. According to Liebling (2004a: 429) '[h]umanistic values mean nothing if they are not translated into day to day practices', and Mathiesen (2008) claims that a strong hierarchical regime in prisons seems to be an obstacle to humane conditions and humanity. On the basis of our findings, it seems to be easier to achieve a humane milieu and humane treatment of prisoners in small prisons than in medium-sized and large ones.

Another aspect that we believe influences the scores in the small prison in a positive way is that many small prisons are located in city centres close to the prisoners' homes. This makes it easy for families and friends to come and visit, and the prisoners can see and listen to the city, thus feeling less isolated. Some of the largest prisons in Norway are located in rural areas, making it difficult for families to visit because there is either no or infrequent public transportation to these prisons. As to the quality of life, then, Baroness Corston's (2007) proposal of locating female prison units in city centres, close to home and easily accessible for visitors, should therefore apply to men as well.

Closed prisons and their moral performance in late modernity

Our study shows that, in general, the standard of the moral performance in Norwegian closed prisons is not as high as one might expect. As the Norwegian system is founded on humanity, legal protection, and equality (Prop. 1 S [2009–10]), and where prisoners' rights in these fields are stated in laws, rules, and recommendations, the expectations *should* also be high. However, as Pratt (2008a: 123) reminds us: 'Of course, one must recognize that however relaxed a prison regime, whatever material comforts are provided, prisoners are still prisoners. There are rules, levels of surveillance, record keeping, denials of choices, deprivation and sanctions that will differentiate any prisoner from free people.' A reasonable question is how positive a prison experience can be, given that we know that imprisonment is painful, and that the experience of pain is deeply relevant for the prison experience (Liebling 2004a). Our findings indicate that prisoners' experience in small prisons is less painful than that of prisoners in medium-sized and large prisons. Considering the importance of the relational aspects for the moral performance of a prison, these results are not surprising, and we see clear parallels to Christie's (1974) study of closely and loosely connected societies. In closely connected societies – as we may find them in small prisons – it is easier for the parties involved to know and relate to each other as people. The social control in such societies happens primarily through daily interaction between the parties involved, and it is often hard to notice because it is an implicit part in the interaction. In looser societies – which seem to be the case for medium-sized and large prisons – it is more difficult for the parties involved to learn to know each other and develop personal contact. Therefore, the control also gets more formalized and discernible, which easily is experienced as more dehumanizing for those controlled. In closely connected societies, inside as well as outside prisons, there is always the risk of being *too* close. In any case, prison officers have to keep some boundaries in order to keep the relationship at a professional level (Bottomley et al. 1994; Hammerlin and Mathiassen 2006; Liebling 2008; Liebling and Price 2001).

When we have presented the study in meetings with prison staff, managers and bureaucrats at the Ministry of Justice, they express that they recognize the differences we have found between small, medium-sized and large prisons. Most likely, this is due to the experience some of them have from working in prisons of different sizes, and to the fact that many of them know Christie's (1974) study – it has been required reading at the staff academy for many years. Besides, in a study of prison officers, Bødahl (1979: 39) concluded that '[s]mall institutions are best'. Despite this 'common knowledge', that the climate in small prisons is better, two of the small prisons in our study, some of the prisons with the best scores, are now closed down in favour of opening Halden Prison. These small prisons were old and had poor facilities, while Halden Prison is one of the most up-to-date prisons in Europe.[9] In the years to come, the plan is to close down several of the smallest prisons with the best scores in our study, because they do not meet the standards of an up-to-date prison. A rebuilding of these prisons is not seen as realistic or economically reasonable. The plan is to build new prisons, none of which will have less than 30 places, preferably more (Kriminalomsorgens kapasitetsplan 2010). We do understand that prisons today have to meet certain criteria for material standards, but while people can be moved, cultures cannot. Some of the new prisons will be small, following our categorization, and the plan is to establish them in central areas. Most likely, however, they will not be as central as the old prisons in the city centres.

The closing down of the smallest prisons may be interpreted as a decline in attention and concern relative to the sociological knowledge of social order in prison (Simon 2000; see also Liebling 2004a). According to Liebling (2004a), the dimensions identified in the studies of the quality of prison life are seriously under threat, due to dominant discourses of punishment and correction that are influenced by the new penology. Rehabilitation is still a central goal of the correctional system, though, but it is now inscribed in what we may in Foucauldian terms call an apparatus of *governmentality*, where prisoners are supposed to learn to govern themselves to become law-abiding citizens (Foucault 1991, 1982; Garland 2003, 1997a). For the prisoners who do not want to change, their time in prison will serve the more modest purpose of incapacitation – to protect society from their crimes. However, within a new penology/governmentality context, rehabilitation of the individual is also about protecting the general society. The reason for rehabilitation is no longer founded in the care for the individual, but in the protection of society from new offences (Estrada 2004; Garland 2001b, 1997b; Johnsen 2006).

The building of Halden Prison is important to the Correctional Service in the management of the increased number of remand prisoners. In 2010 this issue was identified by the Ministry of Justice as the main challenge for the Correctional Service (Tildelingsbrev 2010). The discussion about the pains of imprisonment has been silenced (Schaanning 2009), and in the White Paper to Parliament (St.meld. 37 [2007–8]), for example, pain caused by punishment is hardly discussed at all. In accordance with the new penology, where the individual is responsible for his/her actions *and* the consequences of these actions, pain may be regarded as self-inflicted because punishment is a calculated risk of committing crimes (Johnsen 2006). Efforts to ease the pain seem only to be accepted if they are founded in rights, laws and recommendations, or if they serve the purpose of making society safer by reducing the risk of new crimes. The focus on prisoners *as* prisoners – that is people who live within the very special setting of a prison – and their experiences and thoughts, has no place within the new penology (Liebling 2006). Within the new penology, prisoners are considered to be criminals who get what they deserve, while the prison authorities try to motivate and help the prisoners to change their criminal behaviour. The change, however, is the prisoner's own responsibility. Most likely prisoners' motivation and focus on changing behaviour in order to become law-abiding citizens are influenced by how they feel treated in prison (see also Liebling 2006). This implies that the prison should not disclaim all responsibility for changing prisoners. In order to make the prisoners change, each prison carries responsibility for creating a moral climate in the establishment that eases the pain of imprisonment and helps prisoners to change.

However, it is not on the basis of utilitarian purposes that prisons should focus and improve prisoners' quality of life – it is on the basis of the intrinsic value: 'Prisons should perform well because it is important to treat human beings well' (Liebling 2004a: 473). According to Liebling, prisons in late modernity have a problem with legitimacy, as '[c]urrent penal discourse has apparently swept the concept of legitimacy under the carpet, privileging "economic efficiency" over morality' (Liebling 2008: 75). The study of the quality of life in prison, however, *is* about morality and the treatment of individuals in prison in ways that really matters for them. The study operationalizes the key concepts of legitimacy in prisons in late modernity and places core human values 'at the heart, rather than the periphery, of evaluative knowledge' (Liebling 2004a: 475). This knowledge is important also for Norwegian prisons, because in Norway, as in other countries, prisons are special moral environments even if they are presented as humane. In these environments the power-laden interaction between prisoners and staff needs to be regulated, not only by laws and rights, but also by interpersonal and civic human values.

Conclusion

In spite of a decline in the registered crime rate, prognoses in Norway tell us that the prison population in the coming years is most likely going to increase. In present time, the new penology is influencing the leading discourses regulating crime policy, and this also concerns Norway. We cannot therefore expect studies such as ours – or Booth's (2009) study in England and Wales, which showed that prison size was the most influential factor of the prisons performance on safety, respect, purposeful activity and resettlement – to prevent the building of new prisons and the closing of older and smaller prisons with poor facilities. There is a lot to learn from these studies, however, both for newly built and already existing prisons. The consideration for the individuals' quality of prison life calls for prisons with close social interaction and involvement between the different groups involved. Besides, new prisons should be easily accessible for visitors, and if possible they should be placed in city centres.

In the case of Norway, and in relation to Pratt's notion of Scandinavian exceptionalism, our study has also shown that even if the prison conditions were considered to be humane, the relational performance of humanity – such as paying respect, showing care and being concerned about the wellbeing of another person – cannot be taken for granted. This is an issue that needs to be addressed explicitly. A system that *appears* as humane, based on the principle of normalization and where the essence of punishment is the loss of liberty per se, should evaluate and bring the moral performance of its institutions into focus in order to be legitimatized as humane.

Notes

1 The increase from 1962 to 1982 was 16.4 per cent.
2 The Swedish study was carried out in motivation units for drug abusers, and some of the original questions were taken out of the study. We have therefore not compared our results with results from the Swedish study.
3 We have not altered the item-construction criteria of the dimensions given by Liebling and her colleagues.
4 We are grateful to our colleagues who helped us visiting the prisons.
5 See Roddy Nilsson (Chapter 5 in this book).
6 Another reason that may explain why the Norwegian scores are, from the point of view of the prison administrators, disappointedly low, is that the study was carried out in summertime, when the activity in prisons is generally low (closed schools and workshops, etc., due to the Norwegian summer holiday), and many operational support grades staff work in the prisons during this period. However, we do not believe that these issues fully explain the negative scores in Norwegian closed prisons.
7 The same categorization has been used in other studies, e.g. Hammerlin and Mathiassen (2006).
8 Offending Behaviour courses.
9 Halden Prison was opened after we collected the data and is not included in our study.

References

Andenæs, J. (2004) *Alminnelig strafferett* [General criminal law]. Oslo: Universitetsforlaget.
Baldursson, E. (2000) 'Prisoners, Prisons and Punishment in Small Societies', *Journal of Scandinavian Studies in Criminology and Crime Prevention*, 1(1): 6–15.
Bødal, K. (1979) *Fengselstjenestemannen har ordet* [The prison staff has the floor]. Oslo: Ministry of Justice.
Booth, S. (2009) *The Prison Characteristics that Predict Prisons Being Assessed as*

Performing 'Well': A Thematic Review by HM Chief Inspector of Prisons. London: HM Inspectorate of Prisons.

Bottomley, A. K., A. Liebling and R. Sparks (1994) *An Evaluation of Barlinnie and Shotts Units.* Scottish Prison Service Occasional Papers No. 7.

Christie, N. (1974) *Hvor tett et samfunn* [How closely knit a society?]. Oslo: Universitetsforlaget.

—— (1981) *Limits to Pain.* Oslo: Universitetsforlaget.

—— (2000) *Crime Control as Industry: Towards Gulags, Western Sty*le. London: Routledge.

Corston Report: Executive Summary. London: Home Office (2007).

Danielsson, M., B. Goeransson, L. Krantz and C. Rehme (2006) *Kriminalvårdens innsatser mot narkotika: En studie av klimatet på narkotikaavdelingarna* [The correctional service's measures against drugs: a study of the climate at the units for drug abusers]. Norrköping: Kriminalvårdstyrelsen.

Estrada, F. (2004) 'The Transformation of the Politics of Crime in High Crime Societies', *European Journal of Criminology*, 1(4): 419–43.

Feeley, M. and J. Simon (1992) 'The New Penology: Notes on the Emerging Strategy of Corrections and its Implications', *Criminology*, 30(4): 449–74.

—— (1994) 'Actuarial Justice: The Emerging New Criminal Law', in D. Nelken (ed.), *The Futures of Criminology.* London: Sage, pp. 173–201.

Fengselsloven [Prison Act] (1958).

Foucault, M. (1982) 'The Subject and Power', *Critical Inquiry*, 8: 777–95.

—— (1991) 'Governmentality', in G. Burchell, C. Gordon and P. Miller (eds), *The Foucault Effect: Studies in Governmentality.* Chicago: University of Chicago Press, pp. 87–104.

Garland, D. (1997a) '"Governmentality" and the Problems of Crime', *Theoretical Criminology*, 1(2): 173–214.

—— (1997b) 'Probation and the Reconfiguration of Crime Control', in R. Burnett (ed.), *The Probation Service: Responding to Change (Proceedings of the Probation Studies Unit First Colloquium: Probation Studies Report No. 3).* Oxford: University of Oxford Centre for Criminological Research.

—— (ed.) (2001a) 'Special Issue on Mass Imprisonment in the USA', in *Punishment & Society*, 3:1.

—— (2001b) *The Culture of Control: Crime and Social Order in Contemporary Society.* Oxford: Oxford University Press.

—— (2003) 'Penal Modernism and Postmodernism', in T. G. Blomberg and S. Cohen (eds), *Punishment and Social Control.* New York: Walter de Gruyter, pp. 45–73.

Gottschalk, M. (2006) 'The Long Reach of the Carceral State: The Politics of Crime, Mass Imprisonment, and Penal Reform in the United States and Abroad', *Law and Social Inquiry: Journal of the American Bar Foundation*, 34(2): 439–72.

Hammerlin, Y. and C. Mathiassen (2006) *Før og nå* [Then and now]. Oslo: Correctional Service of Norway Staff Academy, Report no. 5/2006.

Hough, M., R. Allen and E. Solomon (eds) (2008) *Tackling Prison Overcrowding: Build More Prisons? Sentence Fewer Offenders?* Bristol: Policy Press.

Johnsen, B. (2006) 'Forvaring – et barn av sin tid?' ['Preventive detention – a "child" of one's age?'], *Materialisten*, 4: 53–89.

Johnsen, B., P.K. Granheim and J. Helgesen (submitted) 'Exceptional Prison Conditions and the Quality of Prison Life: Prison Size and Prison Culture in Norwegian Closed Prisons'.

Kriminalomsorgens årsstatistikk (2007) [Annual Statistics Correctional Services]. Oslo: Ministry of Justice.

Kriminalomsorgens kapasitetsplan – med enhetsstruktur for fengsler og friomsorgskontorer [Plan of capacity for the correctional service – including structure for prison establishments and probation officers]. Oslo: Ministry of Justice (2010).

Kristoffersen, R. (ed.) (2010) *Correctional Statistics in Denmark, Finland, Iceland, Norway and Sweden*. Oslo: Correctional Service of Norway Staff Academy, Report no. 2/2010.

Liebling, A. (assisted by H. Arnold) (2004a) *Prisons and Their Moral Performance: A Study of Values, Quality and Prison Life*. New York: Oxford University Press.

—— (2004b) 'The Late Modern Prison and the Question of Values', *Current Issues in Criminal Justice*, 16(2): 202–19.

—— (2006) 'Prisons in Transition', *International Journal of Law and Psychiatry*, 29: 422–30.

—— (2008) '"Titan" Prisons: Do Size, Efficiency and Legitimacy Matter?', in M. Hough, R. Allen and E. Solomon (eds), *Tackling Prison Overcrowding: Build More Prisons? Sentence Fewer Offenders?* Bristol: Policy Press.

Liebling, A. and H. Arnold (2002) *Measuring the Quality of Prison Life*. London: Home Office, Research findings 174.

Liebling, A. and D. Price (2001) *The Prison Officer*. Leyhill: Prison Service Journal.

Lokalförsörjningsplan för platsutbyggnad åren 2005–2008 (Plan for Expanding the Prison Capacity in the period 2005–2008). Norrköping: Swedish Prison and Probation Service 2004.

Marianov, V. and F. Fresard (2005) 'A Procedure for the Strategic Planning of Locations, Capacities and Districting of Jails: Application to Chile', *Journal of the Operational Research Society*, 56: 244–51.

Mathiesen, T. (1965) *The Defences of the Weak: A Sociological Study of a Norwegian Correctional Institution*. London: Tavistock Publications Limited.

—— (2008) Contribution and discussion at a debate about preventive detention, Ila Prison 2008 5 November.

Pratt, J. (2008a) 'Scandinavian Exceptionalism in an Era of Penal Excess. Part I: The Nature and Roots of Scandinavian Exceptionalism', *British Journal of Criminology*, 48(2): 119–37.

—— (2008b) 'Scandinavian Exceptionalism in an Era of Penal Excess. Part II: Does Scandinavian exceptionalism have a future?', *British Journal of Criminology*, 48(3): 275–92.

Pratt, J. and A. Eriksson (2009) 'Den skandinaviska exceptionalismen i kriminalpolitiken' ['The Scandinavian exceptionalism in crime policy'], *Nordisk Tidsskrift for Kriminalvidenskap* 96(2): 135–51.

Prison Costs: Opportunities Exist to Lower the Cost of Building Federal Prisons, United States General Account Office (1991).

Prop. 1S (2009–10) Proposisjon til Stortinget for budsjettåret 2010 [Budget Proposition to the Parliament]. Oslo: Ministry of Justice.

Schaanning, E. (2009) *Den tilsiktede smerten: En blindflekk i norsk kriminalpolitikk* [The intended pain: a blind spot in the Norwegian politics of crime]. Oslo: Unipub.

Scottish Prison Service Estates Review, Scottish Prison service (2002).

Securing the Future: Proposals for the Efficient and Sustainable Use of Custody in England and Wales, Lord Carter's Review of Prisons (2007).

Simon, J. (2000) 'The "Society of Captives" in the Era of Hyper-Incarceration', *Theoretical Criminology*, 4(3): 285–308.

Statistics Norway, Crime and the Justice.

St.meld. 37 (2007–8) *Straff som virker – mindre kriminalitet – tryggere samfunn* [Punishment that works – less crime – safer society]. Oslo: Ministry of Justice.

St.meld. 104 (1977–8) *Om kriminalpolitiken* [The politics of crime]. Oslo: Ministry of Justice.

Storfengselsutredning [Report on large prisons]. Oslo: ECON-HolteProsjekt (2006).

Straffegjennomføringsloven [Execution of sentences act] (2001).

Strand, T. W. (2006) 'Mot en senmoderne kriminalomsorg?' ['In the direction of late modernity in the correctional service?'], *Materialisten*, 1: 55–76.

Thornton Hall Prison. Irish Prison Service (2008).

Tildelingsbrev 2010 [The correctional service's letter of commission], Oslo: Ministry of Justice.

12 A harsher prison climate and a cultural heritage working against it

Subcultural divisions among Swedish prison officers

Anders Bruhn, Odd Lindberg and Per-Åke Nylander

The international trend of mass imprisonment (Garland 2001) has not yet reached the same levels in the Nordic countries. However, safe custody, risk management and the expansion of security have become issues of high priority also in Sweden. One reason for this is a number of spectacular escapes from high-security prisons in 2004. These were carried out with the use of high levels of violence, heavy armaments, shootings and by using trucks to force gates, etc. The media debate that followed was extensive. A political consequence was the appointment of a new director general of the Prison Services, a highly ranked police officer. The new political directive to the Prison and Probations Service was 'no more escapes from high security'. In the aftermath of these escapes, and presumably also because of international influences, security measures in prisons have been tightened considerably. In most closed prisons, new electrified fences and new walls have been erected and new airport-like security checks for incoming staff and visitors have been set up (see Pratt 2008b). The number of prison officers specialized in security work has risen. However, at the same time, the number of rehabilitation and treatment programmes has increased. A more 'scientific' approach to 'what works', usually deeply rooted in cognitive behavioural therapy (CBT) and grounded in evidence-based methods, has been a clear policy development in later years (Andersson and Nilsson 2009: 194). A scientific board has been set up to assess the evidence of the treatment programmes. This latter development of 'scientification' is partly an international trend, but also very much in line with a Swedish tradition of social engineering. It is also a revival of the individual treatment idea, the paradigm that dominated prior to the radicalization movement of the 1970s with its focus on social relations and contextual factors. In relation to Swedish culture, these programmes are powerful symbols of the Prison and Probation Service as a 'rehabilitative' institution.

Nowadays, though, the individual treatment idea is based on categorizing prisoners into different risk groups. In closed prisons, the wings have become more specialized – resulting in a division of labour into treatment, regular and specialized security wings. This may be seen as a structural reaction to the dilemma prisons have to handle, enhanced by developments at a political level in later years: the question of security and control versus rehabilitation (Sykes, 1958; Foucault, 1977). But when this kind of division of labour takes place, there is also the risk of subcultural differentiation within an organization with the formation of different groups of staff with different approaches to the dilemma and to their occupational roles. How does this relate to the theme of Scandinavian exceptionalism in prison policy (Pratt 2008a, b)?

In this chapter we will discuss how the improvements in security and a concurrent increase in treatment programmes (and a rehabilitation ideal), with a subsequent division of labour into specialized wings, have affected the prison officer's daily work, especially in relation to the culturally embedded notions of rehabilitation and equality in life chances central to the traditional Scandinavian welfare model. Do prison officers in different kinds of wing think, feel and act differently? Is there a growing 'wing rivalry' based on what prison officers in different wings and with different roles assess as their main task? Or is there, as in many other occupations (police, doctors, military, etc.), a certain *esprit de corps* and feelings of cohesion and community to be found? The questions raised will also be related to Pratt's (2008a, b) discussion of Scandinavian exceptionalism. Is the traditional culture of humane prison conditions at risk in today's development of Swedish prison policy? The theoretical concepts used here to catch the cultural aspects of thinking, feeling and acting among prison officers are social representations, emotional labour and interaction rituals. We will reveal that there are today subcultural gaps between different groups of prison officers in Sweden. At the same time though, we find some important elements of integration. Our discussion is based on a three-year research project on occupational culture, occupational identity and job satisfaction among Swedish prison officers.[1]

Prisons and prison officers in Sweden

Approximately 5,000 prison officers (37% women in 2008) are employed in 55 Swedish prisons divided into five different security categories: closed A–D and open, or category E. Five prisons are classified as 'treatment prisons', two for women and three for men. These facilities are meant for prisoners with a clear motivation for change. Staff are specialized in running treatment programmes and doing motivational work. Most A–D category Swedish prisons have three types of wing: regular, treatment and special security. Treatment wings are focused on drug abuse, violence, sex crimes and criminal behaviour. Security wings aim at handling prisoners who are assessed as having a high risk of causing disorder, threatening others or are being threatened themselves. Since 1992, most prison officers are personal officers responsible for counselling four to ten prisoners, helping and motivating them to rehabilitate and to be able to live 'normal' lives after 'doing their time'. Today, this even holds for prison officers working on a security wing. The 1992 reform was a way of reducing costs for professional social workers in prisons. At the same time though it was intended as an enrichment of the old 'guarding' prison officer role, making it more attractive via the articulation of the rehabilitative side of prison officer work. The role of a personal officer is, therefore, with some exceptions, intended to be an inherent part of the occupational role of rank-and-file prison officers.

The basic level of formal education required to become a prison officer is upper-secondary school. However, prison officers in Sweden today have very different work–life experiences. Almost one-third of them have at least two years of university studies when they become employed by the service. Several of these, of whom the majority are women, have exams from three-year university programmes in social and behavioural sciences. All prison officers receive basic in-service training (20 weeks provided by the Prison and Probations Service). In addition to this and still at the beginning of their employment they attend a university course in sociology and social psychology (10 weeks). In addition to basic training, prison officers in treatment wings often undergo training in managing rehabilitation programmes. Experienced officers in treatment wings are often recruited to be programme managers responsible for recruiting and educating other officers to work with prisoners in rehabilitation programmes. The vast majority working in the wings are of course regular prison officers. They are managed by a principal officer (*kriminalvårdsinspektör*) who most often has an academic degree. Principal officers are normally responsible for several wings/units. Their office is normally in another building or on another floor in the building. There are also client administrators (*klienthandläggare*) in most prisons, most have an academic degree. They review and assess prisoners' requests concerning leave, telephone calls, visits and applications for transfer to treatment wings. They also act as counsellors for the personal officers. In high-security prisons there are special security units that manage all security matters in the prison. There is also a voluntary reaction/emergency force. This group consists of prison officers who receive special training to stop riots and other violent incidents in the prison. They are also expected to assist prisons with a lower-security category if they have problems with riots and violence.

Data and methods

The methodology used by our project is multi-strategic, it uses both qualitative and quantitative methods (Bruhn, 1999; Danermark, 2002). The core of the study is qualitative. Quantitative data are used to complement and support qualitative analyses. We conducted qualitative case studies in five prisons of different sizes and security levels. In total, 25 in-depth interviews, seven focus-group interviews and 120 hours of all-day prison officer shadowing were conducted.[2] The quantitative part consists of a survey of approximately 20 per cent (n = 1218) of the prison officer population, randomly selected. The response rate was 66 per cent (n = 806).[3] The survey questionnaire was developed by means of our case studies, as well as other previously validated instruments (mainly Liebling *et al.*'s measuring staff quality of life – SQL) adapted to the Swedish context.

Theoretical concepts

As stated in the introduction, the concepts of social representations, emotional labour and interactional rituals are closely interrelated in the analysis of how prison officers with different roles and in different wings think, feel and act in their daily work.

Social representations

Our main theoretical concept for exploring prison officers' ways of thinking is social representations. A social representation is a socially developed and shared form of knowledge which has a practical purpose and which affects the picture of reality that is constructed by a certain social group (Jodelet 1995). Social representations are developed in interaction concerning an object of some kind. The concept stresses the collective base for creating and maintaining certain patterns of thought. In a given work context and inside an occupational group, particular 'professional' representations concerning the occupational role and how to perform different work tasks normally develop. 'Being jointly situated on the product side and on the process side, they are a constant reference element, helping individuals to operate in a professional situation' (Piaser and Bataille 2010). When being socialized into an occupation, individuals go through a process where their general social representations of the relevant field transform into professional ones, forming occupational identities based on a more technical/professional understanding of the occupational role. Occupational groups develop their professional representations on a collective level in conjunction with their working conditions and everyday practices. Differences here between individuals and occupational groups may develop as a result of the division of labour, i.e. into different kinds of wing, and other organizational arrangements.

It is not always easy to distinguish a professional representation from a more general, social one; they overlap and permeate one another. In an occupational group such as prison officers the professional jargon is sometimes quite similar to the common language used in public media and discourse. Therefore, what is unique about the professional representation for prison officers is more difficult to discern compared to that of engineers, for example. However, of primary interest here are representations related to the occupational identities of this group, not their uniqueness in relation to the general public. Doctors, nurses, engineers and other professional groups are all socialized via a special education into specific professional identities and cultures before going into 'practical' work. This does not mean that they are not influenced by the culture of the specific organization where they find employment. Prison officers in Sweden, however, are not employed on the basis of such specific occupationally directed formal exams.[4] This means that they are much more 'exposed' to the impact of the occupational culture in the specific work environment where they are located. Their occupational identity will develop very much in relation to their interaction with close colleagues and prisoners and how work is performed in that special place. Professional representations among prison officers therefore can be expected to be formed solely in the day-to-day activities that take place at their organizational unit, while doctors, for instance, have internalized these to a greater degree before entering theirs. This also means that the importance of experienced staff and informal leaders in forming subcultures should be stressed, especially because of the 'flat' organization with no senior officers stationed in the wings.

Furthermore, representations heavily impact emotions and emotional labour, as well as it impacts how acting and rituals are developed and performed.

Emotional labour

Prisons are emotional work environments. In their everyday work, prison officers must manage prisoners' varying emotional states, while controlling their own emotional outbursts. The concept of emotional labour catches this phenomenon: 'This labour requires one to induce or suppress emotions in order to sustain the outward countenance that produces the proper state of mind in others' (Hochschild 1983; Nylander *et al.* in press). Emotional labour concerns managing emotions in accordance with organizational display rules. It is often divided into two modes: *surface acting* and *deep acting*. Surface acting concerns simulating emotions that the performing individual does not feel, a kind of 'faking', not displaying genuine inner feelings. This inconsistency may lead to individual disharmony – so-called emotive dissonance (Hochschild 1983). Conversely, deep acting occurs when the individual makes an emotive effort to feel the emotion he/she is expected to display. This does not give rise to emotive dissonance because more genuine feelings are displayed (ibid.; Kruml and Geddes 2000). Suppressed feelings, such as compassion, may also be produced here, connecting emotional labour to 'real' inner feelings (Crawley 2004a, b). While wholehearted deep acting might lead to exhaustion and stress, but also job satisfaction and a sense of personal accomplishment, surface acting is more likely to lead to self-blame, cynicism and detachment (Hochschild 1983; Kruml and Geddes 2000). The consequences of emotional labour may therefore be very complex (Wharton 1999).

Emotional labour is controlled and supervised in organizations in accordance with formal display rules. Employers exercise control over their employees' emotional work, i.e. through training, regulation and policy (Hochschild 1983). The Swedish Prison and Probation Service Order (2007) promotes 'behaviour that infuses confidence, appearance, showing respect/firmness, and the avoidance of acts of unfriendliness and small-mindedness' (31). 'Be personal but not private' is an expression of official status meaning that prison officers shall act correctly, be honest and humane and show respect but not become too emotionally involved with prisoners. Naturally, the formal rules affect not only how officers act, but also how they think and feel about prisoners. In studies of prison officers' emotional labour a great variety of prisoner emotions are identified, i.e. sadness, anger, fear, frustration and resentment (Sykes 1958; Crawley 2004b; Tracy 2005). General emotional labour strategies found among prison officers include de-personalization and detachment in relations with prisoners (Crawley 2004b), but also that respect makes the work easier (Tracy 2005). Another common strategy entails suppressing 'weak' feelings such as fear or anxiety (Crawley 2004b; Tracy 2005). In our own study we found a clear connection between deep emotional labour and emotional strain in prison work on the one hand and between surface labour and reification on the other (Nylander *et al.* in press). However, the question here is whether today's labour division in prisons leads to different kinds of emotional labour practised in the frame of different kinds of prison subculture.

Interactional rituals

The concept of interaction rituals denotes collective actions performed in collective understanding, which is important for how cultures are constructed and expressed (Collins 1988). Rituals come into existence when two or more people focus their attention on the same action or activity and are aware that 'the other' is attentive in the same way. Actors are physically close and therefore affected by the bodily presence of the other even though they may not be fully aware of this. The persons share a common frame of mind. There are borders to outsiders. All participants know who's in and who's out. The individuals that are involved in the ritual feel group solidarity and feelings of membership. They experience emotional energy, feelings of safety, unity, strength, enthusiasm and power. When symbols and rituals of a group meet disrespect it causes indignation or anger among group members.

Informal rituals which grow out of work practice create strong positive social effects. Formal rituals created by organizational rules for the most part do not create feelings of community and enthusiasm in the same way. These rituals are characterized by supremacy and subordination and they commonly take place in a context surrounded by strict rules and regulations as in prisons, and/or when some individuals have a position to adopt an authoritarian approach and give orders to others that have to follow them. These rituals may produce feelings of power among those who give orders but feelings of alienation and subordination among others. Prison officers are involved in various rituals with prisoners and colleagues. In accordance with the division of labour, and differences in representations and emotional labour, these rituals may take on quite a different character in different units and wings.

In the following, and with the use of the concepts presented, we will discuss the consequences of the division of labour on the occupational culture from, first, a perspective of differentiation and subcultural division; and, second, a perspective of integration, presenting some organizational elements that may work the opposite way, that is, towards an integrated occupational culture (Martin 1992).

The subculture of treatment wings

In treatment wings, staff and prisoners interact closely and quite intensively. The physical environment and interactions are quite different from regular wings and special security wings. The doors to the prisoners' cells are normally open and prisoners and staff are free to move around the wing. The officers seldom have a back office, a backstage (Goffman 1959) where they can 'get away' from the prisoners and talk privately to colleagues. As mentioned, prisoners who apply for rehabilitation at a treatment wing are most often motivated for change. The objective of the staff is to motivate, support and create good relations with the prisoners. This leads to closer relations and a more genuine knowledge of 'the other'. The treatment staff are also doing more deep acting emotional labour than officers in other wings. They allow themselves to show anger when the prisoners misbehave and they have an understanding of prisoner feelings when they show despair and anger when, for example, an application for leave or a family visit is turned down. The two quotations below show the more genuine 'deep acting relationship' that prison officers establish in treatment wings:

> If an application is rejected, it is a kind of natural reaction – they get frustrated and shout at us for a moment. I stay calm because I know they need to 'let off steam'. There is a need to burst out in anger, and then perhaps they come and apologise after a while.
> (Female prison officer, treatment wing)

I: Do you try to control your anger in situations in the wing?
R: I think I did so my first time in the treatment wing. Now I am more confident of my feelings and we [staff] have agreed that it is ok to show our feelings in the wing. But it is my responsibility how I do this – that is, what we say to our prisoners – and we, as staff, must think of that as well. So I think it is ok for us to show our anger, sadness or whatever, but we must do it in a controlled way. Instead of just shouting, I say to the prisoners, 'I get angry when you act like this or talk to me like this'. But I think we have the right to tell prisoners how we feel.
(Female prison officer, treatment wing)

There seems to be an informal display rule in the treatment wing that it is acceptable, maybe even important, to display anger or sadness. Such a rule is not incompatible with formal display rules: one may feel an emotion and display it, but in a 'controlled way'. This deeper mode of expressing emotions is, although controlled, quite honest with respect to inner feelings and should not therefore cause dissonance.

In treatment wings, the prison officers are involved in rituals with the prisoners that seem to create some kind of community spirit between them and the prisoners. They cook together, are involved in group sessions together and watch TV together. This is based on a more positive social representation of the prisoners.

> They have had a tough life but with the right help they can go forward and change (prison officer in treatment wing).
> Also the prisoners create more positive representations of the officers.
> Here we get relationships with the prison officers. We cook together and we eat together (prisoner in treatment wing).

The prison authority management has coined the concept 'dynamic security'. This was before the 'security boom' described in the introduction. This concept highlights how security in prisons ideally is based on a combination of different technical and physical security measures as well as treating prisoners in a humane way – dynamic security is about building good relations and mutual trust. Remarkably, staff in treatment wings often underpin this latter part when talking about security. With security staff it is often the other way around, they emphasize static security – fences, walls, supervision, etc. Thus, security in treatment wings is said to be achieved by the development of good relations and mutual trust between staff and prisoners. This way of working also seems to lead to less harassment and fewer assaults from prisoners. In our survey, one aspect of harassment was measured using the following statement:

> Assaults by prisoners on staff are rare in this prison.

Of the respondents, 45 per cent agreed, 19 per cent neither agreed nor disagreed and 36 per cent disagreed. There was a significant, though not very strong, correlation indicating a higher rate of agreement among staff who work on treatment wings.[5] Prisoners motivated for change are probably less inclined than others to assault others, but officers in treatment wings may also often interpret situations differently from prison officers in other wings. They do not feel insulted in situations of prisoner anger because they might regard the behaviour as 'a kind of natural reaction' in a specific situation i.e. when an application for leave is rejected.

Staff in treatment wings also often regard formal rules and security tasks as obstacles in their rehabilitation work. In one prison, when the prisoners have their outside walk in the afternoon the officers used to walk alongside the prisoners, talking to them. Because of new security rules this was not allowed anymore. One officer monitoring the prisoners during their outside walk commented about this to one of the researchers:

> Earlier we could walk *with* the women. Then we could talk to them about their problems. It was relaxed and a way to build relations. Now we have to stand on the staircase watching the women having their 45 minutes' walk.

So, even if staff in treatment wings have closer relations and perform more deep acting than officers in other wings they have to take into account the formal security regulations. Therefore they are also affected by the double task of prison officer work; security versus rehabilitation. In practical daily work with the prisoners, however, they try to handle this double task with the emphasis on motivation and rehabilitation and a professional representation that all prison work has to be based on positive relations between prisoners and prison staff. The findings from our study indicate that the climate between prison officers and prisoners in treatment wings most often is, taken into consideration the special setting of a prison, based on 'cultures of equality' and based on humanitarian and respectful relations to the prisoners.

The subculture of special security wings

In special security wings, prison officers and prisoner interaction is quite limited and prisoners are constantly monitored and supervised by several officers when outside their cells. The prisoners are allowed to leave their cells one at a time, for exercise, to walk outdoors or talk to their personal officer. The prisoners are both directly supervised by several officers and monitored by officers watching TV monitors in a back office. Officer–prisoner relationships in these wings are built on distance and detachment. Interactions are not relaxed; rather, they should be characterized as distanced and instrumental, building on polite friendliness, a kind of 'low-key' style, and a typical kind of surface emotional labour. The following illustrates what may be constant inner feelings of insecurity, a kind of emotional dissonance:

> We must be very careful in the wing when using humour. You never know what state the prisoner is in and the whole thing might end up going terribly wrong.
> (Prison officer, security wing)

The rituals that staff in the special security wings are involved in are characterized by formal rules and regulations which in turn manifest supremacy and a suborder. The staff and prisoners do not have their meals together, which is often the case in the treatment wings. Meals are served from a serving trolley just outside the prisoners' cells and handed over to the prisoner while in the cell. When prisoners talk to their personal officer or have a meeting with a social worker they sit in a room with glass walls and the interaction is monitored by several prison officers. The meetings are also supervised by officers watching TV cameras in another room. The rituals and interaction between officers and prisoners here is based on distance and detachment. This form of interaction may also lead to cynicism and alienation in relation to the prisoners. As one officer says:

> When the prisoners call on us we sometimes let them wait for a while. They should not think that they can get what they want immediately.
> (Prison officer, special security wing)

In this cultural context of detachment this quotation stands out as an instance of pure exercise of power, and as such it is not in accordance with the Prison and Probation Service's official statement: 'Common for all work in the Prison and Probation Service is the basic value of a humane prison and probation work. You should believe in people's ability to change' (Kriminalvården 2010).These differences in wing cultures seem to be quite far from an earlier Swedish tradition of equal treatment. It is also clear that officers in the latter kinds of wing are often aware of the problem of detachment, cynicism and alienation. As one officer states:

> You should not work here too long as you could become cynical and regard the prisoners as objects.
> (Prison officer, special security wing)

Prison officers in special security units

This kind of security staff seem even more distanced and detached in their relations to prisoners than staff in security wings. They are working all over the prison and their mission is strictly surveillance, control, inspections, responding quickly to emergencies, etc. It is more police-like work and they seldom have the opportunity to create any lasting relations to prisoners at all. Their work is about emotional surface labour at best resting on politeness and a low-key style, avoiding unnecessary conflicts. The performing of work tasks like these, based on such distance, often creates representations of 'the other' as dangerous, manipulative, and highly inclined to escape. These kinds of representation are very much in line with their work assignments. As one security officers says:

> I know that the prisoners always try to cheat us. It is my job to try to stop them. It's more us and them.

The security staff are only involved with prisoners on the basis of formal rituals, such as strip searching, searching for contraband in the cells and using sniffer dogs to conduct searches for drugs. These rituals are also characterized by supremacy and subordination, where power is clearly in the hands of the superior group. When they find contraband, their preconceived opinion is confirmed and their professional representations of the prisoners will be strengthened.

Prison officers in regular wings and open prisons

If differences in culture between treatment and security wings are quite easy to discern, a distinctive subculture on the regular wings is much harder to find. The most important common denominator here is ambivalence in relation to the dilemma of the double task. In regular wings we find a range of emotional labour, different rituals and professional representations about work practices, of prisoners and also of other wings. It seems that this here very much depends on experienced prison officers often functioning as informal leaders setting examples. Why is that? First, as mentioned earlier, there are no senior officers, no first-line management in Swedish prison wings. This makes room for informal leaders. Second, regular wings have to uphold both sides of the dilemma. Staff cannot 'hide' behind specialization. They have to perform both special security measures such as taking urine samples and making visitations at the same time as they are expected to build positive and fruitful relations in an effort to promote rehabilitation. The most obvious part of their rehabilitative role is being a personal officer with extra responsibility for helping some of the prisoners in the wing to prepare for life outside the walls. However, it should also be stressed that there are differences in relation to prison security categories. Regular wings in high-security prisons are more like special security wings while they are closer to treatment wings in others. In open prisons you may say that the whole prison is a kind of hybrid between a regular and a treatment wing. Security is 'softer', there are fewer staff, prisoners are often placed on work practice outside the fences and cooperation with staff outside – working with non-custodial treatment, is extensive. In the regular wings of closed prisons, on the other hand, there are more formal rituals combined with informal ones including prisoners. To sum up: the dilemma of the situation is most obvious in regular wings. Every single prison officer has to find his/her own way of balancing his/her tasks (see Bruhn *et al.* 2010). How this is done depends on both general social representations internalized before entering the service, and professional representations developed at work. Sometimes this is not very conflict laden because original motives harmonize with workplace experiences and a strong group culture at work. Sometimes, however, different representations come into conflict with each other, and sometimes conflicts on how to perform between prison officers at group level are conspicuous.

Representations of other wings

Therefore, our data confirm the presence of subcultural divisions among different wings and roles. These kinds of divisions may lead to 'suspicion' or 'mistrust' between staff in different wings:

> The security unit work very much by themselves. Often we do not know what the security unit does. They are dodging around and also checking the staff.
> (Officer, treatment wing)

> We sometimes call them KGB or CIA.
> (Officer, treatment wing)

These kinds of representation of security staff are quite common among our respondents from treatment wings. They lack knowledge of what staff in the security units do and therefore create images of them based on what they witness on the occasional interaction with prisoners. Security is, as we have seen, a high priority in Swedish prisons nowadays. This has raised the status of the security staff. One treatment wing officer states:

> Sometimes they [security staff] have a negative attitude towards us in the treatment wing. It seems like they see themselves as being of greater value than we ordinary prison officers. They order us around and criticize us instead of working with us.

What is interesting here is also that the officers use the word 'ordinary' to distinguish officers in treatment and regular wings from security officers. This may serve as a way of excluding security staff from all other officers; the latter are seen as performing human service work. Security officers 'belong' to another category.

Among security staff representations of other wings, mostly treatment wings, is that they in some way complicate their work. 'Most drugs are found in the treatment wing' is a common statement. Treatment wings are also sometimes called nicknames such as 'lemonade and cake' or 'the diaper'. 'Lemonade and cake' refers to settings where people only sit and talk and there are a lot of 'mixed up and fuzzy' people there among both staff and prisoners. In 'the diaper', staff are indulgent and caring to the point of almost treating prisoners like infants. These expressions are probably created by a more 'hard-core' prisoner group that is not interested in treatment programmes and change. The problem is that officers are taking over these expressions, and by doing so they also convey a patronizing attitude towards treatment and staff in treatment wings.

In regular wings we find similar representations of security staff as in treatment wings:

> They have a way to put you down, criticize and order you around. You never know what they are doing either.
>
> (Prison officer, regular wing)

This expresses the lack of knowledge of what the security staff actually do. But it is also an indication of status differences. Security officers who 'order you around' are in a different category, not really belonging to the group of 'ordinary' officers. But it is also an indication of a more general problem, which is that staff are sometimes badly informed of what colleagues in other wings or units do. This may lead to suspicion and gossip:

> There is gossip between wings. When you do not know how they work in other wings this is a ground for suspicion.
>
> (Female officer, regular wing)

> We have little understanding as to what they do in other wings. We think that we do good work in our wing and the staff in other wings do things incorrectly. This is because we do not actually know how they work in other wings.
>
> (Male officer, regular wing)

The division of labour obviously leads to a lack of knowledge as to what officers do in other wings. This structural way of 'solving' the double task of prison work in Sweden is therefore a centrifugal force stimulating the creation of subcultural divisions which, in turn, lead to the risk of creating a lack of understanding and a lack of cooperation, even conflicts, between different parts of the workforce.

Professional representations, cultural cohesion and prison officer identity

Earlier we described subcultural divisions between wings. That said, there are some integrating forces as well. Perhaps one of the most important factors promoting similarity in prison officers' occupational approach is the 1992 personal officer reform. As mentioned, most prison officers are personal officers who are responsible for counselling four to ten prisoners. Even prison officers in security wings are often personal officers. We hold that this institution is an important integrating force upholding the rehabilitative side of prison officer work, at least to some extent, also in wings were security tasks are a priority (Bruhn *et al.* 2010). It forces staff in special security wings to develop a closer commitment to the rehabilitation of at least some prisoners. They must provide sit-down counselling, get to know the prisoners' social backgrounds, help them with authority contacts, promote treatment programmes and plan for a future outside the prison. Under such circumstances, the officer cannot keep too great a distance. They may be rejected, but they must at least try to build a more personal relationship with some prisoners. Therefore the personal officer institution guarantees that most prison officers uphold at least some form of rehabilitative approach in their work and in their occupational identity. It should be stressed though that there are of course differences between being a personal officer in a security wing compared to treatment and regular wings. Prisoners in security wings most often have a lot of time left of their sentence and are therefore less motivated to rehabilitate.

In our survey we found that the vast majority of prison officers view personal officer work very positively. At the same time, many officers stress that the time to do a good job here is lacking. Some officers also point out that security work comes first in the eyes of management:

> Today, I think the personal officer's work has become too low prioritized. They have hidden it away, placed it in a corner. It is free though, no one prevents you from working with counselling, but security work comes first.
> (Prison officer, regular wing)

Has security work forced rehabilitative efforts to the margins of prison officer work? To draw such a conclusion would be an overstatement. However, even among highly ranked managers in the service today, the opinion is that security measures now have been given more than its fair share, and that rehabilitation work from now on should be given equal priority.

Traditionally in Sweden the presence of the double task between security and rehabilitation has been relatively strong. Even though methods and ideologies have altered, the basic aim of rehabilitation has all the time been at the centre of the debate on crime and punishment. Further, without being able to make strong empirically rooted comparisons with other countries outside Scandinavia, one hypothesis is that 'rehabilitative' representations about the job are more culturally rooted among Swedish (and other Nordic) prison officers than in many other countries. The fact that so many individuals educated in the field of social and behavioural sciences seek this kind of job together with the above mentioned, more general motives about 'working with people' points to such an understanding. Cultural values of the meaningfulness of doing human care work seem to be quite strong, and this may be related to a traditional commitment to collective interests and society's efforts to create fair life chances and resources for all citizens (Pratt 2008a). Furthermore: only a small minority of prison officers are specialized in performing security tasks, with the vast majority of prison officers being personal officers. The latter is an important mechanism that promotes cultural cohesion and sameness in professional representations.

Thus, occupational culture and identities among Swedish prison officers are strongly rooted in views that their work is to help people rehabilitate into normal life. With the purpose of mapping out professional representations among prison officers we included some open questions in our survey. One was about the qualities needed to do prison officer work.[6] Most frequently cited, and with the strongest links to each other, were 'social ability', 'well organized' and 'empathic'. Also quite strong were 'perceptive', 'calm', 'humane' and 'security conscious'. The pattern differs in an expected, though not extreme, way in relation to wing types and security classes. 'Security conscious' has a conspicuous position only at higher-security-classed prisons (Bruhn et al. 2010).[7]

Conclusion

In many prison studies, the prisoners' culture and staff culture are discerned and discussed each as homogeneous in itself (Ireland 2002). Prisons are normally more complex institutions than that. At the level of staff, which we have discussed here, there are subcultural divisions not only between prisons of different types, but also internally between different wings and units. Labour division will shape subcultures. These subcultural differences are linked to different interactional rituals, differences in social and professional representations and the kind of emotional labour performed.

Boundary lines between subcultures lead to less knowledge, even prejudice, of 'the others', here, those in other wings. But the social representations of 'the others' also mean important feelings of cohesion among colleagues and group mates. The emotional labour seems to be consistent with the differences in work tasks and representations between wings. Certain emotions are more frequent in some wings than in others. The interactional rituals hold power and superiority in relation to prisoners in certain wings and units, but can in other wings have a positive effect on the feelings of community between officers and prisoners. These interaction rituals also strengthen feelings of cohesion between staff at group/wing level. Three main subcultural patterns among prison officers have been presented. Staff in security units stress more formal rituals. They also develop more surface acting when interacting with prisoners, a more detached emotional labour, and their representations of the prisoners are more negative, more 'us and them', 'prisoners are manipulative and not to be trusted'. In treatment wings, where the prisoners are often motivated for change, formal rituals are often seen as obstacles for rehabilitative work built on good relations. Officers and prisoners are involved in rituals together which seem to create feelings of mutual understanding and community. Officers perform more care and deep emotional labour. The representations of the prisoners are more positive based on humanity and respect for the prisoners. In many regular wings, there is a sort of middle ground. Formal rituals have priority, but even here staff and prisoners do things together more easily. The emotional labour in regular wings varies more between depth and the superficial, and the representations about prisoners vary between closeness and distance, respect and suspicion, etc.

These subcultural differences are of course problematic in the sense that all staff should work towards the same objective, which is 'Better out' – the Swedish Prison and Probations Service's official statement. The personal officer institution however works in an integrated way, guaranteeing that many prison officers do at least some degree of rehabilitative work. This prevents too much cynicism and objectifications of prisoners even in wings with many formal rituals and detached relations. The personal officer reform in 1992 may be seen as typical of two main discourses in Swedish society. First, it is clearly established in the Scandinavian model of the welfare state and the striving for equal life chances for every citizen. This ideological–cultural tradition makes it hard for conservative or neo-liberal political currents to sort out 'softer' rehabilitation methods from prison work. The cultural tradition of equality and solidarity runs deep. People who have problems should be helped by society. No one should be left alone and an individual's problems should not only be reduced to the individual capacity. Many citizens therefore also regard working with human care as very meaningful, something that, as we have shown, seems strongly rooted among people seeking work in the prison service. Second, the social context of this reform was an extensive debate on alienation and bad working conditions. Unemployment figures were low and employers in Sweden had problems recruiting personnel, and staff turnover was high. As a result many employers tried to develop more stimulating working conditions. Sweden was in the forefront here with such advanced examples of job enrichment as the ABB T50 project and the Volvo Uddevalla plant.[8] Such job enrichment was one important aspect of the personal officer reform. A study about stress and health among prison officers at this time strongly suggested the improvement of working conditions towards job enrichment, meaning more individual control, responsibility and more interesting work assignments (Härenstam 1989).

Today there are tendencies among large groups in Swedish society towards a more ego-centred individualistic approach. Political forces promoting ideological notions that living on 'the right side of the law' is a matter of individual choice and if you choose otherwise, you only have yourself to blame. As mentioned, a clear political directive with emphasis on increased security has been implemented by the Swedish Prison and Probations Service. This could be seen as a risk to the Scandinavian exceptionalism as Pratt (2008a, b) argues. The picture is, however, more complex. Pratt also has a tendency to overlook significant differences between Finland, Norway and Sweden. To mention just a few: in Norway, many prisons are small and there are no special security staff, all officers are 'generalists'. In Finland no further security categories other than 'closed' or 'open' are used. In Norway and Denmark, men and women are sometimes imprisoned together. As we have discussed in this chapter there are also important differences in and between prisons in Sweden, often related to specialization and security categories. Roughly speaking one could say that a culture of equality, humanity and 'Scandinavian exceptionalism' can be found in treatment wings and open prisons, while the picture is different in regular and security wings, especially in high-security prisons. The development of both more specialized wings and treatment prisons could in the light of subcultural differences among wings lead to the unequal treatment of prisoners. This development may lead staff to aim their effort and rehabilitation work only towards prisoners who show motivation for change leaving the more 'hard-core' prisoners to their own destiny. If so, the culture of equal treatment of all prisoners is certainly at risk. Thus the subcultural differences among prison officers in different wings and units may contribute to a more outspoken acceptance among officers of different conditions for different prisoners and in different wings and prisons. How the political changes in prison policy together with subcultural division and other changes among prison officers will affect what Pratt (2007) refers to as the Scandinavian exceptionalism in the future seems to depend on several different and sometimes contradicting forces.

Notes

1. Financed by the Swedish Council for Working Life and Social Research.
2. Field notes and transcribed individual and focus group interviews were coded thematically using NVivo 8 software.
3. The quantitative data were analysed in SPSS.
4. The above-mentioned short university course is hardly enough in this case.
5. Chi square (4) = 40.9, $p < .001$, contingency coefficient (CC) = .288.
6. 'Name five important qualities you think a prison officer should (ought to) have/be.'
7. The analysis was carried through by the help of the French software Similitude which is constructed for finding patterns of co-occurrences on case level.
8. See for instance Berggren (1990).

References

Andersson, R. and Nilsson, R. (2009) *Svensk kriminalpolitik*. Malmö: Liber.
Berggren, C. (1990) *Det nya bilarbetet*. Lund: Arkiv.
Bruhn, A. (1999) Individualiseringen och det fackliga kollektivet. En studie av industritjänstemäns förhållningssätt till facket. Örebro: Örebro studies 15, Örebro University Press.
Bruhn, A., P.-Å. Nylander and O. Lindberg (2010) 'The Prison Officer's Dilemma: Professional Representations among Swedish Prison Officers', *Les Dossiers des Sciences de l'Education*, 23: 77–93.
Collins, R. (1988) *Interactional Ritual Chains*. New York: Harcourt Brace & Company.
Crawley, E. M. (2004a) *Doing Prison Work: The Public and Private Lives of Prison Officers*. Portland, OR: Willan Publishing.
—— (2004b) 'Emotions and Performance: Prison Officers and the Presentation of Self in Prison', *Punishment and Society*, 6: 411–27.
Danermark, B. (2002) *Explaining Society: Critical Realism in the Social Sciences*. London and New York: Routledge.
Foucault, M. (1977) *Discipline and Punish: The Birth of the Prison*. New York: Vintage.
Garland, D. (2001) *The Culture of Control*. Oxford: Oxford University Press.
Goffman, E. (1959) *The Presentation of Self in Everyday Life*. Garden City, NY: Doubleday Anchor Books.
Härenstam, A. (1989) *Prison Personnel – Working Conditions, Stress and Health. A Study*

of *2000 Prison Employees in Sweden*. Stockholm: National Institute of Psychosocial Factors and Health, Department of Stress Research, Karolinska Institute.

Hochschild, A. R. (1983) *The Managed Heart: Commercialisation of Human Feeling*. London: Sage.

Ireland, J. L. (2002) *Bullying among Prisoners. Evidence, Research and Intervention Strategies*. London: Brunner-Routledge.

Jodelet, D. (1995) 'Sociala representationer: ett forskningsområde under utveckling', in M. Chiab and B. Orfali (eds), *Sociala representationer. Om vardagsvetandets sociala fundament.*

Kruml, S. M. and D. Geddes (2000) 'Exploring the Dimensions of Emotional Labour', *Management Communication Quarterly*, 14: 8–49.

Martin, J. (1992) *Cultures in Organizations: Three Perspectives*. New York: Oxford University Press.

Nylander, P.-Å., A. Bruhn and O. Lindberg (in press) 'Emotional Labour and Emotional Strain among Swedish Prison Officers', *Journal of Criminal Justice*.

Piaser, A., and M. Bataille (2010) 'Of Contextual Use of "Social" and "Professional"', in M. Chaib, B. Danermark and S. Selander (eds) (forthcoming), *Social Representations and the Transformation of Knowledge*.

Pratt, J. (2008a) 'Scandinavian Exceptionalism in an Era of Penal Excess. Part I: The Nature of Roots of Scandinavian Exceptionalism', *British Journal of Criminology*, 48(2): 119–37.

—— (2008b) 'Scandinavian Exceptionalism in an Era of Penal Excess. Part II: Does Scandinavian Exceptionalism Have a Future?', *British Journal of Criminology*, 48(3): 275–92.

Sykes, G. M. (1958) *The Society of Captives: A Study of a Maximum Security Prison*. Princeton: Princeton University Press.

Tracy, S. J. (2005) 'Locking up Emotion: Moving beyond Dissonance for Understanding Emotion Labor Discomfort', *Communication Monograph* 72: 261–83.

Wharton, A. S. (1999) 'The Psychosocial Consequences of Emotional Labor', *Annals of the American Academy of Political and Social Science* 561: 158–76.

Part V
Scandinavian exceptionalism revisited

13 In defence of Scandinavian exceptionalism

John Pratt and Anna Eriksson

In this chapter, we subject the claims for penal exceptionalism in Scandinavia made in Pratt (2008a, b) to self-criticism and review. We thus examine the methodology on which these were based; the reliance on English commentaries rather than untranslated Scandinavian documents; the explanations of exceptionalism that were put forward; its social costs; and the extent to which Scandinavian exceptionalism is now in the process of being undermined by a Scandinavian 'culture of control'. While acknowledging the need for some adjustments and refinements as a consequence of these interrogations, the chapter ultimately validates and reaffirms the Scandinavian exceptionalism thesis.

Methodological issues

Let us first examine the data on which the exceptionalism claims were made. There are two aspects to this, which are considered below.

Prison rates as a measure of punitiveness

The methods by which prison populations are counted vary from society to society. For example, mental health patients are included in the counts of some jurisdictions, in others they are excluded. A similar ambivalence exists in relation to remand prisoners. However, to minimize inaccuracies, all prison statistics referred to by Pratt (2008a, b) were taken from the World Prison Brief website of the Centre for Prison Studies, King's College, University of London. This provides consistency and clarification across societies in that it gives details of remandees, juveniles and foreign prisoners within a given society's prison population, as well as overall rates of imprisonment. In this way, variations caused by different counting procedures are minimized. Furthermore, even if we use alternative measures to gauge levels of punitiveness, as Lappi-Seppälä (2008: 331) does, we finish with the same result: the Scandinavian countries have the lowest rates of imprisonment in the OECD both across total prison populations and also across prison populations with mental health patients, remandees and so on excluded. On this basis we can confidently say that the low imprisonment rates of this region are not statistical artefacts but are valid indicators of incarceration levels.

Prison tourism as a research method

What of the claims that were made about the characteristics of Scandinavian prisons? That is, these are organized around the principle that going to prison is itself the punishment and, thereafter, prison conditions should be normalized as far as possible – hence the arrangements for conjugal visits, dining facilities on the wings rather than in cells, car parks for prisoners in some open institutions and so on (Pratt 2008a: 120–3). These claims were made on the basis of what we might term 'prison tourism'. Visits were made to 16 penal institutions and one after-care hostel in 2006. The tours lasted between two and four hours, in the company of a senior officer. Features of the prison would be explained as the tour progressed and then, in most cases, there would be further discussions with the governor/manager. The prisons were selected to give a good cross-section: maximum and minimum security, men's and women's; closed and open, old and new (another five visits have been made since the 2008 articles were written). One of the reasons for conducting the research in this way was that it would be possible to observe *recurring patterns* relating to officer–inmate interaction, dining and visiting arrangements and various other accoutrements of the material conditions of life that were common across prisons and prison systems in this region. As such, the data that was produced is more substantial than just 'a few sensation programmes' that Bondeson (1989: 15) claimed was what earlier 'tourists' to Scandinavian prisons had based their research on. At the same time, it provides illustrations of what going to prison in the Scandinavian countries *can* involve, as it was designed to do, even if not all prisons will invariably meet such conditions. We would emphasize that it was *the possibilities* of imprisonment that were set out in Pratt (2008a). It was not claimed that all Scandinavian prisons uniformly fit this pattern and it is, frankly, ridiculous to criticize that article on the basis that this was the case.

Nor was it ever claimed that these are 'perfect' institutions: 'one must recognize that however relaxed a prison regime, whatever material comforts are provided, prisoners are still prisoners. There are rules, levels of surveillance, record-keeping, denials of choices, deprivations and sanctions that will differentiate any prisoner from free people' (Pratt 2008a: 123). Bullying and intimidation still take place. Some of the exceptional features of Scandinavian prisons have been turned into local currency by the prisoners: the family visits entitlement is something that can be traded or fought over like cigarettes and phone cards. We also find the strange distortions of time that are probably a universal prison characteristic – in Helsinki Prison in 2006, for example, dinner was served at 3.00 p.m. We are thus not going to find that the 'pains of imprisonment' (Sykes 1958) have been eliminated in Scandinavia. Have they, however, been reduced? It might be thought that the level of prison suicides is one indicator of this. When rates of Scandinavian prison suicides are compared with those of high imprisonment 'Anglophone' societies (specifically for the purposes of this research, England, New Zealand and New South Wales, Australia) the evidence does not suggest this. In 2008 these Anglophone countries all had lower rates than the Scandinavian (International Round Table for Correctional Excellence 2009).[1] We do, though, need to treat these data with caution. There are differences in the constituency of the respective prison populations (for example, Sweden and Norway have significantly larger numbers of foreign prisoners than these other societies[2]). In addition, the actual numbers of suicides in most jurisdictions is so small – usually single figures with the exception of England – that yearly percentage changes can artificially inflate their prevalence. However, if, for the sake of argument, we accept the validity of these data, one inference to be drawn from it is that prison conditions themselves will not necessarily affect prisoners' experiences of incarceration. This has resonance with Bondeson's (1989: 296) claim that 'the pains of imprisonment may vary between various categories of institution, with more or less restrictive atmospheres ... inmates in so called open and treatment-oriented institutions may experience as much pain and react by forming as many defence mechanisms as those in more punitive facilities'. In effect, less restrictive conditions in Scandinavian prisons, particularly the open institutions, might create new pains of imprisonment: the feeling of being nearly free but not free yet can add to prisoners' frustrations (Neumann, Chapter 8 in this book; see also Mathiesen 1965).

Given that any deprivation of liberty, no matter how well appointed the prison in which it is experienced, is likely to be resented (as prisoners who were available for discussion during the prison tours in 2006 confirmed), perhaps this is only to be expected. However, *the exceptionalism thesis does not stand or fall on what effect prison conditions have on prisoners*. Instead, it is *the prison conditions* themselves that is the issue here, rather than their effects; that is, *what is it about the Scandinavian societies* that has made possible these conditions. This is both a sociological issue that requires explanation. And it is a normative issue that relates to the extent to which modern societies are prepared to alleviate the pain of imprisonment and go some way, of their own accord, to respecting the rights of prisoners, even though, for obvious reasons, the vast majority of prisoners would still rather not be there. That said, we do concede that more consideration should have been given to the conditions of remand prisoners while undertaking the research. In Norway and Sweden remandees make up about one-quarter of the prison population. In contrast to the conditions for sentenced prisoners, it is possible for this group to be held in restricted confinement in the Scandinavian countries– sometimes solitary – until the time of their trial. This has been a longstanding practice – in Sweden, for example, it was legislated for in 1864. The original intentions were to prevent contagion from other prisoners, but also to provide the opportunity for confession, where sufficient evidence for prosecution was missing (Nilsson 1999). However, it now seems to have become a routine practice that, apart from anything else, will assist in securing conviction (for obvious reasons). Both Norway and Sweden have been criticized by the European Committee against Torture and Inhumane Treatment for these practices. Indeed, the unusually high level of Swedish prison suicides in 2007 included 12 by remandees but only one by a sentenced prisoner.

Scandinavian languages and documentary sources

Could it not be argued that the exceptionalism thesis is flawed because of Pratt's (2008a, b) almost exclusive reliance on English commentaries rather than untranslated Scandinavian documents? What we have since found is that this untranslated material confirms rather than undermines the thesis.

First, it is clear that some of the material published in English contains 'Anglicisms' – words or phrases that are not translated literally from the Scandinavian languages but that have been given meanings that make them comprehensible to Anglophone audiences. In Swedish, for example, *fångvård* is the term for what in English becomes 'corrective services'. However, the literal translation is 'prisoner care', an understanding that is also reflected in the Norwegian term *kriminalomsorgen*. There are other important language differences in criminal justice and penal administration. The most direct equivalent of the English term for 'sentence' – *straff* – rarely features in Swedish official discourse. Instead, we find the less threatening and non-emotive term *påföld*, literally meaning 'that which follows after', a term that invokes the way in which deprivation of freedom is meant to be the extent of punishment that going to prison involves. Of course, it could be argued that these expressions merely camouflage more sinister developments. But this then begs the question of why the Swedes, in this instance, should be so sensitive about terminology that is taken for granted in the Anglophone world. More likely, surely, and as further evidence of the exceptionalism thesis, it represents different traditions and understandings of the purposes and functions of punishment. For example, the English term 'prison *officer*' refers to the way in which the paramilitary antecedents of this occupation in the Anglophone countries seems more pronounced than in Scandinavia. Indeed, in some New South Wales prisons, there is still a 'parade' at the start of the morning shift. Considerable emphasis is placed on marching in formation at the officers' training school. However, notwithstanding the same historical origins of this occupation in Scandinavia, a different tradition then emerged that has since eradicated most of them. This is implicit in the Swedish and Norwegian terms for prison officer: respectively, *fångvårdare*, meaning, literally, 'prison carer'; and *fengselbetjent*, literally 'prison servant'. Nor are there any parades, marching and so on that would otherwise reflect paramilitary associations. Indeed, in Finland, there are no military insignia at all on prison officers' clothing. This would seem to be of great symbolic importance in the way in which it again is a rejection of the paramilitary traditions of the prison service, while at the same time it reduces the social distance between officers and inmates that a uniform replete with badges, insignia, heavy boots and so on would seem to exaggerate.

Second, previously untranslated Scandinavian official documents confirms these points, while also indicating that penal exceptionalism, as it relates to prison conditions, pre-dates the post-1945 focus it was given in Pratt (2008a) – a somewhat artificial focus made necessary by the lack of English commentaries before that date. It can be traced back to the mid-nineteenth century when, influenced by the Philadelphia prison innovations, great importance was placed on separate cell confinement. Only Sweden, however, had the ability to make it an extensive feature of prison life and between 1846 and 1880 45 such prisons were built (one such prison opened in Norway in 1851 and cellular confinement was introduced to the larger Finnish prisons in 1889). The important point for our purposes here, however, is that in contrast to the way in which it was used as an additional punitive and deterrent aspect of imprisonment in the Anglophone world from the 1860s, it was thought that solitary confinement had productive and redeeming possibilities. As such, it was rigidly enforced to prevent contagion from other prisoners. Inmates could be punished for climbing on their cell window to look outside and, according to Swedish prison regulations, there was to be a layer of dust in the window ledge that was not allowed to be cleaned so that any fingerprints in it could be seen by the prison officers (Rudstedt 1994). In Sweden, prisoners had to wear a hood when they went outside their cell (Rudstedt 1994: 26).[3] Separate confinement remained in use in this region until the 1940s and beyond, during which time, in Sweden, prisoners could be theoretically held for up to three years. In contrast, in England, after being steadily reduced in length during the late nineteenth century, it was abolished altogether as a component of a prison sentence in 1922.[4] Thereafter, it was only available as a punishment for offences against prison discipline, as with the other Anglophone countries in this research.

One of the reasons for the different and more prolonged use of separate confinement in Scandinavia would seem to be related to the place and significance of the Lutheran Church in these societies, in particular the extreme religious homogeneity of Scandinavian society at that time (even if in the twenty-first century the Scandinavian countries are among the most secular in the world) and the centrality of the Lutheran Church in state formation. In its teachings, the individual's relationship with God was all-important. It had thus been the task of local pastors to educate their community so that each member of it could read the bible on their own and come to know God in this way. This knowledge would be examined in classes leading up to the ceremony of confirmation. This was a vitally important test to pass, since it was proof not just of an individual's knowledge of God and his works, but, as well, their trustworthiness and reliability before the rest of their community. At the same time, daily work was understood as service to God. There was a duty incumbent on all to serve others, depending on each individual's capabilities. As regards understandings of crime and punishment, these were based on the belief that all individuals are sinners, if not equal sinners. This meant that crime was understood as simply one of a multitude of earthly sins. There was thus no rigid distinction and division to be made between criminals and the rest of the community – criminals had sinned, but then so had everyone else. Any attempt to make such divisions would have been beyond the parameters of the Lutheran *Weltanschauung*. As Martin Luther (1525: 208) himself had written, 'sin cannot tear you away from [God], even though you commit adultery a hundred times a day and commit as many murders'. It also meant that the way to bring about the redemption of criminals was to bring them closer to God through knowledge of his works, as it was with all other sinners.

And thus while we can see that one of the attractions of separate confinement in prison was that it would bring about the efficient control of prisoners (Nilsson 1999), it also seems to us that this practice is also connected to the work of the Lutheran priests in the prisons: specifically, for their purposes, separate confinement would facilitate the prisoners' communion with God. In effect, we are arguing that from the late nineteenth century into the first part of the twentieth, the pastors and chaplains in the Scandinavian and Anglophone countries performed very different roles, had a very different presence in everyday prison administration in these two groups of societies. In the latter, the work and role of prison chaplains had been markedly downgraded and deskilled, ostensibly in the interests of imposing uniformity across the prison system and as a way of affirming prison governors as the ultimate authority in local governance. At the birth of the modern prison in this country in the 1840s, it had been envisaged that authority would be shared between governors and chaplains, 'each supreme in his own department: the governor as head of the penal, the chaplain of the religious part of the system' (Griffiths 1875: 46). However, under the provisions of the Prison Act 1865 the chaplains were made subservient to uniformed chief officers and had to report to them. Thereafter, they became peripheral figures around the prison, with little of note in their now appended annual reports to the main report of the governor. Numerous prisoner biographies confirm this. For example, Jabez Balfour's (1901: 68) advice from the chaplain on reception was that 'it's lucky for you . . . that you have come just at this time. The governor who has recently left was a very severe man indeed. Things are bad enough at present, and even now I would warn you to be very careful of the warders. You are wholly in their power.' So too, most likely, was the chaplain himself, when he and Balfour witnessed the beating of a prisoner by officers taking place: 'it's no good . . . there's nothing we can do', he remarked (Balfour 1901: 224). In contrast, in all three Scandinavian countries included in this research, it appears that the Lutheran pastors played a more important role in the daily administration of prison life, as the annual prison reports regularly indicate. Here, they were involved in checking each prisoner's educational standard and religious knowledge and status on arrival. Those who had not been confirmed in the Lutheran Church would be expected to attend classes that would lead to this. Education became an integral component of the prison timetable. It was not confined to illiterates, as an optional extra in the evenings after work had been completed, as in England when it was introduced to the prisons in the late nineteenth century. Furthermore, there were no English treadwheels or cranks, no afflictive labour. Instead, prison labour (although of a simple kind; see Nilsson 1999) was intended to be useful – as in the world beyond the prison, it was an indicator of the inmates' service to God and to the well-being of their community. Furthermore, there was no point in depriving prisoners of the means to better themselves through education or make them perform punitive labour that emphasized and symbolized their difference from the rest of the community – there was no difference. In effect, it was as if the prison community had become the last stronghold of pastoral power in Scandinavian society. The previous dominance of the pastors outside the prison had by now been undermined by the growing authority of doctors, civil servants and teachers who represented a newly emerging form of pastoral power in modern society; and by a strong anti-clerical religious revivalist movement.

In these countries it seems to have been only in the early twentieth century that the importance of the pastors began to be undermined as doubts about the consequences of separate confinement increased. The first references to 'prison farms' and 'prison colonies' were made in the Scandinavian countries between 1910 and 1913. From this time onwards there was increasing exploration of relaxed conditions of confinement and collective living. Law changes in Sweden in 1921 made it possible for adult prisoners to work with others outside their cells after one year's separation. The Annual Report of the Prison Service (1941: 41) makes a reference to a psychiatric prison where 'football is arranged between prisoner teams and those from outside'. Swimming pools were now being built where the inmates had 'no natural facilities'. In the Annual Report of the Prison Service (1942: 43) there are to be bigger windows in the cells, 'more light, air and the possibility of a view for the bodily and spiritual health of the intern'. Prison authorities were also becoming more interested in prisoners' mental health rather than their level of religious knowledge. In the Annual Report of the Prison Service (1927), there are references to the problem of 'the mentally weak'. Recidivists now fell into this category, rather than being understood as sinners who had fallen to temptation again. Under their new classification, they could be 'interred' and 'contained' indefinitely until they were 'cured' rather than being allowed to face the temptations to sin again that would come their way when freed. The Swedish Annual Report of the Prison Service (1943: 46, our italics) stated that, as regards those inmates in cellular prisons, 'working in groups is an important means of *minimizing the isolation* . . . They are allowed the cell door open in working hours.' Now, the likely detrimental effect of separate confinement on mental health is a more important consideration for the prison authorities than the opportunity it gave prisoners to be closer to God. Indeed, 1945 legislation abolished cellular confinement in Sweden (Norway followed in 1950; and although some aspects of penitentiary confinement were maintained in Finland until 1971, this had long since been on the basis of deterrence and incapacitation rather than any religious motives). Thereafter, there is more emphasis on socialization and connectedness and increased contact with the outside world. In addition, 'inmates shall be treated with firmness and seriousness, and with respect to their human worth. They should be occupied with suitable work and receive such care that their ready adjustment to society is promoted and that *the harmful effects of the deprivation of liberty is prevented*' (Annual Report of the Prison Service 1946–7: 44, our italics). As such, the redemptive possibilities of imprisonment have disappeared. Instead, for those who have to be sent there, conditions are to be liberalized to offset the harm that this removal from society causes them.

What seems particularly important about Scandinavian prison developments over this period is the way it provided foundation stones on which subsequent penal exceptionalism was built. First, it became a means of reintegrating criminals to society rather than terrorizing them into submission to its rules. Because this mode of confinement was constructed around prisoner's redemptive possibilities and potential, this allowed them access to education and productive work. At the same time, moral differences between prisoners and the rest of the community seem to have been significantly less than in the Anglophone countries, thereby allowing them the opportunity to better themselves during their sentence, rather than insisting that they should spend their time in misery and suffering. Second, from the early twentieth century, as a direct reaction against separate confinement (essential for the pastors to do their work proficiently), we also see the beginnings of those material conditions – such as the provision of swimming pools in some institutions – and greater integration with local community life that have become further signifiers of this exceptionalism. Of course, this did not mean that the separate confinement regimes did indeed make prisoners better people. Prolonged cellular confinement, interspersed only with visits from pastors and teachers, may well have led to madness, as had been the case with earlier experiments in England (Ignatieff 1978; Scharff Smith 2006). But while there are various references to the high level of mental illness in the cellular prisons (see, for example, Annual Prison Report, Sweden 1920), we can find no connection being made between the two in the annual reports of this period.

The point is that, for much of this period, *it was thought* that such regimes *would* produce better people.[5] The sociological task is thus to investigate *how* it was possible to think like that.

The causes of Scandinavian exceptionalism

How was it possible, then, to 'think like that', to think in such a way about crime and punishment issues that the route of penal development was able to embark on a rather different route from that which was taken in the Anglophone world? As was noted in the introduction, Pratt (2008a) took the view that this was the product of longstanding 'cultures of equality' in these societies. The *relatively* egalitarian social relations that were the product were then effectively 'institutionalized' during the post-1945 period by the Scandinavian welfare state model. This does not mean, of course, that there was neither conflict nor injustices in these societies. What it does mean, though, is that the particular social and material arrangements in Scandinavia from the early nineteenth century onwards – including extreme religious and racial homogeneity, state formation, land distribution and late industrialization – were likely to have produced very different ways of seeing and understanding the world, very different tolerances and conduct from a much more class-divided society such as Britain (which also had a different state formation, religious divisions rather than unity, ethnic divisions, much earlier industrialization and so on): in effect, a very different *culture*. By 'culture', we are referring to 'all those conceptions and values, categories and distinctions, frameworks of ideas and systems of belief which human beings use to construe their world and render it orderly and meaningful' (Garland 1990: 195). The end product in Scandinavia was an egalitarian culture that was illustrated in Pratt (2008a) from such sources as memoirs, travelogues and diaries. Norbert Elias (1939, 1979), the most important scholar on the history of Western culture and the structural framework that made this possible, used similar sources, as well as 'manners books', paintings and literature, in his *magnum opus*.

In the Scandinavian context though, how reliable are such sources, coming as they do from largely British and American visitors, who in most cases would not be skilled in the languages of this region? First, these sources also included some notable Scandinavians, commenting on their own societies, saying or implying much the same things as the visitors. Second, the British and American commentaries are perhaps particularly important here because such visitors, by the nature of their backgrounds, would become more aware of arrangements intrinsic to the Scandinavian countries but absent from or different to their own societies: the sources used do not just highlight features of Scandinavian society but, implicitly at least, show *differences* from other Western societies. Third, the various points that were made – the high value placed on education, for example, in Scandinavia – were regularly triangulated. The same themes in these sources occurred over and over again, allowing the long-term developmental course of these values to be sketched in. These sources also demonstrate that the egalitarian features of the Scandinavian countries predate the post-war welfare state: this institutionalized them, but did not create them. As evidence of the material basis of these cultural values, a wealth of studies exists, drawing on economic data, from the late nineteenth century to the present that demonstrate relatively narrow income differences between different social strata of Scandinavian societies and at the same time much larger income differences in societies such as Britain (see, for example, Grimley 1937; Cole and Smith 1938; Nelson 1953; Kuhnle 1978; Kautto *et al.* 1999, Wilensky 2003; Lappi-Seppälä 2008). However, while economic data provide evidence of the structural origins of a particular set of beliefs and values, these do not show the experiences of them during the course of everyday life, nor their consequences. The strength of the kind of cultural explanation provided in Pratt (2008a) is that it is able to do precisely this and at the same time demonstrate the implications of these ensuing sensibilities and mentalities as regards penal development in the Scandinavian countries. Reference was thus made to the *de facto*, at least, abolition of the death penalty in Scandinavia (in peacetime) at least half a century before most of the Anglophone world. And as has now been illustrated above, we can also see these values at work in the nineteenth- and early twentieth-century prison developments in these countries.

Having thus explained the methodological foundations of the causes of Scandinavian exceptionalism, let us now take the opportunity to re-examine, scrutinize and reassess the validity of the causes themselves. We do this by providing a social history overview of these three societies to show how, in more detail than was possible in Pratt (2008a), cultures of equality and the social democratic model of welfare became part of the social fabric of this region.

'Cultures of equality'?

Let us examine Norway first. With economic life based until the late nineteenth century on small, interdependent farming communities, there was never an influential, conservative, propertied elite. As Mary Wollstonecraft (1796: 63) noted, 'the distribution of landed property into small farms produces a degree of equality which I have seldom seen elsewhere'. Not only was the nobility abolished in 1821, but the 1814 constitution gave the vote to 45 per cent of the male population. In effect, the *bønder* class – small independent farmers (the usual English translation of the term as 'peasant' is inaccurate because it implies landlessness) – were given a potential majority in parliament. Laing (1837: 333) observed that 'there is no circumstance in the condition of the people of this country which strikes the observer more than the great equality of all classes, not only in houses, furniture, diet and the enjoyment of the necessaries of life, but in manners, habits and character: they all approach much more nearly to one standard than in any other country'. The inclusionary nature of Norwegian society and the relatively short social distances between one stratum and another can be illustrated with reference to the place of the domestic servant. In contrast to England, where their masters might address them in the third person and where they lived in sections of the house that were entirely shut off from the families they served (Stevenson 1880), in Norway the 1868 *Housemaid's Manual* (quoted by Aubert 1956: 152) stated: 'the master and mistress must, if they want to obey the word of the Lord, look out for their servant's welfare, care for them in case of sickness and other accidents, warn them when they see them on off-paths, and on the whole show an affectionate disposition toward them and set a good example, and not load them with more work than their strength permits them to carry'.

However, there was also a strong cultural component to this egalitarianism, as recognized in Pratt (2008a). Language and literature were of central importance in Norway's quest for national identity and the *bønder* who spoke the *landsmal* dialect (as opposed to the official Swedish language) became heroic figures in this struggle. One of the country's most famous nineteenth-century literary figures, Björnstjerne Björnson (quoted by Barton 2003: 93), described himself as writing 'a plea on behalf of the peasant . . . we had come to understand that the language of the sagas lived on in our peasants and their way of life was close to that of the sagas. The life of our nation was to be built on our history; and now the peasants were to provide the foundations.' In this way, the values of rural simplicity and frugality, rather than upper class extravagance and stylized etiquette, became dominant themes of Norwegian culture. Clarke (1819: 662) observed that 'the people of Trondheim – more polished than any other town in Norway – place themselves *without etiquette* at table: everyone sits as he chooses'. Bowden (1867: 39) complained of the lack of refinement among the Norwegian upper classes: 'it is not considered a breach of good manners to put one's knife into one's mouth and you may afterwards help yourself to salt with it'. While, by the 1930s, more sophistication may have crept into Norwegian society, Rothery (1939: 147) still found that 'while there is in Oslo a certain amount of formal and diplomatic entertaining, where scrupulous attention is paid to the proper seating of guests, to the etiquette of pouring the wines and serving the food, such occasions are restricted a to a very limited circle'. The popularity of holiday homes in the countryside is a reflection of these rural traditions.[6] As is the *matpakke* lunch of bread, cheese and fruit. While this began in the 1930s as a way of encouraging schoolchildren to have nutritious food, it has since become 'a central factor in Norwegian outdoor life' (Aase 2005: 20).

There was also a history of state intervention and regulation. Aase (2005: 110) argues that, in times of crisis, 'the state raised loans that were passed on to industry and commerce. The state was also active in the creation of an institutional apparatus for the provision of credit. Local authorities played an important role in the establishment of savings banks . . . the state played the main role in the development of a communications network which promoted growth and market integration. The purchase of the country's first steamship in 1826 was a state initiative.' The state was also the almost exclusive provider of education, preventing the social divisions characteristic of a public–private mix. Instead, education became a means of strengthening solidarity and egalitarianism. Rothery (1939: 131) thus observed that 'children of the [Norwegian] royal family attend ordinary schools instead of being taught privately'. Castberg (1954: 27–8) wrote that 'the idea is to get children from all sections of the community together in order to lay the basis for a stronger feelings of social solidarity . . . a guiding principle in the school system that basic elementary school education should as far as possible be a common school for the whole nation'.

However, what should have received more attention in this part of the analysis is the place of the Lutheran Church in Norwegian society. It had been instrumental in establishing high standards of literacy before the beginnings of Norwegian state schools in the mid-nineteenth century, for the same reasons as the pastors worked to improve the educational standards of prisoners. In addition, because of the religious homogeneity of Norway (and the other Scandinavian countries), there was no separation between church and state. The church thus sustained the state and solidarity within it, rather than acting as a forum for dissent against it. Its teachings also helped to legitimate a strong central state authority. Belief in the universality of sin and its temptations encouraged government regulation, as individuals could not be relied on to exercise self-control. Hence the period of alcohol prohibition from 1916 to 1927, followed by the establishment of government monopolies (*vinmonopolet*) where it could be purchased, rather than allowing the private sector to profit from and exploit this moral weakness.

Sweden, however, was a more stratified society. Laing (1837: 1) wrote that 'with her splendid court, and her numerous and powerful nobility and clergy, forming distinct orders in her constitution, it must present a curious contrast to the simple and democratic Norway'. There was certainly a much greater class consciousness. Laing (1837: 120) also refers to the 'extraordinary craving for paltry personal distinctions in the middle class – those who can in no other way get at these personal distinctions form themselves into orders, or clubs with all sorts of medals, dresses and other such trifling decorations'. This had become more, not less pronounced during the nineteenth century. Up to then, 'in the greater part of the country, large properties formed an insignificant minority compared to small freehold farms and holdings . . . the life and work of the owners of these and their children were so like those of the agricultural labourers that no marked class distinction was available' (Blomstedt and Book 1930: 221). Thereafter, however, enclosures and new farming practices broke up traditional community life. Many dispossessed peasants moved to the cities, creating a significant working class.

Sweden was also late in moving to a democratic constitution: universal suffrage came into existence only in 1920. Up to then, parliamentary representation had taken the form of a four estate diet: burghers, clergy, nobility and peasant farmers (*bönder*). In 1890 only one quarter of men had the vote. We thus find that while both Norwegian and Swedish migrants to the USA wrote of the opportunities this gave them to lift themselves out of poverty, the Swedes also wrote of the freedom it gave them from the restraints of their class structure (Blegen 1955; Barton 1976). Class antagonisms were also a prominent theme in nineteenth-century Swedish literature (see, for example, Strindberg 1878), as opposed to the bucolic idealism of Norwegian.

And yet, notwithstanding these social divisions, Swedish society still had 'cultures of equality' characteristics. The Swedish aristocracy had not become a ruling elite, detached from the rest of society on large estates. Laing (1837: 180) observed that 'I had formed an erroneous idea of the Swedish nobility. I had imagined they were a rich and splendid class . . . but they are, with few exceptions, extremely poor, living from civil or military employment with small pay. There are few signs of luxury or opulence in Sweden.' Indeed, one of the consequences of the employment of aristocrats in the civil service was that it gave state organizations a high level of prestige. Working in them became a desirable occupation, further legitimating the state's administrative functions (Jenkins 1968). Similarly, during the course of the nineteenth century, social cohesion rather than division was cemented into the Swedish social fabric (as it came to be in the other Scandinavian societies) through a range of interconnecting social movements that often had intra-class membership. Initially there was a religious revivalism movement, a temperance movement and adult education in the *folkskolan* (elementary schools that provided training for all in both rural and urban areas). In the late nineteenth century, trade unions were formed with the onset of industrialization, followed by farmers' cooperatives and employers' organizations. The consumers' cooperative movement also gained momentum at this time (the Swedish king was once a member). Its intention was to keep consumer prices down and undercut the power of monopoly capitalism. By the 1960s, *Kooperativa Förbundet* had become Scandinavia's largest single enterprise, incorporating enterprises such as supermarkets, department stores and restaurants. For much of this period, cooperatives had to be managed on a cash basis, with reserve capital. This meant that 'people were less tempted to buy beyond their means than if instalment buying were a regular practice' (Fleisher 1956: 32). Furthermore, by concentrating on the providing everyday necessities rather than luxury items, it fitted in with the culture of *lagom*. This pervasive Swedish characteristic literally means 'moderation or 'just enough'. It was enforced by both controlling how much an individual could spend at the co-op store, and by the goods that were on sale. In Sweden, as in Norway, over-indulgence or ostentation was frowned upon. The cooperative movement spread to housing in the early twentieth century, with Childs (1936: 51) observing that 'those who were interested in promoting better housing realized . . . that there would be little real progress until the interest of the group [not just the individual] was enlisted'. He goes on to describe (p. 55) apartment blocks with cooperative laundries, nurseries and kitchens. In Stockholm in the 1930s, 15 per cent of all families lived in such cooperative housing. Overall, as Daun (1996: 106) writes, 'popular movements have had an enormous impact on Swedish society, where formal groups and organizations tend to be strong and influential – in contrast with individuals, who are considered weak and often ignored except when representing an organization'. At the same time, interaction between respective social movements also helped to establish a tradition of political consensus and cooperation: each organization would become more powerful it if worked with others. The social movement and 'organization from the bottom of society' tradition, as a member of the Norwegian Prisoners' Association KROM explained to one of us, may also help explain the more conciliatory attitudes and approaches of the prison authorities and mass media to prisoners' rights movements in Sweden and Norway in the late 1960s and early 1970s compared to those in the Anglophone countries (Mathiesen 1974; Fitzgerald 1977).

Cohesion, conformity and egalitarianism were also reflected in education. As in Norway, the Lutheran Church had played an important role in providing educational services (see Laing 1839: 275) before the state became the almost exclusive provider in 1842. Thereafter, 'An Old Bushman' (1865: 119) remarked that 'I like the system of educating youth in Sweden much better than in England. It is freer and much less expensive. In nearly every town there is a public school open to all classes and peasants are admitted on an equality with gentlemen's sons.' The importance given to education as a means of self-improvement according to Lutheran teachings and also, in Sweden, as a means of social mobility, came to mean that 'the writer, the artist, the professor are highly regarded in Sweden. The term "egghead" is unknown' (Shirer 1955: 204). There was also a history of strong state intervention and regulation. The first collection of census data in 1749 had cemented the state into the documentation and administration of everyday life. At the same time, given the unity of church and state, looking after the poor had been a state responsibility since the Reformation. Friis (1950: 141) thus wrote that '[the Swedes] have grown accustomed to the notion that social welfare legislation is the responsibility of the state'. However, the exercise of such state power usually encompassed the whole population – it was not just an attempt to regulate the poor, as in England (Donajgrodzki 1977). As regards medical care, Thomas (1892: 150) wrote that 'the government of Sweden cares for the bodies as well as the souls of its subjects. There is always a physician within easy distance of the remotest hamlets . . . the government gives all doctors in outlying districts a salary proportional in size to the remoteness from business centres.' In the early twentieth century, the state became heavily involved in housing developments. This was not just to give relief to the poor but also to improve the living standards of the middle classes. Cole and Smith (1938: 254) observed that 'there is no official standard of overcrowding in Sweden, and flats and houses of one room and a kitchen are more common than another type. Middle and working class people are alike regards all their rooms, often including even the kitchen, and bed-sitting rooms with divan beds and writing desks, and the standard of a separate bedroom for every person and a common living room is rare.' And, as with Norway, the state became highly prescriptive in setting moral standards. Alcohol was rationed between 1914 and 1955, with each purchase at the government monopoly (*systembolaget*) being entered into a passbook (*motboken*).

In Finland, the pattern of social development differed greatly from the other Scandinavian countries for much of the nineteenth and twentieth centuries. Not only was this country part of the Russian Empire in the nineteenth century (albeit as a supposedly self-governing Grand Duchy) but at the same time it had a Swedish-speaking elite (the product of being part of Sweden until 1809) that constituted about 10 per cent of its population. As the official language of the country was Swedish this meant that all positions of power and influence were held by Swedish speakers. Indeed, the Finnish language had little by way of any formal existence until it was granted official status in 1863. As regards land distribution, up to 1918 a tenancy system prevailed, with only about 100,000 privately owned farms (Alestalo and Kuhnle 1987: 21). Changes in Finnish agriculture in the late nineteenth century – from arable to dairy farming, enclosures and growing mechanization – benefitted yeoman farmers and wealthier tenants at the expense of poorer tenants and landless labourers (*torpare*). If this created the potential for class conflict, then, in addition, tsarist attempts to 'Russianize' Finland from the 1890s, despite existing legal agreements to the contrary, also created the potential for national conflict. Meanwhile, the declining authority of the church as traditional village life fragmented, a young and weak parliamentary democracy (Russian decrees brushed its legislation aside) and the eventual Russian Revolution led to the breakdown of internal order and stability.

In the ensuing power vacuum, Right and Left political factions armed and organized themselves into White and Red Guards, culminating in civil war in 1918. Bloody reprisals followed the victory of the Whites, but from the 1920s to the early 1960s there was a profound political silence over these events (Kekkonen 1999), that gave no opportunity for healing and reconciliation. Contemporary literary sources contained some of the few public references to it, with F. E. Sillanpää (1937: 226) capturing the mood of the time: 'in every phase of every stratum of the Finnish people everything turns mostly to tragedy, a strange thin tragedy. Fate, instead of exterminating the nation, has subjected it to slow torture.' Until the 1960s, Finland remained a poor, predominantly agricultural society, under threat from external enemies. Social and penal reform was largely frozen; indeed, some aspects of penal policy became harsher – separate confinement seems to have lost its redemptive purposes in the 1930s and 1940s and was used as a deterrent against recidivist thieves (Lahti 1977).

However, in other respects, Finland had a cultural and national integrity that had much in common with the other Scandinavian countries. Strode (1941: 207) reported that 'the most casual observer in 1939 could see and feel how profoundly the co-operative movement had stimulated the well-being of the Finnish people ... in the farthest backwoods village the best-looking, neatest, most efficient as well as the least expensive shop was invariably a co-op'. As in Norway and Sweden, alcohol was severely restricted. It was prohibited from 1919 to 1932, before being sold through government monopoly (*alko* shops). As regards income differences, Hampden Jackson (1940: 26) claimed that 'the gap between rich and poor is not so wide as West European countries. There is equal opportunity in Finland in so far as the secondary schools and university education is free and admissions open to talent.' Here, too, the Lutheran Church had been influential in establishing high educational standards: 'elementary schools in Finland date from 1860s . . . before then the priest was the only schoolmaster. It devolved on him to teach people to read, and laggard pupils braced to their task by a law of 1686 – no-one could receive communion without knowledge of the scriptures, nor be married who had not received communion and learned Luther's catechism. Parents expected to take their share in the work of instruction at home, on pain of being fined' (Reade 1915: 178). In the aftermath of this legacy from the pastors, schoolteachers became particularly highly valued members of Finnish society: 'most elementary school teachers have spent three years in college at the state expense; and most secondary teachers have been through the university. It would be difficult to find the equivalent of our [English] uncertified elementary teachers in Finland, or our underpaid broken down schoolmasters and schoolmistresses. *You see, both the people and their administrators are convinced of the benefits of education*' (Travers 1911: 185, our italics). Shirer (1955: 397) later wrote that 'the position of the public school teacher is rather enviable. Salaries are relatively high and if a teacher is the father of a family he receives extra pay.'

But another reason for the high value of education is that, as with Norway, it had become central to Finland's struggle for national identity. Clarke (1819: 510), on a visit to Turku, had found that 'books of any kind are seldom seen: there are no book sellers; nor is it possible to meet with a single copy of the work of the few celebrated authors Sweden [*sic*] has boasted in any of the private houses'. This, however, was because there were virtually no Finnish books available – Swedish was Finland's official language. Between 1543 and 1808 only 174 books had been published in Finnish. Between 1809 and 1853 there were 452; in the next decade, 481 (Lavery 2006: 98). Reflecting the rejuvenation of Finnish culture that was occurring, the Finnish Literary Society was established in 1845 and the Finnish Artists Union in 1846. The symbolism that came to be associated with literary and other artistic works is captured by Hall and Mead (1977: 86): 'Finns respect and revere their artists sometimes with the other side of idolatry . . . the climate of opinion, combined with the emergence from time to time of a great or outstanding figure, or a great work seems to stimulate creative activity and confidence.' Notwithstanding the country's impoverishment at the time, Shirer (1955: 391) reported that 'the Finnish academy . . . pays its twelve distinguished members not only a regular salary but also an annual subsidy, all of which come out of the coffers of the state'.

Here we can see the origins of the respect for intellectuals and expert knowledge that began to reshape penal policy in this country from the 1960s (Lappi-Seppälä 2001) after the defrosting of Finland's social, economic and political structure and its sudden transformation from an agrarian to a modern industrial society. From having the highest rate of imprisonment in Western society up to that time, it was then able to bring this into line with the rates of the other Scandinavian societies.

Finland, because of its geo-political history, had been furthest removed from the ideal type cultures of equality characteristics and its level of imprisonment accordingly rose. However, its dramatic decline as, from the 1960s, as it took on a clearer Scandinavian identity, strengthens rather than weakens the explanatory capabilities of the cultures of equality argument.

The origins and effects of the Scandinavian welfare state

If the social democratic model of welfare (Esping-Andersen 1990) further facilitated the more 'inclusionary' penal policies of this region, what were the origins of this welfare model? Pratt (2008a) puts forward the following explanation for its rise. The endemic poverty of the region, the harsh climate, sparse populations in large territories and the vulnerability of these small states to more powerful neighbours created a yearning for *trygghet* – security. As the then Swedish Minister of Social Affairs (quoted by Fleisher 1967: 197) put the matter, 'nothing good has ever come out of insecurity. Security is the most basic foundation of the individual.' This could be achieved by increasing the power of the state and its welfare apparatus, thereby minimizing the inherent risks the Scandinavian communities faced to their well-being. In the 'people's home' model of welfare that was built, there would be a place for everyone. No one would be disqualified or excluded, there would be solidarity and equality, reducing the potential for conflict and instability and further demonstrating the inclusionary nature of Scandinavian society. As Per Albin Hansson (Berkling 1982: 227), coiner of the 'people's home' *motif* and Swedish Prime Minister 1932–46, claimed: '[this] would mean the breaking down of all the social and economic barriers that now divide citizens into the privileged and the unfortunate, into rulers and subjects, into rich and poor, the glutted and the destitute, the plunderers and the plundered'.

However, while this is one part of the explanation for the development of the Scandinavian welfare state, it overstates the role played by cultural consensus and understates the way in which the welfare state emerged from social conflict. From the 1890s to the 1930s, industrialization followed by economic depression, brought strikes, disorder and violence amid mass unemployment in both Norway and Sweden (for reasons set out in the previous section, the Finnish welfare state did not really take shape until the 1960s [see Kuusi 1964]). The monetarist response of conservative governments to this turbulence was to cut public expenditure and wages. However, the political left had gained strength from the strong labour movements that had links to the rural population (industrial development was not concentrated in the cities) and the temperance movement. When, however, the Social Democrats in Sweden and the Labour Party in Norway came to power in 1932 and 1935 respectively, with the support of centrist rural parties, a Keynesian economic programme was pursued: governments stimulated job creation, thereby increasing tax revenue which in turn fed into welfare expenditure. In Sweden, a state-supported unemployment insurance scheme was introduced in 1934; old age pensions were increased in 1935. The Social Democrats won the 1936 election with the slogan 'Welfare Policy' and 'Remember our Poor and Old people'. These were pointers to what Childs (1936) famously referred to as Sweden's 'middle way' – a form of social organization 'between the extremes of Communism and Fascism' that seemed to rectify free market shortcomings without recourse to tyranny. With subsequent incremental development (such as earnings related unemployment benefits and a free health service) the social democratic model of welfare came into full bloom during the 1950s. In Norway, 1930s welfare reforms included pensions for all at the age of 70, special pensions for the disabled; child allowances were extended post-war and three weeks' holiday with pay was introduced. These and other incremental extensions culminated in the 1966 'people's pension': 'the basic philosophy is that each citizen shall be able to *maintain the standard of living he has maintained during his working life*' (Tveteras 1967: 252, our italics).

Despite initial Conservative opposition to the welfare reforms, amidst concerns about taxation levels and the growing power of the state that were its by-products, what then ensured the popularity of the welfare programme and subsequent electoral successes of Social Democrat and Labour governments, was the way in which its parameters ensured that everyone would receive tangible benefits – this welfare model was not just intended to provide a safety net to prevent destitution. Gustav Möller (1928: 27), made this clear when laying the intellectual foundations of the Swedish welfare state: 'a social insurance system is not intended to help the obviously asocial or antisocial elements; it is instead for that part of our people who belong to the category of good citizens but who need protection against certain special risks, so that these dangers don't cast them down, down to the bottom rung of society. It is intended to protect the home and family against afflictions for which the individual bears no responsibility.' Essentially, then, this welfare model was intended to maintain living standards, rather than merely prevent destitution, as with the subsequent Anglophone model.

Recognition that the origins of the Scandinavian welfare state was not solely the product of a cultural consensus does not then invalidate the effects it produced. Indeed, its inclusionary and egalitarian nature did help to maintain consensus while reducing conflict and diffusing social tensions. Current survey data illustrate the high levels of trust between individuals and social institutions in the Scandinavian countries; relatively low levels of fear of crime and penal moderation (van Dijk *et al.* 2007). It is also clear that there is a strong correlation between levels of welfare expenditure and levels of imprisonment (Downes and Hansen 2006). The Scandinavian countries, with the lowest levels of imprisonment in the OECD and the highest welfare expenditures provide the clearest confirmation of this relationship, while at the same time validating the explanatory force given to his model of welfare in Pratt (2008a).

The costs of Scandinavian exceptionalism

The social costs of Scandinavian exceptionalism are briefly mentioned in Pratt (2008a). More attention should have been given to them. Here we examine two aspects of the price that had to be paid for it.

The pressures to conform

Inevitably, small homogeneous societies have the potential for strong interdependencies, solidarity and inclusion. But they can also demand high levels of conformity. Although Pratt (2008a: 125) refers to complaints by Henrik Ibsen and Gustav Sundbärg about the stifling nature of Norwegian and Swedish society, these are probably overwhelmed by the positive emphasis given to the social characteristics of these societies in the rest of the paper. It should also have been noted that, despite the reverence for artistic and literary figures, both Ibsen and August Strindberg spent most of their working lives outside their respective countries, partly to offset the pressures to conform. Nor was it the case that these feelings of suffocation were experienced only by the intelligentsia. Swedish immigrants to the United States regularly expressed the feelings of release that their adopted country gave them: 'all were exhilarated by the new freedom; from meddlesome bureaucrats, army officers and pastors; freedom for all its citizens to participate in public affairs; freedom from the deadening constraints of social convention. They welcomed US informality' (Barton 1976: 20). These pressures to conform remained for much of the twentieth century. De Mare (1952: 233) wrote that 'the eccentric character in Sweden is rare'. Similarly Fleisher (1967: 342): 'nonconformists often have difficulty fitting into Swedish life'. And Daun (1996: 107): 'in Sweden eccentrics are not regarded with the same positive interest that they allegedly are in Great Britain. Rather, all deviance from the group norms and common group patterns is potentially threatening to the individual. The individual should fit in with co-workers and neighbours.'[7]

The point is, then, that the very solidarity that was instrumental in the development of Scandinavian exceptionalism was also likely to produce strong, informal control systems, leading, for many, to an intolerable insistence on conformity.

The over-powerful state

As we have seen, the state in Scandinavia was generally assumed to be a benign and protective entity, one that would bring guarantees of *trygghet*. Tage Erlander, Sweden's Prime Minister from 1946 to 1969 (quoted by Fleisher 1967: 63–4) thus explained that 'the state is not a threat to or an enemy of the individual. On the contrary, many of his problems can only be solved through cooperation and solidarity, through the state and the municipality'. However, what is again understated in Pratt (2008a) is the way in which these beliefs in the protective state led to practices that threatened individual human rights well-being.

In Sweden especially, as the power of medical professionals grew in all sectors of the criminal justice process, so their diagnoses of mental abnormalities exponentially increased. From 1928 in Sweden there were provisions for the indefinite detention of 'abnormal delinquents' and 'habitual criminals'. Ten recidivists were diagnosed as being 'mentally weak' (and thereby sentenced to indefinite detention) in 1929; the number had increased to 43 by 1932. In 1943, 928 out of 3,000 people arrested were given a mental health assessment. Only 60 were declared sane. The

1956 Penal Code Commission noted that while 47 per cent of murderers had been found to be insane in 1950, by 1953 the number had increased to 80 per cent. Not surprisingly, the Social Welfare Board (1952: 6) reported that 'many penal institutions are provided with mental departments. In fact there has been a strong tendency in recent decades to bring medical sciences, particularly psychology, to bear on treatment. The Prison Board has a department staffed with forensic psychologists, and to an increasing extent the courts order a mental examination of the defendant.' In effect, the more the state invested in mental health expertise, the more this demonstrated the need for further investment and resources. And the stronger the belief in the power of the state and its organizations to solve social problems, the more it concentrated this power on searching for and then trying to rectify what were thought to be individual deficiencies in its own citizens. Some particularly important Scandinavian criminological voices were in the forefront of the struggle to restrict such abuses (see Christie 1961; Mathiesen 1965; Anttila 1972).

Furthermore, and uniquely in post-1945 western Europe, the Scandinavian countries were prepared to use compulsory sterilization and castration laws to regulate what were understood as antisocial tendencies. In Sweden, sterilization had been given momentum by the publication of Myrdal and Myrdal's (1934) *Population Crisis*. Their central theme was that every child should be a wanted child, but they were concerned that the mentally retarded would not practise birth control and thereby bring large numbers of children into disadvantaged circumstances. In these societies, where it was thought that social engineering was the way to produce community well-being, the rational solution was simply to prevent them from having children. This fitted the preventive social policy that the Myrdals, for example, advocated: 'we can prevent – technically it is possible to quite a high degree – illness, crime and asocial tendencies of different sorts' (Myrdal 1945: 11). Legislation in 1935 thus provided for the compulsory sterilization of 'legally incompetent' individuals. There were 63,000 such sterilizations up to 1975, the vast majority women. A castration law was introduced in 1944. There were 43 such operations that year, but by 1946 only 11 and this legislation fell more quickly into disuse, although it remained on the statute books until the 1960s (Broberg and Roll-Hansen 1996). In Norway, there were 41,000 compulsory sterilizations between 1934 and 1977 (here voluntary castration was available for sex offenders). In Finland, there were 1,078 compulsory sterilizations between 1935 and 1955, under legislation allowing this for 'idiots, imbeciles and the insane'. Further legislation in 1950, allowing this to be carried out on eugenic, social or general medical grounds, led to 56,000 more. The 1950 Castration Act (although hardly ever used and repealed in 1958) prescribed this for 'a person who has been found guilty of ... a [sexual] crime or of an attempted crime and who because of their sexual drive, is dangerous to another person'.

The reasons why we find such practices in Scandinavia are inextricably tied into the same social arrangements that led to the penal exceptionalism of this region: investment in the power of a strong central state that engineered uniformity, the high value placed on expert knowledge, and the desire to improve the material possibility of individuals' lives while at the same time ensuring that they would not challenge social cohesion and homogeneity. That said, the presence of such oppressive conformity and a central state authority that post 1945 seems to have been more intrusive and regulatory than in the rest of western Europe does not undermine the Scandinavian exceptionalism thesis: what it reflects, instead, are the social costs associated with this.

'Culture of control' or 'catastrophic criminology'?

Could it not be argued, though, that, whatever exceptional features penal policy may have had in Scandinavia, these are now being replaced by a more punitive penal culture that, from its roots in the US, has begun to spread across the rest of Western society (Wacquant 2009)? On the face of it, we can certainly detect ingredients for the development of a Scandinavian 'culture of control' (see Garland 2001). The new penal language associated with these changing penal values – 'three strikes', 'zero tolerance' and so on – is known in this region (Aas 2005). And, similar to the new arrangement of penal politics in the Anglophone world (Pratt 2007), Left political parties have been willing to abandon social democratic crime control principles of reintegration and instead compete with the Right on the basis of who is the toughest on law and order (see Tham 2001). In addition, welfare state provisions have tightened up and become more restrictive (see, for example, Lindbom 2001) on the one hand, while on the other, income differentials have widened. The tendency towards more heterogeneity has also seen the ascendancy and electoral success of right-wing populist political parties such as the Norwegian Progress Party. Parties even further to the right, with strong racist overtones, such as the Swedish Democrats and the True Finns are also making political headway. Furthermore, media reporting of crime has increased and become more sensationalized (Pollack 2001).

Pratt (2008b) assessed the effects of such changes on Finland, Norway and Sweden and concluded that Scandinavian exceptionalism was most at risk in Sweden. It was in this country that the social arrangements necessary for its existence had been most undermined. As a consequence, we can discern important shifts taking place in the penal values of that country. At the height of the welfare period Frederic Fleisher (1967: 170), in his book *The New Sweden*, wrote that 'the appreciation of restraint, a certain aloofness, and the disapproval of displays of emotion play a vital part in forming the general outlook toward violence'. In contrast, in 2008, there were massive public outpourings of grief at the funeral of 10-year-old Engla Hoglund in 2008. She had been murdered by a man with a history of violent crime. State television broadcast the funeral in full, the first time for any such event, and a special funeral song was composed – 'Living without You'. In effect, as these two contrasting examples illustrate, the restraints on displays of public emotion and, ultimately, public involvement in penal affairs that is evident in Fleisher, and that had allowed the 'experts' so much authority in this country, may now have broken down, paving the way for more populist and punitive influences.

Let us also take note, however, that there were no subsequent nationwide vigilante activities against suspected paedophiles in Sweden after Engla Hoglund's murder, unlike those that that occurred in Britain in 2000 after a similar incident, egged on by sections of the tabloid press (Jewkes 2004). In addition, there are still dramatic differences in the reporting of crime and punishment issues between the Scandinavian countries and the Anglophone world (Green 2008). Furthermore, notwithstanding some tightening of its parameters, there has been no wholesale restructuring of the welfare state in this region. To attempt to do so is to invite political suicide, as the Swedish Moderate Party discovered in the early 1990s. As such, it continues to build social capital and community well-being, thereby countering punitive populist rhetoric and ideology. And while we can see the retreat from social democracy in, for example, Sweden's zero-tolerance drugs laws, the Norwegian Labour party won the 2006 election – and was then re-elected in 2009 – with a cast-iron restatement of social democratic crime policy: '*with good welfare services for everyone*, crime can be prevented and many of the initial incentives for a life of crime can be removed. Given that 60 per cent of violent crime is committed under the influence of alcohol, it is important to adhere to a restrictive drug and alcohol policy. Good psychiatric health care services and an active labour market policy are important for comprehensive crime fighting' (Norwegian Labour Party 2006, our italics).

For these reasons, to follow the path of a Scandinavian culture of control analysis may only mean that this collapses into an episode of what O'Malley (2000) refers to as 'catastrophic criminology'. In such inevitably apocalyptic accounts, we are imagined to be on the brink of a global and political watershed, that leads us into much stormier, uncharted penal territory. However, this is manifestly not occurring. The gulf in prison rates between the Scandinavian and Anglophone countries is widening rather than narrowing (see Pratt 2008a);[8] and for *sentenced* prisoners at least, despite some significant tightening of controls in Swedish closed prisons, material conditions remain comparatively benign and humane. In these respects, the more pertinent issue for sociological analysis is to consider what it is about the Scandinavian countries that provides them with high levels of insurance (if not fully comprehensive insurance) against the contemporary penal excesses that have become a characteristic of much of the Anglophone world. The papers by Pratt (2008a, b) were a preliminary attempt to address such matters and laid the foundations for a comparative research programme on the differential nature of penal development in Scandinavian and Anglophone societies. They were also a contribution to the growing literature on comparative studies of punishment and penal policy (see, particularly, Whitman (2004), Cavadino and Dignan (2006), Green (2008) and Lacey (2008)). Notwithstanding differing theoretical perspectives between its authors, this œuvre is beginning to construct a sociology of low imprisonment societies to complement the voluminous literature on the sociology of high imprisonment.

In retrospect, we acknowledge that some of the features and characteristics that were claimed for Scandinavian exceptionalism may have been overstated, others understated. There was too much emphasis on cultural consensus, not enough on material conflict. The role and influence of the Lutheran Church on Scandinavian society as a whole and in daily prison administration was an important absence and needs further examination. Recognition of these and other matters thus means that some adjustments and refinements need to be made to the exceptionalism framework. However, the overall thesis has been validated in this chapter and the contours and colouring of its themes remain much the same. But if this has been a defence of the theoretical basis of Scandinavian exceptionalism, it also represents a normative defence of this way of responding to crime. For all the shortcomings it has that have been well documented over the years by such distinguished criminologists as Thomas Mathiesen and Nils Christie, and notwithstanding the social costs that had to be paid for it, for those of us familiar with the excesses of the Anglophone penal world that have taken place in recent times and their social costs, it represents a beacon to be defended against the political and economic challenges it now faces.

Notes

1 In 2008, the rates of suicide were New South Wales 0.3 per 1000; New Zealand 0.5; England 0. 73; Finland 1.2; Sweden 0.9; Norway 2.0.
2 For example, foreign prisoners make up 27.5 per cent of Sweden's prison population, but 13.6 of that of England.
3 In England, the masks had been compulsory when introduced in 1842, but were then abolished in 1860. In Sweden, wearing hoods remained compulsory outside the cell until the early twentieth century.
4 In England, the solitary confinement component of a prison sentence was introduced in the 1840s, but was quickly reduced from 18 to nine months. In 1910 it was reduced to three months for recidivists and one month for first offenders before final abolition.
5 Our interpretation thus differs from Nilsson (1999) who emphasizes the social control aspects of this mode of imprisonment: which, of course, is correct; in just the same way that the extraordinary 'hard bed, hard fare, hard labour' regimes introduced to English prisons during the 1860s were another form of social control. Rather than exercise this exclusively in the form of separate confinement, this was embellished with all kinds of additional deprivations. It was a form of social control that mercilessly brutalized prisoners. As Arthur Bidwell (1895: 209) put it, what had been created was 'a vast machine . . . [w]ithout passion, without prejudice but also without pity and remorse . . . it crushes and passes on'. We do feel it necessary, however, to look beyond the social control aspects of these respective modalities of imprisonment and ask why they should take such different forms in these countries: hence the importance we have given here to understanding what appears to be the enhanced role of the pastors in Scandinavian prison administration.
6 In 1970 there were 190,000 holiday homes in Norway. By 2005 this had increased to 375,000. In recognition of the increasing wealth of this country, Aase (2005: 23) notes that 'the main difference from earlier times is that most cabins today have electricity and running water. Many are located next to a skiing resort . . . a new trend is to build luxury apartments in the mountains with outdoor jacuzzi and a panoramic view of the mountains.'
7 For similar comments on Norway, see Martin (1952: 15) and Rodnick (1955: 1). See also Johansen (1989) in relation to Norwegian and Swedish antipathy to Jewish immigration during the Nazi period.
8 For example, in Finland, the rate of imprisonment in 1995 was 59 per 100,000 of

population; in 2009 it was 67; in New Zealand for the same years, the rates were 128 and 197.

References

Aas, K. (2005) 'The Ad and the Form: Punitiveness and Technological Culture', in J. Pratt, D. Brown, S. Hallsworth, M. Brown and W. Morrison (eds), *The New Punitiveness: Trends, Theories, Perspectives*, Cullompton: Willan Publishing.
Aase, A. (2005) 'In Search of Norwegian Values', in E. Magero and B. Simonsen, B. (eds), *Norway: Society and Culture*, Kristiansand: Portal, pp. 13–27.
Alestalo, M. and S. Kuhnle (1987) 'The Scandinavian Route: Economic, Social and Political Developments in Denmark, Finland, Norway, and Sweden', in R. Erikson, E. J. Hansen, S. Ringen, and H. Uusitalo, (eds), *The Scandinavian Model: Welfare States and Welfare Research*, Armonk, NY: M. E. Sharpe, pp. 3–38.
Annual Report of the Prison Service (1927) Stockholm: Sveriges Officiella Statistik Rattsvasen.
—— (1941) Stockholm: Sveriges Officiella Statistik Rattsvasen.
—— (1942) Stockholm: Sveriges Officiella Statistik Rattsvasen.
—— (1943) Stockholm: Sveriges Officiella Statistik Rattsvasen.
—— (1946/7) Stockholm: Sveriges Officiella Statistik Rattsvasen.
Anttila, I. (1972) *Incarceration for Crimes Never Committed*, Helsinki: National Research Institute of Legal Policy, 9.
Aubert, V. (1956) 'The Housemaid: An Occupational Role in Crisis', *Acta Sociologica*, 1(1): 149–58.
Balfour, J. (1901) *My Prison Life*, London: Heinemann.
Barton, H. A. (1976) *Letters from the Promised Land: Swedes in America, 1840–1914*, Minneapolis: University of Minnesota Press.
—— (2003) *Sweden and Visions of Norway*, Carbondale: Southern Illinois University Press.
Bidwell, A. (1895) *From Wall Street to Newgate*, London: Macmillan.
Blegen, T. C. (ed.) (1955) *Land of their Choice. The Immigrants Write Home*, Minneapolis: University of Minnesota Press.
Blomstedt, M. and F. Book (1930) *Sweden of To-day: A Survey of its Intellectual and Material Culture*, Stockholm: A.-b. H. W. Tullberg.
Bondeson, U. (1989) *Prisoners in Prison Societies*, Brunswick: Transaction Press.
Bowden, J. (1867) *Norway*, London: Bibliobazar
Broberg, G. and N. Roll-Hansen (1996) *Eugenics and the Welfare State: Sterilization Policy in Denmark, Sweden, Norway and Finland*, Michigan: Michigan University Press.
Castberg, F. (1954) *The Norwegian Way of Life*, Melbourne: Heinemann.
Cavadino, M. and J. Dignan (2006) *Penal Systems*, London: Sage
Childs, M. (1936) *Sweden: the Middle Way*, New Haven, CT: Yale University Press.
Christie, N. (1961) *Tvangsarbeid og Alkoholbruk*, Oslo: Institute of Criminology, University of Oslo.
Clarke, E. D. R. (1819) *Travels in Various Countries of Europe, Asia and Africa, Part III: Scandinavia*, London: T. Cadell and W. Davies.
Cole, M. and Smith, D. (1938) *Democratic Sweden*, London: George Routledge.
Daun, A. (1996) *Swedish Mentality*, trans. J. Teeland, Philadelphia: Pennsylvania State University Press.
De Mare, E. (1952) *Scandinavia: Sweden, Denmark and Norway*, London: BT Batsford.

Donajgrodzki, A. (ed.) (1977) *Social Control in Nineteenth Century Britain*, London: Croom Helm.
Downes, D. and K. Hansen (2006) *Welfare and Punishment*, London: Crime and Society Foundation.
Elias, N. (1939, 1979) *The Civilising Process*, Oxford: Blackwell.
Esping-Andersen, G. (1990) *Three Models of Welfare States*, Oxford: Oxford University Press.
Fitzgerald, M. (1977) *Prisoners in Revolt*, London: Penguin.
Fleisher, F. (1967) *The New Sweden: The Challenge of a Disciplined Democracy*, New York: David McKay.
Fleisher, W. (1956) *Sweden. The Welfare State*, New York: John Day Company.
Friis, H. (1950) *Scandinavia between East and West*, Ithaca, NY: Cornell University Press.
Garland, D. (2001) *The Culture of Control*, Oxford: Oxford University Press.
Green, D. A. (2008) *When Children Kill Children: Penal Populism and Political Culture*, Oxford: Oxford University Press.
Griffiths, A. (1875) *Memorials of Millbank and Chapters in Prison History*, vol. 1, London: Henry S. King and Co.
Grimley, O. (1937) *The New Norway*, Oslo: Griff-Forlanget.
Hall, W. and W. R. Mead (1972) *Scandinavia (New Nations and Peoples)*, London: Thames & Hudson Ltd.
Hampden Jackson, J. (1940) *Finland*, New York: Macmillan.
Hansson, P. A. and A. L. Berkling (1982) *Fran Fram till folkhemmet: Per Albin Hansson som tidningsman och talare*, Stockholm: Metodica Press.
Ignatieff, M. (1978) *A Just Measure of Pain*, London: Macmillan.
International Round table for Correctional Excellence (2009) *Benchmarking. Trends and Developments 2008–2008*, The Hague: Ministry of Justice.
Jenkins, D. (1968) *Sweden and the Price of Progress*, New York: Coward-McCann.
Jewkes, Y. (2004) *Crime and the Media*, London: Sage.
Johansen, Per Ole (1989) 'Norway and the Holocaust', in Hannu Takala and Henrik Tham (eds), *Crime and Control in Scandinavia during the Second World War*. Scandinavian Research Council in Criminology.
Kautto, M., M. Heikkila, B. Hvinden, S. Marklund, N. Ploug (1999) *Nordic Social Policy*, London: Routledge.
Kekkonen, J. (1999) 'Judicial Repression after the Civil Wars in Finland (1918) and Spain (1936–1939)', in M. Lappalainen, and P. Hirvonen (eds), *Crime and Control in Europe from the Past to the Present*, Helsinki: Academy of Finland.
Kuhnle, S. (1978) 'The Beginnings of the Nordic Welfare States', *Acta Sociologica* 21, 9–35.
Kuusi, P. (1964) *Social Policy for the Sixties*, Helsinki: Finnish Social Policy Association.
Lacey, N. (2008) *The Prisoners' Dilemma*, Cambridge: Cambridge University Press.
Lahti, R. (1977) 'Criminal Sanctions in Finland: A System in Transition', *Scandinavian Studies in Law*, 21: 119–57.
Laing, S. (1837) *Journal of a Residence in Norway During the years 1834, 1835 and 1836*, London: Longmans, Green and Co.
Lappi-Seppälä, T. (2001) 'The Decline of the Finnish Prison Population', *Scandinavian Journal of Criminology and Crime Prevention*, 1: 27–40.
—— (2008) 'Trust, Welfare and Political Culture: Explaining Differences in National Policies', *Crime and Justice. A Review of Research*, 37: 313–87.

Lavery, J. E. (2006) *The History of Finland*, Westport, CT: Greenwood Press.
Lindbom, A. (2001) 'Dismantling the Social Democratic Welfare Model', *Scandinavian Political Studies*, 24: 171–93.
Luther, M. (1525, 1990) *The Bondage of the Will*, New York: Revell.
Martin, A. (1952) *Norwegian Life and Landscape*, London: Elek Books.
Mathiesen, T. (1965) *Defences of the Weak*, London: Tavistock.
—— (1974) *The Politics of Abolition*, New York: Wiley.
Möller, G. (1928) *Trygghet och sakerhet at sveriges folk!: ett socialdemokistiskt program infor valet*, Stockholm: Tidens Bokforlag.
Myrdal, A. and Myrdal, G. (1934) *Population Crisis*, Stockholm: A. Bonnier.
Myrdal, G. (1945) *Nation and Family*, Cambridge, MA: MIT Press.
Nelson, G. (1953) *Freedom and Welfare*, Stockholm: Ministry of Social Affairs.
Nilsson, R. (1999) *En valbyggd maskin, en mardrom for sjalen: Det svenska fangelsesystemet under 1800-talet*, Lund: Lunds Universitet Press.
Norwegian Labour Party (2006) *Crime Policy*, Oslo: Norwegian Labour Party.
O'Malley, P. (2000) 'Criminologies of Catastrophe? Understanding Criminal Justice on the Edge of the New Millennium', *Australian and New Zealand Journal of Criminology*, 33: 153–67.
Pollack, E. (2001) *Medier och Brott*, Stockholm: JMK Stockholms Universitet.
Pratt, J. (2002), *Punishment and Civilization*, London: Sage.
—— (2007) *Penal Populism*, London: Routledge.
—— (2008a) 'Scandinavian Exceptionalism in an Era of Penal Excess. Part I: The Nature and Origins of Scandinavian Exceptionalism', *British Journal of Criminology*, 48(2): 119–37.
—— (2008b) 'Scandinavian Exceptionalism in an Era of Penal Excess. Part II: Does Scandinavian Exceptionalism Have a Future?', *British Journal of Criminology*, 48(3): 275–92.
Reade, A. (1915) *Finland and the Finns*, London: Methuen & Co.
Rodnick, D. (1955) *The Norwegians: A Study in National Culture*, Washington: Public Affairs Press.
Rothery, A, (1939) *Norway: Changing and Changeless*, London: Faber & Faber.
Rudstedt, S. (1994) *I fangelset: Den svenska fangvardens historia*, Kristianstad: Tidens Forlag.
Scharff Smith, P. (2006) 'The effects of solitary confinement on prison inmates', *Crime and Justice*, 34: 441–528.
Sillanpää, F. E. (1937) *Meek Heritage*, trans. Alexander Matson, London: Putnam.
Social Welfare Board (1952) *Social Sweden*, Stockholm: Social Welfare Board.
Shirer, W. L. (1955) The Challenge of Scandinavia: Norway, Sweden, Denmark and Finland in Our Time, Boston: Little, Brown.
Stevenson, J. J. (1880) *House Architecture, vol. II*, London: Macmillan.
Strindberg, A. (1878/1913) *The Red Room: Scenes of Artistic and Literary Life*, trans. Ellie Schleussner, London: Howard Latimer, Ltd.
Strode, H. (1941) *Finland Forever*, New York: Harcourt, Brace.
Sykes, G. (1958) *The Society of Captives*, Princeton: Princeton University Press.
Tham, H. (2001) 'Law and Order as a Leftist Project', *Punishment and Society*, 3: 409–26.
Thomas, W. W. (1892) *Sweden and the Swedes*, New York: Rand McNally.
Travers, R. (1911) *Letters from Finland: August 1908 – March 1909*, London: Kegan Paul & Co.
Tveteras, E. (1967) *Norway Year Book*, Oslo: Johan Grunt Tanum Forlag.

van Dijk, J. et al. (2007) *A Comparative Analysis of the European Crime and Safety Survey 2005*, Brussels: EU.
Wacquant, L. (2009) *Punishing the Poor*, Durham, NC: Duke University Press.
Wheelwright, H. W. (1865) *Ten Years in Sweden: Being a Description of the Landscape, Climate, Domestic Life, Forests, Mines, Agriculture, Field Sports and Fauna of Scandinavia*, London: Groombridge and Sons.
Whitman, J. (2004) *Harsh Justice*, Oxford: Oxford University Press.
Wilensky, H. (2003) *Rich Democracies*, Berkeley: University of California Press.
Wollstonecraft, M. (1796, 1987), *A Short Residence in Sweden, Norway and Denmark*, London: Penguin.

Index

Aase, A. 244–5
advanced liberalism 158
Ailes, R. 68
Allern, S. 66, 67
Amilon, C. 85
Andersen, H.S. *et al.* 50
Anderson, B. 122, 124, 127, 135
Andersson, R. 164, 165; and Nilsson, R. 163, 165, 166, 215
Anglo-American practices 4–5, 58; *see also* United Kingdom (UK); United States (US)
anthropology 13; comparative 102–3; criminal 160
attention deficit hyperactivity disorder (ADHD): biopolitics 157–8, 164, 166; culture of intervention 163–4, 167–8; degeneracy research programme and degeneration theory 158–60; diagnosis of children and adults 161–3; *Diagnostic and Statistical Manual of Mental Disorders* (DSM) 160, 161, 162–3; differentiation and rehabilitation 164–5; epigenetic aetiology 162; as knowledge production 158–63; moral engineering 166; (neo-)liberal governmentality 164, 165–6; in prison population 163; and Scandinavian exceptionalism 156, 167
Austin, P. 87–8

Balfour, J. 240
Balvig, F. 32
Barfoed, L. 45
Barth, F. 112
Berkley, G.E. *et al.* 89
biopolitics 157–8, 164, 166
Björnson, B. 244
Bloch, A.-K. and Mathisen, H.B. 22

Blomstedt, M. and Book, F. 245
Blumler, J.G. and Gurevitch, M.A. 59
Bondeson, U. 24, 64, 236, 237
Borstal system, UK 176
Bourdieu, P. 31, 140, 148
Bowden, J. 244
Braithwaite, V. 178, 180
Bratholm, A. 20, 50
Britain *see* United Kingdom (UK)

Castberg, F. 245
Cavadino, M. and Dignan, J. 2–3, 41, 59–60, 94, 103, 176, 186–7, 193, 194
Childs, M. 80, 246–7, 250–1
Christensen, C.B. *et al.* 42
Christie, N. 2, 6, 201, 208, 209; and Bruun, K. 127
Clarke, E.D.R. 244, 249
Clarke, K. 30
class-specific issues (health visiting), UK 149–51
classification of prisons 216–17
'climate prisons', Denmark 47
comparative perspectives 100–2; anthropology 102–3; criminology 2–4; health visiting, UK *vs* Norway 149–51; media and penal systems 59–61; methodological and theoretical challenges 4–6; prison conditions 17–18; *see also* Jordan and Denmark; Norway and UK
conformity, comparative perspective 252
conjugal relations 24
Connery, D. 87
consensus democracy 70
control: culture of 43–4, 58, 254–6; digital data processing and 18–19
Corston Report 200, 208

costs of Scandinavian exceptionalism 251–4
Crawley, E.M. 219–20
crime news: media convergence thesis 63–5
criminal anthropology 160
Criminal Procedure Act (1887/2002) 20
cultural cohesion and identity of prison officers 226–8
culture of control 43–4, 58, 254–6
culture of equality: Finland 248–50; Norway 243–5; Sweden 245–8; welfare state and 40–2; *see also* immigrants: Norwegian remand prison
culture of intervention 156, 163–4, 167–8
Curran, J. 70, 94; *et al.* 67–8, 72

Dahl, H.F. 121
Dalteg, A. *et al.* 163
Daun, A. 247, 252
de Toqueville, A. 121
deficits in attention, motor control and perception (DAMP) 161–2
degeneracy research programme and degeneration theory 158–60
democratic corporatist media model 60–1, 62, 63, 68; *vs* liberal model 70, 71
democratic systems typology 59
Denmark: Acts 51, 52; 'climate prisons' 47; culture of control 43–4; Danish Institute for Human Rights 109–10; gangs: three strikes proposal 45; human rights violations 45–6, 47; and Jordan *see* Jordan and Denmark: comparative perspective; juvenile offenders 47; liberal and humane prison conditions 39–40, 42; open prisons 39, 42; Penal Code 51; pre-trial solitary confinement 47–53; Prison Commission (1840) 51; prison rates 46; self-catering regime 39, 42; 'tough on crime' policies and penal popularism 43–7, 53–4
Department of Prison and Probation, Norway 24–5
Deputy Police Commissioner (DPC): Danish and Jordanian 107–8
Diagnostic and Statistical Manual of Mental Disorders (DSM) 160, 161, 162–3
digital data processing and control 18–19
drug-related crime 25–6
Durham, M. 88

education: prisoners 19; *see also* training
Eide, E. and Simonsen, S. 127
Eide, M. 64–5, 66
emotional labour 219–20
epigenetics 162
equality *see* culture of equality; immigrants: Norwegian remand prison
Eriksson, T. 82–3, 85, 86, 91
Espersen, L. 43–4
Esping-Anderson, G. 40–1
Estrada, F. 63
European Committee on the Prevention of Torture (CPT) 21, 22, 48–50
European Convention of Human Rights 47
European Prison Rules 52
Evans, M. and Morgan, R. 38
expertise: citizen confidence in 69; governmentality 158
export of ideas/policy transfer 79–80, 92–4, 103–10, 113–15

Feeley, M. and Simon, J. 180, 186, 190–1, 201–2
Finland: culture of equality 248–50; media 63, 64, 66, 67–8, 69
Fleisher, F. 81, 88, 246, 250, 252, 254
Foucault, M. 128, 129, 145–6, 148, 157, 158, 209, 216
Fox, R.G. and Gingrich, A./Gingrich, A. and Fox, R.G. 102, 103, 113

gangs: three strikes proposal, Denmark 45
Garland, D. 58, 135, 175, 184, 209, 215, 242
governmentality 145–6, 148, 158; (neo-)liberal 164, 165–6; and rehabilitation 209
Graubard, S.R. 126
Green, D.A. 58, 59, 64, 69, 70
Greve, V. 44, 45, 46
Griffiths, A. 240
Gullestad, M. 124, 125–6, 127

Hacking, I. 158–9
Hallin, D.C. and Mancini, P. 58, 60–1, 62, 63, 70
Hammerlin, Y. 22; and Mathiassen, C. 209
Harcourt, B. 167
Hardy, J. 61, 62
Hawkins, G. 89
health care 23; European Prison Rules 52; psychiatric illness and 22–3, 156–7,

164, 252–3; *see also* attention deficit hyperactivity disorder (ADHD)
health effects of solitary confinement 50–3
health visiting, UK *vs* Norway 149–51
Herzfeld, M. 102–3, 112, 113
historical perspective 26–7; liberal/humane values 176–7; penal popularism 43–7, 53–4; Scandinavian exceptionalism 26–7, 238–42, 243–50, 252–4; solitary confinement 50–3
Hochschild, A.R. 219
human rights violations: Denmark 45–6, 47; *see also* torture
humane values *see* liberal/humane values; Scandinavian exceptionalism
hunger strikes 24, 139
Huntford, R. 88–9

identity and cultural cohesion of prison officers 226–8
immigrants: Norwegian remand prison: and equality (*likhet*) culture 122–6, 134–6; multicultural reality 126–8; on Norwegian families 134; on Norwegian marginalism 131–2; on Norwegian men 132–3; on Norwegian state 130–1; reaction to otherness ascription 129–30; and welfare state 128–9
institutions, citizen confidence in 69
interaction rituals 220
International Covenant on Civil and Political Rights 20–1
intervention, culture of 156, 163–4, 167–8
isolation *see* solitary confinement
Israel 49–50
Iyengar, S. 62

Jefferson, A.M. 115
Jenkins, D. 87, 246
Jones, H. and Cornes, P. 176
Jordan and Denmark: comparative perspective 100–1; Deputy Police Commissioners (DPCs) 107–8; export of ideas, norms, values and techniques 103–10, 113–15; prison officers 106–8; Prosecutors 105–6, 107; Scandinavian exceptionalism 110–13
juvenile offenders: Denmark 47; media coverage 63

Kärfve, E. 160, 161–2
Kjærsgaard, P. 44
knowledge: ADHD as production of 158–63; export/policy transfer 79–80, 92–4, 103–10, 113–15; public service broadcasting and public knowledge 67–8
Konovalëv, A. 30–1
Kosovan prisoner, Norway 123, 124
KROM (Norwegian Association for Prison Reform) 15–17, 27
KRUM (Swedish prisoner support-group) 91
Kuper, A. 102

Lacey, N. 2, 6, 59, 142, 176, 193, 194
Laing, S. 244, 245, 246
Lakatos, I. 158–9
Lappi-Seppälä, T. 65, 66–7, 68, 69, 235, 249
liberal model of media systems 61; *vs* democratic corporatist 70, 71
liberal/humane prison conditions: Denmark 39–40, 42; *see also* Scandinavian exceptionalism
liberal/humane values, UK: conceptual issues 178–9; contemporary prison service 184–9; decline of 181–4; history 176–7; policy implications of research 192–5; research process 177–8; senior management typology 179–81; senior management views 181–92; silencing liberal voice 189–92
liberalism: advanced 158; (neo-)liberal governmentality 164, 165–6
Liebling, A. 143, 178, 180, 199, 201, 202–3, 204, 205, 208, 209, 210; and Arnold, H. 100, 202, 204; and Price, D. 178, 209
Lijphart, A. 59
likhet culture *see* immigrants: Norwegian remand prison
Lutheran influence: Finland 249; Norway 245; Sweden 239–40, 247

McChesney, R.W. and Nichols, J. 65, 67, 68
macro-sociological approach 14–15
Manjoo, F. 72
Marnell, G. 90–1
Martinsson, B. 86
material conditions 141, 142–3
Mathiesen, T. 23–4, 30, 31, 64, 91, 208, 247
Mbembe, A. 101
Mead, M. 13

media: commercialization 62–3; consensus democracy 70; convergence thesis 62–5; convergence thesis, limits of 65–70; crime news 63–5; democratic corporatist model 60–1, 62, 63, 68, 70, 71; expertise and institutions, citizen confidence in 69; juvenile offenders 63; liberal model 61, 70, 71; news markets 65–7; and penal systems: comparative perspective 59–61; proliferation 62; proliferation of niche-media 72; public service broadcasting and public knowledge 67–8; and Scandinavian exceptionalism 70–2; secularization 63; violent crime 64
Melhuus, M. 112, 113
Mikkelsen, B. 44–5
minimal brain damage (MBD) 161–2
Moller, G. 251
moral engineering 166
moral performance in closed prisons 208–10
Morgan, R. 49–50
Moroccan prisoners, Norway 129–32
Morris, N. 89
multicultural reality 126–8
Myrdal, G. and Myrdal, A. 81, 253

Nelken, D. 1, 4, 5, 6, 142
news *see* media
niche media proliferation 72
Nilsson, R. 53, 80, 81, 82, 114, 156, 237, 239–40; Andersson, R. and 163, 165, 166, 215
Nissen, H. 53
Nordic and Scandinavian countries, definition 14–15
normalization 40, 46, 49, 87, 145, 148, 187, 204–5, 211, 236
Norway: culture of equality 243–5; examples of Scandinavian exceptionalism 15–26; Lutheran influence 245; media 63–5, 66–7, 69; national anthem 124–5; Penal Code 25–6; pre-trial solitary confinement 52–3; prison rates 199; *see also* immigrants: Norwegian remand prison; Norway and UK, comparative perspective; prison size and quality of life, Norwegian closed prisons
Norway and UK, comparative perspective: Bredtveit open prison for women 139, 140, 141, 143–4, 145, 146–8, 151; class-specific issues (health visiting) 149–51; governmentality 145–6, 148; humane conditions and treatment 141, 143–4; material conditions 141, 142–3
Norwegian Association for Prison Reform (KROM) 15–17, 27
Norwegian Bar Association 21–2
Nowak, M. 40, 49

open prisons 25: Bredtveit, Norway 139, 140, 141, 143–4, 145, 146–8, 151; Denmark 39, 42; Sweden 86, 87, 224–5

Pakes, F. 6
Pakistani prisoner, Norway 122–3, 124
Paterson, A. 176–7, 187
Penal Codes: Denmark 51; Norway 25–6; Sweden 85–6, 153, 163
penal popularism, Denmark 43–7, 53–4
penal systems, comparison 59–60
Piaser, A. and Bataille, M. 218
Pind, S. 45
political context of media systems 60–1
political economies typology 59–60
Pratt, J. 1, 2, 3–4, 5–6, 13, 14–16, 121, 126, 127, 129, 139–40, 141, 175–6, 193–4, 199, ; 200–1, 204–5, 208, 216, 229; and Eriksson, A. 29, 136, 204; media issues 58, 65, 69, 70–1, 88; *see also* Scandinavian exceptionalism
pre-trial detention *see* immigrants: Norwegian remand prison; remand
pre-trial solitary confinement *see* solitary confinement
prison conditions: comparative perspective 17–18; liberal/humane 39–40; *see also* Norway and UK, comparative perspective
prison officers: classification of prisons and 216–17; Danish and Jordanian 106–8; emotional labour 219–20; interaction rituals 220; professional representations, cultural cohesion and identity 226–8; regular and open prisons 224–5; research data and methods 217; representation of other wings 225–6; security staff 224; social representation 218–19; special security wings 223; and students, Norway 17–18; subcultural differences 220–2, 223, 228–30; Swedish 215–31; theoretical concepts 218–20; training 18; treatment wings 220–2

Index

prison rates: comparative perspective 3, 5; Denmark 46; as measure of punitiveness 235; Norway 199
prison size and quality of life, Norwegian closed prisons: moral performance 208–10; new penology 200–1; new penology critique 201–2; penal excess 199–200; research study 203–4; research study results 204–5; size-related differences 205–8; UK research 202–3, 204–5
prison tourism as research method 236–7
prisoners: immigrant, Norway 122–3, 124, 129–32; work and education 19
prisonization 23–4
professional representations of prison officers 226–8
Prosecutors, Danish and Jordanian 105–6, 107
psychiatric illness: and care 22–3, 156–7, 164, 252–3; *see also* attention deficit hyperactivity disorder (ADHD)
public service broadcasting and public knowledge 67–8

quality of life *see* prison size and quality of life, Norwegian closed prisons

Rafter, N. 159, 160
Rehabilitation and Research Centre for Torture Victims (RCT) 103, 109
remand 20–1; *see also* immigrants: Norwegian remand prison
Rose, N. 158, 166
Røssland, L.A. 64, 66
Rothery, A. 244, 245
Russia 30–1
Rutherford, A. 180
Ryan, M. 181

Scandinavian exceptionalism: causes of 242–50; costs 251–4; critique of 15–29, 38–57, 93–4; culture of control 254–6; culture of equality 243–50; culture of intervention 156, 167–8; defence of 235–60; historical perspective 26–7, 238–42, 243–50, 252–4; hypothesis 40; macro-sociological approach 14–15; and media 70–2; methodological issues 235–7; over-powerful state 252–4; prison rates as measure of punitiveness 235; prison tourism as research method 236–7; social conformity 252; turning point and alternative measures in penal policy 29–32; *see also* Pratt, J.; welfare state(s); *specific countries*
Scandinavian languages and documentary sources 238–42
Scandinavian and Nordic countries, definition 14–15
Scandinavian Studies of Confinement (SSC) 2
Schaanning, E. 156, 210
Schmuhl, R. and Picard, R.G. 72
secure prisons 25
security and harmony values 178–9, 180–1, 188–9
security staff 224
security wings 223
self-catering regime, Denmark 39, 42
Sellin, T. 84–5
Sherill, M. 91
Shirer, W.L. 247, 249
Simmel, G. 124
Smolej, M. and Kivivuori, J. 63, 64
Snortum, J.R. 90
social conformity, comparative perspective 252
social representation of prison officers 218–19
solariums 24–5
solitary confinement 20–1, 47–50; cells 21–2; history and health effects 50–3
state power 252–4
sterilization 163–4, 253
Stevenson, J.J. 244
Strathern, M. 102
Strode, H. 80–1, 248
Strömbäck, J.: *et al.* 59, 60; and Nord, L.W. 71
subcultural differences, prison officers 220–2, 223, 228–30
suicides 22–3
Sweden: culture of equality 245–8; Lutheran influence 239–40, 247; media 71; open prisons 86, 87, 224–5; Penal Code 85–6, 153, 163; policy transfer process and idea travelling 79–80, 92–4; pre-trial solitary confinement 48–9; reforms (1960s and 1970s) 85–92; reforms and reformers 82–5; and UK 238, 239; and US 80–1, 83, 84, 87–92, 93, 94, 252; *see also* attention deficit hyperactivity disorder (ADHD); prison officers; Scandinavian exceptionalism

technologies of the self 158
Thomas, J. et al. 178
Thomas, J.E. 176, 177
Thomas, W.W. 247
three strikes proposal, Denmark 45
torture: European Committee on the Prevention of Torture (CPT) 21, 22, 48–50; Karama programme, Jordan 103–10, 114–15; Rehabilitation and Research Centre for Torture Victims (RCT) 103, 109; UN Special Rapporteur 40, 49
'tough on crime' policies 43–7, 53–4, 199–200
training: prison officers 18; *see also* education
treatment wings 220–2

United Kingdom (UK) 30; Anglo–American practices 4–5, 58; Borstal system 177; media 61, 63, 64, 65–8, 69; research 202–3, 204–5; and Sweden 238, 239, 252; *see also* liberal/humane values, UK; Norway and UK, comparative perspective
United Nations (UN): Congress for the Prevention of Crime and the Treatment of Offenders (1965) 85–6; Convention on the Rights of the Child 47; Human Development Index 130; International Covenant on Civil and Political Rights 20–1; Special Rapporteur on Torture 40, 49
United States (US) 4, 30, 43; Anglo-American practices 4–5, 58; media 61, 62, 63, 65–6, 67, 68, 88, 94; and Sweden 80–1, 83, 84, 87–92, 93, 94, 252

violent crime 64

Wacquant, L. 4, 127, 193, 254
Ward, D. 88, 89–92
Weiss, R.P. and South, N. 115, 142
welfare state(s) 90, 92–3, 163–4, 250–1; and equality ethos 40–2; immigrant views on 128–9; typology 40–1
Wicker, T. 88
Wilhjelm, P. 50
Wollstonecraft, M. 243–4
women's prisons 200; Bredtveit open prison, Norway 139, 140, 141, 143–4, 145, 146–8, 151
work, prisoners 19

Zedner, L. 4, 6

Taylor & Francis
eBooks
FOR LIBRARIES

ORDER YOUR FREE 30 DAY INSTITUTIONAL TRIAL TODAY!

Over 23,000 eBook titles in the Humanities, Social Sciences, STM and Law from some of the world's leading imprints.

Choose from a range of subject packages or create your own!

Benefits for you
- Free MARC records
- COUNTER-compliant usage statistics
- Flexible purchase and pricing options

Benefits for your user
- Off-site, anytime access via Athens or referring URL
- Print or copy pages or chapters
- Full content search
- Bookmark, highlight and annotate text
- Access to thousands of pages of quality research at the click of a button

For more information, pricing enquiries or to order a free trial, contact your local online sales team.

UK and Rest of World: online.sales@tandf.co.uk
US, Canada and Latin America: e-reference@taylorandfrancis.com

www.ebooksubscriptions.com

ALPSP Award for BEST eBOOK PUBLISHER 2009 Finalist

Taylor & Francis eBooks
Taylor & Francis Group

A flexible and dynamic resource for teaching, learning and research.